AVIAN
ILLUMINATIONS

AVIAN
ILLUMINATIONS
A CULTURAL HISTORY OF BIRDS
BORIA SAX

REAKTION BOOKS

FOR LINDA, MY PHOENIX

Published by
REAKTION BOOKS LTD
Unit 32, Waterside
44–48 Wharf Road
London N1 7UX, UK
www.reaktionbooks.co.uk

First published 2021

Frontispiece: Joseph Wolf, *Rufous-necked Hornbill*, 1866,
chromolithograph.

Printed and bound in India by Replika Press Pvt. Ltd

A catalogue record for this book is
available from the British Library

ISBN 978 1 78914 432 1

CONTENTS

INTRODUCTION

PART ONE
BIRDS IN PHILOSOPHY AND RELIGION

1 Parallel Worlds *18*
2 Phoenix and Thunderbird *32*
3 Bird Divination *50*
4 Bird Souls *79*
5 Migration and Pilgrimage *97*

PART TWO
BIRDS IN HISTORY

6 Nature-cultures *114*
7 Avian Politics *151*
8 Falconry *183*
9 Plato's 'Man' *201*

PART THREE
BIRDS IN ART

10 From Caves to Cathedrals *234*
11 Art or Illustration? *259*
12 Birds, Flowers and Time *287*
13 The Nightingale and the Rose *311*

CONCLUSION
BIRDS AND THE FUTURE

14 Extinction *327*
15 Protection and Revival *359*

References *377*
Further Reading *400*
Websites about Birds *403*
Acknowledgements *405*
Photo Acknowledgements *406*
Index of Birds *408*
General Index *412*

INTRODUCTION

I would that we were, my beloved, white birds on the foam of the sea.
W. B. Yeats, 'The White Birds'

At a pond in the forest, a bird casts off her feathered skin and becomes a woman. A man sees her bathing, falls totally in love, and hides the skin so that she will be unable to resume her avian form and fly away. She agrees to marry him. They have children, and for many years they live together in apparent happiness. One day she finds the pelt, puts it on to become a bird again and flies away. This is the basic 'swan maiden tale', and there are hundreds of variants throughout the world. In Scandinavian versions the wife is generally a swan, but she is a crane in tales from Japan and a dove in ones from the Near East.[1]

Sometimes the genders are reversed, in which case the story is like 'Beauty and the Beast'. There are many legends in Northern Europe of a swan knight, from whom several aristocratic houses claim to be descended. In one, Princess Beatrix of Cleves looks out over the Rhine and sees a white swan with a golden chain around its neck pulling a small boat in which stands a knight. She immediately falls in love with the knight, and they are soon married. They live happily together and have several children, but the knight warns Beatrix never to ask about his family or his origins. One day she carelessly asks him if he will eventually tell his children where he came from. He then takes leave of his family, summons his swan and boat, gets in and vanishes into the distance on the Rhine.[2] Very probably, the knight himself was originally a swan.

These animal paramour tales are about the things we hide from loved ones and even from ourselves. But the main reason why such tales are so widely disseminated is that their foundation is a common experience. When looking at a swan in flight or on the water, you can momentarily feel a profound sense of intimacy with it. Then, as it disappears into the distance, you remember that you are excluded from its domain. This is what I call an 'avian illumination' – an intense identification of a person, or group of persons, with counterparts among birds. The difference between human being and animal begins to fall away, if only momentarily, and the person may then sadly realize that he is grounded.

Flight has made birds seem blessed and, in a very literal way, close to heaven. This is, in perhaps all cultures, an attribute of sages and saints.

Opposite: Giotto di Bondone, The Lamentation of Christ, *c. 1308, fresco. The angels resemble a flock of birds in flight, especially in the ways they express themselves through movement. The artist must have observed birds closely.*

Mircea Eliade has written that the 'ability to turn into a bird is the common property of all kinds of shamanism, not only the Turko-Mongol but also the Arctic, American, Indian, and Oceanian'.[3] Myths and legends constantly tell of transformations of people into birds. Angels embody the human dream of becoming one with birds, not only through their wings but through the flowing, brightly coloured robes that often extend like feathered tails behind them. They even sing like birds. In Jewish, Christian and Islamic traditions angels also have assumed essentially the same role as prophetic birds in Greece and Rome, as messengers between God, or the gods, and human beings.

I once watched two blue jays mobbing a hawk, which was perched on a dead branch beside a stream. The hawk had no doubt invaded their territory and they probably had a nest of chicks nearby. The jays circled the raptor's head and even dived recklessly beneath her beak, as though daring her to pounce. For a while the hawk remained completely motionless. Then she raised her wings, slowly spread them, flapped a few times and hurried away. After the hawk had left, the jays seemed to have disappeared as well, but then I glimpsed one a minute later passing quietly overhead. This was a drama of life and death, yet, for the birds, something that might happen any day.

In Melville's *Moby-Dick*, the seaman Ishmael, who is the author's alter ego, tells of seeing an albatross for the first time. The albatross had become entangled with the ropes of his ship and fallen to the deck. He writes that, 'it uttered cries, as some King's ghost in supernatural distress. Through its

Albatross, from the journal O Panorama *(1837). The sight of an albatross passing overhead inspires the young man to go to sea.*

A crow and eagle enacting an aerial drama.

inexpressible, strange eyes methought I peeped to secrets which took hold of God.' He gazed at the bird in utter amazement, lost in a reverie and unaware of how long had passed. Finally he asked a fellow sailor about the creature, to be casually told that it was not some supernatural being but a rather familiar bird.[4]

The Canadian novelist Graeme Gibson saw a gyrfalcon perched high on a boulder in the Canadian Arctic suddenly descend in pursuit of a passing raven. The latter, which was slower but more agile, constantly rose, fell and twisted in the air. At times it seemed close to being caught but always managed to elude its pursuer. A second raven appeared, poised to intervene if its companion was caught, and a third one circled above. Finally, the gyrfalcon gave up and returned to its perch. The experience was, in Gibson's words, 'close to rapture'. Nevertheless, as Gibson explains, such events can neither be predicted nor entirely recaptured, for we are not aware of them until they are over and self-consciousness has returned.[5] Gibson at least came away with a story of a gyrfalcon and three ravens, but sometimes there is almost nothing to tell. You have seen a pileated woodpecker and feel that the experience is special, but you cannot explain why.

Avian illuminations are often found in the work of poets, for example 'The Windhover' (kestrel) by Gerard Manley Hopkins, which he dedicated 'to Christ our Lord':

LA CRESSERELLE.

> I caught this morning morning's minion, king-
>   dom of daylight's dauphin, dapple-dáwn-drawn Falcon,
>   in his riding
>   Of the rólling level underneath him steady áir, and stríding
>   High there, how he rung upon the rein of a wimpling wing
>   In his ecstasy! then off, off forth on swing . . . [6]

The sighting of a mammal or reptile – however beautiful, rare or rich in symbolism – hardly ever generates such exhilaration, which at times approaches religious ecstasy. This sense of cosmic significance is mostly unique to the human relationship with birds.

Not all avian illuminations are so dramatic or intense, and they may even be below the threshold of consciousness. But even a momentary identification with a bird in the wild can direct us beyond an everyday, anthropocentric perspective to reveal an exhilarating range of previously unsuspected emotional,

Kestrel taking flight, from a book of natural history, latter 19th century.
Opposite: Jules Breton, Song of the Lark, *1884, oil on canvas. An avian illumination.*

perceptual and philosophic possibilities. Such encounters have moved people to interpret the behaviour of birds as messengers from a deity.

The bonds between human beings and birds is vastly older than either of the two parties. Their co-evolution dates back hundreds of millions of years to the point where the lineages of mammals and dinosaurs diverged. Very early mammals literally 'looked up' to birds, or at least their ancestors, much as we do today, though for a different reason. The dinosaurs, most of them at least, did not fly, but they were vastly larger than the rodent-like mammals living alongside them. Very likely, the mammals regarded the ancestors of birds with considerable fear, a bit like what a vole may feel about an owl. Ever since that time, the two groups have been constantly observing, and adapting to, one another.

For humankind, the story of evolution is our epic, our myth of origin. In older books of natural science it was told as a fairy tale. Man was a heroic fish climbing out of the water to colonize the land. He gradually developed legs and learned to stand upright. He domesticated fire, developed new weapons and vanquished large, powerful adversaries. Current books are more detached, more technical and more complex, yet their stories remain full of intense challenges, conflicts and friendships.

But there is no episode in the vast epic of evolution with as much high drama as the extinction of the dinosaurs 65 million years ago, when Earth was struck by a huge asteroid. No event seems more miraculous than the escape

Archaeopteryx, a transitional creature between feathered dinosaurs and birds, drawn by Jan Slovak, late 20th or early 21st century.

A swan in flight.

of a few dinosaurs, which had taken to the air and were well on the way to becoming birds. We have adopted the dinosaurs as surrogate ancestors. In terms of evolution, of course, that is not the case, but we show vastly more interest in dinosaurs than in our early mammalian relatives. We see ourselves as 'dominant', and we think the same of dinosaurs. Finally, we see the evolution of dinosaurs into birds as, in many ways, a sort of resurrection. We hope this for ourselves as well. They mirror, in summary, nearly every aspect of the way we see ourselves as human beings: powerful, vulnerable, wicked and blessed.[7] One might say, then, that dinosaurs are the 'parents' of birds and the 'foster- parents' of human beings.

Let us imagine a person long before recorded history on a hilltop observing birds. At a time when the vaunted human 'sense of self' had only partially emerged, to focus intense attention on something was close to becoming that object. The sky, as the domain of birds, was even more a realm apart than it is today, in effect a transcendent realm. But the human imagination was more vivid and powerful, as well as more profoundly sensuous. Individual identity was porous, while a collective sense of human identity had barely begun to appear. A man was what he ate, but, even more, what he saw. Jays mobbed an

American robin feeding her young.

owl, and two eagles locked talons in a mating dance. Our hero pounced with the falcon, sang with the lark, soared with the vulture and played with the crow. Millennia of what we call 'civilization' have covered up but not effaced that primeval view. Birds still lend themselves to epiphanies, in part because of the ways in which they can suddenly emerge and command attention, whether through a call or a dramatic silhouette against the sky.

Understanding birds and their relations with human beings is like accurately describing a single bird seen in a grove. You hear a call and look around until you glimpse it on the branch of a tree. It is in constant motion, turning, hopping, fluttering about and landing a short distance away. It seems to change colour as it goes from full sunlight into a canopy of leaves and back. A description must take into account many views, synthesize them and then explain why they vary. In a similar way, this book will bring together perspectives drawn from ornithology, graphic arts, history, folklore, literature and so on. I have tried also to weave together facts, stories and images, in something like the way a bird constructs a nest from twigs, yarn, spiderwebs, fur and other materials.

My intent in this book is to show how intimately our bonds with birds are bound up in the matrix of ideas, practices, fears and hopes that make up what we call 'human civilization'. The interconnections are so profound, I will argue, that a world without birds would effectively mean the end of humankind, even if we continued to pass on some approximation of our DNA. Birds have had many roles in human society, including omens, food, bearers of messages, disposers of waste, deities, environmental indicators, pets and models for decorative motifs, but they are most important as embodiments of our aspirations. Terrestrial and marine animals also tell us a great deal about ourselves, but birds, especially, reveal what we wish to become.

It is now spring in the year 2020, and I am writing this from my home in White Plains, New York, near the global epicentre of the coronavirus. Businesses deemed 'non-essential' are closed. Most of the classes I teach have been cancelled, and I usually spend the entire day at home. Somewhere near our apartment is a nest of baby American robins. In normal times their voices might be drowned by the noises of the city, which are pervasive, though, since we are accustomed to them, usually unnoticed. Every morning before sunrise, my wife and I hear the robins calling out in melodious but unconnected chirps. Gradually, from day to day, patterns of notes are starting to emerge, and in a while these will form a song.

PART ONE
BIRDS IN PHILOSOPHY
AND RELIGION

1 PARALLEL WORLDS

It is from a mountain called after the great bird that the
famous bird whose fame will ring around the world will take flight.
Leonardo da Vinci

Considering that we are not closely related to birds in evolutionary terms, it is amazing how much we share with them. Birds and humans rely heavily on the senses of sight and hearing. Both are highly mobile and yet build at least semi-permanent residences, nests for them and houses for us. Their feathers are like our clothes. Birds, like people, are endothermic and bipedal. Birds and humans have elaborate courtship rituals and care for their young. Both groups are relatively monogamous, and the basic unit of most avian and human societies is the nuclear family. Many birds even lock beaks in what looks like a human kiss. Like human beings, birds don't quite seem to be animals; in fact we often speak of 'birds and animals' as though these were separate categories.

Perhaps the most remarkable thing that birds share with human beings is that they form a huge range of flexible social groups. Because many birds migrate for vast distances, they constitute, like human beings, a global community. They can form large flocks, at times across lines of species. Many varieties of birds can also work cooperatively, for example by mobbing an owl. Some, such as rooks and weaver birds, live in colonies analogous to cities. Birds can also form relationships with other, non-avian creatures, such as groups of ravens that travel together with wolves. They enter a vast number of symbiotic relationships with human beings, working together with us to gather honey, hunt small mammals, create music and for many other purposes.

Bird behaviour constantly suggests analogies to many other human practices, resemblances that have inspired many prophecies, poems and scientific theories. Crows gather around the body of a dead companion and call out together in what appears strangely like a human funeral. The courting behaviour of birds involves practices that uncannily resemble dance, music, building, home decoration and other human activities. These similarities amount to a perplexing form of biological, or perhaps cultural, convergence, as though birds had independently developed what we call 'human civilization'.

Opposite: J. J. Grandville, birds preparing for the night, c. 1842, engraving with watercolour.
Birds seem to have a society that in remarkably many ways appears to mirror our own.

Earth and Sky

Our word 'human' comes ultimately from the Latin *humanus*, which is closely related to 'humus', meaning 'earth'. The origin of our word 'bird' is unknown. The Old English word for bird was 'fowl', and 'bird' did not start to replace it until the fourteenth century. Interestingly, at that time 'bird' could also mean 'young girl', a usage that has continued up to the present in British slang and is approximately the equivalent of the American word 'chick'. 'Fowl' comes from the Germanic *fleug*, the source of our word 'fly', and probably originally meant 'flying creature'.[1] That is also the original meaning of the German word for bird, *Vogel*, as well as the Russian *ptitsa*. Humans are creatures of the earth, birds of the air.

Claude Lévi-Strauss has written of birds, 'they form a community which is independent of our own but, precisely because of this independence, appears to us like another society, homologous to that in which we live.' Lévi-Strauss maintains that human relations with birds are the reverse of those with dogs, since, far from constituting a parallel society, dogs assume a place in the human domain. He points out that we give individual dogs names that resemble those of human beings but are a little different, such as 'Fido' or 'Rover'. Precisely because dogs belong to human society, giving them the same first names as

Utagawa Hiroshige, Dancing Swallows, *c. 1878, woodblock print. The behaviour of birds can appear uncannily suggestive of human practices.*

An allegory of ornithology from Histoire Naturelle *by Georges-Louis Leclerc, Comte de Buffon (1773 edn), engraving with watercolours. The two children on the left side aspire to fly like birds.*

men and women risks causing uneasiness with respect to both their identities and our own. By contrast, we do not hesitate to give birds human names such as 'Jenny Wren', 'Robin (or Robert) Redbreast' and 'Polly Parrot', but we then apply the same forename to all members of a given species.[2]

Even domesticated birds such as roosters seem part of a larger avian society, and they never have a place in human hierarchies. In the words of Lévi-Strauss, 'everything conspires to make us think of the bird world as a metaphor for human society.'[3] He gives as an example a bird clan of the Chickasaw people who identify their members with different avian species.[4] To give another example, Boios, a late classical mythographer who influenced Ovid, wrote a book entitled *Ornithogonia,* preserved only in scattered fragments, which regarded all birds as transformed human beings.[5]

According to *The Zhouli* (Rites of Zhou), a book on social organization from the second century BCE, the legendary Emperor Shaohao, inspired by a phoenix that appeared when he took the throne, named all the officers in his realm after birds. The officer in charge of the calendar was named 'Phoenix', while the one in charge of responding to solstices was 'Shrike'. The officer in charge of education was 'Partridge'; the minister of war, 'Vulture'; the chief of police, 'Hawk'; the minister of works, 'Wood Pigeon'; the minister of public affairs, 'Falcon'. Assemblies were called by a group known as the 'Five Pigeons'. Those who administered the department of agriculture were the 'Nine-tailed birds'.[6] The reason was not so much that birds, considered as individuals, resembled human beings as that both had the same patterns of organization.

This is shown vividly in 'The Man Who Was Changed into a Crow', from *Strange Stories from a Chinese Studio* collected by P'u Sung-ling (also written Pu Songling) in the mid-eighteenth century. A young man named Yu Jung has just failed his civil service exams and run out of money when he stops at the temple of Wu Wang, the Daoist guardian of crows, to pray. A man appears, leads him to Wu Wang and says that Yu Jung might fill 'a vacancy in the black robes'. The deity agrees and gives Yu Jung a black uniform. Yu Jung puts it on, changes into a crow, flies away, marries another crow and joins a flock, but one day he is hit by an arrow from a crossbow. He then suddenly finds himself in his human form lying on the floor of the temple, surrounded by sympathetic people who contribute money to send him home. He later passes his exams, returns to the temple, sacrifices a sheep to feed the crows and is again given his black robes.[7] He spends the rest of his life moving back and forth between his identities as crow and human being, together with his wife and sons, but those two worlds are so closely parallel that they seem to be almost the same.

According to the *Book of Saint Albans*, an English treatise on hawking, hunting and heraldry published in 1486, various birds correspond to ranks of nobility. An eagle is for an emperor; a gyrfalcon for a king; a sparrowhawk for a prince; a peregrine falcon for an earl; a saker falcon for a knight; a merlin for a lady, and so on. These pairings were not rules about who could hunt

Theodore Jasper, 'Meadowlarks', chromolithograph from Studer's Popular Ornithology *(1881). The birds are perched on a hill above the people. They exchange glances, perhaps contemplating the men and women with a combination of wonder and frustration.*

with various birds of prey, a privilege that was generally limited only by an individual's budget and skill. Eagles were not used for falconry in Europe, nor were some of the other birds on the list such as the vulture. Rather, the list was a series of equivalent figures, as one ascended a scale of perfection.[8]

In his highly influential *Le monde des Oiseaux* (The World of Birds), first published in 1853–5, Alphonse Toussenel used avian life as an elaborate allegory for human history, recounted from a perspective that was populist, antisemitic and Anglophobic. He began by stating, 'The history of the birds of France is nothing but, starting with the cuckoo, a tedious litany of theft, extortion, murder and pillage.' The victims, in his view, were avian citizens who wished only to live in peace. The raven and magpie, according to Toussenel, are philosophers without integrity who use their verbal facility to corrupt and deceive. The eagle personifies aristocratic privilege and resembles the decadent ruling classes of Rome, Carthage, England and Venice. The vulture, inserting its neck and head into a carcass, is like Jewish bankers, whose oppression penetrated into the most intimate areas of society. The owl is an assassin, 'a sinister bird of murder' that, since it eats its own kind, reminds us of the era of human sacrifice.[9]

We also find the use of birds as an allegorical representation of human society in the 1948 movie *Bill and Coo*, directed by Chuck Reisner Jr, in which all the roles are acted by trained birds. Most but not all of the birds are parakeets, but they are identified with human occupations through accessories such as hats, bow ties, aprons, academic robes, make-up and so on. The movie is set in a small town of the American Midwest called 'Chirpendale'. The hero is a humble taxi driver and volunteer fireman named Bill Singer who saves his sweetheart, an upper-class girl named Coo, and the entire town by luring a marauding crow into a trap.

The parallels are not always so explicit, but the idea that birds correspond to types of human beings constantly surfaces in folklore and literature. The sense that birds exist in a realm parallel to our own is a reason why observing the flight of birds has often been a form of divination. It suggests that every story of birds in the sky corresponds to one unfolding among human beings on the ground.

Totemism

What are we to call this parallelism, this sense of intertwined destinies, between humankind and birds? There is no very close analogue, but the word 'totemism' will probably come to mind. Some words are specialized and have narrowly delineated meanings. Others, like 'totemism', are generalists, which, with a bit of alteration, can fit many contexts. We usually think of this word as designating a relationship between a species and a tribe, yet perhaps birds should be called a 'totem of humankind'.

For many ethnologists of the latter nineteenth century, 'totemism' meant belief in the genealogical descent from another species such as the eagle or wolf. For the anthropologist Claude Lévi-Strauss, it meant using the natural world, with its divisions of living things, as the model for the classification of human beings and their institutions.[10] For the contemporary anthropologist Philippe Descola, 'totemism' referred mostly to primeval animals of the Dreamtime in the culture of Australian Aborigines.[11]

An environmentalist version of totemism is 'biophilia', which Edward O. Wilson defines as 'the innately emotional affiliation of human beings to other living organisms'.[12] Postulating a genetic basis for love of nature seemed to reconcile the romantic and scientific approaches to environmentalism. But while traditional totemism designates the affiliation with specific kinds of animals such as birds, biophilia is more oriented to landscapes and vegetation.

Another variant of totemism, one more oriented to the individual, is Roberto Marchesini's concept of an 'animal epiphany'.[13] For a while the boundary between a person and animal is blurred and almost disappears. Through an animal, a person achieves a renewed sense of what he is and is not. Personal, and even human, identity is challenged, redefined, expanded, yet ultimately reaffirmed.

Yet another concept related to totemism is 'companion species', first introduced by Donna Haraway and widely used today. It refers to species that have co-evolved together and have, over vast periods of time, created a shared environment and relate to one another in both culturally complex and immediately pragmatic ways. The major example is human beings and dogs, though the list of human companion species would also include cats, honeybees and corn.[14]

We have roughly as many companion species among birds as we do among mammals, among them rock doves (pigeons), ducks, geese, swans, chickens, peacocks, falcons and ravens. This handful of varieties joins us to the rest of the approximately 10,000 species of bird. The relationship is in a way like that of an individual who marries into an extended family or clan, acquiring bonds of kinship with many people who are neither blood relatives nor geographically close.

These diverse formulations, in my opinion, do not render the concept of 'totemism' incoherent but, rather, rich in associations. For all their differences, they may be attempts to make sense of a single sort of relationship. As I use the term, 'totemism' designates any close identification of people with a group of animals, particularly to the degree that it involves blurring of boundaries between these animals and human beings. I believe this encompasses, and often clarifies, the previous definitions that I have mentioned. Understood in this way, totemism may be found in virtually all cultures, whether indigenous, modern or post-industrial. The concept is applicable to heraldry, where noble families, and eventually many other institutions, represented themselves through stylized animals such as the wolf, falcon or lion. The totemism of mammals involves assuming a new, or expanded, identity, but that of birds involves living within a different element as well. Birds have always entered our domain, but for millennia we only dreamed of setting foot in theirs.

Daedalus and His Heirs

The story of Daedalus was to become the inspiration for Leonardo da Vinci and almost all others for well over two millennia who dreamed of emulating the flight of birds.[15] In a myth retold by Apollodorus and many others, Daedalus and his son Icarus are imprisoned on orders from King Minos in the Labyrinth, an architectural wonder that Daedalus himself had once designed. Daedalus fabricates wings for himself and his son, and they escape by flying away over the prison walls. Against the instructions of his father, Icarus ascends too close to the sun, which melts the wax that held the feathers of the wings together. He falls into the sea and drowns.[16] Daedalus had also created many wonders such as statues that moved by themselves.

It was common in Greek mythology for human beings to transform into another species. According to a related myth, a nephew of Daedalus named Talos was changed into a partridge.[17] Daedalus was probably a shapeshifter in an older form of the tale of his escape, a shaman who could turn into a bird. As people grew more interested in technology and less in magic, they rationalized his story, making the sorcerer of old into a mechanical genius.

Socrates, the central character in Plato's dialogues, claimed to be a descendant of Daedalus.[18] He believed in the transmigration of souls and did not accord any special status to human beings. For Socrates, reincarnation as an animal could be a reward or simply a change rather than a punishment. In Plato's *Republic*, he speaks of many famous people who were reborn as birds. The Homeric hero Agamemnon, disillusioned with humankind, chooses to be reborn as an eagle. The legendary singer Thamyras is reborn as a nightingale. Orpheus, who was the centre of a mystery religion, elects to be

Albrecht Dürer, Daedalus and Icarus, *1493, woodblock print. Icarus is juxtaposed with a bird diving into the sea, reminding us of one more ability that some birds have but people find hard to emulate.*

reborn as a swan. Meanwhile, many songbirds chose to be reborn as human beings.[19]

The story of Socrates' putative ancestor is echoed in the episode known as 'the allegory of the cave' in Plato's *Republic*, which many consider the definitive statement of his philosophy. Suppose some people, Socrates explains, have been held prisoner in a cave since birth. They are chained to the wall in such a way that they can only look in a forward direction. Behind them is a ridge, where others carry statues of animals and various objects, and still further behind are fires. The statues cast shadows on the cave wall facing the prisoners, who mistake them for reality, since that is all they have ever known. The cave has some resemblance to the Labyrinth where Daedalus was imprisoned, which was a vast underground maze.

If we understand the allegory in literal terms, it will appear absurd. For one thing, the prisoners would not be able to eat, drink and eliminate bodily wastes unless they were constantly waited on by servants. Confined though they are, everything appears to centre around the prisoners, and the elaborate light show is performed strictly for their viewing. But perhaps the cave itself is an anthropocentric illusion. It represents human society, where people are confined by countless expectations, customs, conventions and so on. These limits are embedded in language and so completely internalized that many people can imagine nothing else.

Socrates tells how, one day, a prisoner escapes the cave and ascends to open air. At first, the man is disoriented, but gradually he learns to make out shapes such as those of trees, creatures, rivers, the sun and the moon. He returns to the cave and declares to the other prisoners that what they had taken for genuine is only the shadow of a greater reality, but they are unable to understand what he says. If he insists on telling the captives that their lives are based on illusion, he will infuriate them and even risk being killed.[20]

Socrates' and Plato's Theory of Forms holds that the objects that fill our everyday lives are, like shadows on the walls of the cave, only pale copies

of a greater reality. A philosopher, by contemplating ideas, approaches that reality, while simultaneously detaching himself from worldly concerns. The Theory of Forms has been often maligned as a pretext for focusing on ethereal abstractions and ignoring practicalities. But the philosophy resembles that of many indigenous peoples, most especially that of the Australian Aborigines, for whom events of today are only reverberations of those in the original Dreamtime when the world was created.[21]

If Socrates claimed to be descended from a wizard who could transform into a bird, even an artificial one, that is close to claiming descent from the bird itself. He was an arch-rationalist but also a mystic, and the two sides to his personality were not so far apart as they may seem. Science has always had a side that, while not irrational, can justly be called 'mystical', since it reveals our everyday reality, as known through the senses, as an illusion. Instead of a static object, say, a tree, it presents us with the products of forces, materials and perpetually changing circumstances. The prisoner escaping from the cave is a sort of shaman, and his story has foundations in totemism.

Daedalus as an embodiment of the mechanical arts, relief on the facade of the cathedral of St Mary of the Flower, Florence, from the workshop of Andrea Pisano. Leonardo would have been familiar with this sculpture, which is prominently displayed in his native city.

If Socrates was descended from Daedalus, then Icarus as well was at least his distant relative, perhaps even his ancestor. The escaped captive, rising above his colleagues like a bird in flight, is Daedalus and Icarus in one. At first, when he is disoriented, he is more like the unfortunate son. When he has learned to distinguish objects, he is like the father. When he has survived and returned to the cave, he is Socrates, endeavouring to communicate about the world of forms to those who will not comprehend and are destined to be executed by the Athenians.

Flight

According to Giorgio Vasari, Leonardo would buy caged birds in the marketplace and set them free,[22] but, assuming this is true, Leonardo's prime motivation was not simply to grant them liberty. In an era before reliable telescopes, this was the only way to observe up close exactly how birds take to the air. He wished to uncover the mechanisms of their flight for use in an airborne machine. About 1506 he completed a codex on the flight of birds, which contains many illustrations, along with meticulous notes on things like the construction of feathers and the distribution of a bird's weight. The drawings are very simple and diagrammatic, but they show how the wings move, stretch and contract in departing from the ground or responding to wind as accurately as any previous European depictions.[23] Nevertheless, birds, especially in flight, remain noticeably absent from Leonardo's paintings. He called his proposed mechanism to enable flight a 'bird'. The last entry in his codex predicts that it 'will make the first flight launched from the peak of Mount Cecero … filling all the universe with awe, filling all writings with its fame, and eternal glory to the nest where it was born'.[24] But there is no record of this flight ever taking place.

Even if it might be a legend, the image of Leonardo buying caged birds to release them has an almost uncanny sort of appropriateness. He was the artist of great dreams. His towering reputation (and I do not say this as a reproach) rests mostly on what he should have, could have, might have or would have accomplished rather than on known achievements. Throughout his career he constantly became engaged in grandly ambitious projects. All were either unrealized, like his flying machines, destroyed, like the equestrian

Opposite: Shooting birds from a glider, from Adams Merrill, The Great Awakening *(1899). Conceived not much more than a decade before the Wright brothers tested the first plane, this imagined flying machine illustrates how people at times envied and resented yet aspired to the abilities of birds. The person in this device is claiming the sky for humankind by shooting an eagle.*

monument to Francesco Sforza, of uncertain attribution, like the stairway at the château of Chambord, or severely damaged, like his painting of the *Last Supper*. Birds in flight are a font of dreams and aspirations. Leonardo may have valued the sense of endless possibility more than any consummation of a project. Is that why the *Mona Lisa* is smiling?

The project of Daedalus was doomed outside of myth for many reasons. The human body lacks the light construction, powerful muscles and efficient respiration that enable birds to fly. In 1504, when Leonardo was studying the flight of birds, John Damian, an Italian at the court of James IV of Scotland, constructed a pair of wings. He tried to fly from the walls of Stirling Castle in the manner of Daedalus but immediately fell and broke a bone.

It was only when inventors finally abandoned the avian model, and with it a good deal of romance, that they finally managed to become airborne. This was accomplished in Paris during 1783 in a hot air balloon, a device with no resemblance whatsoever to a bird. The first aeroplane, successfully tested by the Wright brothers in 1903, retained the basic body plan of a bird, with wings and a tail, but the wings, unlike those of a bird, did not flap. Engineers and scientists still study the mechanism of remarkable flyers such as hummingbirds in hope of discovering mechanisms that could be incorporated in their designs for planes, but technology, much like art, has steadily moved further away from the imitation of nature.

It may be that birds have seemed a bit less awe-inspiring since human beings have learned to fly. Nevertheless, our machines still have none of the easy spontaneity of birds, which can leave the ground or change direction

In this engraving with watercolour by J. J. Grandville, jackdaws sketch a statue of the god Mercury, patron of thieves: a satire on the ways human beings borrow from birds.

Glossy swiftlet nesting in a Malaysian cave.

as they please, without preparation or forethought. Sitting in the seat of a passenger plane, even in the air, one feels grounded. There is a lot more to flight than elevation.

Suppose a swiftlet, a small South Asian bird that has adapted to life in caves and, like bats, navigates by echolocation, had entered Plato's cave. The prisoners would have had trouble describing the bird and been puzzled by the way in which it appeared and left. At first they might have said that the swiftlet was a hallucination, but the shadow it cast was real. Suppose the swiftlet and her mate built a nest on the cave wall and then laid eggs, from which chicks eventually hatched. The swiftlet could have directed the prisoners beyond the bounds of their familiar world and perhaps even inspired one to escape.

To imaginatively project yourself into a bird, you must lay aside your own identity. You must, for the moment, forget who you are and what you know. In anthropomorphizing a bird, thinking of it as essentially 'human', we confer a false impression of universality on human or culturally specific ways of thinking. In attempting to see the world as a bird does, we begin to activate unconscious intuitions and vestigial senses. This can produce a flurry of intense emotions such as exaltation, confusion, melancholy and wonder. Finally, we return to our everyday routines with enhanced appreciation.

2 PHOENIX AND THUNDERBIRD

He clasps the crag with crooked hands;
Close to the sun in lonely lands,
Ring'd with the azure world, he stands.

The wrinkled sea beneath him crawls;
He watches from his mountain walls,
And like a thunderbolt he falls.
Alfred, Lord Tennyson, 'The Eagle'

The philosopher of birds, at least for the twentieth century, is Gaston Bachelard. Long ago, scientists rejected the idea that all things are physically composed of earth, air, water and fire, but Bachelard believed these elements are still the basis of poetic imagery. Birds, of course, are quintessential creatures of the air. Bachelard thought that identity is neither fixed nor illusory. Individuals are in a state of perpetual metamorphosis as they are born, wake, sleep, daydream, work and eventually die. One highly visible symbol of such transformations is a bird taking off towards the heavens. According to Bachelard, birds are transformed in flight.[1] They move constantly, varying their form according to the winds. Their colours change as well, flickering as they are touched by light from different directions.

They seem to leave behind their corporeal reality, much as people do in dreams, a phenomenon Bachelard calls 'oneiric flight' (*vol onirique*). This is essentially the flight of the Daoist immortals. Bachelard believes it to be the foundation of poetry, where objects are deprived of mass. The avian alternation of flight with activity on the ground is like the dialogue of imagination and reality that makes up human culture.[2] Finally, there is the building of bird nests, which make use of twigs, grass, string and many other materials from the surrounding area. The nest becomes a centre for the avian cosmos, and making it resembles the human construction of reality from images collected everywhere.[3]

This analysis might help explain the nature of imagined birds. Fantastic animals of the terrestrial realm tend to be relatively simple composites of others. The unicorn is a horse or goat with a horn, while a centaur is a human torso and head on the body of a horse. Fantastic birds are less unequivocally

Opposite: Photograph of an eagle's nest by Francis H. Herrick, 1930s. Some birds such as eagles and ravens will use the same nest for generations, constantly repairing and adding to it.

J. J. Grandville, Phoenix Reborn, *1840s, engraving with watercolours. Grandville imagines a phoenix rising in mid-19th-century Paris and causing a conflagration. He has depicted himself as an owl looking out of the lower right corner of the picture.*

corporeal and more difficult to describe. Their identities are more fluid, and people are more likely to conflate one with another. The Arabian rukh (or roc) is often identified with the Chinese phoenix, Persian simorgh or Greek griffin. Imaginary terrestrial animals are more likely to be actors in stories, while imaginary birds are mostly presences, signalling ill weather or good luck simply by appearing in the sky. The reason why fantastic birds are seldom clearly describable combinations of traits from actual species may be that, as Bachelard has argued, they seem to cast aside their species on entering the sky.

Bachelard adds that oneiric flight is not by means of wings, which are largely symbolic. A casual survey of paintings seems to confirm this, for angels, even in flight, rarely seem to be actively flapping their wings. These are usually either folded or stretched out, almost as though they were worn as a detachable accessory. Angels are really walking on air. Any animal – for that matter, any object – can be given that sort of symbolic wings. Airavata, a white elephant with wings, is the mount of the Hindu god Indra. Pegasus, a horse with wings, is that of the Greek hero Perseus. Most fantastic animals, even primarily terrestrial ones, are usually depicted with wings, including the dragon, basilisk, griffin, hippogriff and sphinx. When people view them as mostly benign, these are the wings of birds, but, in Western tradition, those that inspire fear may have the wings of bats. These appendages are a symbolic statement that the figure belongs not to our everyday world but to a transcendent realm.

Our weightlessness in dreams may truly resemble the experience of birds. Compared to other animals, birds are very light for their size, because their bones and feathers are both hollow. Their ability to fly is due partly to a remarkable sense of balance, and this is also evident when they are at rest. Most birds shift their weight easily, whether in flight, in water or, in most cases, on the ground. Many, such as flamingos, cranes and parrots, can remain perched on a single leg for long periods. Especially in dance, but more subtly in music and other arts, people constantly aspire to the lightness of birds.

Furthermore, birds probably perceive time very differently from human beings. Bachelard points out that a poem creates its own tempo, which has little in common with the sort of time measured by calendars and clocks. The pace of events in poetry is far more leisured than in most experience, yet poetry may concentrate the experience of years into a single moment. In his words, a poet 'constructs a poem based on silent time, on a time which is not labored, rushed, or controlled by anything'.[4] Avian metabolisms are far more rapid than those of human beings, so it seems likely that birds experience time as less rapid. They distinguish individual sounds that pass so quickly that the human ear runs them together. Their experience may be a bit like a film reel played in slow motion.

Human beings measure space and time, but our units never correspond closely to our experience. A distance will seem longer when we are tired, just as an hour seems shorter when we are having fun. Birds probably know space and time far more holistically than we do. In the sky, they do not need to choose a path, but simply fly in whatever direction they prefer or else surrender control and let themselves be carried by the wind. It is not easy for us to imagine this sort of freedom. Birds may not conceive of space and time as something apart from the motions that fill them. Spacetime, in other words, seems to be continually created by a bird in flight, like the currents of water around a swimmer.

Furthermore, although birds wake and sleep like human beings, their way of differentiating between dream and reality may be very different. For people, dreaming and waking are distinct states, even though there is a continuum between them. Like human beings, birds have brains divided into left and right hemispheres. Unlike human beings, most birds are able to rest one hemisphere while the other remains alert. Songbirds, ducks, gulls and some raptors sleep with a single eye open. As Chaucer put it in the late fourteenth century in the opening lines of the prologue to *The Canterbury Tales*:

> And smale fowles maken melodye,
> That slepen al the night with open yë . . .⁵

The visual information obtained from the right eye is processed by the left hemisphere, while the other remains asleep. In addition, gulls and other birds are able to sleep while gliding on the wind.⁶ If sleep and waking are not entirely distinctive states for birds, their perceptions may have the ambience of a dream. To sum this up, just as humans fly in dreams, birds sleep in flight.

Phoenix

Any number of imaginary birds go under the name of 'phoenix', including the Egyptian benu bird, the Chinese fenghuang, the Japanese ho-ho, the Russian firebird, the Arabian rukh and the Persian simorgh. Mythic birds raise the same taxonomic questions as real ones. Is every bird that goes under the name really a phoenix? Can a bird go under a different name, yet still be a genuine phoenix? To answer such questions about physical animals, scientists look to the evolutionary record. The equivalent for imaginary animals is folkloric and literary lineage, but that can rarely be traced with great confidence or precision.

In his book *The Phoenix* (2016), Joseph Nigg has reconstructed the history of the mythical bird with such thoroughness that his study will probably be definitive for a long time to come. It is a long and lively story, involving celebrated authors such as Herodotus, Confucius, Ovid, Gesner, Shakespeare, Milton, Rowling and many others. But the very completeness of the study makes one wonder about gaps in the record. It is a bit like a world tour where you stop in great cities from Tokyo to Rome without seeing the countryside between them. What connects this succession of images? The answer, of course, is mostly oral traditions. The phoenix of legend has been influenced by, and identified with, so many birds, both legendary and real, that any attempt to describe the historical development of the phoenix in a linear way becomes hopelessly tangled. I find it more helpful to think of the phoenix as a product of the continual interaction of many cultures as well as a perpetual work in progress. Its general characteristics include brilliant plumage with flowing tail feathers trailing it in flight. The phoenix is closely associated with fire, the sun and, especially, eternal life.

Even within individual traditions, there is often a great deal about the phoenix that seems indeterminate. In the Christian tradition, for example, it is not very clear whether the phoenix is male, female or androgynous. Neither is it certain whether there is only a single phoenix or many. It is variously described as living in Arabia, Egypt, Ethiopia and India. The exact size and colour of the phoenix are not often specified. Furthermore, for such a legendary creature, there are remarkably few stories about the phoenix. It is sighted from time to time yet appears to take little interest in the affairs of human beings. The phoenix seems to exist in a dimension of imagination where the protocols of scientific description do not apply.

The first known reference to a phoenix can be found in a fragment by Hesiod around the end of the eighth century BCE. In the fifth century BCE Herodotus described the phoenix in detail and equated it with the Egyptian benu. The Chinese phoenix and the benu are of perhaps comparable antiquity, though the origins of both are lost in the remote past. Tracing their histories is a matter of synthesizing scattered pictures, references and traditions, which may

Chinese embroidery showing a fenghuang or 'Chinese phoenix', 19th century.

or may not pertain to the phoenix as we think of it today. According to *Annals of the Bamboo Books*, a Chinese history written around the start of the third century BCE, the phoenix first appeared in 2647 BCE in the court of the legendary Yellow Emperor and then in the palaces of various emperors that followed.[7] Like the Graeco-Egyptian phoenix, it is associated with the sun and has feathers of red and gold. Both are also, in some way, immortal: the Graeco-Egyptian phoenix dies and is reborn; the Chinese phoenix never dies. It is possible that both these figures go back to a solar deity in some primeval mythology. It is equally likely that they blended with one another and with additional figures of legend in stories told along the Silk Road over the centuries.

The Chinese phoenix is known as the fenghuang, with 'feng' being the male and 'huang' the female. They represent respectively yang, the male principle, and yin, the female one. At times the male and female phoenixes are shown together. More often, the Chinese phoenix is female, and she is paired with the dragon, together representing the empress and emperor of China.

Above: Augustus Knapp, illustration of the Rosicrucian cosmos, *early 20th century.*
Note the five alchemical birds in the lower half of the sphere as well as the phoenix and eagle below.
Opposite: Allegory of chemistry from Diderot's Encyclopédie *(1790), engraving with watercolour.*
Long after the tenets of alchemy had been rejected, alchemical symbolism continued to be used to
represent the sciences. Note the phoenix at the summit of the cosmos.

Pl.18.

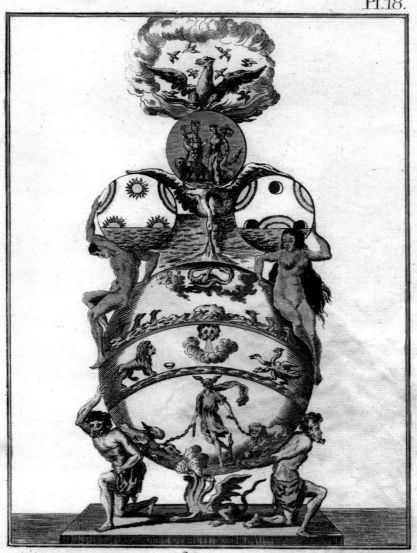

Chimie.

The Chinese phoenix was supreme among birds, not because it possessed some unique characteristic but because it incorporated those of many other creatures. It has the breast of a swan, the neck of a snake and the beak of a swallow. Its feathers are those of a peacock, pheasant and other colourful birds.[8] This amorphous quality is not simply the result of disagreements but is itself an attribute of the bird. The phoenix was, in a sense, all birds, perhaps even all animals. Any bird that was beautiful, exotic and mystical came to be identified with the phoenix.

Since the legend of the phoenix was first recorded, many writers such as Herodotus and Pliny have expressed doubts about its existence, but, though perhaps never very widely believed, accounts of it continued to circulate. Pre-modern writers about the phoenix would simply report what they heard, and they would hardly ever engage in debates about whether the phoenix lives five hundred or a thousand years before being reborn. Nobody argued about whether the home of the phoenix was in Arabia or India. They did not appear to regard such details as worth the effort of disputing. The phoenix had become a sort of paradigm, which might encompass birds with different features.

In Renaissance Europe the phoenix was being revived in a relatively new context. The ultimate goal of the alchemists was to produce the legendary philosopher's stone, which was capable of conveying eternal life. This was at once a material and spiritual aspiration. It was done by means of chemical procedures, which were described not directly but using an elaborate symbolic language. This encryption was needed in part out of fear that the powers of alchemy might fall into the hands of people who would abuse it. It was also because alchemists could be suspected of witchcraft, so it might be necessary to conceal their activity from the uninitiated. The creation of the philosopher's stone, known as 'the great work', was generally divided into five stages, which in turn were sometimes represented by five birds: respectively the crow, swan, pelican, peacock and phoenix.[9] The completed philosopher's stone was also symbolized by the phoenix, which had been resurrected from the ashes. As in Chinese tradition, it seemed to represent all birds in one.

Opposite: Exotic bird against a backdrop of the pyramids, from The Picturesque Dictionary of Natural History, *chromolithograph, 1837. Because Egypt is associated with the phoenix, the artist depicted a red bird of paradise with flowing red and yellow feathers amid marshes by the Pyramids. It is actually indigenous to Indonesia and not the Near East.*

Pl. 459.   1.a.   1.b.

Plate No.1.

EDEN, IN THE MORNING OF CREATION.

Birds of Paradise

As we approach the modern era, there is more emphasis on literal accuracy and classification. Naturalists would include fabulous creatures such as the phoenix and unicorn in their taxonomies, even when expressing scepticism about their reality. At the same time, European traders and explorers were returning home with fantastic tales of fauna in distant lands together with previously unknown sorts of skins and feathers. Scholars tried to identify these in terms of old mythologies: the orangutan might be considered the satyr of Graeco-Roman lore, for example. Many dazzling birds were being discovered in the tropics, and some of these were at least provisionally identified with the phoenix.

Today, what we call birds of paradise are members of the family Paradisaeidae, found in Australia, Papua New Guinea and Melanesia. In the Early Modern era, the term might be applied to just about any colourful bird from a distant land. When their skins were brought back to Europe, the legs had usually been broken off. Scholars understood the absence of legs to mean that the creatures were entirely heavenly and never left the sky.

Very old traditions place the phoenix in the Garden of Eden, which people located somewhere in the East, often in India. In a very widely disseminated, though doubtless inauthentic, letter to the emperor of Byzantium, an allegedly Christian ruler named Prester John boasted of the wonders of his distant kingdom in Asia, including wild men, giants, fauns and the phoenix.[10] This helped establish an expectation of wonders, and what mariners brought back in the Age of Exploration often seemed as fantastic as anything Prester John had described. Just as citizens of the colonial powers viewed indigenous people as either wild or noble savages, they thought of the rainforests alternately as a savage wilderness and a paradise.

According to Antonio Pigafetta, one of the few people to survive Magellan's voyage around the world in 1519–22, the surviving mariners brought back two brightly coloured, dead birds that had been gifted by the king of the Maluku Islands to the king of Spain. He describes the birds with some care, saying that they were about the size of a thrush, with thin legs and long beaks. They did not have conventional wings but a great profusion of many-coloured plumes on their sides. Apart from these feathers, they were tawny in colour. The birds did not actually fly, but they glided on the wind. The natives said that the birds came from a terrestrial paradise and called them 'birds of God'.[11]

'Eden, Morning of Creation', from a religious tract, England (1887).
This picture of the original paradise contains several brightly coloured birds from the tropics.

Other writers soon elaborated on Pigafetta's description and their accounts became ever more fanciful. Konrad Peutinger, an official of the Holy Roman Empire who claimed to have seen a corpse of the bird, sent a picture of it to Konrad Gesner, who published it in his *Historia animaliam* of 1551–8. Gesner, following Peutinger, claimed that the bird had no legs or feet, since it always soared high in the air. According to Gesner, the bird had never been seen alive, but was occasionally found dead on the ground or in the water. The back of the male had a deep crevice in which the female laid her eggs. The male binds her to him while the eggs are hatching, using a long, black thread in its tail. Gesner called it *paradisea* or 'bird of paradise'.[12] Pigafetta's description of the birds, the starting point of all this lore of the bird of paradise, is not sufficient for ornithological identification. The picture published by Gesner, as received from Peutinger, later led Linnaeus to classify it as the greater bird of paradise (*Paradisaea apoda*, or 'bird without feet').[13] I suspect, however, that it was not a dead bird as Pigafetta claimed, since that would have decayed within a few weeks at most. Rather, it may have been some artefact, like many created in the South Pacific, that involved stitching together

the feathers of many birds. The same could be true of the 'dead bird' seen by Konrad Peutinger. Some of the characteristics attributed to birds of paradise by authors such as Gesner, Belon and Topsell are fantastic, but others do belong to various birds in islands of the South Pacific. The phoenix of Renaissance zoology was, like those that came before it, an imaginative composite of many other birds.

Above: Johann Andreas Pfeffel, illustration to Physica Sacra
by Johann Jacob Scheuchzer, showing Adam alone in the Garden of Eden before the
creation of Eve, copper engraving, c. 1731. In the upper left is a bird of a paradise copied
from the one in Konrad Gesner's Historiae animalium *of 1551–8.*
Opposite: Traditional painting of a Chinese dragon and phoenix, 20th century.

The Thunderbird

The Chinese dragon, partner of the fenghuang, lives in a kingdom under the sea but it is usually shown flying among the clouds. It is the bringer of storms and rain. Fire flashes from its limbs as they move, creating lightning. Even more than the phoenix, it is a composite of all animals. It has the horns of a deer, the scales of a fish, the claws of a hawk and so on. In addition, it is a master of transformations, able to assume the form of any other creature. In the words of Roel Sterckx, 'The dragon epitomized the image of the sacred animal as the embodiment of change. It encompassed the boundaries of species, space, and time, and represented all animals in one.'[14] This composite nature also applies to its means of locomotion, which is at once swimming, flying and running.[15] Though usually in the air, it does not have wings. Rather, it is a perfect example of the oneiric flight discussed by Bachelard. For the dragon, the four elements are essentially one.

Above: Huge dragon puppet, from the celebration of the New Year in Brooklyn's Chinatown, 2017. The dragon dances to a sound like thunder, produced by large drums. Opposite: Edward Julius Detmold, rukh lifting an elephant, illustration to The Arabian Nights *(1924).*

Few if any other figures from world mythology are so multifaceted as the Chinese dragon, but many birds, and birdlike figures, have a similar role as the bringer of rain, lightning and storms. These include the Hindu Garuda and the Australian rainbow serpent. The eagle of Zeus, the Greek thunder god, has often been depicted holding bolts of lightning in its claws. The woodpecker makes a sound like thunder when it knocks against a tree trunk with its beak, and Edward Armstrong has argued, on the basis of many fragmentary references in legends, that it was a deity of storms in Neolithic times.[16]

The rukh, or a similar bird of legend, is mentioned in print by the German historian Hieronymus Megiser in his description of Madagascar, published in the first decade of the seventeenth century. He cites reports of indigenous people on the island who say the bird is so large and powerful that it picks up elephants in the air, drops them to their death and then eats them. People who claimed to have seen several estimated its wingspan at sixteen paces. The location on Madagascar suggests that it was originally an elephant bird, which had either perished or was quickly approaching extinction yet lived on in legend. Since the natives also reportedly claimed it came only in certain times of year, it may also have been associated with meteorological phenomena. Megiser identified it with the griffin as described by Marco Polo.[17]

In the second voyage of Sinbad the Sailor, the hero mistakes the rukh for an impending storm. He is stranded on an island, where he sees a huge, white dome, which is entirely smooth. As he walks around it, searching for an entrance, the sun suddenly disappears. He initially thinks that a cloud has covered the sky, and then he realizes that it is the shadow of the rukh, while the dome is one of its eggs.[18]

Many tribes of Native Americans in the United States and Canada, from the Great Plains to the Northern Coasts, have legends of the thunderbird. When this spirit flaps its wings, a storm appears. When it blinks its eyes, there is lightning. The bird is so powerful that it can lift a whale in its talons. A bit like the phoenix, the Native American thunderbird is the centre of esoteric mysteries. Much of its lore is confined to tribal elders, who do not write it down but only pass it on orally to carefully selected heirs. Also like the phoenix, the thunderbird is resurrected. There is a story, told in many versions, of a virtuous young man who became so beloved among his people that those in power saw him as a threat. They tied him to a tree and burned him alive. Soon a thunderbird rose from the ashes. For some Native Americans, the thunderbird is a form taken by Jesus.[19]

Remarkably, all of these embodiments of storms from the Chinese dragon to the Native American thunderbird are basically benign, even for agriculturalists who know well how destructive storms can be. Perhaps that is at least in part because they realize that even the damage done by hurricanes can be outweighed by the blessings of rain. According to Bachelard, the aesthetics of storms is 'basically a poetics of anger', which 'requires forms more animalized than those of clouds driven by a hurricane'.[20] It needs, in other words, a thunderbird. But anger is not the same as malice, and here it is part of a loving, if occasionally troubled, relationship.

To understand the mythic foundations of our culture requires not only learning and imagination but the ability to lay current assumptions aside, in order to think in unaccustomed ways. One must, in other words, forget the eagle is an eagle, so that it can perhaps become a phoenix or thunderbird. Bachelard was one philosopher who preserved that sort of imagination in an era dominated by science, industry and affairs of state.

Especially for somebody who lived through two world wars, Bachelard seems strangely oblivious to politics. He is writing from the perspective of relatively unmediated perception. When he speaks of a bird in flight, he means one seen with the naked eye. He is not talking about one seen through binoculars, much less in a video on YouTube. When he speaks of air, he means an element of pristine clarity. When he speaks of water, he means an ocean without foreign chemicals or floating plastic. This sort of world was already vanishing when he was born in 1882 and is fading from memory today.

Haida thunderbird, Pacific Northwest.

3 BIRD DIVINATION

I could think there trembled through
His happy good-night air
Some blessed Hope, whereof he knew
And I was unaware.
Thomas Hardy, 'The Darkling Thrush'

Souls in Hades, the abode of the dead in Homer's *Odyssey*, have a faded, insubstantial existence until Odysseus gives them pig's blood to drink, which temporarily revives their memories and enables them to speak. The sage Tiresias, who knows the past and the future, towers over the other dead,[1] a bit like the prisoner who escapes from Plato's cave. Tiresias, according to tradition, had been gifted not only with prophetic powers but with the ability to understand the language of birds. In part because they travel widely, birds were considered extremely knowledgeable.

According to Apollodorus, the soothsayer Melampus had befriended two snakes, which during the night approached and licked his ears. On waking he suddenly discovered that, like Tiresias, he could understand the cries of birds flying overhead. They taught him esoteric rites and enabled him to predict the future.[2]

The Old Norse *Poetic Edda*, which was written down in the latter thirteenth century but probably goes back much further in oral traditions, contains similar instances in which heroes learn the language of birds, which then give them prophetic guidance. When Sigurd has slain the dragon Fafnir, he cuts out Fafnir's heart and roasts it on a spit. He touches the heart to see if it is done, burning his finger. When Sigurd puts the finger in his mouth to ease the pain, he is suddenly able to understand the speech of birds. He overhears a flock of nuthatches telling how Regin, his stepfather, is plotting to kill him, and so Sigurd immediately cuts off Regin's head.[3]

Knowing the language of birds is a common motif in fairy tales. In 'The Three Languages', a tale recorded by the Brothers Grimm, a boy announces that he has been learning the speech of birds and other creatures, at which his father, a count, decides that he is useless. His father orders that the boy be taken into the forest and killed, but, guided by animals, he escapes and makes his way to Rome. Two doves land on his shoulders and speak with him, which the cardinals take as a sign from God, and the boy is elected pope.[4] According to Mircea Eliade, 'All over the world learning the language of animals, especially of birds, is equivalent to knowing the secrets of nature and being able to prophesy.'[5] Birds spoke, in other words, the idiom of esoteric wisdom.

The silhouettes of birds against the sky resemble written words, particularly hieroglyphs. When writing with a pen, the hand glides over the surface of the page, a bit like a bird flying over the earth. Quill pens have been used since at least the sixth century CE, but they first became popular in monasteries of the early Middle Ages. When holding one the hand resembles a bird, and, according to Rebecca Ann Bach, 'Quills were part of a culture of writing that related writing and imagination to flight, and when writing with quills, humans consciously took on the powers they attributed to creatures that could actually fly.'[6] In Elizabethan England, the point of the quill was known as the 'neb', a word also used for 'beak', so writing suggested a bird singing in flight.

The Origins of Bird Divination

The Neolithic Revolution began at the end of the last Ice Age and slowly spread across the world. It involved the switch from nomadic populations, with lives based on hunting and gathering, to permanent settlements based on agriculture. This entailed the process known as 'domestication' of vegetation, particularly grains and eventually animals such as the dog, sheep and chicken. There are many theories as to why the Neolithic Revolution took place, but it remains a mystery. Skeletal remains suggest that early agriculturalists generally had poorer health and shorter lives than their hunter-gatherer predecessors.[7] The Neolithic Revolution made people more susceptible to zoonotic diseases

Relief on a rock in Ramsund, Sweden, telling the story of Sigurd, c. 1030. He has just sucked the dragon's blood from his finger and discovered that he can understand the speech of birds.

and predisposed to armed conflict. Towns had to be separated from the surrounding landscapes by walls, which ultimately created a division between what we now refer to as 'civilization' and 'nature'.

The Neolithic Revolution also increased human dependence on weather, since the crops on which they lived could easily be destroyed by intense storms. Birds, which previously may not have been of great interest, became both a major blessing and a threat. People began to pay more attention to the skies and especially to birds, which, through their migration and return, signalled phases of the agricultural year. They helped people to predict the weather, but they also ate grain from cultivated fields.

Animals and even plants are constantly on the alert for the calls or behaviours of other species that might signal danger from predators or sources of food. There is perpetual communication among organisms in a field across

Above: Man-o'-war birds in flight. Photo by Underwood & Underwood, 1930s.
Flying birds form silhouettes in patterns that can sometimes seem like language.
Opposite: Quill pen, photo by Muschki Brichta.

lines of species by means of visual signals, sounds, scents and even, in the case of trees, electrical impulses. American grey squirrels, for example, heed the alarm calls of American robins, black-capped chickadees and other species. They become vigilant and watchful on hearing the calls of hawks, which are their predators, or blue jays, which eat the nuts they have stored, but they are relaxed by the untroubled chatter of harmless birds in a meadow.[8] It is very likely that birds convey information about the weather and even the environment to one another and to other animals. Early human beings were surely similarly conscious of messages that could signal either danger or safety. But as people became more sedentary, reading the natural signs increasingly became a specialism, just like hunting, farming, making war, weaving and almost all other activities.

For Palaeolithic human beings, birds were not a major source of food or a continual threat, and religious practices were centred on the terrestrial realm. Bird divination grew out of the practice of constantly observing the flight of birds in early agricultural and maritime societies for clues to changes in the weather and environment. For farmers, in times when formal calendars were not even in widespread use, observation of birds was necessary to keep track of the agricultural year. Accordingly, Hesiod tells us in *Works and Days*, 'Take heed when you hear the voice of the crane from high in the clouds, making its annual clamor; it brings the signal for ploughing, and indicates the season for winter rains.'[9] If the cranes arrived in early November in flocks, the winter would be early, but if they arrived singly and late, the farmers knew that winter would be delayed.[10] The swallow and cuckoo were the harbingers of spring. Hesiod also advised, 'and if you do plough late, this may be your remedy: when the cuckoo first cuckoos in leaves of oak, gladdening mortals on the boundless earth, then hope that Zeus may rain on the third day without intermission'.[11] The central role of bird divination in the lives of farmers is apparent from the formula for piety and good fortune at the end of *Works and Days*: 'giving the immortals no cause for offence, judging bird-omens and avoiding transgressions'.[12]

Boys on the island of Rhodes chanted a song in spring to the returning swallow, whose arrival signalled fair weather.[13] Many other birds were watched and listened to carefully for signs that might predict the weather, including ravens, crows, sparrows, herons, gulls, ducks, geese, hoopoes, petrels and chickens. In general, agitated behaviour such as very energetic flapping of wings and loud cries suggests an impending storm. Birds can anticipate turbulent weather by sensing an increase in electric currents and subtle changes in air pressure. The use of birds in this way is not much different from observing goldfish or toads to predict earthquakes, which, while controversial, is practised today.

In addition, the sighting of birds told mariners, whose culture transcended geographic boundaries, when they were approaching land. Seamen would often take birds with them on voyages and then release them to judge the nearness and direction of land by watching their flight. In the *Epic of Gilgamesh*, which goes back to about the late second millennium BCE,

*A herring gull comes in for a landing in this photo by C. L. Welsh, USA, 1930s.
As it approaches the ground, the bird artfully shifts its centre of gravity.*

Utnapishtim, who alone with his wife survives a great flood, sends out ravens to see whether land is near.

The biblical Noah does the same, first sending out a raven, which does not return, to look for land. Contrary to what is popularly thought, the failure of the raven to return showed neither defiance of Noah nor failure. Noah had simply been following the practical wisdom of seamen. He doubtless realized that the disappearance of the raven suggested that the boat was at least beginning to approach shore. Having ascertained that, it made sense to send out a less powerful flyer to gauge whether the coast was near. Noah sends out a dove, which returns. After seven days have passed, Noah sends out the dove again, and this time it returns with a freshly plucked olive branch in its beak, so he knows that the flood has receded (Genesis 8:6–12).

When Jason and the Argonauts need to sail the treacherous route through the clashing rocks, they also release a dove, which finds a path that they can follow in safety.[14] In the year 864 the Viking Flóki Vilgerðarson, sailing from Norway, ceremoniously blessed three ravens and then released them in succession from his boat. By following their path, he discovered Iceland.[15] Farmers and mariners both spent their days in the observation of natural phenomena and their survival often depended on understanding meteorological signs correctly. Ploughing at the wrong time could mean a failed harvest, which might lead to starvation. Misjudging the weather at sea could lead to shipwreck. Sailors had fine-tuned their intuition over many years and could read subtle signals, even if not always on a fully conscious level. Their knowledge of the behaviour of birds and other creatures was vast, though it could not be summarized as a set of rules. Their conjectures may not always have been correct, but they were seldom purely superstitious.

According to Debra Herrmann, an expert on avian cognition, 'When it comes to body language, the 9,672 species of birds . . . are more adept at and have more sophisticated means of communicating via visual displays than any other creatures living on the planet.'[16] Many birds engage in mating dances in flight. Pairs of bald eagles lock their talons and spin in cartwheels. Raven couples engage in aerial acrobatics, diving, rising, doing somersaults and circling in the air. Huge flocks of starlings in Scotland synchronize their motions to form beautiful, undulating clouds. Harris hawks coordinate their flights in communal hunting.

Illustration to the story of Noah's Ark, tempera on parchment, England, 1480–90. To strengthen the contrast with the dove, a story was often told in the Middle Ages that the raven failed to return because it was eating corpses. Here it has left only a skull.

The body language and even the facial features of ravens seem to convey a wide range of emotional nuances.

The motions of birds in the air are so evocative that every flight is a sort of story. It has the same rhythmic pattern that we find in a human tale. There is a beginning, when a bird starts to flap its wings. There is a climax, when the bird is in full flight, perhaps engaging in aerial acrobatics or seizing prey. Finally, there is a denouement, as the bird starts to approach the ground, shift its weight and flap its wings more slowly.

Even when the gestures of birds may have no very specific meaning, at least not the sort that can be easily paraphrased, they give all sorts of subtle clues about moods and intentions. They arouse almost intangible fears, aspirations and memories. Paul Shepard points out that the flight of birds closely resembles thought, in that birds 'flash through consciousness connecting with this twig or that branch, are attended to momentarily, and are gone'.[17] The gestures of birds in flight are like the proverbial language of Adam and Eve, in which there is no gap between words and what they represent.

Omens from Zeus and Athena

The Greek word for 'bird' was *ornis*, which is the root of 'ornithology'. *Ornis* could also mean 'omen',[18] and the Latin *avis* had the same double meaning. This suggests that the Greeks and Romans saw avian activity as a sort of representation of our world, filled with intricate parallels. At times these might require learned interpretation, but they might also be intuitively apparent. Birds were a sort of language, only partly decipherable, in which deities constantly talked to human beings.

Divination has never been simply about predicting the future. Rather, it is about knowing a divine will. Before the work of Herodotus and Thucydides, the writing of the Greeks shows little or no sense of historical time. There is no dating in the work of Homer or Hesiod and, consequently, little distinction between past, present and future. Everything takes place in mythic time. The Greeks had little sense of causal determinism, but the will of the immortals, as expressed in omens, lends events a sense of almost inexorable finality.

Illustration to Evart de Conty, Livre des échecs amoureux moralisés *(1496–8).*
This picture is a mélange of ancient and medieval motifs thrown together in idiosyncratic ways.
The figure on the right is the god Apollo, while the three-headed dog at his feet is Cerberus.
In the tree is the prophetic crow of Dodona.

Even among civilizations in the ancient world, the Greeks were a very fatalistic people. They believed that the thread of one's destiny was spun, measured and cut at birth by the three Fates. On another level it was determined by the immortals, who were constantly intervening in human affairs. Along with this belief in fate came the habit of constantly consulting oracles, and the flight of birds was the most popular way in which they told the future.

Crows, kites and vultures might follow armies in anticipation of a meal of carrion after battle, though they had no way to know which side would win nor any reason to care. Similarly, seagulls and pigeons might fly around a warrior camp in hope of being able to feast on scraps from human meals. It may have been possible to ascertain approximately the location and size of an enemy force, and perhaps even its level of activity, by observing where scavengers and other birds congregated. But as soon as it was detached from the contexts of farming and navigation, telling the future by means of birds became less practical and more superstitious.

The oldest shrine consecrated to divination in Greece was that at Dodona, which was known to Homer. Zeus, the Greeks believed, sent messages through the rustling of leaves, supplemented by wind chimes, in a sacred oak tree, which were then interpreted by three priestesses. The Greek historian Herodotus wrote that, according to the priestesses, two 'black doves' (possibly crows) had flown northwards from Thebes in Egypt. One landed at the temple of Zeus-Ammon in Libya. The other came to Dodona and settled in an oak tree, where, speaking with a human voice, it directed people to set up a shrine to Zeus.[19]

Zeus, Athena and others regularly sent birds as omens to indicate fortunes in war. The deities, however, were powerful but not omnipotent. They were also not always trustworthy, and at times they deliberately deceived people. In addition, not all bird behaviour was necessarily significant. Nevertheless, there was almost always a suggestion of impiety attached to denying the significance of omens, as though disbelief in them were itself a slight against the gods, and those who expressed scepticism suffered dire consequences. Bird prophecies in battle could often be self-fulfilling, since they had the potential to rally or panic troops.

For the Homeric Greeks, nature was seldom restful. They saw their own violence reflected in the predatory behaviour of raptors and, occasionally, serpents. In Homer extreme conflict is ubiquitous in both nature and society, and there does not seem to be much difference between the two realms. Human beings do not have any particular qualities that set them apart from, much less above, animals. All life, whether of human beings or other creatures, is

Stained-glass dove surmounting the throne created by Gian Lorenzo Bernini in St Peter's Basilica, Rome, 1657–66.

precarious and easily expendable. There is very little explicit psychology; in fact, the characters in Homer do not seem to have a great deal of internal life, and their personalities are not very sharply differentiated from one another. Their emotions are intense but simple. Even the mightiest are constantly haunted by fear and prone to lash out unpredictably. The Homeric heroes, for the most part, appear almost as predatory beasts, and that is much of their fascination.

The major ontological division in Homer is not between humankind and nature but between mortals and immortals. The deities are constantly quarrelling with one another, yet they maintain a degree of peace by choosing human beings as their champions and having these engage in combat, very much like fighting cocks. For this reason alone, the deities are generally focused on the human world. The way deities use human beings as surrogates to fight their quarrels may not justify wars and feuds, but it places them beyond the need for legitimation. The gods and goddesses absorb the pettiness of human quarrels, making men and women more heroic.

In the works of Homer and many others, bird omens usually appear at critical moments – often just before the climax of an episode – perhaps because that is when people are most in need of guidance. At times when battle was raging and everything hung in the balance, the tension must have been almost unbearable and the appearance of a bird might, even if the omen was not favourable, bring immediate relief. By deflecting blame to the heavens, the birds might have also turned any anger away from the commanders.

Though people in the time of Homer already specialized in interpreting the behaviour of birds, it did not necessarily require esoteric knowledge. There was only one major rule: bad omens are on the left and good ones on the right, a rule that still informs many superstitions in the modern period. In the *Iliad*, when Diomedes and Odysseus set out at night for a raid on Troy, the goddess Athena sends a heron on their right. The two are unable to see it because of the darkness, but they hear its call and immediately understand it as an omen of success.[20]

Just about every major episode in Homer is connected with some sort of prophecy involving birds. Most of the time, divination used to predict the outcome of a battle or adventure involved an entirely different class of birds from those used in agriculture or navigation, as well as a profoundly different sort of sign. The avian activity that people in Homer usually regarded as ominous or auspicious is mostly predatory, and the prophetic birds were usually eagles.

In the *Iliad*, when Hector leads the Trojans in an attack on the Greek ships, his men hesitate before a defensive trench. An eagle flies overhead from right to left across their front line. It holds a large snake, still struggling, in its talons. The snake suddenly bites the eagle just below the neck. The eagle drops the serpent in the Trojan ranks and then flies off with a shriek. Polydamas, a friend of Hector who is skilled in interpreting omens, takes this as a warning that they should not continue to attack the Greeks. He explains that the eagle represents the Trojans, who hold a temporary advantage, while the snake represents the Greeks, who will eventually counterattack and drive them away. Hector replies scornfully that he does not care about the flight of birds. At his orders, the men continue their attack, but, as Polydamas predicted, it does not turn out well for the Trojans.[21]

At the end of the *Iliad*, when Achilles has killed Hector in combat, he leaves the body to rot, but the deities miraculously protect it from decay. Priam, the aged king of Troy and father of Hector, makes the bold decision to approach Achilles' tent and ask him to ransom the body. He prays for a favourable omen. An enormous black eagle (possibly a raven) appears on his right, and he knows that his suit will be successful.[22]

In some passages, however, the interpretation seems superimposed on behaviour that is only striking or unusual. In the *Odyssey*, Telemachus, son of Odysseus and Penelope, complains that the suitors of his mother are devouring the family goods and refuse to leave their home. He prays to Zeus for a sign. In response Zeus sends two eagles, which hover lazily over the people and drift in the wind. When they are directly above the assembly, they turn in arcs, begin beating their wings intensely and look down intently. They engage briefly in combat and then fly off as everyone watches in amazement. An augur interprets the omen as signalling that Odysseus is near and will soon return home, bringing destruction to the suitors.[23] What they saw was probably a mating dance. The enormous golden eagle, which is indigenous to Greece, has a courtship dance that consists mostly of dramatic swoops and dives. The mating pair also raise their talons, engage in mock attacks and chase one another, behaviour that can easily be mistaken for genuine fighting.

Because the sight of their true forms is not easy for mortals to bear, the deities not infrequently assume the form of birds. At one point in the *Iliad*, Athena and Apollo sit in an oak tree like vultures to watch a battle.[24] In the *Odyssey*, the sea goddess Ino appears to Odysseus in the form of a shearwater.[25] In well-known myths, Zeus takes the form of a swan to impregnate Leda and a sparrow to seduce Hera.

Such transformations have suggested to mythographers such as Otto Keller and Hans Blumenberg that birds and other animals were the original forms of the deities,[26] to which they reverted from time to time. Metaphors from birds and other animals are also frequently used to describe the deities: for example, Athena is often referred to as 'owl-eyed' and Hera as 'cow-eyed'. Did the Greeks consider the human forms of their deities more authentic than the bestial ones? Blumenberg has written of the Olympians, 'Even when they appear in human form, there is an "echo" of the animal form and animal countenance. It is not always possible to distinguish between metamorphosis and simile, particularly in Homer.'[27] When Zeus sends an eagle flying over the battlefield, we do not know for sure if the bird is just a messenger or an avatar of the god.

After Homer, avian omens continued to be important in wars. Plutarch reports, for example, that when the general Themistocles was speaking to his troops before the naval battle of Salamis against the Persians, an owl appeared flying to the right of his fleet and then eventually settled on the top of a ship's mast. The event was especially noteworthy, since owls are generally nocturnal. The Greeks, like most peoples, usually considered owls birds of ill omen. However, since they were associated with Athena, patron goddess of the city of Athens, in this case the soldiers took it as a favourable sign.[28] Plutarch also reported that ravens led Alexander and his men to the temple of Zeus-Ammon in Egypt, even providing special guidance for stragglers who had become lost. They later prophesied his imminent death in Babylon, however, when a large flock of ravens flew over and a few fell dead at his feet.[29]

Though less emphasis was placed on raptors, the importance of birds in divination continued in the Roman Empire. According to tradition, Romans chose the site of their city and their first ruler by counting vultures.[30] Suetonius reports in *The Twelve Caesars* that a wren bearing a sprig of laurel in its beak flew into the senate house of Pompey, the former rival of Julius Caesar, where it was torn to pieces by pursuing birds. Augurs interpreted this as a sign of danger to Caesar, who was indeed assassinated shortly afterwards.[31]

Aelian, a Roman who wrote in Greek during the second century CE, recorded many of the more homely and colourful beliefs that were current about birds and other animals. He tells how crows were symbols of faithful, married love, since they never indulged in promiscuous intercourse, and when one crow died its partner would never take another mate. A 'Crow Song' was sung at weddings, in which partners would pledge their fidelity to one another. For the same reason, however, to hear a single crow at a wedding was a bad omen.[32]

People as well as gods frequently changed into birds in Graeco-Roman mythologies. According to Aelian, at the end of their lives storks and cranes retire to distant islands, where, because of their filial piety, they are transformed into human beings.[33] A witch, Circe, turns Picus, the first king of Latium, into a woodpecker for rejecting her advances.[34] Ceyx, king of Trachis and happily married to Alcyone, is killed on a sea voyage. When Alcyone commits suicide out of grief by throwing herself in the sea, the immortals change the couple into kingfishers and then set a period of seven days in winter, known as 'halcyon days', when the sea will remain untroubled so that they can mate.[35]

In the ancient world, even deities occasionally practise bird divination, in a sort of role reversal. There is an inscription on an amulet placed near an Egyptian mummy stating, 'I am the benu-bird, the soul of Re, who guides the gods to the netherworld.'[36] According to some legends, when Zeus was preparing for a battle with the Titans, an eagle flew over predicting victory for the gods.[37] In one legend a raven brought Apollo news that his mistress Koronis had been unfaithful.[38] In *The Golden Ass*, a second-century CE novel in Latin by the North African writer Apuleius, Venus, the goddess of love, had a seagull that would fly around the world and bring her news.[39] Two ravens named Hugine (thought) and Munine (memory) brought news to Odin, the Norse god of battles. Such prophetic birds are clearly not just messengers, or even avatars, of deities, since even immortals rely upon their council.

Our most systematic discussion of soothsaying from the ancient world is probably Cicero's *On Divination*, written in 44 BCE. It is a very thoughtful dialogue in prose between Quintus, who is a sceptic, and his brother Marcus, who accepts traditional beliefs about divination. Marcus claims that his beliefs are shared by all peoples and nations. He distinguishes between 'natural' and 'artificial' divination. The first consists of dreams or words uttered in a frenzy of divine inspiration, which are spontaneous and require little or no interpretation. The second consists of prophecies that require special knowledge. These include telling the future from the flight of birds, astrology, lightning and other phenomena.[40] The division was, and remains, a valid one. By Cicero's time, ornithomancy, as practised by the elites, had become a highly esoteric practice surrounded by complicated rules. Artificial divination usually seems to develop in periods of scepticism, when, in response to doubt, augury becomes increasingly esoteric, intricate and opaque.

But the flight and behaviour of birds does not necessarily require sophisticated interpretation. If a beautiful and slightly unusual bird passes overhead before an important test, one is likely to approach the challenge with greater optimism. One will, in other words, take the bird as something resembling a favourable omen, whether consciously or not. Even when bird divination had become highly esoteric among the elites, a far less intricate form was probably practised by the common people. While the artificial divination of the upper classes was focused on affairs of state, natural divination was about personal concerns. In most eras we have few records of the natural sort of bird divination, for several reasons. Most of the people who practised it exclusively were probably illiterate and lacked access to scribes. Most significantly perhaps, it can only be understood in the context of a rather specific situation, including the hopes and fears of the person who receives it.

Messengers from Yahweh

Much as Zeus would send an eagle as a sign of his presence, the Judaeo-Christian God would often send a dove. In a monotheistic tradition marked by periodic efforts to eliminate vestiges of paganism, idolatry, zoolatry and superstition, the veneration of animals has generated many waves of controversy, but the dove has been hallowed in Judaeo-Christian iconography from early times. Long before even Homer, the dove had been associated with many goddesses of the Near East such as the Hittite Atargatis and the Phoenician Astarte. This association with doves was passed on to the Greek goddess Aphrodite, the Roman Venus and finally the Christian Mary.

Divinity in the Tanakh, or Old Testament, was not entirely lacking a female element. In the first Creation story, God creates the first man and woman in his own image, suggesting that he contains both (Genesis 1:27). But God is consistently referred to by the male pronoun and has been almost invariably depicted as male. This contrasts with the pagan pantheons of the ancient world, which all contained powerful female and male figures. It resulted in a lack of balance and the dove, which had been so long associated with female divinities, provided a longed-for feminine element in iconography.

Arguably the first suggestion of this is at the beginning of the Creation story, when the Bible tells us that, as soon as the heavens and earth had been created, 'God's spirit hovered upon the water' (Genesis 1:2, Jerusalem translation). The phrasing suggests a bird and it is in this way, specifically as a dove, that the line has usually been illustrated. In many passages, particularly from the Psalms and the Song of Songs, the dove is a symbol of beauty and purity. In the latter, the speaker refers to his beloved as 'my dove' and praises her in terms that seem almost impious:

> The maidens saw her, and proclaimed her blessed, queens and concubines sang her praises: 'Who is this arising like the dawn, fair as the moon, resplendent as the sun, terrible as an army with banners?' (Song of Songs 6:9–10, Jerusalem translation).

For rabbinic authorities, the dove often represented the nation of Israel.[41] Pigeons and doves are mentioned as the only acceptable birds for sacrifice in Leviticus (1:14), and they were an option for poor people who could not afford more expensive animals. In the time of Jesus, when other animal sacrifices had long been abandoned, doves for that purpose were still regularly sold around Jewish temples. Like virtually all animal sacrifices, they mediated between human beings and divinity. Doves and pigeons had already long been used to carry messages, and they were also considered capable of carrying communications from human beings to God. This role was not fully acknowledged in a religion that emphatically rejected any suggestion of zoolatry, but it began to become more explicit in Christianity.

God the Father became one part of the Holy Trinity, together with the Son and the Holy Spirit. The first two figures were anthropomorphic as well as masculine. The third was mystical and ambiguous. Though it is never explicitly identified as a dove in Christian doctrine, it has very seldom been depicted as anything else. From early times, there have been debates as to whether the Holy Spirit is masculine, feminine or genderless. The Hebrew word for 'spirit', *rauch*, is feminine, as are its cognates in Aramaic and many other ancient languages.

Nevertheless, the Holy Spirit is referred to with a masculine pronoun in many translations of the Bible and liturgies. However, it is visualized as a dove and its associations are overwhelmingly feminine.

Mary, mother of Jesus, who has often overshadowed her son in Catholic and Eastern Orthodox worship, inherited the symbolism of many Mediterranean goddesses and became closely identified with a dove. According to the apocryphal gospel known as the *Protoevangelium*, she was raised in a temple and educated in the ways of God by a dove. In the same book, as well as other accounts of Jesus, Joseph was chosen as her husband when a dove landed on his staff.[42] The most detailed account of the Annunciation is in the Gospel of Luke, where the angel Gabriel appears to Mary and announces that she has been chosen to bear the Son of God. Mary asks, 'How can this come about, since I am a virgin?' The angel replies, 'The Holy Spirit will come upon you' (Luke 1:34–5). This has usually been represented in Christian art as a dove in a ray of light.

Just as an eagle was often the sign of the presence of Zeus or Jupiter, so the dove signalled that of Yahweh. In the Gospel of Luke, when John baptizes Jesus, 'heaven opened and the holy spirit descended on him in bodily shape, like a dove' (Luke 3:21–2). The voice from the sky then proclaims Jesus the son of God. The story is retold, with hardly any variation, in the other three gospels. As is also often the case in Homer, it is not entirely clear whether the bird is literal or metaphoric. At any rate, countless illustrations would show a dove hovering above the head of Jesus in a beam of light, with God the father looking on in the distance.

In the description of Pentecost a group of Christians from many lands was meeting in Jerusalem,

> when suddenly they heard what sounded like a powerful wind from heaven, the noise of which filled the entire house in which they were sitting, and something appeared to them like tongues of fire; these separated and came to rest on the head of each of them. They were filled with the Holy Spirit and began to speak foreign languages (Acts 2:1–4).

The wind is suggestive of beating wings, though no other bird is explicitly mentioned, but artists have usually depicted the Holy Spirit here as a dove, often at the centre of beams of light, which end in flames. Since most people in pre-modern times were not literate, the visual interpretations of biblical events were in practice more influential than fine points of official doctrine.

La Pentecôte

Tableau de Gaudentio Ferrari, qui est dans le Cabinet de M.r Crozat.

Peint sur bois, haut de 8. pieds 1. pouce, large de 5. pieds 4. pouces, gravé par Frederic Hortemels.

82

The practice of reading the divine will through the behaviour of birds continues in a wide range of different eras, cultures and religious or philosophical beliefs, without a great deal of variation. It is found in cultures that are polytheistic or resolutely monotheistic, rural or urban, authoritarian or democratic. This suggests to me that it expresses an impulse in many ways prior to culture. There is little in the intellectual foundations of Jewish, Christian, Islamic or Buddhist theology that would sanction such fortune telling, but tales of bird divination still appear in those religions.

Bird divination usually does not follow many fixed rules. In most instances it simply involves, at a moment of decision, noticing unusual and dramatic behaviour in birds and then interpreting it as a harbinger of fate. In the Koran, when Cain realizes that he has killed his brother, he does not know what to do. A raven claws the earth, showing how to give Abel a burial, and then Cain repents.[43]

Near the beginning of the Middle High German epic *The Nibelungenlied*, from the end of the twelfth century, Princess Kriemhild dreams that she had reared a magnificent falcon, but two eagles tore it to pieces. Her mother interprets the dream to mean that she will marry a noble man but will lose him soon afterwards.[44] Kriemhild then decides never to marry, but she later changes her mind and the prophecy is fulfilled.

In the early fourteenth-century Japanese epic *Tale of the Heike*, before the sea battle of Dan-no-ura between the Genji and Heike clans, a warlord is uncertain about which side to support. He sets seven cocks that are white, the colour of the Genji, to fight seven that are red, the colour of the Heike, and the white cocks win every time. He takes that as a sign from heaven that the Genji will be victorious, and he lends them his support.[45]

Esoteric traditions adopted, partially secularized and expanded the dense symbolism of the late Middle Ages and Renaissance, where almost every object became charged with meanings. Birds were often used to represent stages of the alchemical transformations, whereby base metals were transmuted into gold. That, in turn, corresponded to stages in the purification of the soul. Descriptions of this process varied greatly from one alchemist to the next. In general, the initial phase of *prima materia*, or primordial matter, was represented by a raven or crow, partly because of its blackness. The intermediate phases, where heated metal takes on many colours, was represented by a peacock, and the final phase, when it was heated to a glowing whiteness, by a dove. These symbols could also be used in divination.

Frédéric Horthemels, Pentecost, *1729–40, engraving. The dove here is so central to the scene that its significance goes far beyond symbolism.*

The most central work of Western esoteric traditions is *The Chemical Wedding of Christian Rosenkreutz*, usually attributed to the German pastor Johannes Valentinus Andrea and written around the start of the seventeenth century. On his way to a royal wedding, the protagonist Christian Rosenkreutz comes to a place where the path forks in three different directions, and he is unsure which to choose. While he is trying to decide, a white dove flutters down and approaches him without fear. He offers it part of his food, and then a raven suddenly attacks and tries to seize the meal, at which the dove flies away. The raven chases it and Rosenkreutz angrily runs after the raven. The two birds lead him along the correct path.[46] It is the way of alchemy, which begins with the raven and is consummated with the dove.

Modern Divination

In the modern period, which historians conventionally date from 1801 through to 1950, people widely thought that superstitious practices such as divination would gradually disappear. Though there were plenty of dissenting voices, intellectuals generally assumed that history was a record of ever-increasing rationality. Cultural anthropologists such as James George Frazer and Bronisław Malinowski believed that human culture inevitably progressed from magic to religion and finally to science, and that we had begun the last transition. Some celebrated the demise of magic and religion, while others lamented it, and most people did a little of both. Early folklorists began to systematically record legends and superstitions, believing this was a cultural heritage which had to be recorded soon to prevent it from vanishing forever.

In retrospect, the ease with which folklorists were finding legends and magical practices should have alerted them that these were not dying out. The daily horoscope remained a popular feature in most newspapers, and tabloids such as the *Weekly World News* were as at least as full of legends as the folk books of the Early Modern period had ever been. They seem to come from a folkloric substratum of a society, which may not be greatly affected by whether a country is officially Christian, Islamic, Buddhist, Communist, Fascist or anything else. Ideas such as the transmigration of souls constantly surface in folklore and literature, whether the favoured system of belief has a place for them or not.

The incessant scrutiny of traditional beliefs, as well as a mistrust of intuition, in the modern period has sometimes led to a rebirth of what Cicero called 'artificial divination', in which the art of prophesy is formulated in terms of complicated rules. One example is the counting of magpies, which is first attested in a quatrain recorded in 1780 in Lincolnshire, England:

> One is for sorrow,
> Two is for mirth,
> Three for a wedding,
> And four for a birth.

Later versions are considerably varied: in one such, three is for the birth of a girl and four for a boy. Additional lines, going up to about eight, were added to predict a person's fortune or destiny in the next life. In American versions, crows instead of magpies were used.[47]

But it is hard to say how much these charms were a matter of amusement and how much they were believed. Even when folklorists conscientiously document the gender, class and ethnicity of their informants, much of the context of their tales is inevitably lost. The existence of several variants suggest that people may simply have changed the verses to conform to their expectations. Perhaps the major purpose of such divination was to give people the confidence to carry through on decisions that they had, half-consciously, already made.

The German fairy tales recorded by the Brothers Grimm in the early nineteenth century contain some of the most extravagant magic in all of literature, including several examples of ornithomancy. Perhaps the best example is the story of 'Faithful Johannes'. An old king has assigned his servant Johannes to look after a young prince, who has just abducted a beloved bride, in an episode that perhaps goes back to a Viking raid. The young couple are about to marry when Johannes overhears three prophetic ravens telling in great detail the hazards that await them. A beautiful horse will be waiting for the prince, but it will fly away with him and never return. A beautiful wedding dress will be waiting for the princess, but it is really made of pitch and will burn her to death. At the wedding dance, the princess will fall as if dead and may only be revived by a magical formula. Johannes shoots the horse, burns the dress and then revives the princess, but when he tries to explain his deeds, he is mysteriously turned to stone.[48] The hero of the story certainly suggests an augur or shaman whose magic practices survived into the modern era, where they were no longer understood. The Brothers Grimm themselves believed that the tales contained remnants of an archaic mythology, and scholars still debate whether the magic is more an ancient inheritance or a Romantic invention. Perhaps it might be most accurate to call it both, for the imaginative appeal of such enchantments has never faded.

Up through the late nineteenth century and the early twentieth, even urban people could still often mark the time of day, particularly dawn, by the crowing of a rooster. This was part of a daily routine and any abrupt break in the pattern signalled a major change, usually for the worse. In Ireland at the end of the nineteenth century, if somebody set out on a journey and a crowing rooster met him in the doorway, people thought the trip should be postponed, for it otherwise would not turn out well. In the West of England in the late nineteenth century, people said that if a cock crowed at midnight, the angel of death was passing over a house.[49] To see a dead pigeon was considered a sign of bad luck in Britain. Swallows and other birds entering a window or flying down a chimney were also often considered ominous.[50] But the accounts of such superstitions are so fragmentary that it is hard to know whether they are more representative of a shared belief or an individual response to an unaccustomed situation.

It may not matter a great deal if people believe in, or have even heard of, superstitions. Unusual events that involve impressive birds appear charged with meaning, enough so to change anybody into a soothsayer. In England at the beginning of the twentieth century, one informant reported that an old owl flew in through the door at a wedding, alighted briefly on the bride's chair, and then flew three times around the room and out the window. Everyone spontaneously took this as an unfavourable omen. The person who reported this apparently did not usually give credence to superstitions, for she added in retrospect, 'Of course, nothing happened.'[51]

Native American author Evan T. Pritchard uses the term 'bird medicine' for the practice of understanding bird behaviour in terms of messages and even portents. According to him, it is not necessarily tied to any system of beliefs and does not follow any strict rules. It is, in his opinion, universal, though most developed in Native American cultures.[52] For those who are receptive to their guidance, birds may appear in many capacities, such as role models, teachers, messengers and storytellers, though there is no way of summoning them at any particular moment. One day, the author tells, he was driving to a job interview at a university and was lost. Suddenly he saw a red-tailed hawk gliding directly in front of the windscreen, which seemed to be guiding him. After about a mile, it flew away, and he immediately knew that the job would be his.[53]

According to an account by Pritchard's Mi'kmaq relative White Wolf, when her mother died, a small bird perched on her headstone during the funeral. When the minister gave her eulogy, the bird turned towards him and appeared to listen intently. As the body was lowered into the earth, it looked down into the grave. Finally, as the ceremony was ending, it chirped a few

Faithful John listens to the prophecies of ravens in this illustration by Walter Crane to Household Stories *by the Brothers Grimm (1886). Motifs in the story seem to go back to Viking times or earlier, though the picture is in the spirit of Victorian medievalism.*

FAITHFUL·IOHN

IT HAPPENED, AS THEY WERE STILL
JOURNEYING ON THE OPEN SEA, THAT
FAITHFUL IOHN, AS HE SAT IN THE FORE
PART OF THE SHIP, & MADE MUSIC, CAUGHT
SIGHT OF THREE RAVENS FLYING OVER-
HEAD.   THEN HE STOPPED PLAYING &
LISTENED TO WHAT THEY SAID TO ONE ANOTHER

times and flew away. White Wolf always believed that the spirit of her mother entered the bird and came to say good-bye.⁵⁴ The funeral appears to have been Christian, but that made little difference in interpreting the behaviour of the bird, for such divination seems to belong mostly to a level of awareness that is prior to formalized beliefs.

All birds from the sparrow to the heron are used in natural divination, as understood by Cicero. The messages they bring are far from trivial; in fact they can be matters of life and death for individuals. Nevertheless, at least in Western culture, a single variety of bird is used predominantly to express epic concerns such as the fate of nations or even the destiny of humankind. As we have already seen, for the Homeric heroes this was the eagle of Zeus. In Christianity, the bird of destiny became the dove, representing the Holy Spirit. In modern, largely secular culture, it became the raven.

The eagle was a fitting, and perhaps almost inevitable, choice for a warrior culture, because of its fierceness, power and predatory behaviour. The dove signalled a break with the pagan world of the past, since it was in so many ways the opposite of the eagle. It was distinguished not by power but by beauty and grace. It was also a sacrificial bird, appropriate to a divinity that took human form and embraced crucifixion. Why the raven became the bird to express the destiny of nations in the modern world is less immediately clear. Part of the reason is doubtless that, in an era that emphasized intellectual accomplishments, ravens stood out as perhaps the most intelligent of birds.

Ravens' body language and even their faces seem to express a vast range of emotions. Both the eagle and the dove are birds that inspire admiration, yet, in more personal ways, they are not easy to relate to. Their features are fixed in a single expression, and their personalities, at least from a human point of view, can seem one-dimensional. Perhaps that is why they are especially suited to represent other, anthropomorphic powers. The raven, as befitting a society without clearly defined religious beliefs, can seem to express emotions and simultaneously embody fate. It is particularly important in the folklore of Germany, France and Britain.

The raven was important in Germanic and Scandinavian cultures from very early times. Just as the Romans had marched into battle carrying the standard of the eagle, the Vikings carried a flag with a raven. The Valkyries, warrior maidens who brought those who died in battle to Valhalla, were associated with ravens. Old sagas often speak of killing adversaries in battle as 'feeding the ravens'.

According to a popular German legend recorded by the Brothers Grimm, the Holy Roman Emperor Frederick Barbarossa (reg. 1155–90) is not dead but sleeping in the Kyffhaüserberg, a ridge in the Kyffhaüser hills in Thuringia. When he finally emerges, he will hang his shield on a dead tree, which will then immediately sprout new leaves, and a new age will commence. Every hundred years he checks to see if the ravens are still flying over the mountain and, on learning that they are, he goes back to sleep.[55] At the beginning of the Franco-Prussian War of 1870–71 the new flag of the united German nation was unfurled on the mountain, at which the ravens reportedly 'fled screaming from their usual haunt'. The event was probably staged, but at any rate it suggested to spectators that Kaiser Wilhelm I was the second coming of Frederick Barbarossa, who would restore his people to their former glory.[56] After the death of Wilhelm in 1888, a huge monument was erected on top of the Kyffhaüserberg. It featured a sandstone sculpture of Barbarossa on the lower level, with a far larger copper statue of Wilhelm on horseback at the level above, the whole topped by a tower with an imperial crown.

In France there is a legend of a raven (in some versions a crow) that can be recognized by its partially grey plumage and appears to rulers just before a catastrophe in which they will be deposed or killed. The raven first appeared to Queen Marie Antoinette in about 1786 in her Petit Trianon retreat at Versailles, and it constantly followed her whenever she went outdoors. After she was arrested, it disappeared for a while, but then appeared to Napoleon's second wife, Marie Louise, in almost the same place. She reported this to her husband, who was alarmed and said she should leave the Trianon. She did so, but she returned in 1814 after Napoleon had been defeated and sent into exile on Elba. She was walking there with her father and reminiscing about former days when they heard the loud call of the raven behind them. She fainted. As we all know, Napoleon briefly returned to power, only to be defeated once again.[57] For a while the raven continued to live at the Trianon, where it was fed by servants and pointed out to tourists.

Adolphe Thiers, president of France's Third Republic, saw and recognized the raven in 1872 when he was staying at Versailles. He denied being afraid, but the bird followed him to the Elysée Palace in Paris, where it reappeared before the assassination of French president Marie-François Sadi Carnot in 1894. About two years later the raven reportedly appeared before, and furiously flapped its wings at, the next president, Félix Faure.[58] Directly afterwards Faure abruptly collapsed and died while engaged in sex with a prostitute. Subsequent sightings of the raven have inspired rumours and widespread fear.[59]

But it has been in Britain that the prophetic aspect of the raven has been most enshrined. Ravens were brought to the Tower of London in the early 1880s, in part to make a connection with Bran the Blessed, a Celtic raven deity whose body, according to legend, is buried there to protect London from invasion. The first ravens were supplied by the Earl of Dunraven, who strongly believed in ghosts. Iolo Morganwg, a Celtic scholar, forger and occultist, had convinced the Dunraven family that their castle in Wales was the home of the original Bran, who had been an actual person. Bringing ravens to the Tower may have been an attempt to assert a sort of spiritual claim on the Tower on behalf of Bran.

The Tower of London was, and still is, marketed to tourists essentially as a Gothic house of horrors, using grisly stories of tortures and executions. The ravens were probably used by the Yeoman Warders, who lead tours, as props for stories of bloody rulers, romantic rebels, ghosts and maidens in distress. A guide might say something like, 'They chopped off her head, and ravens immediately descended to pluck out her eyes.' A real raven might then add to the ambiance by croaking in the background.[60]

After a while people forgot about the origin of the ravens, and they became enveloped in even more mystery. During the Second World War they were used clandestinely as spotters for enemy bombs and planes, which helped inspire a legend that Britain, or at least the Tower of London, would fall if the ravens ever left the Tower. Like so many other legends, this one was pushed

Raven at the Tower of London.

into the remote, indefinite past. Official publications by the Tower told visitors that the ravens had been in the Tower since ancient times, and that their wings were clipped by Charles II because of an ancient prophecy.[61] Only in the twenty-first century has the Tower conceded that the ravens are a modern institution, but that story lives on even in the days of COVID-19.[62]

Animal divination remains popular. It received a big boost when Paul the Octopus, a resident of an aquarium in Oberhausen, Germany, successfully predicted the winners of all seven of Germany's football matches as well as Spain's final victory in the 2010 World Cup. This was an instance of artificial divination, as the term had been used by Cicero, and a more complicated one than even the Romans ever imagined. In an elaborate procedure devised by scientists to eliminate bias, before each game Paul would be placed in a tank between two jars of mussels, each with the insignia of a soccer team, and the one he selected was the predicted winner. In the following years a large range of animals began to be used in divination, especially for sporting events, including hedgehogs, cows and elephants. Tower of London Ravenmaster Chris Skaife announced over his Twitter account that he was training the popular raven Merlina to predict the winners of the Olympic Games in 2012. Apparently, that was not among her talents, for the project was eventually dropped.

Peter Doherty has recently, in a book with the visionary title *Their Fate Is Our Fate*, made a scientifically argued case that birds are the best monitors of important changes in the environment. As he puts it:

> In the course of just living, the free-flying and readily observed birds sample the atmosphere, the oceans, the plants, the forests, and even insect life. If any one of those is compromised, the first place that such effects may become obvious is in the health and number of birds, both within and between species.[63]

Birds have the major role in spreading vegetation. They ingest seeds and eliminate them together with their dung, which serves as fertilizer. They also carry seeds and pollen for great distances in their feathers. Some, especially corvids, also cache nuts, some of which they forget and allow to grow into plants. Vegetation, and ultimately all life, suffers from the absence of birds.

I think the sages of the ancient world must have had an intuition of this, even though they expressed it in mythological terms. If migrating birds failed to show up in their usual numbers, for instance, they could sense that something might be wrong. They spoke mostly of individual birds in part because they understood that a single avian appearance in the sky at a tense moment was more dramatic than a gradual trend. They freely blended their observations with intuition, just as contemporary storytellers do. Counting birds to ascertain the health of the ecosystem, as we do today, is not entirely different from the way augurs of old scanned the sky for warnings. In both cases, it is hard to know just where reason leaves off and imagination begins.

4 BIRD SOULS

Thou awakenest in beauty, magnificent falcon of morning.
Egyptian hymn to the sun-god Re

The biblical prophet Isaiah called Egypt the 'country of whirring wings' (Isaiah 18:1, Jerusalem translation). Perhaps no other civilization has accorded birds such prominence in religion, art and just about every aspect of life. Egypt had, and still has, an extraordinary abundance of birds. It is directly on a major migratory path for birds, including hundreds of thousands of white storks that still pass by twice a year on a journey from the Arctic region and much of Europe all the way to Southern Africa.[1] Many, possibly most, of the prominent Egyptian deities were at times depicted either in the form of birds or at least with avian features such as wings. In one popular creation myth, Geb, god of the earth, took the form of a goose and (despite his gender) laid a cosmic egg, from which the sun was hatched.

Animals and birds were depicted in virtually every aspect of Egyptian life, as pets, divine messengers, livestock, game, hieroglyphs, decorations and so on. Francis Klingender writes, 'One of the most remarkable features of Egyptian religion is the tenacity with which totemic associations with animals, wild as well as domestic, were retained down to the Christian era.'[2] Juliet Clutton-Brock goes even further, stating, 'The people of ancient Egypt were more involved, as a nation, with wild and domestic animals in cultural and religious ways than any other civilization before or since.'[3] Egyptian art certainly celebrates a vastly greater variety of animals, and in far more situations, than the cave artists of Palaeolithic times. More than seventy species of birds alone have been identified in Egyptian paintings, sculptures and reliefs.[4]

Egyptians shared the fascination of earlier and concurrent cultures with large, powerful animals, especially felines and bovines, but they also paid attention to small ones such as insects. They probably emphasized birds, from swallows to vultures, more than any other kind of creature. The hieroglyphs consisted largely of stylized animals, and more than sixty of them are complete or partial images of birds.[5] Animals and birds decorated objects used in everyday life such as combs, toys, bowls, vases, musical instruments, boxes and games. They could be imposing statues in temples or humorous cartoons. Animals figure in Egyptian mythologies at least as prominently as people, perhaps a good deal more.

What this indicates is not simply that the Egyptians loved animals. They did, but that love was only part of a vast range of feelings for other

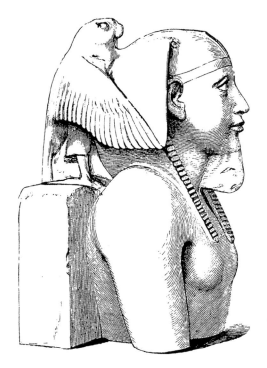

creatures, which could also include fear, rivalry and amusement. Every human representation of another creature is at least subtly suggestive of qualities that human beings wish to either incorporate into or banish from their own identities. That applies, for example, to national birds, names of sports teams and prints on T-shirts. Each contains an element of totemism, even when, as in contemporary times, this is muted and well beneath the threshold of consciousness.

The pharaoh was closely associated with a falcon and often depicted with one. Thoth, the god of wisdom, was most often shown with the body of a man but the head of an ibis, but he could also fully assume the form of an ibis or a baboon. Many female deities were depicted as vultures: Nut, goddess of the sky; Mut, goddess of motherhood; Nephtys, goddess of mourning; Nekhbet, guardian of upper Egypt; and Wadjet, guardian of lower Egypt. Maat, goddess of balance and harmony, was depicted as a woman with wings, and sometimes represented by an ostrich feather.

Cyclical Time

According to Klingender, 'Whereas Mesopotamian art was chiefly devoted to the exaltation of cosmic strife and to the commemoration of great historical events ... Egyptian artists of the Old and Middle Kingdoms, up to 1500 BCE, ignored time and change in their works, which exalt the peaceful round of daily life and its sustaining rituals.'[6] The Mesopotamian *Epic of Gilgamesh*, which goes back to the third millennium BCE, is about coming to terms with the inevitability of death. There is nothing comparable in Egyptian culture, where death held little terror. Although the Egyptian underworld contained demons, their depictions of death do not convey the horror that we often find in, say, the more graphic European Baroque, Maya and Tibetan

Stone statue of the god Horus in the form of a falcon sheltering Pharaoh Khafre, c. 2480 BCE.

representations, full of skeletons, grimacing faces, streams of blood and severed heads.

The Egyptian conception of time was cyclical. They had many creation myths, yet no myths about the end of the world. Their lives were governed by the rhythm of the seasons, particularly as reflected in the annual rise of the Nile and the flooding of the Delta, which deposited fresh soil and was essential to agriculture. Even Re-Horakhty, the sun-god and often the supreme deity of the Egyptian pantheon, was not immortal in the same way as Zeus and the Olympians. He died at dusk, then travelled through the underworld to be 'reborn' the following day. By about the sixteenth century BCE the goal of Egyptians was not precisely to live eternally but to join Re in this eternal rotation.[7] The sky and the underworld are simply phases of the sun's daily journey.

According to anthrozoologist Aaron Katcher, animals do not go through our continual developmental stages of infancy, childhood, youth, adulthood, middle years and old age. In contrast, among animals, especially in the wild, the first three of these stages blend and last only a short time. Old age is almost unknown and, if it occasionally is reached, does not involve any change of role. Most of life is lived in the single level of maturity. In the absence of any sequential progression, animals experience time as cyclical. A major reason why we crave contact with animals, according to Katcher, is that they offer relief from linear time, with all the pressures it entails. He writes that the stability that we seek in animals 'is the constancy of cyclical time, life in the cycles of day, month, season, lifetime'.[8] This is especially applicable to migrating birds, which leave and return seasonally every year. In a culture such as that of Egypt, where time is understood as cyclical for human beings, this difference between people and animals, and the attendant fascination, does not exist. The boundary between human beings and animals was very fluid in Egypt and did not need to be mediated by biology or philosophy.

Pictures of marshes in the Nile Delta, found in many Egyptian tombs, celebrate life's abundance. People are hunting, fishing, fowling, cutting papyrus and gathering flowers. One of the best examples is the painting from the tomb of Nebamun, dated from about 1350 BCE. The departed noble stands in a small boat moving into the reeds. In his right hand he holds three birds, probably decoys, by the feet. His left hand is raised to hurl a throwing stick, carved in the form of a snake. Some birds scatter before him while others remained perched on the reeds. In front of him a cat, which may be a pet, has caught no fewer than three birds, one with its hind paws, one with its front paws and the last in its mouth. A goose stands at the prow of the boat with its beak slightly

Drawing after a relief from the tomb of Ptah Hotep in Egypt, c. 2400 BCE, *showing people trapping birds and fishing.*

open, perhaps honking to warn companions. Behind Nebamun is his wife, Hatshepsut, holding a bouquet. She is dressed very elegantly but in a long gown that is entirely inappropriate for a hunting expedition. Below him is his daughter, picking a lotus flower. An accompanying hieroglyph explains, 'Taking enjoyment: seeing the good things . . . the works of the marsh goddess Sekhet'.[9]

Peter Dance has complained of such art that 'A depressingly large number of the animals depicted on cave walls, tombs and limestone edifices have arrows or spears sticking in them.' He contends, on that basis, that the paintings are an anthropocentric celebration of dominance,[10] and it is not hard to see how he got that impression. The idealized figure of Nebamun, together with his family, is the centre of attention, and the patriarch shows no compunction about killing. Our contemporary culture predisposes us to understand Nebamun and his family as representing humankind, with the birds symbolizing nature, but those were not symbolic distinctions that the Egyptians habitually made.

The pictures show the rhythm of life and death. Through hunting birds, Nebamun participates in death; through his wife and daughter, in the generation of life. The scenes are intended to represent him at the height of his powers and happiness in the expectation that such days may come again. In the words of Dorothea Arnold, 'In essence such scenes served as symbols of the power of nature to renew itself constantly, a cycle in which the Egyptians wished to participate.'[11] This is also why the tomb paintings often feature frightening predators such as crocodiles and wild cats. But the Egyptians were not anthropocentric; in fact, they did not even have an equivalent for our word 'animal'. Divinities, animals and human beings did not belong to clearly differentiated spheres. Animals, like people, might become gods through death and mummification,[12] while deities might take the form of animals. Both people and animals could be treated with tenderness, reverence or pragmatism.

But a less anthropocentric perspective is not necessarily either more humane or more environmentally sound, any more than an anthropocentric one guarantees kindness towards fellow human beings. Biocentrism, humane treatment of animals and environmental soundness are three distinct qualities that do not necessarily coincide. While the use of birds and other animals in

Painting in the tomb of Nebamun showing him hunting birds together with his wife and daughter,
c. *1350* BCE.

Egypt was generally respectful and even reverent, the Egyptians captured and killed them on a massive scale. According to a contemporary record, Ramses III (reg. *c.* 1187–1157 BCE) donated 680,714 birds to temples in the course of his reign, to be kept in domestic flocks and to provide offerings for ceremonies.[13] The cemetery in Saqqara contained over four million individual mummies of ibises, and there were additional millions at Abydos, all of which had been sacrificed to the gods.[14] At least 42 additional species of birds have been identified from mummified remains in Egyptian tombs, while those of an additional ten species were placed in tombs to provide food for the deceased in the afterlife.[15] In more secular contexts, the Egyptians could be ruthlessly pragmatic in their treatment of animals. Reliefs picture them force-feeding cranes and other animals in order to fatten them up for the table.[16]

The fact that the Egyptians had no hierarchy of species does not mean they were egalitarian. Modern Western culture is, in its ideals though not so much in practice, egalitarian and has relatively rigid conceptions of identity. It constantly uses the most restrictive markers of identity from Social Security numbers to fingerprints and sequences of DNA. The individual, understood in a very limited way, is the ultimate unit of concern. The culture of ancient Egypt had very fluid notions of identity, which is shown by the way deities might be identified with one another and depicted in multiple forms. Nevertheless, the culture was unabashedly hierarchical. Human beings were not equal to one another; nor were individual animals of a species given the same status. The lack of equivalence is suggested, among other ways, by the imposing scale of their monuments, such as the pyramids or the statues of the pharaohs at Luxor.

Just as the pharaoh represented the sun-god Re, so individual animals might be an incarnation of a deity, such as the Apis bull that was a vehicle for the god Ptah. Such animals would, of course, be treated with awe and constant solicitation while alive and then ceremoniously buried when dead, but that status did not extend to all members of its species. The Egyptians probably felt that that all bovines lived through the Apis bull just as all people of the kingdom lived through the pharaoh, in something like the way all Christians, partaking of Mass, become one in Christ. There was a practice remarkably reminiscent of holy communion at the temple complex of Thoth, god of wisdom, during the second century BCE, which, according to an account by a temple priest, contained a preserve with 60,000 living ibises. Workers at the temple would eat in a hall before a statue of Thoth in the form of an ibis. They conceived their bread as an offering, rather like the eucharist, with its spirit being absorbed by the deity.[17]

The Soul Bird

The idea of a soul is implicit in the idea of reincarnation, also known as the 'transmigration of souls'. The concept of a soul may be intangible, yet it is also vivid. It is perhaps that intense yet fleeting nature that first led to its conceptualization as a bird in Egypt. This image was probably inspired, at least in part, by the way vast numbers of migratory birds would appear in Egypt every year, almost as though resurrected from the dead.[18]

The Egyptian term *ba* is usually translated as 'soul', and that is a good working definition, though inevitably inexact. The Egyptians thought of the *ba* as a manifestation of the body, at once physical and spiritual, rather than as something apart from the bodily realm. The Egyptians depicted the *ba* as a small bird with a human face, often shown hovering over a coffin. Starting in

After an Egyptian relief, the jackal-headed Anubis, god of the dead, hovering over a coffin as the ba *or 'soul' takes flight.*

the Middle Kingdom, miniature statues of the *ba* were often placed in a coffin with a mummified corpse. It could consume offerings of food and drink left for it in a tomb. It could also fly about the world. The large head and especially the eyes suggest an owl. The pattern of its plumage often resembles that of a hoopoe, while its erect posture suggests a falcon or hawk.

Like a guardian angel, the *ba* could speak to an individual, offer advice and even engage in dialogue with a person,[19] as in this Egyptian poem, probably from the second millennium BCE:

> *The swallow*: Day breaks, what is your path?
> *The girl*: Don't, little bird! Are you scolding me?
> I found my lover in his bed . . .[20]

In Egypt the swallow was an attribute of the goddess Isis and the sun-god Re, both of which were associated with resurrection and new beginnings, and this bird tells the girl that she must now change her life.[21]

Opposite: Painted wooden statue from an Egyptian tomb showing the ba *of the deceased, c. 331 BCE.*
Above: Limestone relief showing a swallow, 400–430 BCE.

The concept of the soul as a bird was based on an analogy between flying and human thought. Both take the subject to distant places and confer a sort of ethereal presence. But the *ba* was not a theological construct. The Egyptians expressed what they thought of death, immortality, time and so on not in terms of abstractions but of images. The iconography of Egypt is extraordinarily supple. For that reason, much of the symbolism was carried over into, or at least influenced, Christianity. The all-seeing eye of Re or Horus became that of the Judaeo-Christian God. Images of Isis holding the infant Horus, her child with the god Osiris, became the Madonna and child. The Egyptian ankh resembles the Christian cross. People in Western tradition have envisioned the soul in many other ways – as a butterfly, a tiny person with wings, a mist or a sort of cherub – but the *ba* is probably the original motif from which these subsequent representations are derived.

For the Egyptians, deities as well as people had 'souls'. The ibis was the soul, the *ba*, of Thoth, god of wisdom; the *benu*, or heron, was that of both Osiris, god of the dead, and Re, god of the sun. The centre of worship for Re was the Temple of the Sun in Heliopolis, near present-day Cairo, which Egyptians held to be the location where the cosmos was first created. According to one myth, the cry of the *benu* had started the progression of time. The *benu* became known as the 'phoenix' when the Greek historian Herodotus reported a legend that when one died, its son would carry the body to Heliopolis, place it in a coffin of myrrh and then deposit it in the temple. Gradually, in Roman and

Anubis, the jackal-headed god of the dead, weighs the heart of the deceased against an ostrich feather. Meanwhile, the soul, in the form of a bird, looks on. Egyptian, c. 1250 BCE. Egyptian scenes of judgement convey solemnity but little or no terror.

A harpy from Greek mythology, based on an illustration to Ulisse Aldrovandi,
Monstrorum historia *(1538).*

medieval times, this developed into the legend that the phoenix would live
for an extremely long time, often five hundred years, build a funeral pyre and
immolate itself, and then rise again from the ashes.

　　There is not much to connect the *benu* to the phoenix beyond the
location in Heliopolis. Herodotus describes the bird as red and golden, and
compared it to an eagle, while a heron is white and very differently built. But
the legend of the phoenix retains a notion of cyclical time very similar to
that of Egypt.[22] In Christianity and, in large part, Graeco-Roman religion,
an individual had but a single terrestrial life. In Christian religion, one might
be reborn and enter into heaven, perhaps after a stay in purgatory, or else be
consigned to hell. But in Egyptian religion, as in the legend of the phoenix, the
cycle of death and rebirth might be eternal.

Perhaps because the Greeks initially had trouble grasping Egyptian concepts of eternal life, the *ba* entered Greek mythology as an autonomous mythological figure. The Sirens are figures of Greek myth that very closely resemble the *ba*, figures with the bodies of birds and human heads. Though initially of both genders, they became entirely female. In the *Odyssey* they sing sweetly and entice sailors, who are then wrecked on rocky coasts. Forewarned before he passed them, Odysseus has his sailors block their ears with wax and tie him to the mast, so he will be able to hear their song and survive.[23] Although the Homeric view of the afterlife was bleak, stories of the sirens show how the prospect of death could still be seductive.

The harpies of Greek mythology have the same form, but they are not in any way seductive. Their faces are those of maidens but hideous, filthy and distorted by insatiable hunger. They sometimes have the breasts of women, but otherwise the bodies of raptors with long claws for tearing flesh. In the story of Jason and the Argonauts, as told by Apollodorus in the second century BCE, they torment a blind soothsayer named Phineus who has been punished by the gods by swooping down whenever he tries to eat, snatching most of his food and leaving a terrible stench on the rest, until they are chased and killed by the sons of the North Wind.[24] Except for their claws, the harpies suggest vultures, just as the sirens resemble songbirds, both of which are important in Egyptian culture and mythology.

But the idea of a soul did eventually enter Greek culture. Butterflies and moths, unlike birds, undergo a metamorphosis, and the winged creature emerging from a chrysalis is suggestive of a soul leaving the body. The Egyptian *ba* largely gave way to depictions of the soul as a butterfly, which has predominated not only in Graeco-Roman culture but in East Asia, and it is also found in Native American tribes such as the Hopi. The idea of the soul as a bird has frequently resurfaced in folklore. It largely vanished from Christianity, which instead believed in resurrection of the body, until the Early Modern period, when it was revived by Descartes and others.

The concept of a bird soul continued to surface in more folkloric contexts. According to legend, the Assyrian queen Semiramis was raised by doves. When she died, her soul left in the form of a dove and entered a passing flock.[25] In the first century CE Pliny the Elder wrote that the soul of a man named Aristaeus was seen flying out of his mouth in the form of a raven,[26] a bit like the Egyptian *ba*. In the ancient world, the idea of a bird soul did not remain confined to Egypt but became widespread through much of Mesopotamia, Eastern Europe and Siberia, where it was associated with the spiritual flight of shamans.[27]

Bede tells that in 627 CE, when the Saxon king Edwin was considering converting to Christianity, one of his counsellors compared the soul to a sparrow:

> Your majesty, when we compare the present life of man on earth with that time of which we have no knowledge, it seems to me like the swift flight of a single sparrow through the banqueting-hall where you are sitting at dinner on a winter's day with your thanes and counsellors. In the midst there is a comforting fire to warm the Hall; outside, the storms of winter rain or snow are raging. This sparrow flies swiftly in through one door of the Hall and out through another. While he is inside, he is safe from the winter storms, but, after a few moments of comfort, he vanishes from sight into the wintry world from which he came.[28]

The counsellor went on to argue for the new religion, with its promise of resurrection after death.

The novel *Precious Bane* by Mary Webb, set in Shropshire during the Napoleonic Wars, documents many folk beliefs among rural people. When the father of the narrator, Prue Sarn, is being buried, she sees a white owl 'like a blown feather for lightness and softness'. Her mother says that the bird is her father's spirit looking for his body.[29] The idea of the soul as a bird has appeared especially often in Slavic folklore. Jacob Grimm, for example, noted a belief among the Czech people that when a person was cremated, the soul flew out of his mouth and continued to perch nearby until the body had been consumed by flames.[30]

The soul bird appears in the fairy tale 'The Juniper Tree', recorded by the Romantic painter Philipp Otto Runge and included by the Brothers Grimm in their collection of fairy tales, and it describes rituals that could ultimately be derived from ancient Egyptian religion, perhaps continued as a mystery cult in Roman and Christian times. A man and his wife pray for children and they eventually have a son, but the wife dies and the husband buries her under a juniper tree. After a period of mourning, he remarries and has another child, a girl named Marlene. The second wife kills the son in a fit of rage, and then, to conceal her crime, cuts up the body, cooks it in a stew and feeds it to her husband. Marlene takes the bones of the boy, wraps them up in silk and ritualistically buries them under the juniper tree, which immediately becomes animated. The branches are filled with mist and flame, out of which a magnificent bird appears, which sings gloriously, ascends to the sky and

vanishes. It flies about, and people, enchanted by its song, give the bird gifts of shoes, a golden chain and a millstone. It then returns and drops the millstone on the wife, killing her. It gives the shoes to Marlene and the chain to the father. It changes back into a boy, and the three sit down to dinner.[31]

The bird resembles the Egyptian phoenix, as described by Herodotus and others. The burial rituals in the story are described with unusual care and precision, suggesting that they may at one time have been actually practised. But perhaps the strongest tie with Egyptian practice may be a relatively circular conception of time and death. The soul does not go to heaven, hell or purgatory, as it would in Christianity. Rather, it is reborn to carry on its former life on earth. Another possibility is that the phoenix rising from mist and fire may at one time have alluded to some alchemical transformation. Both the cryptic style of the tale and the symbolism of the phoenix, as well as Egyptian motifs in general, were very characteristic of alchemical writing in the Early Modern era.

The idea of the soul returning as a bird keeps reappearing not only in European cultures but in many others as well. In several African legends, a young wife who has been killed by an enemy flies to her husband's dwelling in the shape of a songbird and sings to him of her sorrowful fate.[32] Our Western idea of the self as composed of soul and body seems simple, even unsophisticated, compared with other concepts from many civilizations. The Tzeltal Maya of Chiapas, Mexico, for example, see the self as a sort of ecosystem in which the body is inhabited by four to sixteen souls, which may take a range of forms, including meteors, animals and other people. One sort of soul they believe is found in all human beings is called the 'Bird of the Heart', which is imagined as a hen, rooster, pigeon or grackle. Sometimes fiends entice it to leave the body through the mouth, at which point it becomes a normal bird. To kill, cook and eat the Bird of the Heart causes a person to grow sick and die.[33]

Regardless of what people may claim to believe, the idea of the soul as a bird still resonates today. *In the Company of Crows and Ravens* by scientist John Mazluff and artist Tony Angell tells how the latter was startled one morning by a crow hammering on his roof, a behaviour that was, in his experience, unprecedented. When he went out to investigate, the crow immediately descended and stood on the porch before him, directly meeting his gaze. Angell started to go back inside to wash his hands, but the crow cawed insistently and

Illustration by Kay Nielsen to 'The Juniper Tree' by the Brothers Grimm, c. 1925. Marlene has ceremonially buried the bones of her brother under the juniper tree, and the boy is suddenly reborn as a wonderful bird.

then nipped him on the shoulder. Its demeanour reminded Angell of a friend who was gravely ill, and he asked, 'Freddy?' The crow replied by gazing at him insistently. The next day Angell learned that his friend had died the day the crow arrived.[34] Was it the spirit of his friend? The idea might at first sound loopy, and there is no way to either confirm or disprove it. At any rate, the book was published by Yale University Press, and it had an enthusiastic reception in both popular and scientific circles. Tony told me that out of more than fifty reviews only a single one even mentioned the incident, and that appraisal was not disparaging.

The Holy Spirit (or Ghost) in Christianity regularly appears in the form of a dove at transformational moments in the Christian story such as the Annunciation, the Baptism of Christ and Pentecost. That bird is essentially the *ba*, the soul, of Christ, just as the *benu* was that of the Egyptian sun-god Re. Even when initially rejecting the idea of a soul apart from the body for human beings, the Church accorded one to God.

The Animal Gods Reborn

Christianity broke with most Jewish practices that linked animals with divinity, particularly with sacrificial and dietary practices. On the level of official doctrine, this left animals with little more than metaphoric significance.[35] On the level of folk religion, it left a void that could be filled by all manner of legends and stories. Though it may now impress us as charmingly naive, *Physiologus* (The Physician), written in Alexandria, Egypt, between the second and fourth centuries CE, presented a view of animals that transformed Christianity and, in some respects, even opened the way for scientific investigation. Like modern scientists, the author was not content with recording information and events but looked for underlying patterns. But the dynamics that he uncovered were not physical laws but moral allegories.

The animals in *Physiologus* embody qualities, attitudes and aspirations. The original *Physiologus* consisted of about fifty relatively short chapters, most of which were devoted to a specific variety of animal. The Egyptian influence is most overt in the chapter on the phoenix. The author tells that the phoenix, which lives for five hundred years, signals to the Egyptian priests of Heliopolis when it is preparing to die. They then pile up brushwood on an altar. The phoenix comes, mounts the altar, sets the wood on fire and immolates itself. The priests return the next day and find a worm in the ashes, but on the second day they find a small bird. On the fourth day it is the size of a huge eagle. It greets the priests and then flies back to its home in India.[36]

The account of the rite somewhat resembles that by Herodotus but differs in many details. Unlike Herodotus, the author was not writing from another continent; in fact Heliopolis, now incorporated into Cairo, is only about 220 kilometres (135 mi.) from Alexandria, so he could easily have visited the temple. Since the author uses the present tense, it is very likely that some rites of the ancient priesthood were still practised, or at least had been passed on in oral tradition, when he wrote.

Much as in ancient Egypt, solar imagery is constantly used in *Physiologus*. Another mythical bird that probably has an origin in Egyptian lore is the charadrius, which the author says is completely white. If a man is ill and the charadrius turns its face away from him, that is a sure sign that he will die soon. If he is going to recover, the charadrius stares at him. The man should then stare back at the charadrius, which takes on the illness and flies up to the sun, burning away the disease. The charadrius, the author explains, is Christ, who takes on the sins of the world.[37] The charadrius also has some resemblance to the god Horus, who takes the form of a falcon and is closely associated with the sun. But the solar symbolism was being shifted to the eagle, which, *Physiologus* tells us, restores itself three times in its lifetime by flying up to the sun, where the failing parts of its body are burned away.

Ancient Egyptian religion had several vulture deities that were female but none that were masculine. These deities were primarily protectors, painted hovering over a pharaoh or other person. At times they were depicted with their wings around a pharaoh in a sort of shielding embrace.[38] Horapollo, a former priest in old Egyptian religion who wrote at about the same time as the author of *Physiologus*, maintained that all vultures were female and became pregnant by the North Wind.[39] *Physiologus* seems to assume something of the sort when it speaks of vultures using the feminine pronoun and discusses their pregnancy.[40] Medieval bestiaries would compare the vultures to Mary, who also had a virgin birth.[41]

Like the animal deities of Egypt, the creatures in Physiologus were allegorical embodiments of human choices and attributes. *Physiologus* also tells how the mother pelican kills its young in anger but later, overcome by sorrow, opens her own breast so that the infants may be revived by her blood. The owl, according to *Physiologus*, symbolizes the Jews, since it is afraid of the light of Christ, and the hoopoe is a model of filial devotion, since it cares for its aged parents.

As the European Middle Ages progressed, *Physiologus* became the most popular of books, translated with embellishments into almost every European language. By the twelfth century these developed into the medieval bestiaries, moralized accounts of well over a hundred different animals. We now think of *Physiologus* and the bestiaries as profoundly Christian, and perhaps they have become so, but that is only because Christianity has a remarkable ability to absorb other traditions. The fantastic animals of the bestiaries were the Egyptian gods reborn.

When people speak of 'animals' they refer primarily to non-human mammals, but only peripherally to humans and to birds. When philosophers wish to discuss the objective existence of objects, they conventionally mention tables, mugs and stones. When they wish to discuss the nature of consciousness, they mention dogs or cats. They do not often mention birds. In respect to the usual categories of Western thought, birds have always been a bit of an anomaly, since they seem neither bestial, human nor divine.

Do animals have souls? There has never been an official Christian doctrine on the question. The implicit position of ecclesiastical Christianity is that they do not, for such souls, if they exist, are ignored almost entirely. The implicit position of folk Christianity is that they do, since there are countless tales in which they not only talk and perform magic but seem to live on after death. In the late Middle Ages, as doctrine became more rigidly inclusive, Aquinas and later Descartes proclaimed that they did not have souls, and this denial is widely blamed for a decline in the status of animals. It may not have had much impact on the status of birds, however. The concept of a soul has become largely abstract but not entirely so. The word still evokes images, usually of a small birdlike figure. Birds in folklore are often shapeshifters.

But how can birds *have* souls when they *are* souls?

5 MIGRATION AND PILGRIMAGE

Migration is an expression of the human aspiration for dignity, safety and a better future. It is part of the social fabric, part of our very make-up as a human family.
Ban Ki-moon, Secretary General of the United Nations 2007–16

In *The Hero with a Thousand Faces*, Joseph Campbell wrote that mythology consisted of variations on a single story that he called 'the monomyth'. The first stage was 'departure', where the hero receives a calling that will lead him away from the community of his birth. The second was 'trials and victories of initiation', which is followed by the third and final stage of 'the return and reintegration into society'.[1] He went on to describe the tales of a vast number of mythic heroes from Gilgamesh to Buddha in terms of that basic structure. Though Campbell himself may not have recognized this, this cyclical pattern of departure, challenges and eventual return corresponds very closely to an animal migration, a paradigm that is prior even to the evolution of humankind yet intimately tied to our concepts of adventure, destiny and heroism.

Many kinds of animals migrate, often showing navigational skills that at least match those of any human explorer and overcoming hazards that should bring acclaim to any hero. Green turtles migrate from Brazil to tiny Ascension Island in the middle of the southern Atlantic Ocean. Monarch butterflies migrate about 4,000 km (2,500 mi.) from the United States to an area in Mexico where they hibernate in oyamel fir trees, returning to the same trees every year. Bluefin tuna shuttle between the Gulf of Mexico and Norway. But the creatures best known for migration are birds. The Arctic tern, to give one dramatic example, spends winters in Antarctica and then travels every year to breeding grounds in Iceland. Since ancient times, people have greeted the return of migratory birds such as swallows and cuckoos as a harbinger of spring.

Bird migration is usually in relation to a fixed home, which for birds means a nest. With some, such as bald eagles and ravens, this may be used for many generations. Boris Pasternak, quoted by Gaston Bachelard, speaks of 'the instinct with which, like the swallow, we construct the world – an enormous nest, an agglomerate of earth and sky, of life and death'.[2] This dialectic between domesticity and wanderlust runs through human civilization.

The patterns of bird migration today were generally established at the end of the last Ice Age. Prior to that, journeys had not been so long, since the relatively temperate parts of the globe were not so extensive.[3] Long avian migrations therefore began just as humans started to become sedentary.

Perhaps this helped make birds a focus of human nostalgia. Just about all human culture is pervaded by elusive feelings of longing for a time in the past that we miss intensely yet cannot quite remember. This may be, at least in part, an expression of a vestigial migratory instinct. The sight of migrating geese appeals at once to our nostalgia for an era that, in retrospect at least, appears as one of wonderful adventures.

Up to Neolithic times, when people began constructing permanent settlements, all human beings were migratory or at least nomadic. Before reliable maps, paved roads and compasses, people guided themselves on long journeys in something like the manner of migratory animals, using a combination of remembered landmarks, observation of the sky and intuition. Though their methods did not have the efficiency of a GPS, merchants, soldiers, pilgrims and pioneers seem to have got around remarkably well. The conflict between early agriculturalists, who became sedentary, and herders, who remained nomadic, is the basis for the biblical story of Cain and Abel.

In many early tales, people follow birds to a place of destiny. According to legend, the Sabines followed a woodpecker to the site of their future city, which they then named Picenum or 'woodpecker town'.[4] In Japanese tradition, Jimmu, the descendant of the sun goddess Ameratsu and first emperor of Japan, followed a mystical crow to Yamoto, where he built his capital. The eagle holding a snake which today decorates the Mexican flag commemorates a legend that the Aztec gods sent an eagle to mark the site where Mexico City was to be built. At the beginning of the Irish epic *Táin Bó Cuailinge*, King Conchobor and the nobles of Ulster are lured by magical birds to a fairy mound, where they find the infant Cúchulainn, son of the sun god Lugh.[5] The original name of the sites of the cities of Lyon, Leiden and very possibly even London is *Lugdunum*, a Romanization of the Celtic *Lugdon*, meaning 'hill of ravens'. The locations for these cities could easily have been chosen by following a flock of birds.[6]

Bird migration resembles the wandering of the few remaining nomadic ethnicities in the world, such as Gypsies, Bedouins and Irish Travellers. The largest survival of nomadism is the culture of mariners, which has continued from ancient times until at least the twentieth century in a close relationship with birds. It drew from countries across the globe and was, apart from the exclusion of women, very cosmopolitan. Songs of the sea are, as we might expect, full of nostalgia for distant homes and sweethearts. An example is the maritime ballad sometimes known as 'Ocean Burial', which goes back at least to the mid-nineteenth century. It begins, 'O bury me not in the deep, deep sea.' The speaker, a young sailor about to die, recounts how, listening

An Arctic tern engaged in its epic journey.

to 'The free, wild winds, and the songs of the birds', he remembers his childhood home.[7]

Sailors would constantly watch birds for many purposes, such as judging nearness to land, predicting the weather, ascertaining the presence of marine life, setting the course of the ship, and doubtless also relieving the loneliness of a long voyage. In the lore of sailors, gulls, gannets, kittiwakes and other aquatic birds are the souls of people drowned at sea. In parts of Scotland, people were told not to kill gulls, since they might be the souls of the departed. Such beliefs were sometimes transferred to other birds, and they are the foundation of Coleridge's poem 'The Rime of the Ancient Mariner'.[8] People in Brittany said that the souls of tyrannical skippers would roam the seas forever as storm petrels.[9] For sailors, who might feel almost lost in time, the sight of migrating birds could be a welcome reminder of terrestrial seasons.

Migration or Hibernation?

People have always been amazed at the precision with which birds arrive at fixed times of the year, which was so reliable that people could tell the time

Fisherman drawing in hibernating swallows with their nets. Illustration to Historia de gentibus septentrionalibus *by Olaus Magnus (1555).*

for planting or harvesting by their arrival. It seemed that either the birds themselves must be divine or else they were guided by a god. In the Old Testament Yahweh asks Job, 'Does the hawk take flight at your advice when he spreads his wings to travel south?' (Job 39:26, Jerusalem translation). For the ancient Egyptians, the arrival of many birds in spring and autumn was part of the seasonal rebirth of the world.

The birds simply disappeared and then came back at the appointed season, but nobody knew where they went or how. In *Huainanzi*, a collection of texts on nature and philosophy collected in the early second century BCE by Chinese scholars, the seasonal appearance and vanishing of many birds is attributed to metamorphosis. Swallows, it reports, enter the sea and become clams. According to traditional Chinese calendars used as late as the eighteenth century, hawks transformed into pigeons in early spring and field mice into quails a bit later.[10] In ancient Greece, some believed that cuckoos transformed into hawks in late spring, an idea that Aristotle reported but declined to either endorse or repudiate.[11]

Aristotle, in *The History of Animals*, had also written that some birds such as swallows and kites did not migrate but hibernated through the winter. According to him, swallows had been found lying in holes without their feathers, and kites were seen emerging from concealment in spring.[12] Aristotle has a reputation as the most consistently accurate writer on natural history in the ancient world, and many scholars have regarded this as one of his relatively few egregious errors. The report about kites seems relatively understandable, since they are ambush predators which rely on their ability to suddenly appear as though from nowhere. The one about swallows is harder to explain. Swallows were highly visible, since they regularly nested in the eaves of houses, but their ability to find their homes after a long absence in distant lands may have seemed almost unbelievable. Perhaps the swallows Aristotle found in holes were fledglings that had fallen from their nests.

In part because of the belief that they hibernate and reawaken, swallows became symbols of the resurrection in Christianity. Medieval European painters would sometimes show swallows nesting in the eaves of the stable in which Christ was born and hovering over the cross as he died. Reports that swallows spend the winter buried in leaves, in the decaying wood of hollow trees or even on the moon continued to circulate well into the modern era.

In the early sixteenth century Olaus Magnus, Bishop of Uppsala in Sweden, wrote in *Historia de gentibus septentrionalibus* (Account of the Northern Peoples) that swallows hibernate in water, and illustrated this idea with a picture of fishermen pulling up swallows and goldfinches in nets. From the sixteenth century through to the nineteenth, there was an ongoing debate in scientific circles between 'migrationists', including Pierre Belon and John Ray, and 'hibernationists', including Carl Linnaeus and Georges Cuvier, about where birds went in winter.[13]

Part of the reason the problem proved intractable for so long is that the methods of natural scientists were not very well suited to addressing it. Apart from collecting specimens, they generally did not spend very much time outdoors. Classification of items such as feathers, nests and bird skins was often very systematic, but observation of birds in a natural environment remained anecdotal. This began to change in the latter eighteenth century with the work of Gilbert White, curate of several parishes in Hampshire, including his birthplace of Selborne. He lacked formal education in the natural sciences, but in ways that proved an advantage, for established methodologies could not distract him from careful observation of wildlife in Selborne. He was the first to observe that swifts copulate in mid-air and that male and female chaffinches congregate in separate flocks in winter.[14]

In a letter of 4 August 1767, White discussed a report that a chalk cliff had fallen on the beach during a storm and swallows were found among the fragments of shattered stone, but came to no firm conclusion as to whether or not they had been in hibernation.[15] Migration received a boost in 1822 when a stork was found in the far north of Germany with a huge arrow made in

Central Africa embedded in its neck. The question was largely settled in the second decade of the twentieth century, when swallows banded in England were discovered in South Africa.[16]

Looking back, it does not seem very surprising that avian hibernation once seemed more reasonable to many people than the idea that birds could find their way across continents for hundreds, even thousands, of kilometres. Plenty of animals from bats and bears to garter snakes and box turtles hibernate. Perhaps we should really be asking why birds do not. The reason is probably because birds have a very high metabolic rate, which makes it harder for them to enter a torpid state.

Nevertheless, although hibernation by birds is extremely rare, it is not totally unknown. The common poorwill, a type of nightjar found in the American West, Mexico and a small area of Canada, is the one bird that actually does hibernate, and that is enough to prove that hibernating birds do exist. Others, such as hummingbirds and swallows, can slow their metabolism as the temperature becomes colder and food less readily available.

Human beings, for that matter, may stay indoors more than usual, sleep more, curtail their physical activity and slow their metabolism in winter to a point where one might speak of them entering a 'semi-dormant state'. Some birds, particularly those that nest in holes rather than the open air, may do the same under unusual conditions, such as a disruption of the usual succession of seasons. Well into the twentieth century there were still occasional reports of swallows hibernating,[17] and these probably continue today.

How Do Birds Migrate?

What enables migratory birds to find their way around the world in all sorts of weather and then later return to their nests? The study of bird perception has been greatly refined over the last half century. Researchers have performed a vast array of systematic experiments in which birds were deprived of certain senses and then tested. They have also done displacement experiments, in which birds were transported from their accustomed migratory routes and then carefully observed to see whether, and how, they could find their way home. These studies have yielded spectacular results, and we have learned much about the perceptual world of birds that seemed almost unimaginable in the mid-twentieth century. Until relatively recently, researchers widely assumed that the migratory ability of birds would have a single explanation, which might be something like visual memory or inherited mental maps. But, as our methods of investigation grow more refined and precise, the problem of how birds find their way in migration simply seems to grow more complicated and difficult.

A kestrel can see and pursue a beetle 50 metres (165 ft) away,[18] and many birds have comparable visual abilities. Human beings have three kinds of cones in their eyes, while birds have four, which very probably enables them to see colours that are inaccessible to us. Many birds from pigeons to eagles can also see the polarization of light. Birds have an internal compass that enables them to orient themselves by geomagnetic fields,[19] and they can detect subtle changes in atmospheric pressure. Birds can also orient themselves by heavenly bodies, as well as create mental maps based on olfactory memories.[20]

Additionally, birds distinguish many variations of sound that human perception runs together.[21] When a bird calls, the syrinx, its voice organ, can make two calls or melodies at once, which human beings cannot differentiate but other birds can. What sounds like 'tweet' to us can be a succession of ten tonal variations, which is roughly the equivalent of a substantial sentence.[22] Different abilities are important for migration depending on the species of bird and the circumstances.[23] But the capacity of birds to find their way depends on integrating many diverse facilities around a single task.

For people, and animals as well, it can be hard to distinguish sharply between feeling, volition and perception. Feelings are responses to mental images and are never without some sensual associations.[24] In an analogous way, perception is always accompanied by feelings in the background, even when these are subtle and below the threshold of consciousness.[25] Just as birds can often perceive sights and sounds that are inaccessible to us, they may also have emotions we do not generally share. We can hardly begin to imagine what a red-tailed hawk feels as she sits for hours looking down, occasionally shifting her position, and scanning the landscape for prey. Integrating many senses is a more complicated ability than using any one alone, and this blending makes it just about impossible to reduce bird behaviour to a simple pattern of stimulus and response. What links together all of the sensuous impressions seems close to what we designate by the sometimes helpful yet notoriously vague concept of 'consciousness'.

Migration and Pilgrimage

What is it like to be a bird? There are essentially two ways of approaching the question. One is the analytic approach, in which one learns as much as possible about the various senses and habits of a bird and then tries to synthesize this information. The other is the holistic, or artistic, approach, in which one

attempts to answer the question in one great leap of intuition. The analytic approach produces mostly theory, while the holistic one creates mostly stories, and both are useful to our understanding of avian life.

Birds such as the storks that nest in Mecca have been considered holy in Muslim culture, since migrations resemble pilgrimages. In the twelfth-century Persian epic *The Conference of Birds* by Sufi poet Farid ud-Din Attar,

Opposite: Habiballah of Sava, illustration to The Conference of Birds *by Farid ud-Din Attar (c. 1600), ink and watercolour with gold and silver.*
Above: Illustration from Gordon C. Aymer, Bird Flight *(1939). People have often welcomed storks nesting in unused chimneys.*

the hoopoe summons the other birds to undertake a pilgrimage to the simorgh, which is the ruler of birds. According to Islamic legend, the hoopoe is the bird that carried messages between Solomon and the Queen of Sheba. He tells the other birds that the simorgh first appeared one night in China and then let one of its feathers float down to earth. From that one feather, people (or birds) have ever since endeavoured to imagine it. The simorgh, also known as the 'luan', is a fabulous bird of Chinese mythology, which is, for most purposes, a variant of the fenghuang or 'Chinese phoenix'. The luan had five colours on its feathers and a song with the same number of notes. It was the ancestor of all other birds except the fenghuang.[26] The simorgh was frequently depicted by Persian artists with long flowing feathers of red, gold, blue and other colours.

In response to the call of the hoopoe, many of the birds decline to leave and make excuses. The nightingale is unwilling to leave the rose, which he loves; the owl is too attached to the treasures in abandoned ruins, while the peacock is too preoccupied with memories of paradise. The parrot, hawk, duck, partridge, finch and other birds also decline, and the hoopoe criticizes their rationalizations. After a while a huge flock of birds sets out and passes through

Above: Naked-footed night owl, from William Jardine, The Naturalist's Library *(1830s), engraving with watercolours. In both Europe and the Near East, people have long thought of owls as haunting ruins, especially of old castles.*
Opposite: Hoopoe, from Brightly and Childs, The Natural History of Birds *(1815).*

HOOPOE.

seven valleys representing the seven stages of the Sufi path – search, love, gnosis, trust in God, unity and bewilderment, culminating, finally, in mystical annihilation.

On the way the birds tell stories to keep their spirits up, which are mostly about love among human beings. A humble dervish conceives a mad love for a princess, who first pities him but spurns him in the end. A sheikh falls in love with a haughty Christian woman, who torments him and provokes him to blasphemy, but then she finally converts to Islam. A sultan falls in love with a fisher boy, but then, falsely believing his companion has been unfaithful, almost kills the young man, who is saved by his ministers, and then the two lovers are united.

Finally only one bird out of every thousand has survived. The rest have perished from hunger, thirst, heat, drowning or a predator's jaws. Only thirty exhausted, bedraggled, frightened birds are left, but a herald refuses them admission to the simorgh's presence. On leaving, they see themselves reflected in a lake, and their reflections form an image of the simorgh, showing that God is to be found within yourself. It is a mystical epiphany in which the distinctions between man, bird and God fall away. The style of *The Conference of Birds* is at once intensely sensuous and austere. It is filled with extremely colourful, evocative imagery, yet the sensuality seems fleeting and fragile, a bit like rainbows on a misty day.

Migration and Providence

To watch a bird is to become a bird. That, at least, is how it was for William Cullen Bryant in his poem 'To a Waterfowl', first published in 1818. It begins:

> Whither, 'midst falling dew,
> While glow the heavens with the last steps of day,
> Far, through their rosy depths, dost thou pursue
> Thy solitary way?
>
> Vainly the fowler's eye
> Might mark thy distant flight, to do thee wrong,
> As, darkly seen against the crimson sky,
> Thy figure floats along.
>
> Seek'st thou the plashy brink
> Of weedy lake, or marge of river wide,

> Or where the rocking billows rise and sink
> On the chaféd ocean side?
>
> There is a Power whose care
> Teaches thy way along that pathless coast –
> The desert and illimitable air –
> Lone wandering, but not lost.

The poet does not even need to tell us that he is also solitary, frightened and longing for a place of peaceful contemplation. After a few more stanzas, the poem continues:

> He, who, from zone to zone,
> Guides through the boundless sky thy certain flight,
> In the long way that I must trace alone,
> Will lead my steps aright.[27]

As the bird is guided by God to its destination, Bryant believes that he is being led, through all his uncertainties and tribulations, by a divine power.

The poem is written in a tradition, stretching from Aesop to the bestiaries and beyond, which regards nature as a book in which it is possible to read practical, moral and religious lessons. The point of this one is perseverance. Just as the bird continues its long flight despite danger, exhaustion and uncertainty, so the poet must move forward in the journey of life. Just as the waterfowl trusts to nature and does not despair, so the poet must place his trust in God.

'Instinct' is the secular version of 'providence' and both these explanations might be begging the question of what exactly it means to trust in God. That does not suggest passivity here, since the waterfowl is constantly exerting itself, flapping its wings over long distances. That is no counsel for the poet either, since he is deeply aware of what hazards, both open and concealed, he may face. He must trust subtle intuitions, a bit like the migratory senses of a bird.

Migration Today

As human society around the globe has become increasingly urban and industrial, people have felt a growing nostalgia for the rural past. In 1856 Jules Michelet wrote,

Geese foraging during migration.

> Would to Heaven that Napoleon in September 1811 had taken note of the premature migration of the birds to the North. From the storks and the cranes, he might have secured the most trustworthy information. In their precocious departure, he might have divined the immanency of a severe and terrible winter.[28]

Through the reference to Napoleon's disastrous campaign in Russia, Michelet was also criticizing human arrogance, which leads us to believe that we always know better than animals. He was lamenting that humankind, apart from some country people, had already drifted so far from the natural world that they were unable to recognize the wisdom of birds.

Even for many rural people, the flight of birds had, by the nineteenth century, ceased to be an important sign of the optimal time for planting and harvesting, but migratory birds were still enthusiastically welcomed. At the start of the twentieth century, migrating storks were still protected and even pampered, especially in Germany and the Netherlands. Spaces were set aside for their nests near houses and on top of roofs.[29] The birds were a reminder of natural rhythms, which people missed in their lives. But two world wars, each followed by a rapid burst of industrialization, damaged not only the environment but patterns of custom as well.

Nevertheless, the example of a migratory bird can inspire us to rediscover abilities that have slipped from our awareness. One of the best examples from literature is in the late W. G. Sebald's novel *Austerlitz*. The protagonist, a young boy in Wales who goes by the name Dafydd Elias, learns from a schoolmaster that his legal name is Jacques Austerlitz. Much later, when he is in middle age, he intuitively senses that he may have been sent away from Germany on a train by Jewish parents shortly after the Nazis came to power, later to be adopted by a British couple. Using no systematic plan, but aided by faded half-memories, coincidences and scraps of information, he retraces the route of his childhood and comes to Prague, where he chances upon his old nanny. She tells him that his real parents were indeed Jewish and had sent him away at the age of four, shortly before they were taken to a concentration camp.

Like a migratory bird, Austerlitz seems to be guided by sensual intuitions, which are mostly beneath the level of consciousness, as he retraces the journey of his childhood. The book is full of avian images. There are white cockatoos imported to a British country estate, brightly coloured finches in an aviary near a train station, birds that fall on ice and die during a harsh winter, and so on. Austerlitz himself says of pigeons, before he undertakes his own journey, 'no one knows how these birds, sent off on their journey into so menacing a void, their hearts almost breaking with fear in their presentiment of the vast distances they must cover, make straight for their place of origin.' A friend of his releases a white homing pigeon, anticipating that it will find its way back to the aviary. At first it does not show up as expected, but finally it is found walking back with a broken wing, perhaps an anticipation of Austerlitz's own journey.[30]

Austerlitz was written around the start of the twenty-first century, a time when political and environmental upheavals were making ever more people into refugees. Most of the new migrants are fleeing northwards because of climate change or social turmoil to Europe and North America. A combination of xenophobic resistance and bureaucratic complexity has made their journeys especially hazardous. For birds, migration has always been dangerous, yet in the twenty-first century they face more obstacles than ever before. Foremost is habitat destruction. In addition, electric grids may interfere with their magnetic sense, and light pollution obscures visual cues.

Even people who are not refugees must contend with a high degree of insecurity. Recently the posthumanist philosopher Rosi Braidotti has used the word 'nomadic' to describe ways we negotiate a world in which all traditional markers of identity such as gender, ethnicity and species have become questionable.[31] Today, migration may less resemble the sort of archaic epic described by Campbell than the daily routine of contemporary human beings, who must constantly struggle with confusion, disorientation and stress. Migrating geese hold many secrets, but the greatest one is their serenity.

PART TWO

BIRDS IN HISTORY

6 NATURE-CULTURES

He watched their flight; bird after bird: a dark flash, a swerve,
a flutter of wings. He tried to count them before all their darting
quivering bodies passed: six, ten, eleven: and wondered were they
odd or even in number. Twelve, thirteen: for two came wheeling down
from the upper sky. They were flying high and low but ever round and
round in straight and curving lines and ever flying from left to right,
circling about a temple of air.
James Joyce, *A Portrait of the Artist as a Young Man*

Peregrine falcons and ravens are very much at home on the rooftops of our skyscrapers, which are a bit like their favoured habitat of seaside cliffs. A bit lower down, occasional hawks make their homes in places like fire escapes. Pigeons, sparrows and other birds take advantage of any crevice in places such as the awnings of shops and the lattices of bridges to build their nests. The biblical Tower of Babel, which may be based on the Great Ziggurat or Etemenanki dedicated to Marduk at Babylon,[1] would certainly have supported much bird life on its many terraces, especially since these had gardens. The occasional cracked or fallen brick could have opened a place of shelter for a nest.

According to the biblical account, people of the world settled in Babylon, and then:

> 'Come,' they said, 'let us build ourselves a town and a tower with its top reaching heaven. Let us make a name for ourselves, so that we may not be scattered about the whole earth.' Now Yahweh came down to see the town and the tower that the sons of man had built. 'So they are all a single people with a single language!' said Yahweh. 'This is but the start of their undertakings! There will be nothing too hard for them to do. Come, let us go down and confuse their language on the spot so that they can no longer understand one another.'

He then scatters people once again around the world (Genesis 11:4–9, Jerusalem translation).

The biblical story of Babel does not explicitly mention birds, but its symbolism is connected to them. To aspire to reach heaven is to emulate birds. Birds are the most vocal of creatures, yet different species have distinctive calls and songs, which are like languages. It is almost as though Yahweh were to say to humankind, 'You wanted to be birds, and so that is what you will become.'

People constantly have trouble accepting the cultural division of humankind today, a discontent that drives repeated attempts to convert or conquer the world. Perhaps the Babylonian Empire, by establishing a language of law, administration and commerce, created an illusion of human unity, which was eventually destroyed as the domain collapsed. The Roman Empire would eventually unify a substantial part of humankind under one

J. J. Grandville, illustration to a fable of Jean de La Fontaine entitled 'The Swallow and the Spider', 1844, engraving. Birds go about their lives in secluded places on tall buildings, mostly oblivious to human beings.

government and even, to an extent, impose its own language. In the biblical Book of Revelation, 'Babylon' is sometimes used as a code for 'Rome'. In ways, the story in Revelation parallels that of Babel, though the scale of conflict is much grander. Human hubris has gone from being a relatively practical problem to – from a Christian perspective – a sin. Before the first great battle between the armies of good and evil, the book tells us:

> I saw an Angel standing in the sun, and he shouted aloud to all the birds that were flying overhead in the sky, 'Come here. Gather together at the great feast that God is giving. There will be the flesh of kings for you and the flesh of great generals and heroes, the flesh of horses, and their riders, and all sorts of men, citizens, and slaves, small and great.' (Revelation 19:17–18, Jerusalem translation).

The account goes on to say that the followers of the Beast and the False Prophet were killed and 'all the birds were gorged with their flesh' (Revelation 19:21). For many peoples of the ancient world a proper burial was necessary for the deceased to be at peace, and to be eaten by birds was the ultimate indignity, although Zoroastrians and Tibetans have deliberately exposed their corpses for that purpose. Alone in the Bible, this passage seems to suggest that birds accept the God of humankind and understand at least the language of the angel. Birds have often been classified mostly by diet, but here they will share a single meal.

Ethnocentrism

We are now at the end of an era in which the dominance of the West, especially the British Empire, made human culture appear far more homogeneous than was ever actually the case. It was a time when theorists explained significant differences in customs by saying that unfamiliar ways were 'primitive' or less 'advanced'. Even if human cultures varied, in other words, they were still on the same trajectory. The loss of Western dominance is a bit like the fragmentation of humankind after the Tower of Babel. During the era of colonization, Westerners, for the most part, regarded other cultures with a combination of demonization and idealization, which combined to create a smug sense of superiority.

This ethnocentrism, in my opinion, is very much in evidence in discussions of animal awareness today. For one thing, researchers often take the understandings that prevail in Western culture for granted. When they ask whether animals can 'understand time', they mean linear time, which is largely confined to Western culture. When they ask whether animals 'comprehend death', they mean in the same way as a member of the secular, Euro-American intelligentsia. When they ask whether animals have 'morality', they mean that of the intelligentsia in the twenty-first century. When they ask whether animals have a 'sense of self', they mean the sort of identity that prevails in contemporary capitalism. Perhaps some ethnocentrism is inevitable, but these perspectives are by no means universal even among human beings.

Even without considering elephant graveyards and crow funerals, it is very hard to see how all animals could be unaware of death, considered simply as a state in which bodies no longer function. It is simply too easily observable and an almost daily experience in the wild. Many vultures will eat only carrion, so they must be able to distinguish between the living and the dead. But human responses to death are by no means always confined to grief. They may also, for example, regard it as an adventure, an opportunity to reunite with loved ones, or a cosmic joke. Some cultures take a very casual attitude towards death, and funerals can be marked by a very wide range of behaviours such as fighting, joking and casual conversation.[2]

Animals probably also have many differing perspectives on death, many kinds of morality, and perhaps almost endless views of what constitutes an individual being. Like God or the position of an electron in quantum physics, the nature of the individual, the soul, seems to hover between corporeal reality and nothingness. People have variously held it to be an essence, a social construction or an illusion. It might be interesting if ethologists were to study animals in the same way as anthropologists study human societies, asking questions such as 'How do they comprehend death?', 'What are the foundations of their morality?' and 'What, if anything, defines their concept of an individual?' They would then learn philosophically from animals, as do many indigenous peoples.

The account of Babel in Genesis can be misleading in that it makes culture the product of a divine judgement rather than a response to an environment that includes fauna, flora, weather and topography. Even when the Bible was written, people had already started to think of culture as something apart from nature. If that were the case, it might indeed be possible to impose homogeneity on humankind, but culture consists largely of responses to the natural world.

Just as environmental factors divide human beings into geographically defined groups, they also mediate between them. Ignoring the environmental component may often have made differences seem more intractable than is actually the case. To rectify this, Bruno Latour speaks not of human 'cultures' but of 'nature-cultures',[3] a term that has now been adopted by many anthropologists and philosophers. The diversity of birds not only mirrors that of human culture, but helps to create it. Different groups of people identify intensely with, and relate to, different birds.

Detached from their environmental context, human cultures become abstract, self-contained systems of signification, which can seem almost incommensurable. It is plants, animals and landscapes that provide organic links among cultures. These serve as relatively stable points of reference, which people of different cultures may use in communication. The symbolism of animals, while it does vary considerably, is perhaps the closest thing that humankind has ever had to a universal language. In many divergent cultures, for example, eagles and big cats are symbols of royalty.

As human beings engage in trade, they take animals and their lore with them across the globe. This may be in the form of menageries, which have, from the earliest civilizations on, been a showcase for great wealth and power. It may also be in the form of pets such as cats and dogs. Most often, it is probably in the form of images which then, unable to be checked against the living creature, continue to develop in the realm of legend. Both East Asia and Europe had long lacked indigenous rhinoceroses, but the accounts of them, amplified in legend, developed into different kinds of unicorns. Whenever animals, or even just their images, are exported, they take some characteristic ways of thinking with them, enabling them to mediate between cultures.

Birds are especially suited to being cultural ambassadors. Many varieties of lizard are confined to a very specific geographic area, perhaps a few dozen acres or less of a particular rainforest. Birds, with their power of flight, cover a far vaster area and are also much more easily visible. Lizards thrive by closely adapting to very specific habitats, while birds, a bit like human beings, make use of several. Through their narrow ranges, lizards tend to separate nature-cultures, while birds bring them together.

Our bonds with birds are in constant, and relatively rapid, evolution. They also reflect the relationships among human beings, divided along lines of culture, geography, history, gender and so on. The fascination with birds of paradise among Europeans of the nineteenth century was due, in addition to their beauty, to their association with exotic places such as Indonesia, New Guinea and Australia. Some birds are associated with religions, such as the dove with Christianity. Some are national symbols, such as the American bald eagle and the English robin. Sparrows have traditionally been associated with common people, while peacocks and pheasants suggest luxury.

But what is human? Many of the traditional definitions such as a 'tool-using animal' and 'rational animal' no longer seem plausible, while others such as 'the animal with language' have been at least seriously placed in question. Still others such as a 'possessor of a soul' have come to seem almost unintelligible to many people. There are various legal, biological and poetic definitions, which are largely incommensurate.[4] Our humanity is defined less by characteristics, whether mental or physical, than by relationships. We exist, in other words, within a nexus of bonds with animals, plants, machines, earth and sky. Our bonds with birds, of course, are only a part of this fabric of relationships, but it is a unique and important one. With this in mind, I will attempt to trace in part a few of the historic relationships between human beings and birds.

Ravens and Crows

Every human relationship to another species is unique. We relate to dogs, cats, lizards, silkworms, sheep and chickens in very different ways, with respect to use, obligations, symbolism and so on. These are relationships that have evolved for centuries or even millennia. Many relationships with animals that we call 'domestic' were originally forms of symbiosis, in which neither partner fully understood the reason for their association but both profited from it.

At least since the Industrial Revolution most of these relationships have largely evolved to ones of domination. The one likely exception is our relationship with dogs, which are now, at least in Western countries, thoroughly integrated into contemporary human culture. With their own television shows, designer clothes, hotels, gourmet foods, psychiatrists and so on, dogs now enjoy most of its amenities, though they may suffer from the same feeling of purposelessness that pervades our society.

Our relationship with crows and ravens is unique among our bonds with animals in that it has remained very reciprocal from the start. Other animals may find human beings useful, but only corvids (crows, ravens and their relatives) seem to find us interesting. They are the anthropologists among avians. As one walks along the street, one may notice them perched on a telephone wire or a streetlamp, carefully observing as men and women pass by. According to David Quamen, this is because crows, a bit like human beings, have intelligence that greatly exceeds what is required for their evolutionary niche. In his words, crows 'are dissatisfied with the narrow evolutionary goals of that tired old Darwinian struggle'.[5] Crows have the sort of intellect that goes beyond even problem solving and leads them at least to the boundaries of myth, poetry and philosophy.

But their interest in human beings also has practical advantages. Chimpanzees are seldom or never able to understand what people mean by the gesture of pointing a finger, but crows, like dogs, can understand that without being taught. The crows in the city of Sendai in Japan understand the meaning of traffic lights and have figured out how to take advantage of them. They place walnuts in front of the wheels of cars when the light is green and wait. After the light changes to red and cars have broken open the nuts, they swoop down and eat them. Crows know at what time unsold food will be taken out at supermarkets and gather to receive it. They pick up paper bags near fast food restaurants by the bottom and shake them to see if anything is inside. Ravens in Yellowstone Park have figured out how to unzip hikers' knapsacks. Once my wife and I saw a small flock of crows gathered around a leader, who circled with a small package and then dropped it at our feet. It turned out to be a small sandwich wrapped in cellophane, and he seemed to be asking us to unwrap it for him, which we promptly did.

Crows often leave gifts for people who befriend them. A celebrated example is a girl named Gabriella Mann, just eight years old when this was reported, from Seattle, Washington, who formed a close relationship with the local crows. At the age of four she began sharing her boxed lunches with them, and she now feeds them regularly in the family garden. They have, in return, brought her dozens of small objects, which she stores in boxes, including pieces of beach glass, beads, earrings, buttons and charms. Once her mother lost the lens cap of her camera in an alley, and the crows returned it by placing it on the edge of her bird bath.[6]

In the fairy tale 'The White Snake', from the collection by the Brothers Grimm, the hero comes across three baby ravens that have fallen to the ground and are dying of hunger. He kills his horse in order to feed them. Later, the young man must bring an apple from the Tree of Life to win the hand of a princess he loves but is faced with execution should he fail. When he has almost succumbed to despair, the three ravens he saved bring him the apple.[7]

Scientist John Marzluff has shown that crows not only recognize human faces and remember them for years but can even pass down their memories, with good associations or bad ones, to their offspring. They remember the faces of those who annoy them and scold as the offender passes by.[8] For both animals and human beings, memory is not simply a matter of something like snapping pictures with a camera. To remember something requires, first of all, being able to perceive it as a coherent whole, not simply as a mass of disconnected details.

Engraving showing the Prophet Elijah in the wilderness fed by ravens, 1702. Ravens in the wild can form relationships with groups of people or individual human beings.

To remember human faces, corvids must also be able to interpret them, in other words to read human expressions. To remember further usually requires that the subject attach importance to what is remembered, which for corvids includes both caches of food and human features.

This sense that corvids are perpetually observing us runs through their treatment in literature, and a good example is the Scottish ballad 'The Twa Corbies':

As I was walking all alane
I heard twa corbies making a mane:
The tane unto the tither did say,
'Whar sall we gang and dine the day?'

'In behint yon auld fail dyke
I wot there lies a new-slain knight;
And naebody kens that he lies there
But his hawk, his hound, and his lady fair.

'His hound is to the hunting gane,
His hawk to fetch the wild-fowl hame,
His lady's ta'en anither mate,
So we may mak our dinner sweet.

'Ye'll sit on his white hause-bane,
And I'll pike out his bonny blue e'en:
Wi' ae lock o' his gowden hair
We'll theek our nest when it grows bare.

'Mony a one for him maks mane,
But nane sall ken whar he is gane:
O'er his white banes, when they are bare,
The wind sall blaw for evermair.'[9]

The ravens understand the relationship of the knight to his lady, his hawk and his hound, and they have been keeping track of each. This is in much the same way as people, at least poets and scientists, observe birds.

The raven is important in the mythologies of peoples within or near the Arctic Circle including Vikings, Siberians and Native Americans of the American/Canadian northwest coasts, and similarities suggest that their traditions may all go back to a cult of the raven in very early times.[10] Among the Haida, Tlingit, Kwakiutl and similar tribes, Raven is a major deity. There are many legends about how Raven stole the light of heaven, and then released it in the forms of sun, moon and stars. He is also a creator of humankind from formless matter found in clams. People in many cultures claim that ravens communicate with them, leading hunters to game with calls or showing the

Illustration by Arthur Rackham to 'The Twa Corbies', c. 1919, watercolour.

way. Ravens have also been used to lead ships in the direction of land and to warn of storms. The Dene people and medieval hunters would both leave part of their kill for ravens.[11] They are the guides, teachers, friends and sometimes the scourges of humankind.

Perhaps it is the phenomenon of 'crow funerals' that most intimately seem to tie the culture of crows to that of humankind. Other crows will gather around a dead crow, call out for a while as though in mourning, and then fly away. The behaviour follows a clear pattern, which is not dictated by practical necessity in any obvious way and seems ritualistic. Do they gather around the dead for the same reason as human beings? Perhaps, but what exactly is that reason? In both crows and humans, the behaviour is hard to explain beyond the vague statement that it somehow relieves our grief.

According to John Marzluff and Tony Angell, mates and close relatives of a crow may express grief at crow funerals, but most of the crows are gathered to obtain information about how it died and any imminent danger. They are also considering ways in which the social organization of crows may be affected by the absence of a specific member.[12] As in human society, we cannot necessarily assume that a single event will have the same significance all of the time or for every participant. It could even be that individual crows, like human beings, understand death in highly contrasting ways. At any rate, crow funerals may always lie at the intersection of science and mythology.

Above: Raven rattle used for ceremonial dances, Tsimshian Indians,
Pacific Northwest, 19th century.
Opposite: Victorian trade card advertising yarn, United States, 19th century.
Crows have often been associated with African Americans. Interestingly, in a society
pervaded by racism, this advert views blackness as positive.

When chaplain Norman Hood died in his room in the grounds of the Tower of London in 1990, the ravens in the Tower reportedly held a funeral for him. They gathered near the royal chapel of St Peter ad Vincula, where they otherwise never came, called out for a while and then fell silent.[13]

Owls

Crows are constantly contrasted with owls in folklore and literature. Crows are diurnal, most owls nocturnal; crows constantly chatter, while owls are known for their soundless flight. Among crows, the males are a bit larger than the females, but with owls it is the other way around. Crows have a reputation for intelligence, owls for wisdom, and the two qualities are by no means the same. Some kinds of intelligence may be measured, and scientists have confirmed, through extensive testing, that crows are among the brainiest of birds, rivalled only by some parrots. Wisdom, by contrast, is relatively intangible, and there is no test to determine whether or not owls live up to their reputation. Crows have a vast range of associations and symbolic meanings in human cultures, from playful sages to sombre harbingers of doom. The significance of owls, by contrast, is remarkably consistent in cultures throughout the world. They are associated with night, witchcraft, death and wisdom, and almost all myths of owls are variations on those themes. No other bird evokes such deep ambivalence in folklore throughout the world.

The owl is probably the bird most often depicted by visual and graphic artists, but it is not nearly as prominent in folktales or literature. Owls were associated with many goddesses in antiquity, but these are mostly figures on the fringes of official pantheons, which often assist with witchcraft. A sort of prototype for these is the Old Babylonian figure in fired clay known as the *Burney Relief* or, popularly, the *Queen of the Night* in the British Museum. It shows a naked woman with wings and a conical hat. Her legs end in talons like those of a bird, probably an owl. Beneath them are two lions, and two huge owls are at her sides. She is staring straight out at the viewer with large eyes reminiscent of those of an owl.[14] Her identity is unknown, but scholars have suggested Inanna, queen of heaven, Ereshkigal, ruler of the underworld, and Lilith, demon of the wilderness. Lilith also became the first wife of Adam in Jewish folklore and is referred to by the prophet Isaiah as a 'screech owl' (Isaiah 34:14).

Athens was among the few places in the ancient world where a positive view of the owl, based on its reputation for wisdom, generally prevailed. The owl was identified with Athena, patron goddess of the city, and its image was

Queen of the Night, Old Babylonian relief, 1800–1750 BCE.

placed on many coins. Athena was a goddess of war and capable of being bellicose, ill-tempered and, despite being female, misogynistic. Her visage, and even her wisdom, had the severity of a formidable predator. But it is mostly sculpture and painting that connect Athena with the owl, and she is not closely associated with the bird in myths.

In the rest of the ancient world, owls were usually forms taken by witches or omens of doom. According to folklore, they predicted the deaths of many Roman emperors by perching on their homes and hooting.[15] Among the Aztecs, owls were messengers of Mictlantecuhtli, the god of death, and people considered their cries to be dangerous omens.[16] For Hindus, owls can be emissaries of Yama, lord of the underworld. Among Australian Aborigines of West Victoria, the owl is a herald of the bogey Muurup, who devours children,[17] though Aborigines also credit the owl with wisdom. In a tale from Fraser Island, the owl sat very quietly while Yindingie, the creator god, passed out gifts among birds, so it was at first overlooked. On becoming aware of the owl, Yindingie thought initially that nothing was left, but then bestowed the gift of understanding.[18] In Navajo stories, owls often come to the aid of heroes, though they can also be harbingers of death.[19]

There are many varieties of owl in Africa, and they are far more often heard than seen. When they become visible, it is usually as a pair of gleaming eyes, which, in part because they face forward, seem disconcertingly human. Much of the traditional culture of sub-Saharan Africa is based on the contrast between the village, a place of relative security, and the adjacent bush, which is the domain of sorcerers and dangerous beasts. The Badyaranké of Senegal and Guinea consider an owl visiting a village at night to be a witch.[20] The Wuli of West Central Africa regard the owl as a form taken by magicians intent on murder.[21] When Mobutu Sese Seko arranged for the execution of the democratically elected president Patrice Lumumba in Zaïre during the late 1960s, his secret agents became known as 'the owls'.[22]

Smaller birds may gang up on any large raptor, but this 'mobbing' behaviour is particularly common with owls that appear during the day. The other birds will fly around the owl, harass it and even attack it, usually causing the unwelcome bird to fly away, which has suggested many diverse comparisons drawn from human society. Aristotle noted this behaviour and mentioned a special enmity between the owl and the wren, but also said, perhaps with irony, that the aggressive way the small birds buffet the owl and pluck its feathers was popularly called 'admiring'.[23] For Aelian, the owl was itself a witch. Its call was an incantation, enabling it to attract small birds that remain 'stupefied and seized with terror'.[24] Medieval bestiaries compared the owl, which generally avoids sunlight, to Jews, who reject the light of revelations, implicitly likening birds that mob it to righteous Christians.[25] The visage of an owl could also signal an aristocratic contempt for the masses. On a Hungarian shield from about the start of the sixteenth century in the Metropolitan Museum, New

Martin Schongauer, Ornament of an Owl Mocked by Day Birds, *1435–96, engraving. The owl was associated with sin, and here it may even represent the Devil. Here the owl holds one small bird in its mouth while the others chase it away.*

El sueño de la razon produce monstruos.

York, is a picture of an owl with the inscription, 'Though I am hated by all birds, I, nevertheless, enjoy that.'[26]

Over the coming centuries the European aristocracy would slowly but inexorably lose most of its power to the middle class, while retaining, and perhaps even increasing, its glamour. As human beings subdued, or at least pretended to subdue, the natural world, its manifestations such as storms or large predators could not evoke more than a piquant shudder. The old terror

briefly returned in Goya's famous engraving of 1799 entitled the *Sleep of Reason Produces Monsters*, showing a man bent over his desk, his head buried in his arms, as owls and a few bats swarm around him, while his cat looks on helplessly in the background. It is hard to tell whether this is due to artistic inspiration or a mistake in anatomy, but these owls, especially the one directly above the man's back, can shift their pupils so as to look out of the corner of their eyes. This makes them seem disconcertingly human, a bit like ghosts, and especially terrifying.[27] Romantic melancholy, which was popular among poets and artists of the time, disintegrates into primeval terror.

By the nineteenth century owls had become associated with Romantic landscapes, often featuring ruined castles in deep woods or on craggy mountain sides. The birds of night retained just enough associations with sorcery or imminent death to inspire a quiver of nostalgia. The heightened romanticism of Goya was gently satirized by the artist J. J. Grandville in a wood-engraving of 1854, showing a gentlemanly owl and a rather ladylike, elderly bat leaving a crumbling mansion at dawn, with the caption 'Les lumières leur font peur' ('They are frightened by the lights').[28] There are, however, many other owls and bats above the distant horizon. There is a pun here, for the word *lumières* ('lights') can also be applied to philosophers of the Enlightenment. One interpretation of the

Above: Shield with an owl, Hungary, c. 1500. The noble for whom this shield was made identified with the owl, and being mobbed by smaller birds became a point of aristocratic pride.
Opposite: Francisco Goya, The Sleep of Reason Produces Monsters, 1797, brush and ink.

print might be that these philosophers have, by inveighing against superstition, overly glamorized it, while at the same time exaggerating the ease of banishing old beliefs.

In the middle of the twentieth century, however, as people drifted ever further from the natural world, owls were denied both their nature and reputation. In Disney Studios' 1942 film *Bambi*, a diurnal owl cheerfully mentors baby rabbits in a sunny field. In the Harry Potter books, published in the late twentieth century, owls are used to carry letters at Hogwarts School of Witchcraft and Wizardry, but the description makes the birds sound much more like carrier pigeons. These owls are diurnal. They live not in a forest but a place called an 'owlery', essentially a dovecote. They are no longer solitary but usually appear in large flocks, bringing messages to students of magic in the dining hall.[29]

Like many people, I am thrilled by the ability of J. K. Rowling's Harry Potter books to inspire children who were raised on the Internet to not only read hefty books but to consider what life was like before mobile phones, and even moveable type, were invented. In this instance, however, I think the Ministry of Magic at Hogwarts has gone a little too far. It sometimes seems to insist that all magic be regulated and institutionalized. But I wish it would allow owls a little enchantment or, failing that, at least a bit of individuality.

Owls may well have the keenest senses of any animal. Their huge eyes, which never move in their sockets, suggest the possession of wisdom, and they are in some ways as powerful as they are big. In addition, their eyes, like those of cats, are luminous in the dark. Owls are able to see well by the light of the moon and stars, even when these are partly obscured by clouds. They are not especially

J. J. Grandville, illustration to Les métamorphoses du jour *(1854) entitled* 'Les lumières leur font peur'.

good at visual acuity, the ability to pick up detail, but they can distinguish shapes at great distances and are particularly proficient at detecting motion. Barn owls have shown visual sensitivity at least 35 times that of humans.[30]

But owls hunt primarily by the use of sound, and their hearing is even more remarkable than their sight. The tufts that many have on their heads are often mistaken for ears, but their real ears, further down on the head, are simply openings covered by feathers. They are surrounded by concave facial discs of feathers, which often make the eyes look even larger than they are yet actually serve to filter sounds to the ears. They are asymmetrical, with one a bit lower than the other. The difference in time of sound reaching the two ears can be only 30 millionths of a second, yet that is sufficient to tell an owl exactly where a vole is located.[31]

People have long wondered at the ability of an owl to zero in with great precision on a snake moving beneath a cover of leaves from a distance well over 30 metres (100 ft) away. If we were able to hear every leaf separately as a wind blows over a meadow in the autumn, it is likely that our capacity for thought and imagination would be overwhelmed. It could be that the sensory richness and intensity of an owl's world does not allow for, or require, thought of a more human variety. Owls have not tested well on mental abilities like problem solving, and perhaps that is why. It seems to me, however, that distinguishing which sounds of the forest were made by wind ruffling leaves and which by a potential prey requires a kind of intelligence.

So, are owls really wise? They remind me of the famous quotation by George Eliot from *Middlemarch*: 'If we had a keen vision and feeling of all ordinary human life, it would be like hearing the grass grow and the squirrel's heart beat, and we should die of that roar which lies on the other side of silence.'[32] I am not sure if even owls can hear the heartbeat of a squirrel, but they come far closer than we do. There may not be as much difference between thought and sensation as people usually think. Research has confirmed that sensation is pervaded by emotion and perhaps even volition as well, so it does not seem entirely unreasonable to regard the sensual acuity of owls as a sort of wisdom. At any rate, owls seem to occupy a liminal place, a realm of night, where evil may become good and foolishness turn into understanding.

Parrots

About 1650 the Flemish artist Jan Brueghel the Younger depicted the serpent of Eden as a red parrot, a scarlet macaw, in his oak panel painting entitled *Earthly Paradise*. Eve and Adam are monkeys, possibly howler monkeys,

high up in an apple tree. They are seated near the centre of the painting on a large branch with a secondary branch rising between them, which gives an iconographic resemblance to the biblical Tree of Knowledge. The parrot is perched further to the left on the same limb of the tree, looking on as the simian Eve takes an apple, which she will probably offer to her mate.

Lower down, a pair of blue and white parrots are perched in a smaller tree. The scene, with a meadow of grass that looks as though it might be freshly cut, resembles an aristocratic park more than a jungle. Birds and animals, mostly in pairs, are at rest. A majestic lion lies between a cow and a deer, and does not trouble either herbivore, since, according to tradition, all animals were herbivores before the Great Flood.[33] Adam and Eve had at times been associated with monkeys at least since the late Middle Ages, but identifying them so overtly in this way, even if it is only allegorical, anticipates the theory of evolution.[34] The Serpent of Eden in the Bible is clearly no ordinary snake, and painters sometimes depicted it as a dragon or even a woman with a serpentine tail.

Was Brueghel, however, suggesting that the scarlet macaw was an evil creature? Clearly not. The biblical account was secularized to a point where it appears not as a moral parable but simply as a tale. The picture shows the moment when humankind emerged from the realm of nature, at least approximately as this was imagined by contemporary Europeans. That change in status could be viewed as either a blessing or a curse, perhaps both at once, but in this case it is only history.

And why a parrot? Brueghel's depiction of the serpent of Eden as a parrot was original, but it had plenty of basis in tradition. If you do not count Balaam's ass, which becomes the mouthpiece of an angel, the serpent is the only animal in the Bible that can talk like a human being. A long tradition running from Aristotle to Descartes made humanity the animal with language, but parrots seemed to challenge that, since they were often taught to speak. A parrot, of course, has a long tail, which, especially when hanging down, has some resemblance to that of a serpent. And perhaps Brueghel understood the idea of a Fall in an unusually literal way. On becoming fully human, our ancestors would cease to live in trees, an idea that may be an anticipation of evolution. Most importantly, the serpent spoke only to Eve and, in pictures of Eden, she often seems to have a sort of intimate understanding with the creature, expressed in furtive glances between them.

Brueghel the Younger, Earthly Paradise, c. *1615, oil on panel. Adam and Eve as monkeys and the serpent of Eden as a snake.*

Puck

WEEK ENDING MAY 9, 1914
PRICE TEN CENTS

Blue-bird lady though you be,
  With your hat perched careless-wise,
No such likeness do I see,
Blue-bird lady though you be;
You are more than that—to me
  You're a Bird of Paradise!
Blue-bird lady though you be,
  With your hat perched careless-wise!

Parrots were, and still are, also closely associated with human females. Women, like parrots, would often be valued one-dimensionally for their appearance, and both served as status symbols. For most of Christian history, believers had thought of the serpent as male, but in the thirteenth century that changed. The creature was frequently depicted with the face of a woman, often as a double of Eve. The scarlet macaw painted by Brueghel could be of either gender, but it is on Eve's side of the branch.

Parrots have long been kept as animal companions for their capacity for human speech. In the *Panchatantra*, a Hindu-Persian collection of tales written down around the third century BCE but probably much older in oral traditions, a talking parrot is cared for by Indira and the other gods more or less as a pet, though it does not appear to be caged.[35] Aelian wrote that they were kept at royal courts in India but never caged or eaten, because 'the Brahmins regard them as sacred and even place them before all other birds.'[36]

The first mention of a birdcage is from a Greek text of the eighth century BCE, now lost but cited some nine centuries later, and wicker cages were regularly depicted on Greek vases of the fifth and fourth centuries BCE.[37] Cages were independently developed in the Americas, and the zoo of Motecuhzoma, eventually burned by the Spanish, had a huge aviary. Parrots were first brought to the Mediterranean world by Alexander, whose armies had reached the boundary of India, and caged parrots became popular in Greece, Rome and Egypt. They were valued for their bright colours and their exotic

Opposite: Cover of Puck, *9 May 1914. The little rhyme in the lower left corner compares the 'Bluebird Lady' with her brightly feathered hat to a bird of paradise. Exotic birds have long been associated with women.*

Above: Bird Peddler, *ink and pigment on scroll, China, late 15th or early 16th century. The vendor offers intricate cages, gilt perches and other paraphernalia relating to the keeping of birds, as children frolic around him.*

associations but, most of all, their ability
to convincingly mimic human speech.
Even as they became relatively familiar,
these parrots never lost their association
with India. Parrots appear in Roman
mosaics, often flying free, and there
may once have been significant feral
populations.[38]

After the fall of Rome, pet parrots
declined in popularity, but they again
became stylish when the Spanish
discovered new breeds in South America.
Foremost of these was the Scarlet macaw,
the very species that was painted by Jan
Brueghel the Younger. It had already been
partially domesticated by several tribes of
Mexico and the American Southwest.
Macaws and other parrots were a major
motif on the pottery of the Mimbres
Indians, from the late eleventh and early
twelfth centuries.[39] When Europeans
began to import them, these birds had
already become accustomed to a human
presence. Birds in cages became an

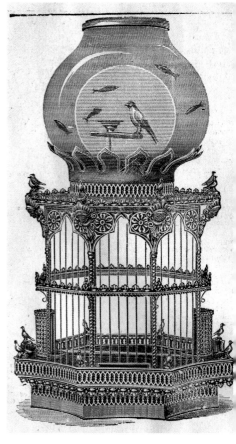

accessory in prosperous middle-class and aristocratic homes from the
seventeenth to the nineteenth centuries, and some of the cages were so
opulent, with intricate carving or metalwork, that the birds in them seemed
to be only an excuse for their display. They were often constructed as pagodas,
perhaps to emphasize their origin in an exotic land. By far the most prestigious
pets were parrots.

In the 1470s the German artist Martin Schongauer produced an
engraving known as *Madonna and Child with the Parrot*, an example of which

*Above: Intricate birdcages have long been as much a status symbol as the birds within them.
This one from a catalogue of the Iowa Bird Company in the early 20th century shows a parrot
in a sphere and an aquarium.*
Opposite: Martin Schongauer, Madonna and Child with the Parrot, *late 15th century, engraving.
In this German picture, with her right hand, the Madonna holds open the Bible, perhaps to announce
the coming of the Messiah. In her left, she holds the infant Jesus, who has a parrot perched on one
hand. The Madonna has her eyes focused on the child, while the infant Jesus gazes very intently at the
bird, which is probably telling him of events to come.*

Above: Albrecht Dürer, Adam and Eve, *1504, engraving. In his right hand,*
Adam holds a branch of mountain ash, the Tree of Life, on which is perched a parrot.
Opposite: Hans Baldung Grien, Madonna with Parrots, *1527, oil on panel.*

Giambattista Tiepolo, Young Woman with a Macaw, *c. 1760, oil on canvas.*

is now in the Metropolitan Museum of Art. It shows Mary opening a Bible with her left hand and holding the Christ Child with her right. She is looking at the infant Jesus, who is gazing intently at, and listening to, a parrot perched on his right hand. Parrots were closely associated with Mary, on the ground that their natural call was 'Ave', the greeting of the angel Gabriel appearing to Mary to announce that she will bear Christ. Here the bird seems to have a prophetic role. Just as, according to tradition, the Bible predicts the coming of the Messiah, the parrot in the engraving is foretelling his story.[40]

In 1504, still more than a hundred years before Brueghel's *Earthly Paradise*, Albrecht Dürer made his engraving of Adam and Eve in Paradise. Eden is a primeval forest rather than a garden. Eve is taking the fruit, a fig, from the serpent with her right hand as Adam looks on, his left hand open to receive it from her. She has also broken off a twig from the Tree of Knowledge, which she holds behind her back in her left hand. Adam has his right hand around a twig from the Tree of Life, a mountain ash, on which a parrot is perched.[41] The snake and parrot, which Brueghel would later combine in a single figure, seem to be acting almost in concert, to represent the fall and redemption of humankind. In the *Madonna with Parrots* by Hans Baldung Grien, painted in 1533, Mary is an aristocratic young lady, with carefully arranged hair and a pearl necklace. She is nursing the Christ Child, who looks directly out at the viewer, as an African grey parrot nibbles on her neck, which might seem erotic to us but was intended as an allusion to her primeval innocence.[42]

Ladies of means would often have their portrait painted together with a pet parrot, and such pictures were to become ever more common over the centuries to come. In most of them, the parrot comes across as a surrogate

Gustave Courbet, Woman with a Parrot, *1866, oil on canvas.*

Plyctolophus Leadbeateri. Agapornis Swinderianus.

SCOTCH FANCY CANARIES.

BUFF PIEBALD.   YELLOW PIEBALD.

YELLOW PIEBALD.

Vincent Brooks Day & Son Lith.

Opposite: Frontispiece for the ornithology section of William Jardine, The Naturalist's Library
*(1848), engraving with watercolours. The colourful cockatoo and parrot are associated with distant,
romantic kingdoms. The figures bathing in the background represent a sort of primeval innocence.
Above: 'Scotch Fancy Canaries', illustration from* Cassel's Canaries and Cage Birds *(1880),
chromolithograph. Cage birds were often bred simply for novelty, and at times had physical problems
as a result.*

Leadenhall Poultry Market, London, from Harper's Weekly, *16 March 1876. The peacocks may be destined to stroll in aristocratic gardens but in transit they, like chickens, are kept in cramped cages where they cannot even turn around.*

boyfriend or husband. A caged bird, especially a parrot, became a symbol of erotic longing. Its release from the cage, even when still within the home, could suggest the discarding of sexual inhibitions. In a painting from about 1760 by Giambattista Tiepolo entitled *Young Woman with a Macaw*, a seductive lady, with one bared breast, possibly a courtesan, is affectionately stroking a parrot. She seems to have been looking at her beloved pet and perhaps even talking to it, when somebody, perhaps a lover, approached. She is turning her head, showing surprise but no loss of composure.[43] In *Woman with a Parrot*, painted in 1866, Gustave Courbet depicted a naked woman sprawled luxuriously on a bed, with her hair extended in all directions. She has one arm raised where her parrot has just landed on her hand.[44]

In addition to their speech and brilliant colours, parrots in Europe acquired glamour from their association with jungles in the far corners of the colonial empires. Tropical birds in general seemed to epitomize the barbaric splendour that explorers associated with exotic lands. Europeans were fascinated with the secretary birds, ostriches and weaver birds of sub-Saharan Africa, the bower birds and birds of paradise of New Guinea, the lyrebirds and kookaburras of Australia, the hummingbirds and toucans of

Latin America. But of the greatest interest of all were parrots, which could come from just about anywhere in the tropics. Their capacity to imitate human speech suggested enough intelligence to make them interesting, and it was flattering as well. To 'parrot' means about the same thing as to 'ape': to imitate without understanding. For Europeans, both the colourful bird and the large primate represented indigenous people. Teaching a parrot to speak was, in a symbolic way, a bit like bringing 'civilization' to 'savages'. Even the scientific knowledge gained by studying these creatures was a trophy of conquest.

The parrots ushered in a new era of pet-keeping, especially in Europe and North America. As people became increasingly urban, their contact with animals in the wild and on farms diminished, but this was in some ways compensated by taking tame animals into their homes. People have done this since the Neolithic era, but the scale of modern pet-keeping was unprecedented. Also new was the way animals were no longer expected to work at tasks such as hunting or catching mice but were generally retained only for companionship or status. For those of the middle class, parrots were often too expensive and demanding. In the Early Modern era parrots were rivalled in popularity by the canary, a small yellow finch from the Canary Islands, a Spanish archipelago off the coast of northwest Africa. In the nineteenth century the most popular avian pet worldwide became the budgerigar, a diminutive parakeet introduced from Australia.

The treatment of these pets reflected all the paradoxes and contradictions of human society. They were often kept in filthy, cramped conditions in markets, but they could sometimes be physically pampered in homes. They were bred, often at the cost of their health, in all sorts of unusual colours and shapes because of fads or their owners' whims. Parrots and their relatives continued to represent a fantasy of extravagant luxury.

In the late decades of the twentieth century, Irene Pepperberg systematically taught words and the associated concepts to her African grey parrot, named Alex. A chemistry student at Harvard, she was feeling disillusioned with her major when she purchased Alex and conceived the idea, at the time rather quixotic, of contributing to science by teaching it not simply random words but human language. Working with Alex over the next thirty years, she taught him to identify colours, shapes and materials, as well as numbers up to six. He learned over one hundred English words.[45]

When he died at the age of 31 in 2007, Alex's last words, which he said every night, were 'I love you.' His death was announced on major newscasts and his obituary was carried in just about every American newspaper. Alex was a media sensation.[46] He had become, in the minds of many, perhaps the foremost emissary between the human world and the animal kingdom. The story of Alex appealed to the human imagination, specifically to the longing to converse with animals, which runs through myths and legends throughout the world.

The public was fascinated less with Pepperberg's accomplishments than with her relationship with Alex. This was in part because the work took place on the fringes of the scientific community. Had Pepperberg, like most scientists, worked only in a laboratory as part of a team, comparing results obtained with several fairly anonymous subjects, her accomplishments might have aroused little interest beyond a handful of specialists. Since much of the research was in her home and centred on a single, highly personalized subject, it seemed far more romantic. On the cover of Pepperberg's autobiography, *Alex and Me*, is a photograph of the pair that is reminiscent of many portraits of women with their parrots over the centuries. She is sitting on the ground with her knee raised and Alex perched on it. Pepperberg has turned her head to face the viewer with a knowing smile, while Alex stares dreamily into the distance.

In the twenty-first century it has become less generally acceptable to keep birds in cages, at least without constant avian companionship. Researchers might also find the emphasis on learning human speech, rather than problem solving, as a measure of intelligence to be narrow. Nevertheless, the story of Alex and Irene has a fascination that goes well beyond its significance as science. It appeals to us as a fairy tale akin to 'Beauty and the Beast', where a woman initiates a wild yet ultimately good-hearted man into civilization.

Indigenous Traditions

Every genus, species or folk taxonomy of birds involves a special sort of bond with people, of a sort that has evolved over centuries or millennia. Each entails a unique set of images, rights, privileges and expectations. When talking about such relationships, it is hard to separate nurture from nature or tradition from biology. There are instances in which the relationship between humans and birds has altered avian behaviour to a point where the changes may have become hardwired. Swallows have been known since ancient times to make their nests under the eaves of houses. Today most populations of barn swallows in North America have abandoned trees and will only nest in human structures.

The honeyguide has developed a close symbiosis with several peoples in Central Africa. The Yao of Mozambique let out a rumbling call to summon honeyguides when they are ready to look for honey. The birds appear and then lead them to beehives in cavities of trees. The Yao extract the honeycomb and the birds feed on what they leave behind.[47] Pastoralist peoples of Kenya believe the honeyguides take the initiative, come to them and summon them by dancing when there is honey nearby.[48] Most of the peoples who collect honey deliberately leave behind a bit of honey for the birds, though a few do not. In any case, the honeyguides benefit, for they have the ability, unique among vertebrates, to eat and digest the wax of the honeycomb, which is of little use to human beings.[49]

The behaviour, at least on the side of the birds, appears to be inborn, since honeyguides are brood parasites like cuckoos and cowbirds. They lay their eggs in the nests of other birds, so they are not very likely to have learned how to work with humans from their parents. If we count this relationship as an instance of 'domestication', it may well be the earliest one. The honeyguides, however, have a similar relationship with the honey badger, which suggests that the bond with them may have been mostly on the initiative of the birds.[50]

The relationship is also a dramatic example of indigenous knowledge, which does not derive from Western paradigms yet commands respect. Environmental concerns today are international and cross-cultural. They require Western conservationists to work closely with people who ultimately share many of their concerns yet see the natural world in very different terms. Their taxonomies may correspond roughly to ours, but never with great precision. They may understand 'humanity' in radically different ways, and surround birds as well with different associations. Their knowledge of fauna and flora is never systematic in the same way as Linnaean taxonomy, but it may be based on far more extensive observation than most scientists have time for. It also tends to be oriented around practical tasks such as hunting.

Western ornithological knowledge is not infallible; nor is any indigenous tradition. When there are disagreements, all parties can work together in dialogue. Whether there is a misunderstanding or one party turns out to be in error, all are likely to deepen their understanding in the process. This is the foundation of the emerging discipline of ethno-ornithology, which attempts to study birds from the comparative perspectives on birds of many cultures.[51] But birds in ethno-ornithology are, in perhaps a slightly more visible way than usual, simply filling a role they have had since before the Tower of Babel – mediating among cultures (or 'nature-cultures').

Symbols shift their meaning with the context in an organic way, a bit like birds and animals themselves. Like living things, they are also constantly changing and evolving. They occupy a liminal area between the subjective and objective realms. No, a scarlet macaw is really neither the Serpent in Eden nor the Virgin Mary. But such comparisons, if we think about them for a while, can tell us a lot about relationships between macaws and human beings. It is a way of nourishing a bond that, like a partnership between married people, need not necessarily be always harmonious to be profound. Just as married people relate, through one another, to adopted elements of ethnicity and heritage, so we relate, through a macaw, to distant lands and to the natural world.

We might say that, in the world of birds, crows are the scholars; owls, the priests; parrots, the poets. Crows show intellect; owls, silent understanding; parrots, verbal facility. Actually, that is wildly oversimplified at best, but my larger point is that each variety of birds has a unique territory in the human psyche, even if the boundaries are not clearly marked. If they become extinct or we lose all contact with them, something or someone else will fill the void, but never with the same vitality. The huge machines of the Industrial Revolution are a bit like the great mammals that, in part through human agency, were driven to extinction before the rise of civilization. The alarm clock may remind us of a rooster, and the burglar alarm is like a barking dog. Tamagotchis and other electronic pets may be modelled on parrots, as well as monkeys, dinosaurs and just about any creature. But, in comparing the copy to the original, one sees that something precious has been lost.

I will close this chapter with a tale from the Australian Aborigines, in which all three birds discussed in this chapter appear, together with the great eagle hawk, who serves as a chair of their meeting. In presenting the tale, Sonia Tidemann and Tim Whiteside observe that it is very unusual among Aboriginal stories in addressing the fear of death. This concern, they believe, may have only appeared with the arrival of missionaries. Perhaps the Aborigines once felt so deeply connected to their ancestors that individual death did not appear terribly significant. At any rate, this makes the story one more example of how birds often mediate among cultures.

A young cockatoo tumbled from a high tree and collapsed. The animals all tried to wake it in vain. At a meeting called to investigate what happened, they first turned to the owl, who had a reputation for wisdom, but it was silent. The eagle hawk took a pebble, tossed it into a river, watched it sink, and then said that the cockatoo, like the pebble, had entered another sphere. The other creatures were not satisfied, so they turned to the crow, who knew a great deal, for an explanation. The crow took a weapon for hunting, tossed it into the river, and then watched as it sank and then rose again. The crow explained that, in the same way, we enter another sphere but return. Then eagle owl asked for volunteers to enter the realm of death to learn the truth. The insects volunteered. When larvae returned as dragonflies and caterpillars as butterflies, all knew that the crow was right.[52]

7 AVIAN POLITICS

The wren, the wren, the king of all birds,
St Stephen's Day was caught in the furze;
Up with the holly and ivy tree,
Where all the birds will sing to me.
Sung at the ceremonial parade with the wren in Cork, Ireland

teach at Sing Sing Correctional Facility in Ossining, New York, a monumental structure from the early nineteenth century when security was a matter of stone and iron rather than of digital technology. Ravens nest on the rooftops and walls of the ruins that still form part of the enormous Sing Sing prison complex. Flocks of tree swallows often pass over the prison yard beside the Hudson River in autumn. Their appearance can seem, in such a setting, almost prophetic. Inmates have told me that crows used to congregate there in huge numbers whenever there was an execution, especially when Julius and Ethel Rosenberg were electrocuted for espionage in 1953.

Auburn Correctional Facility, a bit further north, is older still and inmates are constantly shuttled back and forth between the two prisons. Veterans of Auburn first told me about the infestation of crows that roost around the walls there in winter, which scientists have estimated to be in the tens of thousands. Local people have tried everything from banging on pans to shooting in order to get the crows to leave, but with no more than limited and temporary success. The prison is built on the site of a Cayuga village, and some of the inmates have told me that the crows are the spirits of departed Native Americans.

I have not been able to find any record of crows gathering at Sing Sing for the execution of the Rosenbergs. The antiquity of the roost at Auburn is very questionable as well. Searching in several databases, I have been unable to find references to large numbers of crows roosting around Auburn before the late 1990s. Furthermore, crow roosts tend to shift constantly. When towns are inundated with crows, this often causes a minor panic and people fail to realize that the visitors are just temporarily passing through. Some infestations may last only for part of a year. Crows repeatedly return to other sites for years, occasionally for about a decade, but I have never heard of crows continually returning to the same roost for anything remotely close to a century. As is so often the case, people push legends back into the remote past, which seems to add both romance and authority.

The idea that the crows are the souls of Indian villagers is in line with American Indian lore, both traditional and contemporary. Among Native

American elders, especially the Iroquois, a council of crows, even a small one, was a sign that they should convene as well. Today, large gatherings are said to be the spirits of those in tribes or villages that have disappeared.[1] The students who told me the legend of the crows at Auburn were Hispanic and African American, not Native American. I did not think to ask them, but it is possible that they heard the story from Native people. It is also likely, however, that it was created independently by people of other ethnicities.

This sort of convergence would not be surprising, since crow roosts are remarkably suggestive of a busy village or city of human beings. Except when they settle into place or leave, each crow seems to be following his or her own agenda, as people might do in a marketplace. It is not hard to see how that image would appeal to prisoners, whose days are heavily regimented. They must wear the same clothes, follow orders, keep to strict schedules and abide by innumerable rules.

The originally Chinese story of the Herdsman and the Weaving Maiden, told in many versions throughout East Asia, gives another mythological explanation for the flocking and roosting behaviour of corvids in autumn.[2] In a Korean version, the sun-god has a daughter, who weaves the most beautiful cloth in the world but never leaves her loom. He searches the world for a proper husband for her and settles on a young herdsman who is completely devoted to his cattle. After the marriage, the man and wife are so happy together that they spend all their time strolling through meadows, completely neglecting their work. Angered, the god places his daughter, who becomes the star Vega, in the Western heaven and the Herdsman, the star Aquilla, in the Eastern heaven, separated by the Milky Way. Moved by their entreaties, he decrees that one day a year they may meet. They are at first overjoyed but then find the night has become too dark and the river of stars between them too wide. They cry, creating heavy rain and flooding the land. Finally, crows and magpies come and form a bridge. The lovers cross on each side and are reunited in the centre.[3]

Scientists have intensively studied the roosting behaviour of crows for decades, but they are far from being able to explain it entirely. Reasons why crows roost include protection from predators, the chance to exchange information about food sources and the opportunity to find mates. There might not always be a single reason, and the motivations could be almost as diverse as those of people congregating in New York's Central Park. In the case of Auburn Correctional Facility, part of the reason for the flocking of crows might be the bright lights along the walls at night.

These legends of the crows at Auburn and Sing Sing sound as if, with a few adjustments, they could have belonged to Assyrian, Graeco-Roman

Vincent van Gogh, Wheatfield with Crows, *1890, oil on canvas.*

or medieval times. For the most part, the folklore of birds has changed surprisingly little over the millennia. As explained earlier, we think of birds as a sort of parallel to the human world, with institutions that correspond to our own. Inevitably this makes them appear as kings, capitalists, anarchists, courtiers, housewives, ministers, hermits, Communists, artists and all of the other sorts of people that make up human society. Are these images illusions? In the end, the answer is mostly 'yes'. I don't think we can or should entirely refrain from anthropomorphizing birds, but we should try not to get too carried away. Inevitably we will project our hopes, fears and aspirations into any description of avian society, and reflection on them tells much about ourselves.

Early Fables

Aesop, the half-legendary author of fables, had, according to tradition, been a slave on the island of Samos during the sixth century BCE and was granted freedom for his skill in telling stories. Many of these fables, such as 'The Tortoise and the Hare', 'The Ant and the Grasshopper' and 'The Fox and the Grapes', are still familiar to almost everyone. In general, they model the realm of animals after that of human society, in which species correspond to various groups of people, divided by rank, prestige, profession, gender and so on. Accordingly, the lion is king, while the fox is a courtier. The eagle rules among birds. All animals are constantly competing with one another, not only for survival but status as well. The fables express subtle anxieties about our identity, both as individuals and members of groups.

*J. J. Grandville's engraving of Hesiod's fable of the Nightingale and the Hawk
as retold by Jean de La Fontaine, 1844.*

The oldest fable that has come down to us in Greek literature is from Hesiod's *Works and Days*. It is roughly contemporaneous with the period in which Aesop is alleged to have lived, but it is not usually attributed to him:

> Here is how the hawk addressed the dapple-throat nightingale
> as he carried her high in the clouds, grasping her in his claws;
> impaled on the curved talons, she was weeping piteously, but he
> addressed her sternly: 'Goodness, why are you screaming? You
> are in the power of one much superior, and you will go whichever
> way I take you, singer though you are. I will make you my dinner
> if I like, or let you go. He is a fool who seeks to compete against
> the stronger: he loses the struggle and suffers injury on top of
> insult.'[4]

The moral seems at first to be that 'might makes right', but the author immediately contradicts that lesson by telling his brother, Perses, not to engage in violence but lead a life of righteousness. Hesiod is describing a period of lawlessness that he believes will come to an end. The hawk is showing hubris, which almost always leads to destruction in fables. The fable seems incomplete, and Hesiod may have left out an ending in which the hawk is punished by fate. Perhaps the story was already so well-known at the time that Hesiod could assume the reader was familiar with it.[5]

The fable may contain a reference to the tale of Tereus and Philomela, especially since Hesiod references that story in the same work.[6] According to an ancient legend, Tereus, king of Thrace, was married to Procne, a princess from Athens, who entreated him to invite her sister Philomela to visit. Tereus agreed, but then raped Philomela and, so that she would not tell what happened, cut out her tongue. Philomela wove the story into a tapestry and then showed the picture to her sister. Together, they took revenge by killing Itys, son of Tereus and Philomela, and serving his body to his father for dinner. Tereus pursued the two sisters, but the gods, wishing to end the carnage, changed Tereus into a hoopoe, Procne into a nightingale and Philomela into a swallow.

J. J. Grandville, engraving of the story of Philomela and Procne as retold by Jean de La Fontaine, 1844.

Roman versions of the story reversed the names of the two sisters, perhaps because Philomela, deprived of speech, had communicated through art as the nightingale does through song. There was a belief in Greece, found in Aeschylus, Aristotle and others, that the hoopoe begins life as a hawk.[7] The hawk chasing the nightingale may be an allusion to Tereus and Philomela.

Cloud Cuckoo Land

The comic poet Aristophanes uses much the same sort of satire in many of his plays, especially *The Birds*. As the play begins, two former citizens of Athens, Pisthetaerus and Euelpides, are wandering about, led by a crow, in search of the legendary king Tereus. They are tired of all the bickering of their fellow Athenians, especially of the constant lawsuits. Since he became a bird, they think that Tereus might be able to advise them.

When they arrive, Tereus tells the visitors of the carefree lives of birds, but then Pisthetaerus has an idea. First, he tells Tereus and the other avians that the birds are older than the gods and by right ought to rule. He goes on to say that they should build a city in the sky, blocking the scent of sacrifices rising to the immortals, and thus they can starve the gods into submitting to their sovereignty. Tereus gives Euelpides and Pisthetaerus a root to chew, which enables them to grow wings. The birds name their city in the sky 'Cloud Cuckoo Land'. After several more incidents, the gods submit and accept Pisthetaerus as their ruler, and he then marries Sovereignty, the daughter of Zeus.[8] Poultry is served at the wedding feast and, for all the pomp, Pisthetaerus' power seems far from secure at the end.

In many respects, comedy is the most evanescent of forms, since humour is dependent on very ephemeral references and subtle associations which are familiar to an author's contemporaries but might not be to later generations. *The Birds* is surely full of allusions and jokes that even classical scholars can hardly hope to ever reconstruct and, even if they could explain such passages in the abstract, it is not likely that we would respond to them in the same way as Aristophanes' fellow citizens. On the other hand, his city in the sky seems in ways like London or New York of today, with all the pretensions, delusions, huckstering and petty quarrels. A few episodes seem almost eerily contemporary. When Pisthetaerus first conceives the idea of Cloud Cuckoo Land, several Athenians immediately show up in the hope of making a fast buck, including a surveyor who wants to divide the air into lots and sell them.

Furthermore, the play also reveals aspects of the relations between human beings and birds. We still regard them with a combination of reverence,

Drawing after a Sumero-Akkadian seal showing Nintura in Battle with the Anzu bird, second millennium BCE.

exploitation, envy and perplexity. The form may be different, but the spirit of the play is close to the fables of Aesop, which still make good sense today. As is so often the case, the humour comes from events that are totally preposterous yet have an uncanny ring of plausibility. *The Birds* appealed to nostalgia for contact with the natural world, which was already quite palpable for city people in Aristophanes' time. They must also have looked up from time to time and admired birds, both for their special abilities and the complexity of their society.

At the same time, they must have been aware of the dangers of such nostalgia. The play is about the descent into primeval chaos, as every distinction between birds, deities and human beings is placed in question. It may contain a distant echo of the story of the monstrous Anzu bird of Mesopotamian myth, which is usually portrayed with the head of a lion and the body of an eagle. When the god Enlil was bathing, the Anzu stole the Tablets of Destinies from him, thus gaining supreme power. The other deities were terrified, and Nintura, a god of war, alone dared to challenge the monster. He was victorious after a long battle, restoring the cosmic order and establishing himself as the supreme divinity.[9] The tale of the Anzu Bird and Nintura may well contain elements of burlesque, much as Aristophanes' play does, since it also shows the gods as foolish and not particularly brave.[10]

Aristophanes' *The Birds* is so blasphemous that it is hard to imagine how it would have been tolerated, even acclaimed, outside of a period in which many customs and values were temporarily placed in abeyance. When Aristophanes was writing, theatre had not been entirely separated from ritual. Comedies and tragedies were both performed as part of the festival of Dionysus. Like the Roman Saturnalia, the medieval Feast of Fools and Carnival in parts of Latin America and Europe, this involved a cancellation, even an inversion, of hierarchies. As with the Romans, masters would serve their slaves and, as in the Middle Ages, an outcast was temporarily appointed king.[11] The festivals largely go back to the Babylonian *Sacaea*, part of the festivities leading up to the New Year, which celebrated the triumph of the god Marduk, representing order, over the female demon Tiamat, representing chaos. That tale in turn was much the same story as the victory of Nintura over Anzu,[12] and the two gods were conflated.

The Assembly of Birds

At times in the fables of Aesop, groups of animals, particularly birds, form their own governments, as in the fable of 'The Vain Jackdaw':

> Jupiter determined, it is said, to create a sovereign over the birds; and made a proclamation that, on a certain day, they should all present themselves before him, when he would himself choose the most beautiful among them to be King. The Jackdaw, knowing his own ugliness, searched through the woods and fields, and collected the feathers which had fallen from the wings of his companions, and stuck them in all parts of his body, hoping thereby to make himself the most beautiful of all. When the appointed day arrived, and the birds had assembled before Jupiter, the Jackdaw also made his appearance in his many-feathered finery. On Jupiter proposing to make him king, on account of the beauty of his plumage, the birds indignantly protested, and each plucking from him his own feathers, the Jackdaw was again nothing but a Jackdaw.[13]

One way to read this story is as a veiled criticism of human hubris, more specifically the way we appropriate qualities of animals such as the strength of a bull and the speed of a horse for our own purposes. Like the Jackdaw, we try, in other words, to beautify ourselves by wearing their feathers and fur but will be stripped naked in the end.

The Jātakas, a collection of tales in Pali written down around 300 BCE, centres mostly on previous lives of the Buddha in animal form. He is the king of a tribe of monkeys who sacrifices himself so that the others may thrive. He is a young parrot who takes grain from a field to feed his elderly parents, showing such filial devotion that the farmer ceases to object. He is the king of quails who counsels his subjects not to fight, knowing the exertion would release traps set by human beings.

In one of the tales, terrestrial animals have chosen the lion as their king, and the birds fear that, without a sovereign, their society will degenerate into anarchy. They initially choose the owl. The crow objects, complaining of the owl's ugliness. The owl flies after the crow, and then, when both are gone, the birds choose as their king the 'golden mallard' (possibly the mandarin duck).[14]

In *The Panchatantra*, a collection of animal tales written down about 200 BCE and traditionally attributed to the Brahmin Vishnu Sharma, all of

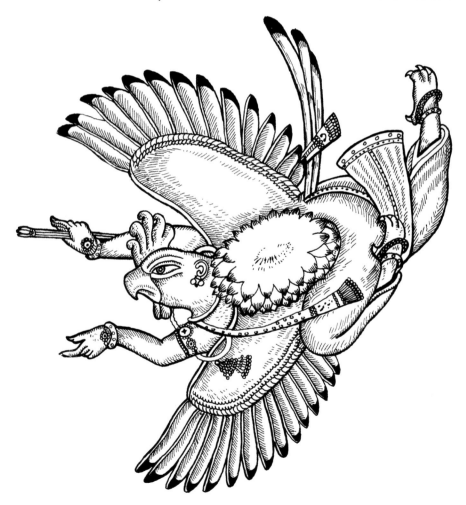

Garuda, the king of birds in Hindu mythology and religion.

the birds call an assembly. Their king is Garuda, and has the torso of a man but wings and beak of an enormous eagle. They complain that he is too preoccupied with the affairs of the deities Vishnu and Lakshmi to pay much attention to the concerns of his fellow birds. They are impressed by the wizened visage of the owl, as well as his ability to see at night, and they choose him as their monarch. As the owl is about to ascend the throne, the crow arrives. He objects that the owl has none of the beauty of the peacock or swan; in fact his features appear grotesque and malicious. Besides, the owl has none of the prestige of Garuda, whose very name is enough to frighten enemies. The birds cancel the coronation, and the owls have been enemies of crows ever since. Crows mob owls by day; the owls attack crows by night.[15]

In *The Owl and the Nightingale*, a long twelfth- or thirteenth-century poem in Middle English, the nightingale and owl trade insults as they compete for status as lord of the night. The nightingale says that the appearance of the owl is filthy, while its screeching is hideous. The owl replies that, unlike the nightingale, it is useful, since it rids churches of mice. Its hooting calls sinners to repentance, while the song of the nightingale only inspires people to lechery. The nightingale replies that it sings to celebrate the glory of God. He then adds that the owl, when killed, will be stuffed and used as a scarecrow. The owl replies that, unlike the nightingale, it helps people even in death. But between the taunts, the two engage in sophisticated debates about morality.

Finally, the owl has had enough and threatens to call other raptors such as the hawk to attack his adversary. By then it is starting to get light and other birds including the thrush and woodpecker gradually appear. The wren, who is the king of birds, arrives to settle the argument. He advises the adversaries to take their case to a wise man named Nicholas of Guildford, who may be the author of the poem. The nightingale and owl agree, and off the birds go to find him.

Throughout the poem the nightingale is perched on a flower. This suggests a garden, the usual setting for poems and tales of courtly love. The owl is on a branch covered with ivy, suggesting a monastery. The two birds seem to represent the values of chivalry and the Church respectively. Perhaps the poem presents a dialectic disguised as a quarrel, since both parties ultimately seem to share the same basic values, despite their difference in emphasis.[16]

Different species stand for various classes, occupations and philosophies. Are the debaters really birds or are they allegorical representations of people? Are they referring to actual human institutions such as churches or are these analogies to places in a meadow or forest? Is Nicholas a man or a bird? The boundaries between bird and man are so blurred here that the answers to these questions do not seem to matter.

In a meditative lyric poem in Middle High German entitled 'Lament for the World' (*Weltklage*), the Minnesinger Walther von der Vogelweide (1170–1230) points to birds as a model for human society. He looks out over the fields, streams and forests, and finds that all the creatures from the stag to the worm have their enmities, which lead to brutal fights. The birds are no different, and they would have destroyed themselves, except that they have agreed upon a government with kings and rule by law. The nobles and servants among birds know their appointed roles. Walter goes on to contrast that order with the Germany of his day, ruled by countless petty, feuding princes.[17]

The brilliant plumage and regular patterns of behaviour of many birds suggest the splendour of a royal court with its costumes and rituals.

The Avian Parliament

In *The Parlement of Foules*, a long poem in Middle English written by Geoffrey Chaucer around 1380, the narrator contemplates the mysteries of love, with all its power and peril, something of which he has no experience himself. He begins to read *The Dream of Scipio* by Cicero, in which the Roman general Scipio Africanus takes his adoptive grandson, Scipio the Younger, above the firmament, where they look out over the cosmos. Africanus tells the other that it is futile to spend one's life in pursuit of glory, since earth is only a minute speck in comparison with the heavens. In addition, the planets will eventually return to their initial positions. The past will be forgotten, and time will begin again, so bliss may be attained only through a life of virtue.

The light fails, and the narrator falls asleep over the book. Scipio Africanus appears to him in a dream, takes him to an ancient temple of Venus

Sir Walther von der Vogelweide, from Manessischen Liederhandschrift *(c. 1304).*

and then disappears. The narrator sees images of Cupid readying his arrows, Venus herself, and mythological figures from stories of sacred or profane love. It is St Valentine's Day, when birds choose their mates, and he sees them collecting in a meadow. They arrange themselves in an orderly manner with birds of prey at the highest level, followed by those that eat worms or insects, the water birds and those that live on seeds. They stand beside the goddess Nature, who introduces a beautiful female eagle. Three male eagles woo her in the language of courtly love, each telling of his loyalty and devotion. By this time the other birds have all chosen their mates and are impatient to leave, but a representative of each social level offers up advice about which suitor should marry the female eagle, and they argue in spirited, and sometimes angry, terms. Nature silences them and then asks the female eagle to choose a suitor, but the bird replies she is not ready. At her request, Nature puts the selection off until next year, and then the birds sing in honour of Nature and the summer to come. The narrator awakens to find the birds have flown away and resolves to study more.

As I interpret the poem, the narrator in his dream fulfils Scipio's prophesy that when the stars and planets are realigned, time will finish and begin again. In entering the pagan temple, he is returning to the past. Finally, in the meadow, he has become the original Adam in Eden, who, according to the first biblical creation story, was made before Eve. That may be why the speeches of Nature and the various birds contain no references to the works of human beings. Like the first man before eating the forbidden fruit, the narrator can understand the speech of animals. According to tradition, birds and animals did not eat meat until after the great Flood. Here raptors and their prey mingle without fear or violence, though the merlin does accuse the cuckoo of committing murder by laying eggs in the sparrow's nest.

The order of nature is perfect, with each sort of bird spontaneously assuming its proper place in the assembly. For late medieval and Renaissance men and women, the harmony of the cosmos consisted of an elaborate network of analogies, signatures and correspondences. Just as, they believed, man was the noblest of terrestrial creatures, so the dolphin was first among sea creatures, and the rose was foremost among plants. In the same way, the eagle was the most exalted of birds. Others choose their mates without thought, but the eagles do so, like men and women, with deliberation. They follow elaborate rules of chivalry. Eagles and human beings have not only free will but, as the final request of the female eagle shows, the ability to delay gratification.[18]

In the late Middle Ages and Renaissance, society was increasingly organized in a hierarchical manner and this was reflected in descriptions of the animal kingdom. This pyramidal schema aligned with the proverbial food chain. The monarchs and nobles identified with predators, as befitted a warrior caste. Birds that eat worms or insects are in a sense also predators, so they are next in rank. Last come birds that eat seeds and grain, which correspond to the peasantry. For the fabulist Marie de France (1160–1215), rank seemed to reflect inherent worth. In her animal tales, the higher orders of animals reflect the virtues of chivalry, while the lower orders are foolish and ignorant.[19]

Chaucer uses essentially the same method of ranking, even though he may be describing a primal time before predation. For him, however, the order of birds seems to be far more a matter of organization than superiority. Just as in *The Canterbury Tales* he did not accord greater humanity to those higher on the social scale, he does not show the higher birds as either morally or intellectually superior. The rhetoric of the eagles is a mostly affectionate satire of courtly ways, and their sincerity is uncertain. The modest seed-eaters, represented by the turtle dove, offer a council of fidelity that is less pretentious than those of the three male eagles but at least as eloquent. Kings should act in a royal way, while peasants should behave according to their station, not because the monarchs are better people but since that is what divine providence has ordained. In the same way, different birds may be equally valued, though each, to use a more contemporary phrase, is confined to a certain ecological niche.

Chaucer's method of classifying birds by what they eat, which goes back at least to Frederick II of Sicily (reg. 1198–1250), is surprisingly scientific. The Christian allegories that were the foundation of the medieval bestiaries are missing entirely. The allegorical frame of the work, with Nature personified, is remarkably like what we would find in books of natural history through the early twentieth century, when the frontispieces of books would show Nature as a pagan goddess surrounded by various animals. Nature is the ruler of the birds in *The Parlement of Foules*. Like a feudal monarch, she has her position as a representative of God. The birds collectively resemble the English Parliament of the day, which was still largely advisory, though gradually acquiring more power.

As a cultivated man who had visited Renaissance Italy, Chaucer may well have realized that St Valentine's Day had been a Christian appropriation of the Roman holiday Lupercalia, which was both a celebration of Rome's founding and a festival of fertility. His reference to the legend that it is the day when birds choose their mates is among the first that has come down to us, but there were many others from both England and France in his era and in subsequent centuries. The ecclesiastical calendar was being partially secularized, perhaps even paganized, and Valentine's Day was becoming a time for lovers to exchange tokens of their devotion. People were learning from birds.

The Eagle, King of Birds

The eagle displays immense power, freedom and royal dignity in flight. When seen perched on a tree or rock, we notice the great size and fierce gaze of the eagle immediately. The exalted status of the eagle is also due to the fact that it avoids human beings and consequently is usually only observed at a distance. Eagles generally fly alone, enveloped in majestic solitude.

Contrary to what is popularly believed, they are not by any means the highest flyers among birds, but they seem majestically aloof from human concerns. That may be why they have been most popular as a symbol in areas often contested by mighty empires such as those that once ruled in Babylon, Rome and Mexico, in which the rulers were set apart from common people by pomp and pageantry. The motif of an eagle as king has been less common in societies where power was decentralized, such as those of the Celts and Vikings, both of which preferred the raven. There are not very many stories that centre on eagles, but they are ubiquitous in royal symbolism.

In most of the Mediterranean the ruler of birds has been the eagle. This status was established, perhaps, in 'Etana', one of the earliest literary texts. It tells how Etana, one of the early kings of the Near East, rode up to heaven on the back of an eagle to meet with the deities in heaven.[20] The eagle was the only creature that the Hittites, often the major rivals to the Egyptians, considered divine. At the investiture of Hittite kings, an eagle was held above the monarch and his consort, as a priest recited a blessing. The eagle was then released to fly up to the sun-god and the storm-god, telling of the royal couple in all their glory.[21] The double-headed eagle, originally an ancient Hittite symbol of royalty, was passed on and eventually adopted by both the Russian and Austrian empires. The eagle was an attribute of Zeus, the supreme god of the Greeks, and Jupiter, his Roman equivalent. It decorated the standards of Roman legions and, much later, the armies of Napoleon.

A great many Roman generals and emperors had eagles prophesy their future greatness. Suetonius reported that when Tiberius came to Rhodes, an eagle, never previously seen on the island, perched on the future emperor's house. He also wrote that two eagles appeared fighting in the sky before the battle of Bedriacum. When one of them was victorious, a third eagle appeared and drove the winner away. Accordingly, two rivals for the title of emperor of Rome would fight one another to exhaustion, leaving the way for a third, Vespasian, to claim the throne. Plutarch told a story, though expressing scepticism, that the commander Marius, as a young man, once had an eagle's nest with seven chicks fall on his cloak. An augur interpreted this to mean that he would attain the consulship, the highest office in the land, seven times.[22]

Just as secular powers appropriated the cross, the Christian Church adopted martial symbols such as the eagle. That became the symbol of St John the Evangelist, who, in his gospel, immediately soars towards mystical heights. In Christianity the eagle also borrowed much of the symbolism of the Egyptian falcon-god Horus, which had been closely associated with the Pharaoh and the sun. Medieval bestiaries told that the eagle would look directly at the solar disc. In the sixth sphere of Heaven in Dante's *Paradiso*, the souls of just rulers such as Roman Emperor Trajan and the biblical King David together form an image of an enormous eagle.[23]

Garuda, the king of birds in much of Hindu mythology, is a blend of human and aquiline features. Often, he is a man with the beak and wings of an eagle. The eagle is often associated with sovereignty among American Indians, particularly of the Northern Hemisphere. Indians of the American West often identified the eagle with the mythical thunderbird. Huitzilopochtli, the Aztec god of the sun, was at times depicted as an eagle. But, however intuitive it may at times seem, according royal status to the eagle is far from universal. In ancient Egypt the falcon has been regarded as supreme among birds. Around the Arctic Circle, including parts of Europe, Siberia and North America, it has usually been the raven, which also decorated the banner under which the Vikings marched into battle. In China the phoenix has symbolized the empress and, more generally, the royal family.

The idea of the eagle as a king was carried throughout most of Europe, first by the Roman empire itself and later by the Graeco-Roman literary culture that followed it. But, particularly on the fringes of the empire, it probably was never profoundly integrated into folk culture and, consequently, not very difficult to challenge.

The Wren, Pretender to the Throne

Illuminations in the Sherborne Missal, a late fifteenth-century manuscript from Dorset in England, show most of the birds that were common in woods and meadows, but only the wren is singing. Its beak is wide open; we can see its tongue.[24] In most of Europe, especially in Celtic areas apart from Scotland, the rival of the eagle for royal status is the wren, a diminutive bird that is unlike it in almost every respect. The wren is small and flies only for short distances but sings beautifully. While the eagle nests high on cliffs or in trees, the wren nests in low branches or in crevices including holes in the ground. The eagle is a

solar symbol, while the wren is a chthonic one. Though sporadic, unpredictable patterns of flight make the wren difficult to catch, it is very familiar to country people.

The role of the wren as a challenger of power goes back very far. In one of the Sumerian proverbs, which are among the oldest literary works that have survived, an elephant boasts of being supreme among animals. The wren replies that, within its own domain, it is just as great.[25] There are scattered literary references to the royal status of the wren. Aristotle mentions an enmity between the eagle and wren, suggesting, possibly with a touch of irony, that the eagle may be resentful because the wren is popularly referred to as 'the king'. Popular names given to the wren contain the word for 'king' in many languages including Latin, Greek, Spanish, Danish, Welsh and Swedish. In French the bird is called *roitelet*, meaning 'little king'; in German it is *Zaunkönig*, meaning 'king of hedges'. The Irish synonym, *dreolin*, originally meant 'druid's bird', which suggests comparable status. This has also been proposed as the origin of our English word 'wren',[26] though that derivation is disputed.

The idea of a diminutive bird challenging the eagle for the avian crown must have been partially inspired by the common sight of a small bird chasing a larger one. If forewarned about their presence, birds that are less fast and powerful but better at manoeuvring can often drive hawks, owls and other raptors away. In his *Morals*, Plutarch made a passing reference to an Aesopian fable of a wren perched on the shoulders of an eagle, which suddenly flew up and overtook the larger bird.[27] The story that Plutarch alludes to is not found in any edition of Aesop that has come down to us, but it has been recorded by folklorists innumerable times, and in many variants, throughout much of Europe. The best-known version is probably from the fairy tales of the Brothers Grimm, which is simply entitled 'The Wren'.

It tells how, in remote times when they spoke a common language, all birds held a great assembly to elect their king and decided that the office should go to whoever could fly the highest. The contest began on a morning in May. The contenders ascended into the air together, but after a while all had grown tired and given up except the eagle. As he finally began to descend, the other birds all proclaimed the eagle king. But at that moment the wren, which had been hiding in the eagle's feathers, flew out and ascended so high that he could see God sitting upon the throne of heaven, and he shouted out, 'I'm the king!'[28]

The wren of the story is like many heroes of folktales such as Tom Thumb or the Clever Little Tailor, who achieve victory over a larger and more

Photo by the Brown Brothers showing an eagle in the distance carrying a rabbit, 1930s.

PLATE 23.

Stewart delt.

WREN.

Lizars sc.

powerful adversary through trickery. Through most of the year, people treated the wren in a way appropriate to its royal status. It was protected by custom, and numerous superstitions promise dreadful punishments for anybody who kills or harms a wren. In Wales popular sayings threatened anyone who destroyed a wren's nest with a life of ill health or even eternal damnation. If anyone killed a wren, their house would burn down. The murderer of a wren could be shunned by the community in Cornwall. In parts of France, a person who so much as touched a wren in its nest would, according to legend, be struck by lightning.[29]

But once a year, usually on St Stephen's day (the day after Christmas), this protection was revoked. Men hunted the wren, killed it with sticks and stones, and paraded it through town on a pole, often with its wings nailed to boards so that the bird looks a bit like Christ on the cross. The ceremony is very widespread, subject to considerable local variation, generally uses primitive weapons and is impossible to explain in terms of modern values, so it is probably very old. The consensus among folklorists is that it may well go back to Neolithic times,[30] though lack of documentation makes this impossible to prove. Edward Armstrong, in his detailed study of the wren hunt, concluded that it was a heritage of the megalith builders and had been carried to Britain during the Bronze Age.[31]

The story of the competition between the eagle and wren has been recorded numerous times from oral traditions and usually with only minor variants. By contrast, there is a huge variation in stories that have been used to explain the annual hunt of the wren. The Brothers Grimm added a second part to their tale, according to which the birds initially refused to recognize the wren as king. Instead, they decided that whichever bird can go furthest into the earth should be their ruler. The wren ran into a mousehole and shouted, once again, 'I am king!' The other birds decided to imprison the wren and set the owl to guard the hole, but the wren escaped when the owl fell asleep.[32]

Many reasons are given for killing the wren. In one tale the wren betrayed Christ, who was hiding in a garden, with its loud song. In another, the bird betrayed St Stephen, who was escaping from prison, by wakening his jailer. In a third, the Jacobite army in Ireland was planning a surprise attack on the troops of King William III when a wren landed on an English drum, sounding an alarm and waking up the troops.[33] All of these tales sound like rationalizations for a ceremony whose original purpose and origin have been lost.

Forms of the ceremony are still practised on the Isle of Man and elsewhere, in large part in order to preserve a connection with the past. It is also

Wren, from William Jardine, The Naturalist's Library *(1830s), engraving with watercolours.*

conducted in part for the benefit of tourists. Because people have objected to killing the wren on humane grounds, the bird is usually not killed, and feathers, a dummy or a caged bird may be paraded instead. The ceremonial hunt is no longer conducted by grown men but by boys. It is also often accompanied by elements of burlesque, rather like Groundhog Day in the United States. Thick ropes may be used to hoist the body of the wren and the mummers will feign great exertion. This sort of irony provides emotional protection against charges of childish superstition, but it may be that participants, together with some spectators, find the ceremony more deeply moving than they are often willing to admit.

The ceremonial killing of the wren is among the oldest, clearest and most authentic instances that we have of a sacrificial offering. Since the latter nineteenth century sacrifice has been the subject of a massive amount of scholarly literature by James George Frazer, René Girard, Marcel Detienne and countless others. A sacrifice is essentially a substitute who takes on the role, status and eventual punishment of another. An animal sacrifice is killed in the place of a human being. A good example is the biblical story in which Abraham was called to sacrifice his son Isaac to God. An angel then stopped the patriarch at the last moment and pointed to a ram, which he then killed in place of the boy.

In an analogous way, the wren is accorded the status of the king and then killed in place of the true monarch, represented by the eagle. According to Klingender, this is an instance of the sacred hunt of the Middle Ages. The hunted animal was generally a stag, and the outing culminated with various parts ceremoniously distributed to different participants, including dogs, according to their role. Finally, the head of the stag was given to the lord of the manor. On a symbolic level, this was his own head, indicating that he had died, been resurrected and might continue to govern. The body of the sacrificed wren was solemnly buried in a churchyard on the Isle of Man. In parts of France, it was presented to the lord of the local manor or the mayor of a town. In some areas, despite its diminutive size, the wren was divided among the participants and eaten, a bit like the transformed body of Christ at Mass.[34]

But for all the learning and brilliance expended on interpreting sacrificial rites, it is far from easy for us to grasp their significance today, when very few people centre their lives on the agricultural year. According to Girard, who is Catholic, this is because the coming of Christ has rendered sacrifice obsolete. By taking on the sins of the world and undergoing crucifixion, Jesus rendered all future sacrifice unnecessary, though the world has moved only slowly towards its abolition.[35] But, rather than mandating an end to sacrifice as

Girard claimed, Christ has provided a paradigm in terms of which, in Western culture at least, subsequent sacrifices have been understood.[36] Christ has been commonly called 'the king' and at times depicted with a crown, yet people have never thought of him as administering a kingdom in the manner of a real monarch or president. Pagan as the wren sacrifice may seem, it is now overlaid with Christian symbolism, and the resemblance to the story of Christ is unmistakable.

It is also not simply our alienation from the agricultural year, and more generally from the natural world that renders sacrificial rites difficult to comprehend. Another obstacle is the institution of kingship. What does it mean to call the wren 'king of all birds'? Surely far less for us than for people in an era when kings actually ruled. It is true that every country has a head of state who continues to represent it in a somewhat mystical way. And perhaps elections, with their modern pageantry, also enact a sort of royal execution and resurrection.

The Turkey for President

In 1782 the newly independent government of the United States designed the official seal for the nation. It prominently displayed the bald eagle, which then became the national bird, pictured on coins, walls of government offices and official documents. In a letter of 1784, Benjamin Franklin jokingly complained that the eagle was a bird of bad moral character and expressed a preference for the turkey, which was so valiant in defending its young.[37] At least since that time, the turkey has at times continued to rival the eagle as the national bird of the United States, in much the same way the wren challenged the eagle in Europe.

The natural abundance of the New World initially seemed without limits, and that blessing appeared to distinguish America from Europe. When colonists from overseas first arrived in what was to become the United States, turkeys seemed to be everywhere and almost absurdly easy to kill. The turkey is a symbol of natural abundance, of America as the 'New Eden', in which the bounty of nature is endless. In the words of Jack Santino:

> The turkey is a symbol of deep, almost maternal nourishment. In our American tall tales, animals are giant. Game abounds. Hunters fire a single shot into a tree and birds fall for 24 hours. In the early days of the Republic, America seemed to have everything, and more of it than anywhere else.[38]

The turkey is traditionally the main dish in the feast on Thanksgiving Day, the fourth Thursday in November. This is officially a celebration of the successful harvest of the pilgrims in their Massachusetts colony during 1621, but the day is also colloquially known as 'Turkey Day'. President Abraham Lincoln proclaimed Thanksgiving a national holiday on 3 October 1863, a few months after the Battle of Gettysburg, which was the turning point of the American Civil War. The purposes of the holiday, perhaps all not fully conscious, included unifying a divided country, re-establishing continuity with the past, reviving the myth of America as a place of primal innocence and preparing for westward expansion. Americans, in other words, might soon return to shooting at turkeys rather than at one another. The turkey was in effect a sacrificial substitute, intended to help end an era of violent conflict.

The holiday has always involved a strong element of nostalgia, as a celebration of rural life in a country that since its inception has been steadily becoming more urban. Overhunting had already made wild turkeys rare in seventeenth-century New England. By the 1670s they were almost gone from Massachusetts. When Thanksgiving became a national holiday, turkeys had become extinct in New England, and only a few scattered pockets remained in less-populated areas of the country.[39] Almost all Thanksgiving turkeys came from pens in the late nineteenth and early twentieth centuries, but people could still pretend they had been hunted in the wild.[40] Many postcards showed hunters searching for turkeys in idyllic landscapes.

This sacrificial symbolism of the Thanksgiving turkey is apparent from American postcards of the late nineteenth and early twentieth centuries. They show a ritualistic cycle of reverence, contempt and reconciliation, which is characteristic of blood rites. The victim is exalted in status and then killed in scorn, to eventually be resurrected in nostalgic memory.[41] The pattern has been documented in many cultures, but the best example may be the ceremony of the wren in Britain and parts of Continental Europe.

On one postcard from this period, the turkey is given a crown or other insignia of exalted, even royal, status. It is lovingly fed by young girls in festive dresses. It stands proudly with an outspread tail amid pumpkins and fruits of the season. A parade of turkeys march carrying American flags, and a turkey replaces the eagle on the official seal of the United States. Uncle Sam passes a royal sceptre to a turkey, which sits crowned upon a throne above the words 'Ruler of the Day'. One American postcard issued in 1910 shows a turkey with a

American postcards from about the first decade of the 20th century.

Thanksgiving Day

RULER·OF·THE·DAY

large crown hovering above its head, perched on a heraldic shield with the stars and stripes of the American flag.

After the adoration comes the execution. On one postcard, a little boy dressed as a pilgrim aims his blunderbuss at a wild turkey. On another, a cherubic toddler holds an axe, ready to behead the turkey. Still others show the live turkey beside an axe and soon to be decapitated, the fate of the English King Charles I as well as other deposed monarchs and pretenders to the throne. The ritualized regicide of Thanksgiving celebrations is partly a re-enactment of the American revolt against a British king.

On farms, children of eight or even younger would be charged with killing, gutting and plucking poultry in preparation for cooking.[42] Postcards suggest that the chore of killing the turkey was a channel for filial rebellion, since a mature male and female turkey are often shown together with a sort of parental dignity, at times watching over the human children. From the beginning, the United States has been in perpetual, and ritualistic, revolt against its Puritan heritage. Every generation protests against this legacy and thinks it is the first to do so. Like other parental figures, the Pilgrim mother and father on the postcards are at once subjects of reverence and objects of derision, and a male and female turkey serve as sacrificial substitutes for them.

Occasionally the sacrificial turkey is also identified with Native Americans, recent immigrants or ethnic minorities. In one postcard, a Pilgrim

American postcard from about the first decade of the 20th century. A common motif on such cards was children beheading or shooting turkeys.

family in an incongruously modern home of about 1900 is seated around the table for Thanksgiving dinner, and a Native American is gazing wistfully through the window. In his headband is a feather, associating him with the bird about to be consumed. In another, a young man whose Turkish fez marks him as a foreigner is being chased away from an American girl by a turkey.

Since the end of the Second World War farming has become far more mechanized, to a point where the turkey on the Thanksgiving table is barely recognizable as a bird. Self-basting turkeys, which require no killing and minimal preparation, are the standard in supermarkets, and for most people there is still little or no connection between the Thanksgiving turkey on a plate and the ones in the forest or field.

A twentieth-century twist on the celebration, made official by George H. W. Bush, is to have the president of the United States ceremoniously 'pardon' two turkeys on the White House lawn before going off to eat another one. What they are pardoned for is never specified, but traditions surrounding the turkey suggest it may be for attempting to usurp power. It has challenged the eagle as the national bird. It has even challenged the republic as a sort of provisional ruler. As power in a democracy becomes ever more diffused and concealed, the idea of regicide loses its traditional dread and enticement, but the symbolism of blood sacrifice also takes ever more indirect forms. In this case, a formerly intimate ceremony is transformed into a public event, perhaps a bit like a televised service in a megachurch.

In many ways, the original American Thanksgiving celebration is now anachronistic. It honours primordial nature in an era when sophisticated technology pervades virtually all human activity. Furthermore, we are now increasingly aware that the bounty of nature that it celebrates was never really limitless. The orgiastic consumption of food that once characterized the holiday increasingly appears crass. Like many ritualistic practices today, this one needs to be reconsidered. Nevertheless, Thanksgiving remains the least commercialized and most spiritual of major American holidays, with little of the ceaseless marketing that accompanies Halloween and Christmas. Its deeply obscured foundation in blood sacrifice is, in my opinion, still felt through all of the permutations and may still help to connect contemporary men and women with the natural world.

Today, it requires more violence against the natural world than ever before to maintain one person in Europe or North America, at least if he or she requires what we call a 'middle-class lifestyle'. At the same time, we have developed an unprecedented ability to conceal this violence from ourselves. It is inscribed in our needs for power, space, food, clothing, entertainment

and so on. This sort of violence has been ritually acted out and sacralized in such ceremonious practices as the stag hunt of European kings and nobility, the wren hunt of the peasantry, and the Thanksgiving dinner of mainstream Americans. Many people object that these customs provide a sanction for violence and even find them barbaric. But the advantage of ritualization is that it keeps people aware of the violence and its consequences. It provides a larger perspective, places killing under some control and sets limits to the destruction it may cause.

Above: American boy dressed as a pilgrim proudly holding a dead turkey with an axe near his side, 1922.
Opposite: American postcard from around the start of the 20th century. The father here is dressed as a pilgrim, though in incongruously bright colours. The home and the manners and dresses of the girls are clearly those of a prosperous, middle-class family around 300 years after the colony at Plymouth Rock. A Native American is looking longingly through the window, and his feather associates him with the bird that is being carved.

Pecking Order or Murmuration?

As Europe embraced modernity in the nineteenth century and the early twentieth, there was a growing nostalgia for the Middle Ages, which was idealized by writers and painters from the Pre-Raphaelites through to the twentieth-century German poet Stefan George. In an increasingly technocratic society, people thought of the Middle Ages as an era of brilliant costume, graceful ritual, simple piety and grand adventures. In addition, people looked on medieval times as an era where all sectors of society from kings and nobles to peasants were united in an organic whole by bonds of loyalty. It was easy to see a reflection of these values in birds of the meadow on a summer day. Plumage gave birds the splendour of a medieval court, and their behaviour often appeared ceremonious. Such romanticizing involved ignoring, or somehow idealizing, the stark reality of predation and many other difficulties that birds encounter, but it had been inscribed in literary tradition by many poets from Walther von der Vogelweide to Geoffrey Chaucer.

In the 1920s the Norwegian researcher Thorleif Schjelderup-Ebbe observed domesticated chickens and found that certain birds could peck others with impunity. The social organization of these birds, then, seemed to constitute a 'pecking order', in which the relative status of each bird was determined by how many the creature could peck or be pecked by without retaliation. Here, for the first time, seemed to be an analogue to human hierarchies that was tangible enough to be measured and quantified.[43] Some contemporaries objected that the observations were of domesticated animals living under artificial conditions, and should not be extended to those in the wild. But the concept of an animal hierarchy quickly entered into behavioural literature and was applied in studying the social life of a vast range of creatures.

The appealing simplicity of a hierarchical order probably made several subsequent authors overlook the finer points of Schjelderup-Ebbe's work. Contrary to what is often supposed in both popular and professional literature, his model of bird society was far from being a simple pyramid. While he theorized that a dominance relationship always exists between any two birds, he also pointed out that these relations were not necessarily transitive. Bird a, for example, might dominate bird b, while bird b would dominate bird c. Bird c, however, could dominate bird a, so the relation of dominance constitutes more of a circle than a triangle. This is possible, in part, because dominance is dependent not only on physical abilities but on transitory factors, such as the relative tiredness of two birds at a time of confrontation. In a flock of ten or more birds, he held pyramidal pecking to be 'a rarity'. There would seldom be any bird that was not pecked at all. Nevertheless, it was possible to construct a system of relative ranking in a flock by tabulating the number of others each bird was able to subordinate.[44]

But the suggestive power of the idea of a natural hierarchy usually obscured such fine points. The geometric structure of it appealed to scientists, and medieval associations appealed to romantics. In the United States and most of Europe, the notion was enthusiastically applied to the study of apes. In the context of social Darwinist theory, the idea became overlaid with all sorts of eugenic and racialist associations.[45]

As Donna Haraway has written, 'dominance is to primatologists what kinship has been to anthropologists – at once the most mystical, most technical, and discipline-grounding of a field's conceptual tools.'[46] That was, at least until recently, true of zoology in general, where grand concepts of dominance do not seem to synchronize well with the excruciatingly specific empirical tests. I am inclined to suspect that the whole idea of dominance may ultimately be an illusion, which may tell us more about the people who use it than about the birds it allegedly describes.

But there was no other test for dominance that approached being as clear as the 'pecking order' that Schjelderup-Ebbe had observed in chickens. In *Man Meets Dog* by Konrad Lorenz, the apparently cheerful informality almost obscures an obsessive emphasis on hierarchy. Misreading, or at least simplifying, the theory of Schjelderup-Ebbe, for example, he states that there is an exact hierarchical order prevailing among birds, and even draws a pyramid to illustrate it. His favourite birds were jackdaws, and he approvingly describes their society as so hierarchical that 'Very high caste Jackdaws are most condescending to those of lowest degree and consider them merely as the dust beneath their feet.'[47]

Though the book was written at the end of the Second World War, it reflected the ideas developed by Lorenz when he had been the major theorist of Nazi Germany on issues relating to animals.[48] An entire society organized in a pyramidal structure with a single leader at the top became an ideal in Nazi Germany. Early in the regime that society attempted to combine all the bureaucracies of different professions, clubs and so on into a monolithic hierarchical structure through a policy of *Gleichschaltung* (synchronization).

One need not be a professional sociologist to see that no society, including that of Nazi Germany, has ever been organized in this manner. Far from having a simple chain of command, the Nazis ended up with a muddled system of authority in which figures such as Himmler, Goebbels, Goering and many others were constantly competing with one another, and nobody knew who

Murmuration of starlings in Scotland.

was really Hitler's second-in-command. Virtually all societies have many overlapping hierarchies, which may reflect professional distinction, age, birth and many other factors. Authority, in consequence, is largely situational.

The entire idea of a 'pecking order' does not provide more than a vague metaphor, even applied to organizations such as corporations and the military, since people at every level are given not only different privileges but subject to different restrictions as well. The ability to peck another bird with impunity does not tell us anything about leadership, which is the capacity to stimulate others by example. Contemporary Western culture, for all its egalitarian ideals, is, completely across the political spectrum, obsessed with almost endlessly nuanced gradations of rank and status. As part of that society, I am unable to lay this preoccupation aside at will, but I do not wish to project it onto birds.

Finally, the pecking order of the barnyard is only one of many social organizations that may be suggested by birds. Another, which is diametrically opposed, is that of starlings in Britain and Scandinavia. Hundreds of thousands of starlings will fly together in a huge cloud known as a 'murmuration', which constantly changes, assuming myriad graceful patterns. It forms because every change in direction or velocity by one starling is immediately passed on to those alongside it. Nobody knows the reason for this behaviour, though it may be a way of confusing predators.

I wondered for years why starlings in the United States never seemed to form murmurations until one day, when watching a small flock, I realized that they actually did. Their flights were not in straight lines or in smooth, predictable curves, but they turned, plunged and rose in unanticipated ways, constantly coordinating their motions with one another. The sight was not nearly as spectacular as a murmuration of many thousands of starlings in Britain or Scandinavia, simply because only a dozen or so individuals were present, but their dance was just as graceful. All of the birds were at once leaders and followers, so, especially for people drawn to egalitarian ideals, the murmuration can represent a sort of utopia.

8 FALCONRY

Turning and turning in the widening gyre
The falcon cannot hear the falconer;
Things fall apart; the centre cannot hold ...
W. B. Yeats, 'The Second Coming'

n 1190, during the Third Crusade, a prized gyrfalcon belonging to King Philip II Augustus of France flew up the walls surrounding the besieged Muslim city of Acre and was claimed by Sultan Saladin. At first Philip requested the return of his falcon as a courtesy but was rebuffed. Then he sent a party of envoys, splendidly attired and announced by trumpets, to offer 1,000 gold crowns in exchange for the falcon. Once again, the sultan refused.[1]

Perhaps there may have been some covert, even unconscious, diplomatic manoeuvring going on between the two rulers. Prized falcons were frequent gifts between sovereigns. Philip may have been signalling, in a very colourful way, that he might have been willing to lift the siege if the falcon was returned. A successful exchange for the lost falcon might have established a precedent that could at least have led to further negotiations. Saladin and his army, on the other hand, could have taken the desertion of the falcon as a sign from heaven that the Crusade would fail. To return the falcon could have damaged their morale. But the motivations of both king and sultan may have been simpler: perhaps both simply felt that the falcon was too precious to lose at almost any price.

If the departure of the falcon was an omen, this is one instance where bird divination may have proved mistaken, for the crusaders did eventually take Acre. Or maybe it was right, since the crusaders would in time be driven away. But how did falcons come to be so valued in both Christian Europe and the Islamic Near East?

Origins

Routes of diffusion indicate that falconry probably originated somewhere on the Eurasian steppes during the second millennium BCE. It then travelled east, west and south. The earliest depictions of falconry come from Hittite reliefs and seals in Anatolia from the late second and first millennia BCE, in one of which a deity carries a falcon perched on his arm with a dead hare in its beak.[2]

King Konrad the Younger engaged in falconry, from Manessischen Liederhandschrift *(c. 1304).*

Representations of falconry later appeared in China and then spread to Japan, India and eventually Western Europe.

Falconry, as we know it today, is too elaborate to have appeared all at once, and it surely went through many stages before it arrived at its present form. It was almost completely unknown in Greek civilization, but Aristotle refers in his *History of Animals* to a related practice in Thrace. Men placed themselves at strategic points in marshes and then beat the undergrowth so that birds flew upwards. Then the hunters summoned trained raptors, which swooped down and drove the small birds back into the bushes. The men observed where the small birds landed and then killed the prey by striking the area with clubs. Finally, they threw a few of the dead birds to the raptors. There is a similar account in a book entitled *Marvels*, often falsely attributed to Aristotle, which reports that the hawks killed the prey and drop it at the hunters' feet.[3]

The practice of using raptors to drive or flush out game, as described by Aristotle, may be the survival of an early stage in the development of falconry, perhaps a plebeian version of the aristocratic sport. Depictions of falconry from the Hittites in Anatolia and from the Eastern Han dynasty (25–220 CE) in China show men holding beaters, which could have been used to strike bushes and as clubs.[4] People have also used raptors to drive other birds into nets. Falconry, as it developed in medieval times, may have been less efficient but was more elegant. People would catch fewer birds, since they could only hunt them one at a time, but they would have the thrill of identifying with the raptor as it rose and then descended. The practice of falconry was carried to Europe and the Near East by nomadic peoples such as the Scythians, Huns and Magyars, and it had become widespread there by about the start of the second millennium CE.

Many civilizations including Egypt, Greece and Rome had been slow in adopting falconry. In the latter two civilizations, this was probably due to a relatively unsuitable climate and terrain. Falconry is most adapted to flat, open areas without dense vegetation, where it is easier to keep track of a raptor's flight and game is relatively scarce. The terrain of Greece and Italy was too uneven. Given the high regard in which falcons were held in ancient Egypt, one might have expected falconry to be popular there, but it did not even have the appearance of utility. Birds were common around the marshes and could easily be caught in great numbers using throwing sticks, nets and traps.

Many raptors have been used in falconry, also known as 'hawking'. Among the Kazakh people of Mongolia, use of golden eagles is common. Barn owls have often been used in England and later the United States. But the general preference has been for falcons (especially peregrines and gyrfalcons)

Unknown Mongolian hunter on horse with a golden eagle.

and hawks (especially goshawks, merlins and sparrowhawks). Falcons are pursuit predators, which rely on speed, while hawks are ambush predators, which rely on surprise and stealth. Falcons have longer wings and more sharply curved beaks, and they are faster flyers. Hawks are slightly larger, have broader wings and longer claws, and are better at manoeuvring in forests. Falcons generally stun prey with their talons and then kill and tear it with their beaks, and they specialize in attacking other birds. Hawks kill prey mostly with their talons, and they are preferred for hunting small mammals such as rabbits.

For a sport that is popular in such a variety of kingdoms and cultures, the practices of falconry are remarkably standardized. The falconer wears a heavy leather glove or gauntlet on which the falcon can perch. Short, thin leather straps known as jesses are attached to each leg of a raptor, usually with a ring or 'swivel' at the end. When the raptor is on a perch, the jesses are fastened to a long leash. When the raptor is on the falconer's glove, it is attached to a short lead held by the falconer. A bell is also attached to the bird, so that, should it fly away, it might be possible to locate it. In early medieval times the eyes of falcons were stitched closed with a linen thread to keep it calm during transportation. By the high Middle Ages the stitching was replaced by a leather hood, which was placed over the bird's eyes during periods of inactivity.

A lure is an object swung on a long rope to train the raptor to pounce. It replaced captive birds such as pigeons, which were previously used in training, since it allowed the falconer far more control. In medieval times the lure was constructed by cutting the wings off a dead bird, drying them and then stitching them together with leather thongs. Food was attached to it, so that the falcon would receive an immediate reward on catching the lure. Today it is often simply a leather cushion, and the raptor may receive meat directly from the trainer upon completing a task.

Falconry and Erotic Love

Dogs reputedly regard their owners with unconditional love. Falcons are almost the opposite. They show hints of affection such as jumping to a perch when the owner enters a room, and falconers are grateful for even the most ambiguous signs of favour, but these expressions are a gift. The lack of demonstrative behaviour was part of the appeal of falcons in medieval times, particularly because they were almost invariably kept in an aristocratic setting, where emotional control was valued highly. There is something that seems noble in the intense but dispassionate gaze of a falcon.

Most of the care falconers bestow on their birds is not returned, and for that very reason falconry is an opportunity to practise 'selfless' devotion. As one present-day falconer in New York City puts it, 'the hardest part of being a falconer is unreciprocated love.'[5] This unconditional dedication was expected not only from a believer to God but from a vassal to his king and a knight to his lady. Believers, vassals, knights and dogs rarely if ever really attain the ideal of selflessness, but it is little wonder that falconry was central to the society of the high Middle Ages.

Falconry and jousting were the quintessential sports of chivalry. Both depend on accuracy and speed. As the falcon would bring credit to his handler, so a jousting knight would bring honour to his lady. Falconry may have taught additional lessons such as delaying gratification, since a bird would rarely kill its prey on the first attempt. The activity may have helped to ease the intense competition at court, since it is

Aplomado falcon, native to the American Southwest, at the Renaissance Fair in Tuxedo, New York, 2017. Raptors do not lose their regal bearing when employed in falconry, and there is no question of human domination.

A falconer with a great-horned owl at a medieval fair at the Cloisters, Fort Tryon Park, New York City, c. 2010. The man gazes at the bird with affection and uncertainty, but the owl stares out in search of prey.

a sport in which there is no loser apart from the prey. But the foundation of falconry was, and still is, the thrill of identification, as the falcon suddenly soars downwards towards its quarry. If the raptor strikes the victim, the falconer experiences a momentary union with the natural world in all its magnificence and brutality. There is a sense of transgression, as often with sexual activity, yet that is absorbed into the perceived purity of nature. As Helen Macdonald has written, 'By skilfully training a hunting animal, by closely identifying with it, you might be allowed to experience all your vital, sincere desires, even your most bloodthirsty ones, in total innocence.'[6]

Chivalry blended violence and eroticism in extravagant fantasies. Ever since Homer's *Iliad*, and doubtless long before, war and blood sports have been heavily eroticized. 'Venery', the late medieval word for hunting, comes from 'Venus', the name of the Roman goddess of love. The association between hunting and eroticism may well be universal in human cultures, but the European Middle Ages accomplished that in ways that were especially colourful. Tournaments were re-enactments of an idealized court such as that of King Arthur and his knights. In addition to heraldic insignia on their

helmets, a knight would carry a piece of clothing of his lady such as a sash, veil or detachable sleeve on his lance. During tournaments ladies would at times throw down their accessories, to a point where they had only a simple, sleeveless tunic left.[7]

Unlike jousting, falconry was practised regularly by ladies as well as knights, who would ride out together in parties, announced by trumpets and accompanied by their entourages, to engage in sport for the entire day. Inevitably falconry became a focus of erotic symbolism far more varied and subtle than that of jousting tournaments. In many medieval pictures of devoted couples, one person, either the man or woman, holds up a falcon.

This may be a bit like the way couples or families today may be photographed with a dog, which represents their bond. Nevertheless, the comparison highlights huge differences. For one thing, dogs appear to share or reflect human emotions, while falcons appear almost impervious to them. Looking back from the perspective of many centuries, the age of chivalry may inspire nostalgia, but it nevertheless seems profoundly foreign. The combination of emotional delicacy, refined manners, exalted ideals, brutal rivalries, cruelty, barbaric splendour and religious piety has an enduring fascination but is hard for people to empathize with today.

Above: Juvenile northern goshawk in flight. To identify with such a bird, even momentarily, is a thrill.
Opposite: Persian painting of a woman, possibly a princess, holding a precious gyrfalcon, probably 19th century.

The emotional intimacy of lovers with their falcons and hawks is shown in the Scottish ballad 'The Gay Goshawk', first recorded by Walter Scott, in which the hawk not only speaks and understands the language of people but sings sweetly, perhaps a bit like a thrush. It begins as a knight named William confides his sorrow to the hawk:

> O waly, waly, my gay Goshawk
> Gin your feathering be sheen!
> And waly, waly, my master dear,
> Gin ye look pale and lean!

The knight tells the falcon that he is in love with a lady but her parents will not allow them to meet. He tells the falcon where to find and how to recognize her, and then instructs it to catch her attention by singing from a birch tree in her garden. The falcon does accordingly, delivers a love letter to the lady and asks her to meet his master at a church. She takes a sleeping draught and is taken to the church to be buried. William is waiting there for her, and she revives in his presence.[8]

In scenes of falconry, erotic interest is not always so idealized. One of the *Devonshire Hunting Tapestries*, probably produced in Arras, northern France, in the early fifteenth century and now in the Victoria and Albert Museum, shows very detailed scenes of falconry alongside various amorous activities. One lady strokes the tiny lapdog in her arms, oblivious to her male companion. A young girl, doubtless destined for a political marriage, is carefully watched by her chaperone, who appears improperly attracted to her. A man, ostentatiously dressed in velvet and gold, fixes his eyes on a woman who looks past him indifferently. One nobleman and his lady, both on horseback, ignore the hunt and gaze at one another.[9]

Why would falconry represent romantic love? We should remember that the Middle Ages was a time when human life expectancy was about thirty years or less, and poultry came from the barnyard rather than the supermarket. People were used to predation and death, which carried less terror than they do today. Falconry, like other forms of hunting, was often criticized during the Middle Ages but for frivolity rather than cruelty. The falcon falls suddenly from the sky, immobilizing and then soon killing its prey. The raptor is an instrument of death, but then, so is the bow and arrow wielded by Cupid. The

Sir Walter von Teufen with his wife, from Manessischen Liederhandschrift *(c. 1304). For medieval couples, falconry was a way to affirm their bond.*

Falconry, as depicted in a Devonshire tapestry, early 15th century. The man on the left is attired in eye-catching splendour, but he is unable to catch the attention of the lady, who is only interested in a falcon.

strike of the raptor suggested the suddenness and intensity with which one might fall in love.

The Sacred Hunt

In some ways a day spent in falconry by those connected with a medieval manor house was a bit like a corporate picnic today. Both the manor house and the corporation are highly hierarchic organizations, and the distinctions of rank would be relaxed a bit yet ultimately reaffirmed. Like the picnic, the manor house might feature sports, games and contact with the natural world. But everyone knows that the corporate hierarchy is pragmatic, transitory and, if one stops to consider the matter, ultimately trivial. For people of the Middle Ages, falconry was a reaffirmation of the cosmic order.

Much of the success of Christianity lay in the way it managed to channel the archaic symbolism of the sacred hunt, which had been mostly banned from

Judaism yet retained its power over the imagination. In the Eucharist, eating the body of Christ was a bit like dividing up the meat after a successful hunt. Medieval and Renaissance tapestries showed people ritualistically going about the hunt of the stag or unicorn, both of which could represent Christ, with expressions of great solemnity.[10]

Hunting by means of raptors could be at least as complex and might involve even more specialized skills. Some methods of hunting involved two or even three falcons, and every step needed to be carefully coordinated. The Holy Roman Emperor Frederick II gave very detailed directions for hunting a crane with falcons. The raptor would be laboriously trained to separate one crane from the flock and then bring it down, but the crane might still be alive and struggling. Horsemen and dogs would come to the falcon's aide and kill the crane, all of which had to be done with enormous care to avoid injury. When the crane had been killed, the falconer would place his falcon on its breast. He would then cut open the crane and present its heart, still beating, to the falcon as a meal.[11] Another method used in Early Modern Italy was to fasten the tail of a fox to a Eurasian eagle owl, which flies low to the ground. One falconer would release the owl, which would soon swoop down. A kite would attack the tail, and then a second sportsman would release a falcon to pounce upon the kite.[12]

In his epic *The Conference of Birds*, the twelfth-century Sufi poet Farid ud-Din Attar compared the jesses of a falcon to the bond of the individual to God, the lure to love and the moment of descent to a glimpse of eternity. He also compared placing a mask over a hawk's eyes to an inward turn, away from earthly concerns and towards the spiritual. The lifting of the mask was a mystical epiphany. These comparisons were not intended as part of any comprehensive allegory: a bit later in the poem the hoopoe, who leads the birds, reproaches the hawk for being overly attached to courtly ways.[13] But the very inconsistency is intended to direct the reader towards a mystical reality beyond the realm of appearances.

In the West, the church regarded falconry with a similar ambivalence. Some members of the clergy, including popes such as Leo II, were avid falconers, though others railed against the sport. A Latin bestiary of the early to mid-twelfth century states, 'The hawk (here not distinguished from the falcon) is the image of the holy man, who seizes the Kingdom of God.' It then compares the way birds moult and grow new feathers to rebirth in Christ. Then comes an extended comparison of mews, where falcons and hawks are kept for the hunt, to a monastery: 'The hawk's perch signifies the rectitude of life under monastic rule, because it is suspended high above earthly things and separates monks from earthly desires.'[14]

Christ is represented by both the lion and lamb. In a similar way, the Holy Spirit was represented by the dove and, rarely, the falcon, two creatures joined in the dance of predator and prey. In sculptures in the church of Notre-Dame de Croaz-Batz in Roscoff, Brittany, for example, the Holy Spirit is represented by a dove when the Archangel Gabriel appears to Mary in the Annunciation but as a falcon at Pentecost,[15] no doubt because that raptor descends from the sky with a grace and speed that can appear almost otherworldly. One anonymous Spanish lyric of the Middle Ages equates a peregrine not only with the dove of the Annunciation but even with Christ himself, saying that he descended from the heavens to enter Mary's womb and be reborn. In the mid-sixteenth century the Spanish mystic St John of the Cross used a peregrine grasping its prey in the sky as a metaphor for the mystic union of the soul with God.[16]

People of the Middle Ages believed that domestication rather than wildness was the original state of animals in relation to human beings. Adam and Eve had lived in harmony with, and even talked to, animals prior to being driven out of Eden. By bringing animals into the human domain, one was recreating at least part of that primeval harmony. A highly secularized version of that idea is offered by Vicki Hearne in her defence of training animals, especially dogs and horses, to execute intricate routines. Many regarded, and still regard, these accomplishments as unnatural and/or exercises in human domination. Her answer was that we human beings suffer from our isolation from other creatures, but by allowing themselves to be trained, the animals were answering our call, and we have an obligation to respond accordingly.[17]

In a similar way, the intricate coordination of man and bird, together with dogs and horses, in falconry involves, among other things, very nuanced communication, which offers a little relief to our collective loneliness. Helen Macdonald takes a very similar position in writing of her hawk, Mabel:

Her eyes can follow the wingbeats of a bee as easily as ours follow the wingbeats of a bird. What is she seeing? I wonder, and my brain does backflips trying to imagine it, because I can't ... This hawk can see colours that I cannot, right into the ultraviolet spectrum. She can see polarized light, too, watch thermals of air rise, roil, and spill into clouds, and trace, too, the magnetic lines of force that spread across the earth.[18]

Prince holding a falcon, Persian, c. 1820. The features of falconers depicted in both the Islamic and Christian worlds are often surprisingly delicate, even spiritual.

Given such radical difference in perception, there cannot be any realistic question of domination, which is ultimately an anthropomorphic illusion. A feeling of domination comes when a person projects his own will onto another creature, and then imagines triumphing over it. In fact, one can no more dominate a hawk than wrestle the wind into submission. But it is amazing that precise coordination between human being and bird is possible despite radically divergent ways of knowing the world.

Rank and Status

Egyptians had once considered the pharaoh the representative of the falcon god Horus.[19] By the fourteenth century CE that land had become Christian and then Muslim, and the religion of ancient Egypt had been long forgotten, yet perhaps the tradition of identifying the ruler with a falcon remained. According to the medieval scholar Al-Nuwayri, only the Mamluk sultan of Egypt, whose domain included the Levant, could legally purchase the gyrfalcon, which had to be imported from northern Europe, and others could not even fly one without with his special permission.[20]

Rulers of the thirteenth century, from Genghis Khan to Frederick II of Sicily, included dozens of falconers and hundreds of raptors in their entourages, which travelled along with them. Frederick based his treatise *The Art of Falconry* largely on Arabic texts, as well as on considerable observation and experience. At the beginning of the first volume, he states that falconry is nobler than other forms of hunting, since it requires more skill, takes more time to master and does not require artificial implements such as snares and traps.[21]

Falconry was a central aspect of courtly life and part of the education of a noble. Knights and ladies would carry falcons on their wrists as a symbol of status and sophistication, even when they had no intention of using them to hunt.[22] But falconry did not need laws or rules to maintain its aristocratic exclusivity. The notorious expense was quite enough. In thirteenth-century England a falcon could easily cost half the yearly income of a knight,[23] and the cost of buying and caring for the most prized falcons might be almost endless. In 1530 Emperor Charles V granted the island of Malta to the Order of St John of Jerusalem, the Knights Hospitaller. As payment, he required

Advertisement showing a woman with a falcon cap, 1928. At the time, it was not terribly unusual for women to wear taxidermized birds on their hats, but they were usually songbirds rather than raptors. The head on the cap may or may not be from an actual bird, but it seems intended to convey a combination of assertiveness and glamour.

only a falcon every year, which was delivered to him on the feast of All Saints Day.[24]

Falconry remained popular for many centuries, but gradually declined, together with the aristocratic order. It was a sport that very few people had the leisure and wealth to pursue actively. Furthermore, it entailed a kind of conspicuous consumption that was widely resented. Firearms made it possible for farmers and others to kill falcons and hawks because of the threat they might pose to livestock, their association with aristocracy or any other reason.

To some extent, hunting game birds with dogs may have replaced falconry. It also requires extensive training of an animal, which must first locate a hunted bird. After the bird has been shot, the dog must fetch the body and present it to the owner. Like falconry or hawking, hunting ducks or pheasants with dogs requires a great deal of skill. It also provides people with a link to the natural world and, to an extent, even the human past, but its ambiance is middle or working class. Hunters with guns do not like competition from raptors, whether or not the birds are in the service of a noble, and so they often shoot hawks or falcons on sight. It may be, however, that the status of being endangered has given peregrines, along with other raptors, a new glamour, making them nostalgic symbols of a vanishing heritage. Falconry itself is experiencing a revival, and it is probably more popular than at any time since the Industrial Revolution.

A Singular Relationship

Many of our relationships with animals have a prototype, even a model, in relationships among human beings. Bees, for example, are a bit like a foreign land, ruled by a monarch, and beekeepers are ambassadors. The dog is a member of the family, at times a sort of surrogate husband, wife, sister or brother. Falconry follows a distinctly different pattern: the apprenticeship. Through much of the Middle Ages, trades, like social positions, were simply passed down in the family. Gradually, however, technologies became more complicated, fashions more ephemeral and social organization less static. Not only princes but blacksmiths, bakers, coopers, tailors, stationers and others had to adapt. Apprenticeship was a way of making sure that practitioners learned not only a traditional craft but newly developed techniques as well.

An apprentice would spend a period of perhaps three to seven years with a master craftsman and receive lodging and food in return for labour. During this time he or she would learn the trade and then, with a bit of luck, eventually open a shop. In Europe falconry began to become popular around the eleventh century, the same time as apprenticeships, and both would gradually fade into relative obscurity during the modern period.

One thing that distinguishes our relationship with raptors is that it involves very little or no breeding, intentional or otherwise. Falcons and other birds are generally taken from their nests as chicks or caught as juveniles. They are trained and used in falconry for about three to seven years (the approximate time of most apprenticeships) and then finally released back into the wild. Since they are generally solitary, except during mating, they adapt very well to being released. Their powers may be slightly diminished, rendering them less optimal for sport, but they are still very capable of providing for themselves. They may even have picked up some techniques of hunting that they would not have learned in the wild, and they are certainly able to mate. The sport is based on a continuous exchange between the world of nature and that of humankind, in which neither is affected in the end.

Helen Macdonald has written, 'Falcons are trained entirely through positive reinforcement. They must never be punished; as solitary creatures, they fail to understand hierarchical dominance relations familiar to social creatures such as dogs and horses.'[25] An even more direct reason why they must not be mistreated is that a working falcon is capable of leaving at any time. Falcons traditionally carry a bell to help the keeper locate them if necessary, and today many also have tiny radio transmitters fastened to their feathers, but these will not be of much help unless the falcon wishes to return.

Falcons and hawks do receive a great deal from their arrangement with human beings, including the assurance of a steady food supply, shelter from storms, veterinary care and even protection from other predators. From our point of view that may seem to be at the cost of freedom, yet that judgement may be overly anthropomorphic. We ourselves often feel constricted by the bonds of human society, with its nearly endless laws, customs and points of etiquette. In response, we construct the idea of nature that is, or at least ought to be, a place of absolute freedom. We expect animals to treasure that freedom above all else, and then may feel disappointed when they don't. But we are really just endeavouring to impose our values upon them.

I once had a long conversation about this with a falconer at the Red Hawk Native American Pow Wow, an annual event held in Harriman State Park in New York State. She told me that having a falcon leave permanently during a falconry outing is not unusual, and most falconers accept it as an occupational hazard. An hour or so later, however, she did lose a falcon and did not accept it with the equanimity that I expected. She went to the microphone, called to the falcon and pleaded with it to return.

Given the enormous financial and emotional investments that knights and ladies made in falcons during the late Middle Ages and Renaissance, to have one disappear into the sky forever was a great loss, but some at least accepted it with stoicism and good humour. Here is a poem from about the mid-twelfth century by Der von Kürenberg, a poet about whom we know almost nothing, in my own translation from the Middle High German original:

> I nurtured my falcon for a year and more;
> I tamed him; he followed my commands.
> But, when I adorned his feathers with gold,
> He ascended high and flew away.
>
> Since then, I have seen the falcon.
> Silken jesses trailed from his feet.
> His feathers gleamed golden red.
> May God bring lovers together.[26]

The poem has been interpreted in many ways. Although most falcons used in sport were female, the one here is referred to using a male pronoun. The speaker, and even the author, might be a woman, and the falcon could represent either her son, who has married, or her husband, away on a Crusade. It may also be that the two strophes are meant to represent the voices of different speakers, conceivably a woman and her maid. The way that I am inclined to understand the poem, however, is simpler and more literal. The lady (or gentleman) believes that the lost falcon is guided by God and hopes that it will find a mate.

Medieval hunters would identify with a stag, even as they killed it, and the entire chase was pervaded by religious mysticism. By contrast, the focus in falconry was on the predatory birds. After being killed, the prey would usually be unceremoniously stuffed in a bag. The hunt for the stag humanized the victim – and, by extension, the entire natural world – by enacting a mystical drama of sin and redemption. In falconry, by contrast, people identified primarily with the raptor, which, for all its grace and power, remained profoundly alien. They temporarily cast off much of their humanity to more fully participate in the rhythms of nature. Falconry was in summary a sort of holiday from being human, akin to what Aldo Leopold has called 'thinking like a mountain'.[27] This is also doubtless why falconry is being revived today, as people confront the realization of the enormous devastation that people have wreaked on the natural world and one another.

9 PLATO'S 'MAN'

Follow the chicken and find the world.
Donna Haraway, *When Species Meet*

According to Diogenes Laertius, Plato, in a lecture at his Academy, defined 'man' as a 'two-footed featherless animal'. The following day, Diogenes of Sinope arrived, held up a plucked cockerel and said, 'This is Plato's man.' Apparently some listeners took this gesture as a scientific criticism of the definition, for they added the qualification 'with broad, flat nails' to render it complete.[1] But the addendum would hardly have settled the matter, since one would simply have needed to file down the claws of the cockerel to make it once again into a 'man'. One must wonder if perhaps Diogenes Laertius, or whoever told him the story, had suffered a lapse of memory. The lecturer sounds a lot more like the empiricist Aristotle than the metaphysician Plato. At any rate, Diogenes of Sinope seems to be exposing the seemingly scientific definition of the lecturer as ultimately symbolic in the end.

To pluck the feathers of a cockerel was like belittling human pride. Before the advent of industrial farming, cockerels were thought of as lords of the barnyard, as is expressed in the saying 'cock of the walk'. They exuded pride in their stride and their calls. In more recent times, cockerels have become faded and even white, but at the time of Plato they still had the brilliant plumage of the jungle fowls from which they descended. Even cockerels, however, were not invulnerable, and the same was true of the grandest of human beings. The Tabwa, a Bantu people of Central Africa, express this in a proverb: 'A chief is like a cockerel; his people are his beautiful plumes; plucked, he is not worth much!'[2] In his interpretation of Plato, Diogenes may also have been suggesting that people are, in essence, birds that have lost the power of flight. In place of both human hubris and scientific detachment, he presented a tragic vision. Man was an unnatural, pitiable creature, a domestic bird soon destined for the cooking pot. Poor cockerel. Poor humankind.

The nature of animal symbolism is widely misunderstood. It is not the projection of human meanings on to animals. Rather, it is a record of centuries of human interaction with animals, to which both parties have contributed. It is also not a simple list of equivalencies. It is contextual, and a single animal can have a very wide range of significations. By far the best example among birds is the chicken; that is, the cockerel (or rooster) and hen. In a way Diogenes of Sinope was, or eventually became, more right than he ever could have realized. The cockerel was indeed humankind, since it has represented almost every

Agnes Miller Parker, Catte and Chyken, *1920s, woodcut. The cat and cockerel, two animals known for their self-confident bearing, eye one another wearily in this Scottish image.*

aspect of human activity. To call a person 'chicken' is to accuse him or her of cowardice, yet cockerels have from time immemorial been celebrated for their fighting spirit. Chickens have been used as symbols of virility, maternal care, esoteric wisdom, royalty, time, clairvoyance, pedigree, modernity, human callousness and a great deal more besides.

A Unique Bond

We relate to dogs, cats, lizards, silkworms, sheep and chickens in very different ways, with respect to use, obligations, symbolism and so on. These are mostly, or at least were originally, symbiotic relationships that have evolved for centuries or even millennia. The word 'domestication' can be misleading, since it suggests that these bonds were initiated solely on the side of human beings. The term 'companion species', coined by Donna Haraway,[3] is now often used for other creatures, including plants, that have culturally and biologically co-evolved with people for long periods of time.

In the study of human-animal bonds, our relationship with the dog usually gets the most attention, since it is arguably both the oldest and the most intimate that we have. Estimates of the age of the relationship vary greatly from more than 100,000 to about 15,000 years. Our relationship with avians is in some ways even harder to trace very far back in time. Birds and human beings have co-evolved for longer than dog and man, at least since dinosaurs and mammals branched off from a single evolutionary line about 200 million years ago. Ever since that time, the two groups have been constantly adapting to one another. Over a span of aeons they have at times switched roles of predator and prey. They have related to one another in many capacities, as rivals and as partners. Birds have been contributing to our culture long before there was a human species. When they were dinosaurs, we were relatively small marsupial-like balls of fur.

Marcus Gheeraerts, Turkey and Rooster, *1567, woodcut, Netherlands. The rooster has long had the barnyard as his domain, but here he faces off against a newly imported turkey.*

Our domestic cockerel and hen are descended from the red jungle fowl, to some extent mixed with the grey jungle fowl and possibly other closely related birds.[4] The red jungle fowl is not only brilliantly coloured but able to run quickly, fly well and perch in high trees, abilities that were lost as people selected birds for size, both as fighters and as a source of meat. It is difficult to say exactly when and where the domestication took place, since it seems to have been a very gradual process in which one cannot mark off any decisive turning point. People practising agriculture left seeds that attracted the birds, which were then exploited by human beings. It was a simple and perhaps inevitable process that could have happened in several places or been spread out over a wide area.

The region where domestication took place was Southeast Asia, perhaps India, Thailand or Vietnam. This began about 10,000 years ago, and the chicken gradually spread around the world. By 6000 BCE the cockerel and hen had reached China.[5] Possible written references indicate that it had reached Mesopotamia by about 2500 BCE, though it does not start to appear in art there until the latter half of the second millennium BCE.[6] By the seventeenth century BCE it had reached the kingdom of Sudan. In Egypt there are a few possible references to chickens from the Middle Kingdom (2160–1788 BCE), but they are disputed.[7] The first unmistakable pictures of red jungle fowl date from the New Kingdom (1580–1090 BCE). The birds are depicted with great care and in ways designed to display their splendour as a pet, tomb offering and decoration.[8]

The chicken gradually spread to Greece, Persia and Rome. To feed a cockerel became a means of divination in antiquity. Roman armies brought cockerels with them when they went on a campaign. Before a battle, they would offer wheat to the birds. If the cockerels ate vigorously, dropping crumbs, that would indicate that victory was at hand. If they declined the wheat, it was an omen of foreboding, especially if they refused to leave their coop.[9] Pliny had written of cockerels, 'Day by day, they rule our magistrates . . . They order and forbid battles, providing the auspices of all our victories.'[10] Whether defeated or victorious, Roman soldiers helped to spread the chicken throughout their entire empire.

Etymological and genetic analysis indicates that chickens had reached Latin America from Polynesia in pre-Columbian times. The Araucana, a unique, tail-less Chilean breed that lays blue eggs, may be derived mostly from a pre-Conquest variety, though that is uncertain.[11] In 1520 Hernán Cortés brought a large flock of European chickens to Mexico, from where they spread

Parmigiano, Diogenes with a Featherless Cock, *1500–1530, woodblock print. We could consider this print an early study in comparative anatomy, since it vividly shows the physical resemblances between birds and human beings.*

rapidly across the New World. There are now roughly 20 billion chickens kept by people throughout the world, almost three for every human being.[12]

It would be misleading to speak of this domestication having a purpose, since it was not an intentional act, but the benefits of the chicken have been many. The most obvious is as a source of food. Its excrement has been used as fertilizer and its feathers as decorations. A cockerel can crow at any hour, but it does so most often at dawn and dusk, so it has been important as a means of keeping time. But the sport of cockfighting was initially its most important use.

At least until the modern era, the cockerel has overshadowed the hen in iconic importance. This is due in part to the original bright red, blue and golden brown of its plumage, crest and wattle. The call of the cockerel is exuberant if not especially musical, and it seems to proclaim, 'Look at me!' These factors combine with its stride to create a lordly demeanour. Edward Topsell, an English clergyman writing in the early seventeenth century, compared the cockerel to 'an armed soldier, having his comb for a helmet, his spurs for a sword, his beak for a spear, his tail for a standard, and after combat his own voice to proclaim his victory'.[13] Chickens are polygamous, so they can appear a bit like an emperor with his concubines. Could the chicken be somehow linked with patriarchy? The audience for cockfighting around the world is overwhelmingly, and in some places almost entirely, male.

The Fighting Cock

I have wondered whether the cockerel held up by Diogenes to symbolize humankind might have been the loser of a recent cockfight. The sport of cocking has accompanied the domestic chicken as it spread across the globe, sometimes officially encouraged and at other times forbidden, but almost always at least clandestinely practised. It is especially popular in Southeast Asia, where the domestication of the chicken first occurred. It showcases archetypically masculine behaviours, caricatured to the point of parody, and it is frequently overlaid with rituals which often seem connected to sacrifice and fertility. Two cockerels, placed together, will spontaneously begin to fight. They have natural spurs on their legs, which their handlers usually replace with metal blades, and the duel is likely to continue until the death of one participant.

Cockerels are very well adapted to the sport, not only because of their fierceness towards one another but because they are, in most respects, difficult to humanize. Their eyes have a reptilian intensity and reveal nothing about their inner state, and they show no great affection for human beings. They have an emotional distance that may be charismatic in a warrior but is disastrous

LI.

Vo régardez Milédy !

J. J. Grandville, two anthropomorphic cockerels fighting over a female, c. 1847.

for a family man. They are beautiful but not cuddly or cute. Cockers love and admire them but in a relatively detached sort of way. They nurture them when alive, and often honour them when dead with household shrines and odes. While gamecocks may be role models, symbols and even idols, they are not thought of as friends or pets, even by the most devoted cockers.[14]

Cockfighting became popular in Greece long before chickens and eggs became a dietary staple. According to Aelian in *Varia historia*, the general Themistocles was leading the Athenian army marching against the Persians, when he noticed some cocks fighting. He directed his men to halt and said to them, 'These birds are not fighting in defence of their country, nor for their ancestral gods ... nor for glory or for freedom, nor for the sake of their children: they are fighting so as not to be beaten by their rival, and because each refuses to submit to the other.' Themistocles and his men went on to victory, and the Athenians then passed a law stating the cockfights should be held annually for the public.[15]

The report, generally confirmed by other sources, is paradoxical since the great general disavows the more exalted reasons for combat, usually invoked before a battle, inspiring his men with raw egotism and stubbornness instead. But he was a supremely successful commander and must have had a fine grasp of military psychology. He apparently sensed that the frenzy of battle provided greater motivation than any solemn appeals to patriotism. The cockfight stripped war down to its brutal essence, showing what the older soldiers could not often say but the young ones had to know.

For human warriors, the sort of martial spirit modelled by gamecocks brings great acclaim. Nothing in martial history is more moving or more highly honoured than people who fight to the death against enormous odds, knowing full well that defeat is inevitable, as the Spartans allegedly did at Thermopylae, the Americans at the Alamo and Irish rebels at the Easter Rebellion of 1916. But for gamecocks this is simply expected and, no matter how spirited its resistance, a cockerel is devalued by a loss.

The bloody spectacle of cockfighting displays a primal, indiscriminate fury that may be a driving force in all civilizations yet which none can fully acknowledge. Fred Hawley, who has extensively studied cockfighting in the United States, compares the pampering of cocks prior to a fight to the care given to victims of an impending human sacrifice by the Aztecs and other Mesoamerican civilizations. He writes, 'As with the Native American peoples of Meso-America, it would seem that the blood of the sacrificial "victim" feeds the gods, and indeed, renews fertility, the cosmos, and the earth itself.'[16] Anthropologist Clifford Geertz writes in his study of cockfighting in Bali, 'A cockfight, any cockfight, is in the first instance a blood sacrifice offered, with appropriate chants and oblations, to the demons in order to pacify their ravenous, cannibal hunger.' He adds that cockfights are held at the start of every festival and in response to natural disasters such as plagues or volcanic eruptions.[17]

Cockfighting represents the antithesis of just about any civilization, at least as they prefer to be viewed. It is the undercurrent of nihilism that so often seems to run through even the most refined philosophies. In the United States, where I live, that corresponds to extreme forms of social Darwinism, expressed in the adage 'survival of the fittest'. Beneath all of the qualifications, this presents a view of culture as the outcome of brutal, amoral competition, where 'might makes right'. This violence is a dimension of our society that we have been able neither to unequivocally banish nor accept, but cockfighting provides some relief by enabling us to indirectly acknowledge it. That is why cockfighting continues despite bans in many countries such as the UK and the United States.

According to Geertz, Balinese society is a matrix of competing groups such as castes, villages, clans and temples. It is common for people to gamble heavily on the outcome of important cockfights, and their betting follows intricate rules that are an expression of loyalties. You do not bet, for example, against a cock belonging to your kin. Through the wagers, the spectators become personally involved in the cockfight, which expresses all the covert tensions between groups, even when they may be allied. When the fight ends, the backers of the losing cock are temporarily shamed. Since the bets are based more on affiliation than sober calculation,[18] the gains and losses even of high-spending gamblers tend to level off eventually. The only abiding change is for the losing cockerel, which will end up in a stew cooked for the household of the winner. In the end, social tensions are neither heightened nor alleviated, but they are 'made endurable by being transmuted into play'.[19] This is a mock battle held in place of a real one.

Contemporary cockers regard the world as chaotic and decadent, as perhaps they have always done. They see cockfighting as a link to a heroic past,[20] and often believe they are misunderstood and even persecuted by a hostile society. In England cockfighting was prohibited in 1830 mostly because it was associated with drunkenness, gambling, brawling and urban squalor. In other places, however, cockfighting has been a way to sublimate, rather than act out, impulses towards interpersonal violence. Traditional cockfighters are well-behaved at matches from Bali to Mexico and the United States. Cockfights in these locales are conducted according to strict rules, and the judgements of the referee are seldom questioned.

In the late twentieth century, anthro-zoologist Hal Herzog studied the society of cockfighters in the rural areas near his home in North Carolina. He found that they are ordinary people whose illegal activity rarely extends beyond the cockpit. But, entering the twenty-first century, the combination of technology and unfettered capitalism are starting to overturn customary restraints. Like human athletes, fighting cocks are injected with steroids and fed expensive drugs that are usually provided by drug cartels.[21]

Like other groups with forbidden passions, cockers rationalize their activity in many ways, saying that it is natural, that heroes such as George

A coat of arms from the Middle Ages.

Cockfighting in 19th-century England was notorious for contributing to drunkenness, brawling and disorder.

Washington engaged in it or that it builds character, but the need to make excuses betrays a defensiveness about their sport. The most convincing defence of cockfighting was made by comparing the treatment of fighting cocks to that of broiler chickens in modern times. Gamecocks are raised with great care for about two years before they are even prepared to fight. Keepers make sure that they have a healthy diet, sufficient exercise and even air conditioning. Broiler chickens are kept in cramped quarters, in conditions designed to fatten them up as soon as possible, after which they are immediately slaughtered. Ironically, cocking evokes greater outrage than industrial farming, even though gamecocks lead a far better life than broiler chickens.[22]

It seems likely that, in certain contexts, the sport of cockfighting may even contribute to a more humane treatment of animals. It inspires people to intimately identify with the birds, and it endows their lives with vast, even cosmic significance. It sacralizes their killing, but it prevents the cockerels from being killed or abused outside of the ritualized context. But, even if they have had relatively good lives, they are likely to end them in pain and disorientation.

The Call of Triumph

When checking our calendars or looking at our watches, we take the nature of time for granted, but our ideas about time have been very gradually constructed over millennia. There were many pre-modern methods of measuring time, such as hourglasses and candles, but the crow of the cock at fairly regular intervals probably first divided the day into segments, and without it we might not have clocks today.

Among the most famous, and also most puzzling, last words ever said are those of Socrates, as recorded in Plato's dialogue *Phaedo*. Socrates has been condemned to die by drinking poison and spent his last day discussing philosophy with his students and friends. When the conversation appears finished, he calls for the poison before the appointed time, calmly drinks it and feels his powers gradually fade. In his final breath, he says, 'Crito, we ought to offer a cock to Asclepius [the god of healing]. See to it, and don't forget.'[23] The cock, because it crows at dawn, is a virtually universal symbol of resurrection. Most of the dialogue has centred on the destiny of the soul after death, so perhaps the offering alludes to Socrates' expectation of immanent rebirth.[24]

In the Book of Job, Yahweh asks, according to the Jerusalem translation, 'Who gave the ibis wisdom and endowed the cock with foreknowledge?' (Job 38:36). The attribution of wisdom to the ibis is borrowed from Egypt, where the bird was closely associated with Thoth, inventor of the arts and the sciences. For the cock, the ascription of foreknowledge is due to the bird announcing the morning by crowing even before the sun has begun to appear. Scientists today believe this is due more to circadian rhythms than to any sensory abilities, but this was a complete mystery in ancient times. For many Christian writers, it suggested that the cockerel had some sort of esoteric knowledge.

The cockerel is one of the twelve animals in the Asian zodiac and is closely identified with the sun. In one Japanese myth, sun-goddess Amaterasu retires in anger into a cave, leaving the world in total darkness. The other deities try in vain to bring her back with pleas and enticements. At last they take a cock to the door of her cave and direct it to crow. Amaterasu thinks the day has begun without her and opens the door to see what has happened, at which light again fills the sky.[25]

According to a Chinese myth, in the reign of the first Emperor Yao, six suns fill the sky and burn crops. At the request of Yao, the archer Ho-Yi shoots down five of the suns. The remaining one seeks refuge in a cave, and no threats and inducements can induce the sun to leave. Finally, people bring a cock. When it crows, the sun is so enchanted with the beauty of the sound that he returns.[26]

An intense awareness of time pervades the story of Jesus in the Bible, which is one of the first narratives to convey a sense of a high drama gradually unfolding slowly through a series of relatively minor events. Jesus predicts to his foremost disciple, 'I tell you, Peter, by the time the cock crows today you will have denied three times that you know me' (Luke 22:34). Later, when three people recognize Peter, he does as Jesus had foretold. The cockerel crows as he is speaking, and Peter goes outside and weeps bitterly (Luke 22:55–62).

Because of this passage, Christians understood the crow of the cockerel as a call to repentance. A twelfth-century English bestiary, echoing words of St Ambrose, waxed unusually poetic about it:

> The cock's crow is a pleasant thing of a night, and not only pleasant but useful. It is nice to have it about the place. It wakes the sleeping; it forewarns the anxious; it consoles the traveler by bearing witness to the passage of time with tuneful notes. At the cock's crowing the robber leaves his wiles; the morning star himself wakes up and shines upon the sky. At his singing the frightened sailor lays aside his cares and the tempest often moderates. At his crowing the devoted mind rises to prayer and the priest begins again to read his office.[27]

Before electric lighting, the night was much darker and more frightening than it is today. There was something reassuringly familiar about the cockerel's call.

Like postmodernists today, late medieval and Renaissance authors were fascinated by ambiguity, irony and paradox. They would construct allegories with many layers of meaning to produce works a bit like a house of distorting mirrors at an old-fashioned amusement park. Geoffrey Chaucer, in the story recounted by the nun's priest in his *Canterbury Tales*, looks at the crowing cockerel through more intricate layers of irony than any deconstructionist. The story is a beast fable of the sort traditionally attributed to Aesop, expanded into a mock-heroic epic with all the inflated rhetoric of chivalry. The protagonist is the cockerel Chanticleer, who rules over the barnyard of a poor widow and is accompanied by seven hens. He dreams of a terrifying beast resembling a red and yellow dog, which wants to kill him. He tells the dream to Pertelote, his favourite hen, who scornfully reproaches him for cowardice. She quotes the Roman philosopher Cato, who claims that dreams are without meaning, and says that Chanticleer merely needs a laxative to purge him of ill humours. She then continues with a discussion of herbal medicines. Chanticleer replies with a learned discourse, in which he cites Macrobius, the Bible and many stories from antiquity to prove that dreams can contain prophetic warnings. But eventually he forgets the matter and spends the afternoon copulating with the hens.

Later the beast, a fox, comes to the barnyard and says that he means no harm but merely wishes to hear the cockerel's beautiful voice. He tells Chanticleer that he was a friend of the cockerel's father, who would close his eyes, stretch out his neck and sing beautifully. He asks Chanticleer to do the same. When Chanticleer obliges, the fox immediately grabs him by the neck and starts to carry him away. The hens begin to cry, bringing dogs, geese, cats and other animals. Chanticleer suggests to the fox that he taunt his pursuers. The fox starts to oblige, opening his mouth, and Chanticleer escapes. The moral is that one should not trust flattery.[28] The fox, which lives in burrows, is traditionally linked with chthonic powers, while the cock is associated with the sun, so perhaps the story alludes to a solar eclipse. On the other hand, it is still an everyday sort of occurrence in a dilapidated barnyard.

First among the many ironies here is that the narrator himself constantly engages in flattery, just what he says should not be trusted. The cockerel's comb, the priest says, was redder than fine coral, and its shape was like a crenellated castle tower. The body of the cockerel was golden, set off by feathers of brilliant black and white. Chanticleer had no peer in crowing, and his voice was merrier than any organ. His call told the hours more faithfully than any clock.[29] So could the narrator himself be a sort of fox? Or might the priest represent Chanticleer himself? He is a priest of the nuns and, like the cockerel, a male constantly surrounded by females. And what is one to make of the learned discussions among barnyard fowl? Is this a mockery of human learning? Some of the suggestions are uncomfortable, but the story is told with such good humour that we are not likely to mind. What I have said hardly begins to elucidate all the levels of irony, and, rather than persist in the futile pursuit of unambiguous answers, we are likely in the end to take the tale, together with its moral, naively.

In *Oration on the Dignity of Man* (1486), the manifesto of the original humanistic movement, Pico della Mirandola commends the sayings of Pythagoras, whom he calls 'wisest of men':

> Finally, Pythagoras will command us to 'feed the cock'; that is, to nourish the divine part of our soul with the knowledge of divine things as with a substantial food and heavenly ambrosia. This is the cock whose visage the lion, that is, all earthly power, holds in fear and awe. This is the cock to whom, as we read in Job, understanding was given. At this cock's crowing, the erring

man returns to his senses. This is the cock which every day, in the morning twilight, with the stars of morning, raises a *Te Deum* to heaven.[30]

The injunction to 'feed the cock' is a reference to the old Roman practice of using cockerels to foretell the outcome of a military engagement, but Pico was here talking about a spiritual one.

Even highly learned men might tell fantastic tales about a crowing cock with little or no irony and scepticism. Ulisse Aldrovandi, the sixteenth-century Italian zoologist, recounts that two gentlemen were once served a roasted cockerel. One of them took a knife, cut it into pieces and covered it with sauce and pepper. His companion remarked, 'You have cut up the cockerel so thoroughly that even St Peter, if he wished to, could not put him back together'. The other replied that would be beyond the ability of even Jesus Christ. At that moment, the cockerel suddenly jumped up, thoroughly alive and covered with feathers. It began to crow, throwing sauce on the two diners. The pepper turned into spots of leprosy, and they died shortly afterwards.[31]

In Shakespeare's *Hamlet*, when day breaks and the ghost of the protagonist's father disappears, Marcellus says:

> It faded on the crowing of the cock.
> Some say that ever 'gainst that season comes
> Wherein our Saviour's birth is celebrated,
> The bird of dawning singeth all night long.
> And then, they say, no spirit dare stir abroad.
> The nights are wholesome. Then no planets strike,
> No fairy takes, nor witch hath power to charm,
> So hallowed and so gracious is that time.
> (*Hamlet*, Act i, sc. ii, lines 156–64)

Vanishing at the crow of the cock suggests the ghost may be an infernal spirit, though its status is never resolved in the play.

But for all the vigour of its call and splendour of its plumage, the behaviour of the cockerel can still seem robotic, in pecking grains, mating constantly, calling the hours and fighting until death. That only added to the

French political cartoon, late 18th century. The Latin expression says, 'All animals are sad after coitus except the cock.' The animals represent European states and, led by the French cockerel, they are attacking Britain. Perhaps because of its possessions in India, Britain is represented by a tiger.

La France

L'Espagne

OMNE ANIMAL POST COÏTUM TRISTE PRÆTER GALLUM.

Tu la voulu

GD in.º

L'Amerique

L'Angleterre

fascination with the bird in the Early Modern period, when timepieces were regarded as the epitome of mechanical engineering. The cosmos could be thought of as a machine and God as the supreme watchmaker. Cockerels were often used to decorate clock faces and weathervanes. They seemed to exemplify the ideas of many eighteenth-century *philosophes* about humankind by being at once mechanical, organic and utterly exuberant. During the French Revolution the cockerel replaced the fleur-de-lis, which the new regime thought was too closely associated with royalty, as a symbol of France. The substitution was based on a pun. The Latin *gallus* can mean either 'cockerel' or 'Gaul' (France). They also saw the crowing cockerel as announcing a new era for humanity, which, the new government believed, would be inaugurated by the Revolution.

As states grew increasingly industrialized and urbanized, however, the cockerel became a nostalgic symbol of traditional rural life. People were woken by alarm clocks and learned the time through watches, so the crowing of the cock lost its utility, but the call may have gained in symbolic importance. It was imitated by bugles, used to wake soldiers and Boy Scouts. A cockerel calling appeared in cartoons, on cereal boxes, on weathervanes and on calendars, in fact anywhere people wished to appeal to a longing for country ways. In 2019 holidayers in the picturesque town of Saint-Pierre-d'Oléron on the island of Oléron off the west coast of France sued the owner of a cockerel named Maurice because the crowing kept waking them in the morning. Tens of thousands across France signed a petition in support of Maurice, and a parliamentary representative called for rural sounds to be officially classified as a national heritage.[32] Later that year the courts ruled in Maurice's favour.

As a verb, 'to crow' can mean 'to boast', a signification that was already established in Middle English. The idea that the crow of a cock expresses pride is, according to ethologists, close to the truth. The call serves to mark territory, and to signal a readiness to defend it.

The Domestic Chicken

In literature and the arts, the cock has received most attention, while the hen was largely taken for granted. This is especially so in early representations of the birds in places such as Egypt, Greece and Mesopotamia. People quickly noticed the brilliant plumage, fighting spirit and song of the cock. Only later did they appreciate the prolific egg laying of the hen. In Egypt chickens and eggs did not become a staple of the diet until the Ptolemaic period (305–30 BCE), roughly a millennium or so after they had been introduced. This happened at about the same time in Greece and a bit later in Rome.

Once their culinary potential was recognized, chickens rather quickly became the first animals, apart from silkworms and bees, to be raised in an almost industrial manner. Elamite tablets from Persepolis in Iran seem to refer to a royal hen house, where chickens were raised on a large scale.[33] Around the end of the fourth century BCE the Egyptians developed a method of hatching eggs by taking them early from the hens and placing them in large ovens to incubate, producing chickens at a rate that Roman contemporaries found astounding.[34]

But the Romans carried the industrialization of farming further than any other civilization of the ancient world. They had enormous plantations with orchards tended by slaves, in which all the trees had been grafted. They also had huge hen houses that were described in detail by Varro in *De re rustica* (On Country Matters) during the first century BCE. A flock of two hundred chickens would be in a pair of connected buildings. They would have large windows that admitted light and air but were covered with a lattice to keep out raptors and other predators. The chicken farmer continually tended the hens, looking after their welfare but also intervening regularly in the process of laying and hatching eggs. The farmer would turn the eggs in the nest every other day to make sure they were evenly warmed. He would also redistribute eggs, and later chicks, regularly from one hen to another in order to make sure that no bird had too few or too many. When the time for slaughter approached, the farmer would place hens in a dark, narrow space and feed them a special diet in order to fatten them up quickly.[35]

Such houses kept the fowl out of the sight of most people, which could facilitate the growth of legends. Aelian, writing in the second century CE, was one of the most entertaining writers of the ancient world and also one of the most wildly inaccurate. He reports that a temple of Heracles and a temple of Hebe, his spouse and the goddess of youth, are separated by a clear stream. Cocks are kept in the shrine to Heracles and hens in that of Hebe. Once a year at mating season, the cockerels fly across the water, mate with the hens, and then return. When the eggs have hatched, the cocks carry off the male birds and rear them, while the hens take care of their daughters.[36] But if several cockerels lived together, they would fight continually and, in any case, they do not take care of the young. The account shows how much some people had drifted out of daily contact with the lives of food animals, even if it is not so far as today.

Aelian's account also illustrates the separation of genders, which is central to the way people have always thought of chickens. They exemplify, in fact caricature, gender roles. People have often regarded any blurring and confusion of these roles among chickens with either horror or contempt. In

the Early Modern era cocks that laid eggs and hens that crowed might be put to death. A further illustration of this is the legend of the basilisk, also known as the 'cockatrice', which Alexander Neckam, writing around 1180, called 'an evil unique in the world'. According to him, it was hatched from an egg laid by an old cock and incubated by a toad. The basilisk, in traditions going back to antiquity, was able to kill with only a glance, and birds allegedly fell from the sky when the monster looked upwards.[37] The basilisk was generally represented with the beak, cockscomb, wattle and claws of a cockerel, the tail of a snake and the wings of a bat.

In the Early Modern era, when there was a mysterious death, a basilisk would be suspected. In 1587 two young girls died in a cellar in Warsaw. A man who had already been condemned to die was sent into a cellar wearing an outfit covered with mirrors, so the basilisk might see itself reflected and die, with the promise of a complete pardon if he survived. The convict picked up a snake, as he had been directed, using the blades of a rake. The serpent was carefully examined and judged to be a basilisk, the poison of which had been weakened by contact with the sun.[38]

Though the basilisk retained most of the physical characteristics of a cockerel, it was the opposite in many ways. The cockerel was solar while the basilisk was chthonic. The monster was reportedly found in caves, wells and cellars. Cockerels were associated with order, since they divided up the day, modelled exaggerated sexual roles and called people to repentance. All monsters contain projections of intimate fears, and the basilisk was an apocalyptic image of disorder, an unnatural creature created by a confusion of genders and species. Just as people saw the wolf as the opposite of the dog and the Antichrist as the contrary of Jesus, they thought of the basilisk as a sort of anti-cockerel.

Hen Mania

After the fall of the Roman empire, chickens reverted to their former semi-domesticated state. They would be left to forage in the barnyard, where they might become prey to hawks or foxes but retained considerable freedom. Much of the appeal of chickens was that they required hardly any care. As in Chaucer's tale of Chanticleer, they were often associated with poor and little-tended but lively barnyards. Theft of cattle could lead to epic confrontations, but chickens hardly seemed worth stealing. But this changed during the Modern period, particularly in Britain and the United States.

Printer's device of Michael Furter showing a basilisk, Basle, 1500.

One reason was that the small properties where chickens had been raised were increasingly consolidated into large estates. Another was the development of techniques of scientific breeding by Robert Bakewell and others during the latter eighteenth century. Yet one more was the importation of previously unknown varieties from distant parts of the globe.

Domestic animals from dogs to cattle were bred intensively. Victorian breeders gloried in their newly discovered human power to alter differences, which had previously seemed ordained by natural law, among creatures. Creating new breeds using exotic imports was also a way to appropriate the cultural legacies of exotic lands. For cows and sheep, breeding was generally intended to produce the most meat with the minimum expenditure. For canines, it was usually for appearance. For barnyard fowl, breeding reflected all of these aspirations. Breeding did not always have a clearly articulated goal, and animals could be bred largely for their novelty or for whimsy, as some of the profusely feathered varieties of poultry certainly attest.

Part of the impetus came from the importation of cochins, an ornamental chicken from China, which caught the imagination of Queen Victoria and her husband Prince Albert, in the 1840s.[39] Cochins had thin legs covered with feathers, slender necks, calm dispositions and a wide variety of

Prize chickens from Cassells Poultry Book *(1872).*

Chromolithograph of Andalusian cockerel and hen. Many of these images of poultry suggest Victorian ladies and gentlemen, proud of their pedigree and out for a little stroll.

colours that were unlike anything the royal couple had previously encountered. From 1845 to 1855 Britain and the United States went through a fad known as 'hen fever', in which people became obsessed with the appearance and utility of new breeds. This was an explosion of enthusiasm similar to the Dutch tulip mania of the early seventeenth century. Chickens quickly shed much of their ancient and medieval symbolism as they absorbed the values of the emerging commercial culture. Huge poultry shows were held in cities such as London

Chromolithograph by Harrison Weir showing 'Captain Heaton's Champion Modern Game Stag-Cock', England, 1902. Although it was illegal in Britain at the time, both the name and the powerful thighs indicate that this rooster was bred for fighting.

and Boston. Criteria incorporating both aesthetic and utilitarian characteristics were drawn up for judging both individuals and breeds. Birds were bought and sold at extravagant prices.

Herman Melville in his 1853 story 'Cock-A-Doodle-Doo!' not only satirized hen fever but made it into an allegory on human aspirations. A man beset by financial problems hears the wonderful call of a cockerel chanting the glory of God, which is so heavenly that he forgets his woes. It is, he tells us, 'the crow of a cock who had fought the world and got the better of it and was resolved to crow, though the earth should heave and the heavens should fall. It was a wise crow; an invincible crow; a philosophic crow; a crow of all crows.'

Like the white whale in Melville's novel *Moby-Dick*, the cockerel inspires an obsessive quest. Searching for the cock, the man visits the poultry yards of the wealthy but finds that nobody has even heard of it. At last he finally locates the cockerel in the possession of a poor man whose wife and children are hopelessly ill. Its appearance is as magnificent as its voice. As the cock crows, the man, his wife and children die. It then ascends to the roof, lets out a final call and itself expires. The narrator buries the family and cock and has inscribed on their tombstone the words of St Paul, 'O death, where is thy sting? Grave, where is thy victory?'[40] Hen fever (which may, in the story, be understood in an almost literal way) was a manifestation of the proverbial American Dream, with all its glamour, futility and pathos.

About two years after the story was published, hen mania collapsed as abruptly as it had begun. Exotic poultry, which shortly before could fetch almost any price, were practically given away. But the standards, values and infrastructure that hen mania had created remained largely in place. Poultry

Cochin rooster running.

Several fancy breeds of chickens displayed at a poultry show, Harper's Weekly *(10 April 1869).*

shows continued, though on a more modest scale. Techniques of poultry breeding developed during hen fever were still used, though more in the service of pragmatic goals than dazzling novelties. They shifted from the cock to the hen, as well as from sensual splendour and cosmic symbolism to ensuring an inexpensive supply of protein.

The Chicken in America

The cockerel and hen were at least as important to the livelihood and culture of people in Central Africa as to those in Europe or Asia. In the origin myth of the Yoruba in West Africa, an ethnicity to which most enslaved Africans in America had belonged, the orisha Odua, a legendary king and ancestor of the people, placed a bit of soil in the primordial waters. On it he then placed a cockerel, which, by scratching, spread dirt to create the earth.[41] Cockerel masks, representing ancestral wisdom, are used in ceremonies by the people of Burkina Faso and other countries in Central Africa.[42] Chickens are still ubiquitous in African village life and are able to run relatively freely. Despite their familiarity, they remain rich in cultural significance. Chicken, usually a cockerel, is the meal with which to honour guests.[43]

Throughout Africa, the chicken has also long been the sacrificial animal. One reason is the bird's extraordinary genetic plasticity. As in Europe and

North America before modern industrial farming, there have been scores of colourful breeds, each with a characteristic plumage, voice and behaviour. This made it relatively easy to customize an offering according to the deity, the situation or the desired outcome.[44]

Fried chicken, cooked in palm oil, had long been a staple in West Africa. When enslaved people were taken over to North America, they brought their cuisine with them. In Virginia slaves were prohibited from owning larger animals such as horses and cows, but they were permitted to keep chickens, in part because that was an activity that had little status. They sold chickens to their masters, to neighbours and to one another. Chickens became part of an underground economy and even a form of currency. Eventually the dish spread to White Southerners and gradually the rest of the United States.[45]

Food shortages during the First World War and the international depression that followed it compelled people to turn to previously underutilized sources of nutrition, and the chicken was foremost among them. Running for president of the United States in 1928, Herbert Hoover campaigned using the slogan 'A chicken in every pot'. Finally American researchers developed the broiler chicken, first raised industrially using massive doses of antibiotics during the Second World War and perfected in the early 1950s.[46] Variants of it, marketed by fast-food chains, have quickly spread around the world.

The success of broiler chickens in feeding large numbers of people, including the underprivileged, is obvious. The negative consequences for the welfare of the animals are vast and unprecedented. In the second half of the twentieth century, ever more chickens were crammed into vast, windowless facilities. Large broiler farms produce several hundreds of thousands per year.[47] They have been increasingly genetically engineered and drugged to make them put on a maximal amount of weight in a minimal amount of time, so hens, which previously had a lifespan of ten to fifteen years, are now fattened and slaughtered in six weeks.[48] Their beaks are trimmed so they do not peck one another to death. Egg-laying hens are placed in battery cages where they sometimes do not have room to turn around. In summary, they are almost entirely objectified: a publication of the U.S. Department of Agriculture stated in 1975 that growing broiler chickens was 'industrialized in much the same way as the production of cars'.[49]

Government and industry were unequivocally enthusiastic about industrialization of the chicken industry, and it initially inspired hardly any protests from the public. Nevertheless, advertising from the late 1940s and '50s suggests that attitudes towards industrial chicken were a good deal more complicated than they seemed. As chickens were being almost completely objectified in agribusinesses, advertising of them went in precisely the opposite direction. Cockerels and hens were being anthropomorphized, or 'humanized', more than ever before. Advertisements for chicken meat and restaurants regularly featured chickens in human roles, often dressed up in clothes and even speaking English. If a restaurant was selling chicken as prepared in the American Southwest, it would show a cockerel dressed up as a cowboy. If the recipe was Mexican, the cockerel would wear a sombrero; if Italian, the cockerel would be dressed as a gondolier.

In the late 1940s The Chicken Hut, a popular eatery in Washington, DC, adopted the motto 'Where chicken is king'. On its menu was a cockerel wearing a crown, royal robes and eyeglasses. A wing was stylized to look like a hand, which held a sceptre with a fork on one end and a spoon on the other.

Brass rooster, Edo peoples, Benin, 18th century. This rooster has the dramatic simplicity that is characteristic of animals in traditional African art.

A smaller chicken, probably a hen, was bowing down before His Majesty as another cooled him with a paper fan. Though not many people would have been able to consciously make the association, it suggested a king of fools, destined soon to become a sacrificial offering.

Some of the advertisements seemed to use the cruelty of industrial farms as a selling point. In an advertisement for a restaurant called The Roost in Atlantic City, New Jersey, an obviously terrified chicken, the gender of which is not clear, stands before a judge and jury, with a sergeant at arms and a secretary nearby. All of those officials are chickens as well, but they are not naked; they are wearing cloth suits. The judge points angrily at the defendant, who looks up pleadingly; the judge says, 'Guilty – sentenced to fry.' Perhaps having a chicken pronounce the sentence, as well as using humour, may be a way to assuage unacknowledged guilt about industrial chicken on the part of customers.[50] In the 1970s Perdue Chicken sold its industrially raised birds with a piquant hint of sadism, using the slogan 'It takes a tough man to make a tender chicken.'[51]

Under conditions of such overcrowding, diseases can spread very quickly, and the congestion was only made feasible through massive use of antibiotics. But over time these lose their effectiveness and so they need to be made even stronger, putting both animals and human beings increasingly at risk. Bacteria constantly mutate in response to the antibiotics, becoming ever more resistant to treatment. Before the Second World War, villages throughout the world would often raise unique varieties of chicken. The genetic uniformity of chickens in most countries today, together with the rapid pace of communication, also renders them easily vulnerable to pandemics.

Sweden banned growth-inducing antibiotics in 1986 and the European Union followed in 1999. Around the start of the twenty-first century Perdue Chicken determined that antibiotics had in any case lost their effectiveness and decided to stop using them.[52] In 2014 the restaurant chain Chick-fil-A decided to ban meat grown with antibiotics and other giant companies such as McDonald's, Subway, Costco and Walmart have followed.[53] These businesses still have chicken produced on the industrial model, but this is being widely challenged as well. The early twenty-first century brought a revival of farmers' markets, where people can buy locally raised meat from smaller farms. Keeping chickens in gardens and backyards has become increasingly popular even in cities.

Finally, there is the emerging alternative of *in vitro* meat, produced not from living animals but cultures in laboratories. Ironically, this is a culmination of industrial farming. After having been objectified for decades, chickens will truly become objects. Those who protest about industrial farming have

CHICKEN DICTIONARY

HOT ROLLS AND BISCUITS from our own sunny **BAKERY** served with all CHICKEN SPECIALTIES

As the world's outstanding authority on the preparation and serving of Pampered Chicken . . . we present this colossal compendium of the ways in which you can enjoy our "Bluebloods of the Barnyard." Just stick a pin anywhere into this side of the menu . . . you can't lose!

1 Chicken ARROZ CON POLLO
It's an old Spanish custom . . . Chicken with Rice . . . plus toothsome vegetables . . . plus an exotic Latin sauce. You'll say "Si Si, that's for me!"
$1.50

2 Chicken BOILED EN POT with Matzoh Balls
Smart chickens always get boiled with Matzoh balls! And if it's good enough for the chicken, it's good enough for you. (You eat everything but the pot!)
$1.35

3 Chicken BAR-B-Q
A real Southwestern gustatory delight . . . with a Barbecue sauce that'll have you smacking your lips. Served with Potatoes and Cole Slaw, of course!
$1.35

4 Whole BROILED Baby Chicken
Tender as a maiden's first kiss . . . broiled to a delicate glaze, and graced with Potatoes Alumette and vegetables, for your Epicurean excitement.
$1.50

5 Chicken CACCIATORE
You go out and "catch-ya" a chicken, then "tore" it apart, cook till tender, and serve with Spaghetti. Don't try to pronounce it . . . just sort of inhale it!
$1.50

6 Chicken EUGENE under bell
Chicken in Ermine . . . firm, plump breast of proud poultry, tenderly roasted and served with Ole Virginny Ham . . . to say nothing of the vegetables and Potatoes Julienne. Folks, this is really living!
$1.75

7 Chicken FRICASEE Burgundy **with Midget Meatballs**
Probably Mother never knew about Burgundy in Fricasee . . . so you're in for an amazing new enjoyment of a favorite old-time dish.
$1.50

8 FRIED Chicken Southern style
A half fryer, carefully rolled in smooth batter, and reverently skillet-fried until the crust is just crisp enough to hold the meat together. With vegetables, potatoes or cole slaw. It's really Solid South!
$1.25

9 Chicken a la KING
Poultry in regal raiment . . . flavored with Sherry wine . . . fit for the King, and not a bad choice for the Queen, either. With Green Peas, it makes a royal repast.
$1.25

10 Chicken MEXICAN
You'll believe in the "Good Neighbor" policy after you try this treat from "South of the Border." And don't wait until Manana to try it.
$1.25

11 Chicken a la MARYLAND
You'll sing "Maryland, My Maryland" at the taste of these large morsels of chicken, fried to a sizzling golden tan, and flanked with vegetables and Corn Fritter.
$1.35

12 Chicken PAPRIKA
It's a regular Hungarian Rhapsody . . . large, luscious hunks of chicken stewed to an unrivalled tenderness in a savory sauce. Served on a bed of vegetables and tender Spaetzle.
$1.35

13 Chicken PARISIEN
A dish that will always make you think of Gay Paree! An old-world delicacy with a true Gallic flavor, that will make you say "Oo La La . . . Oui Oui!"
$1.40

14 Chicken POT PIE
Gobs of chicken meat and vegetables cooked in a tasty gravy, covered with a flaky crust that imprisons the gusty juices . . . just waiting for you to break in.
$1.25

15 POTTED Chicken with dumplings
The real old-fashioned article . . . with the kind of dumplings mother wished she knew how to make! With Lima beans, it's a he-man dish!
$1.35

16 ROAST STUFFED Chicken
The good old reliable . . . roast to a crispy glazed brown, and filled with a special savory stuffing; served with vegetables and potatoes.
$1.35

17 Chicken TETRAZZINI
No wonder this was the favorite dish of the famous opera star. After all, what could be bad about mouth-watering chicken served up with colorful vegetables, mushrooms and tender Spaghetti?
$1.50

SO . . . WHAT DO YOU WANT US TO DO WITH ALL THE **CHICKEN LIVERS?** →

We serve thousands of chickens . . . and every chicken has a liver! That's why our 'Chicken Liver Specials' are super-fresh and extra-generous. THE MOST FOR YOUR MONEY.

OUR DAILY LUNCHE

usually objected to highly processed foods such as frankfurters, but artificial chicken and beef will be among the most heavily processed staples available. As Donna Haraway has put it, 'Genetically engineered muscles-without-animals illustrate . . . designer ethics, which aim to bypass cultural struggle with just-in-time, "high technology" breakthroughs . . . But remember, Chicken squawks even when his head has been cut off.'[54]

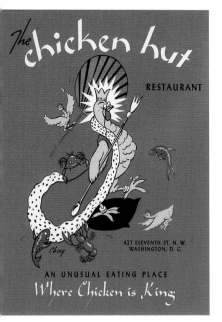

Lack of dung from chickens could force farmers to rely more on artificial fertilizers, which tend to exhaust the soil. Since cultured meat would not be protected by an animal's immune system, it might require increased doses of antibiotics. How successful manufacturers will be in addressing such problems remains to be seen. In any case, it would not be wise to assume in advance that *in vitro* meat will not have negative consequences, much less that it will always be produced and consumed with altruistic concerns and complete efficiency.

Every major new technology from plastics to the mobile phone has had initially unsuspected effects. Broiler chickens were initially greeted with unadulterated enthusiasm as a manifestation of progress and a way to feed the world, and it took decades for people to realize that the conditions for raising them were inhumane and entailed long-term hazards for human health. We can only guess what the environmental, medical, cultural, psychological, nutritional and economic effects of producing *in vitro* meat on an industrial scale may turn out to be.

Meanwhile, the breeds that caused such a frenzy during the mid-nineteenth century are cultivated only by a small number of small farmers, largely as a cultural patrimony. Haraway has argued for the preservation and revival of breeds as a means to encourage, in her words, 'ongoing chicken–human lives that are attentive to complex histories of animal–human entanglements, fully contemporary and committed to a future of multispecies naturalcultural flourishing in both wild and domestic domains'.[55] Every breed

From the menu of The Chicken Hut, a popular restaurant in Washington, DC, in the 1940s. Note the way recipes are identified with different ethnicities.

is a record of the history of bonding with other species, with all the beauty, silliness, compassion and folly that may entail.

Taste is not simply a matter of chemicals but even more of associations, as connoisseurs of wine and cheese know well. It can encode information about an environment and connect people with the past. A major reason for the blandness of broiler chickens, which people have never been able to assuage with additives, is that they have no history, at least none that one would care to contemplate. Aggressive advertising often obscures this problem but has never been able to solve it. The lack of associations has been relatively tolerable because the Industrial Era tends to decontextualize just about everything from art to sexual attraction, in order to render judgements objective and results quantifiable. The usual response has been to overwhelm the meat with extra ingredients or sauces. Heritage breeds are almost never bland. And what about *in vitro* chicken?

511 BOARDWALK
ATLANTIC CITY, N. J.

Would it move people to think back nostalgically on the factories of the industrial era? Would it deprive them of spiritual nourishment? Would it remind them of hens and cockerels? Or would it enable them to forget the birds entirely?

The Future of the Chicken

Because it has proved so adaptable, the embattled partnership between chickens and humans is likely to continue. For the Asian villagers who first entered into a bond with the cock and hen, their Christian use as a symbol of resurrection must have been inconceivable, and early Christians surely could not have imagined the industrial chicken farms of today. In a similar way, we probably cannot imagine forms that the partnership may take in time. But surely, whatever comes cannot be worse than our treatment of broiler chickens.

Menu cover for The Roost, a restaurant specializing in chicken in Atlantic City, New Jersey, 1946–7.

Perhaps someday when broiler chickens are a fuzzy memory and scholars are debating what the 'old Americans' meant by their concept of 'sexy', the world will be full of feral chickens that have, for the most part, reverted to the ways and appearance of red jungle fowl.

Broiler chicken production, with its highly regimented assembly lines and intense use of chemicals, epitomizes the industrial era, which, historians agree, is now either over or at least rapidly drawing to a close. In the approximately 10,000 years or more in which they have partnered with humankind, chickens have been given an amazing range of significance. They have been archetypal warriors, insignia of royalty, soothsayers, promises of resurrection, lords of the barnyard, national symbols, sex symbols, nostalgic icons of rural life, an endless banquet, symbols of progress, corporate logos, indictments of industry and far more. The meanings are perplexingly diverse, but there are esoteric connections. The frequent use of the cockerel as a sacrificial offering in Alexandrian Egypt, for example, is related to its use as a symbol of resurrection in Christianity, and both are subtly connected to the 'hen fever' of the mid-nineteenth century.

Even the popularity of chicken meat and eggs during the twentieth century may not be as utilitarian as it seems. The act of eating is always overlaid with all sorts of aspirations, daydreams and taboos. When they attend a chicken dinner, people are attracted by the mystique of progress, the hope of resurrection or the promise of sexual potency. In the words of Andrew Lawler, 'The chicken is . . . an uncanny mirror of our changing human desires, goals, and intentions.'[56]

Diogenes of Sinope, who challenged Plato's definition of man, was the sort of relentless critic that every society needs at least occasionally. Accounts of him are largely legendary, but they describe him as combining an austere morality with a sharp wit, as well as being totally unimpressed by glamour, wealth and power. Though revered for his writings, he reportedly elected to live in a barrel. Perhaps the best known of the many anecdotes reported about Diogenes is that Alexander the Great once came to pay his respects and said, 'Ask any favour that you choose.' Diogenes replied, 'Cease to shade me from the sun.'[57] If that philosopher were here today, he might point to a broiler chicken in a fast-food restaurant and say once again, 'That is man.'

PART THREE

BIRDS IN ART

10 FROM CAVES TO CATHEDRALS

I would like to paint the way a bird sings.
Claude Monet

Rock art has been created in Africa, Eurasia, Australia and the Americas, but only works in the innermost recesses of caves have survived from Palaeolithic times. These primarily feature paintings of mammals such as great cats, horses and bison, but only a very few birds. The oldest known cave paintings are on the island of Sulawesi in Indonesia. They contain a hunting scene painted about 44,000 years ago in which one figure may be a human with a beak like that of a bird, perhaps either a disguised hunter or a mythological figure.[1] The figure could also, however, be a monitor lizard.

The oldest clearly identifiable representation of a bird that we have is a small mammoth ivory figurine from the Hohle Fels cave in the German province of Baden-Württemberg, which has the extended neck of a waterfowl. The statue dates from about 33,000 years ago. Its neck is straight and its wings are pointed backwards, as though the bird were diving for fish.[2] The oldest surviving painting of a bird may be the image of an owl, painted more than 30,000 years ago, on the walls of the Chauvet cave in southern France. The image shows the back of its torso, with its head turned completely around and facing the viewer, a startling and unusual posture.[3]

Another of the oldest birds in cave art is from the Grotte Cosquer near Marseilles in France, dating from about 25,000 years ago, which zooarchaeologists identify as a great auk or related bird.[4] Since auks are flightless, people may have associated them more with mammals than with other birds. At any rate, the depiction is unusually humanized. The wings are a bit higher than those of a great auk and they are spread out like human arms, almost as though gesturing to the viewer.

There is a family of nesting owls – mother, father and chick – engraved in the wall of the Trois-Frères cave in France, which dates from the upper Palaeolithic era. It is especially remarkable, and perhaps even a bit anthropomorphic, because family groups are otherwise almost unknown in cave art. All three figures are shown from the side, but with their heads turned to directly face the viewer.[5] In a rather uncanny way, it suggests a modern family portrait.

Museum replica of an owl engraved on the wall of Chauvet cave, 2800 BCE.

Towards the end of the Palaeolithic era, figures that combine human and avian features become more common. The most mysterious work of cave art of all may be the 'bird-man' at Lascaux. It shows a person lying down before a bison, the hind quarters of which are pierced by a spear, with the point coming out of its lower belly like a phallus. The man has a bird's beak, or is wearing a mask with one, and seems to have an erection. Beside him is a wand with an image of a bird at one end. The image is dated to about 14,000 years ago, and probably pertains to some sort of hunting ritual.[6] The man may be in some sort of shamanic trance, and perhaps the bison is his dream or vision. There are also many figurines found in several locations around the Mediterranean and Central Europe that depict women with beaks and other avian features.

Bird-woman figurine, Cyprus, 1450–1200 BCE.

The meaning of such images is unknown, but they suggest that birds were culturally important in esoteric mysteries of at least some societies during the late Palaeolithic era.

Abstract patterns, stray lines and relatively crude figures are often found near the entrances of decorated caves. They might be comparable to the gargoyles carved around the portals to medieval cathedrals. Or perhaps they are essentially doodles, with which artists practised for their major works. At times the lines suggest birds, but it is hard to identify them with confidence.

In every location, those birds that appear are almost all either flightless ones, such as the cassowary and great auk, or owls. Why are there almost no prehistoric depictions of birds in the air? The reason may be partly technical. Birds such as vultures, hawks and albatrosses soar with their wings outstretched, their bodies carried by currents of air but otherwise almost still, making their outlines at least consistent, but smaller birds such as sparrows in flight present us with constantly changing perspectives as they energetically quickly turn, bend and change direction. Their motion may have been too rapid and too unpredictable to be recorded. The artists may also have felt that in so terrestrial a setting birds of the air simply did not seem to belong.

Egypt, Greece and Rome

Egyptian images of birds from the Neolithic Age consisted mostly of highly abstract outlines in symmetrical patterns on pottery. By the early third millennium BCE they were starting to develop a highly diverse tradition of animal art. Egyptian civilization was the first to regularly depict birds in flight. This was a culmination of a very long trend in which religious thought increasingly centred on the heavens rather than the earth. When people of the ancient Mediterranean wanted to know the will of the gods, they would look up at the sky. By night, they saw stars and planets; by day, birds and clouds. Accordingly, astrology, especially in Mesopotamia, and ornithomancy, especially in Greece, became the favoured means of prophecy.

The Egyptian art of birds and other animals is found in several media from wall paintings to miniature sculptures. It is at times delicate and often realistic. The pictures show careful observation, not only of avian anatomy but of habits such as preening, diving or calling. The creatures appear soulful and often, particularly in the case of pets, are shown with a great deal of affection. Nevertheless, many of them are in static poses. The closest equivalent in historically more recent times may be the art of heraldry, which also combines realistic representations with highly complex symbolism and associations.

Drawing after a detail of a wall painting in the tomb of Neferherenptah, Saqqara, Egypt, c. 2550 BCE. The bodies of the birds are nearly identical, but an impression of motion is conveyed by the positions of their wings.

People in Egyptian art are generally painted from multiple perspectives, a bit like those in Cubism. We see the legs in profile, while the torso and arms are viewed from the front. The head is also in profile, except for the eyes, which face forwards. Every part of the body, in other words, is shown from the angle that seems to convey the strongest impression or most information. The same is true of avians. Birds in flight are frequently included in tomb paintings and reliefs showing human activity in the marshland. The tails of birds are usually seen as though from below, while their heads are in profile. The exception are owls, which, because their eyes are so dramatic, are shown from the front. The wings of birds are usually in highly symmetrical – and, therefore, somewhat rigid – positions. Most often they are stretched out on both sides, as though seen from below, though at times both wings are pointed either upwards or downwards. At times the Egyptians would paint a bird in flight as seen from the side, with the wing closest to the viewer pointing down and the other outstretched to the side, a pose that was more dynamic yet still conventionalized. Even while flying, the birds seem suspended in space and time.

Introductory science texts we read as children in primary school will have illustrations on just about every page. It seems strange to us that Aristotle, who described the anatomy of animals with care, never, so far as we know, used pictures to illustrate his books of zoology and ornithology. Pliny the Elder does mention some botanical illustrators of the ancient world, though none of their pictures have survived.[7] The lack of motion must have made it relatively easy to show vegetation in an abstract, diagrammatic sort of way, but this would have been harder with terrestrial animals and harder still with birds. An illustrator of birds has to contend with their constant motion, a wide range of colours, subtle variations of shade, possible iridescence, intricate patterns of plumage and plasticity of form.

Perhaps the graphic arts in Greece may not have been fully up to the task. They did not compare in versatility with the paintings in Egypt, Etruria, Rome or Crete, and the graphic arts were far less cultivated in Greece than either literature or sculpture. Painting was mostly done on vases used to ship wine or olive oil. These works were splendid but limited and did not carry a great deal of status. They were heavily centred on human beings and anthropomorphic deities. The subjects were usually taken from mythology. Horses were also relatively common, and there were occasional roosters, owls and mythological creatures, but the variety of animals was relatively small. The colours were generally confined to black, white, red and brown.

There was also some wall painting, but very little of it has survived. In an account by Pliny, set around the end of the fourth century BCE in Athens, the artists Zeuxis and Parrhasius hold a contest. Zeuxis paints grapes so vividly that birds fly down and try to nibble at them. Parrhasius then paints a curtain so realistically that Zeuxis asks that it be drawn back. Finally, on realizing he has been fooled, Zeuxis concedes the prize to his rival, saying that he may have deceived the birds but Parrhasius fooled him.[8] The account is of doubtful accuracy, for birds do not try to nibble at paintings or photographs of food. They see colours that are inaccessible to human beings and, when it comes to *trompe l'oeil*, are sometimes harder to trick than people. In his emphasis on realism, Pliny may be projecting a Roman aesthetic into Greek culture of a few centuries earlier.

The Greeks may not have had the technical means that would enable artists to sharply differentiate between related species. A broader reason why pictures were not used to illustrate natural history is that Greek graphics were centred around narrative and symbolism. Greek painting existed to tell stories, not to convey other sorts of information. Even in the paintings of Zeuxis and Parrhasius, as reported by Pliny, realism was a way of generating narrative, not of conveying facts. Scientific illustrations are supposed to enlighten people, not to fool them. Roman mosaics such as those at Pompeii are also based on careful observation of animals, most of which can be identified by species, but their purpose was primarily decorative.

Even today, the graphic illustrations that accompany works of ornithology are not particularly realistic. The pictures are generally more abstract than lifelike, and excessive foreshortening or shading are regarded as distractions. Though enhancing scientific works with illustrations seems common sense to us now, it would take over a millennium before it became the norm. Zoological illustration involved reducing a dynamic, three-dimensional organism to a two-dimensional, motionless artefact. Though we now take that for granted, it was a complex process that could only be perfected over generations. It involved a great deal of abstraction, which in turn entailed the development of many conventions and barely conscious habits of thought.

Ornithological illustration differs from most art in that it is intended to depict a specific variety of bird, not an individual. It is a portrayal of a type. In the field, or in a photograph, the light may change the colour of plumage, but an ornithological plate has to make sure it is easily recognizable. Art in Western traditions generally prefers exceptional subjects or events, while zoological illustration is confined to typical ones. The artist must disregard anomalies such as birds with unusual plumage or behaviour for their species. The whole concept of zoological, or ornithological, illustration is based on an implicit theory of ideal forms.

Roman mosaic from the basilica in Aquileia, Italy, showing a rooster and tortoise warily eyeing one another, early 3rd century CE.

Aviaries, Bestiaries

In the Christian era direct imitation of nature was long inhibited by a fear of violating the biblical prohibition against 'graven images'. Especially in Byzantine civilization, many techniques were used to deliberately avoid an impression of realism in painting. Many icons employed reverse perspective, in which figures in the background appeared larger than those in the foreground. Several scenes of the same story were often combined in a single picture. Faces were without expression and postures were static.

Animals were stylized in much the same way. Artists may have felt particularly uneasy with respect to drawing birds, which so easily suggest divinity. Early medieval art did not show them often. When it did, their individuality was usually obscured by heavy use of symbolism and stylization. Nevertheless, Byzantine and Western medieval art was like photography in that it endeavoured to show scenes fixed in time. But by presenting events in the perspective of eternity, such art opened the way for zoological illustrations, which were also centred on description rather than narrative.

In much the same way that zoological illustrations would later enhance natural history books, icons and stained-glass windows illustrated the contents of the Bible and other religious works. The pictures did not so much tell the stories, something that was left to religious authorities. They simply highlighted key moments. They used the poses that would convey most information, the frontal view with human beings and the side view for birds, except for owls, and most animals. They also, like books of natural history, 'labelled' people and events, using familiar symbols. St John would have an eagle at his side, while St Roch would have a dog. One result was that people on entering a church might feel exalted above temporal concerns. It was a bit like contemplating the stars in the days before light pollution or viewing photographs of Earth that have been taken by spacecraft today.

Medieval bestiaries were usually accompanied by illustrations, even though the pictures did not always correspond closely to the texts. One early thirteenth-century English bestiary describes sirens as 'deadly creatures, which from the head down to the navel are like men, but from the lower part to their feet are birds'. The accompanying illustration, however, shows sirens as mermaids with fish tails rather than bird wings.[9] All of the illustrations are highly stylized, but many are zoologically fairly accurate.

Fanciful though they may seem to us, bestiaries developed the basic format used by popular books of natural history today. First of all, they did not simply cover a few charismatic species but a full range of animals, known

Owl mobbed by other birds, from an English bestiary, 1230–40.

through local experience, legend and rumour. They organized chapters according to species and then illustrated them with graphics. They also worked from many implicit assumptions, which we now take for granted but could not be assumed by writers of the ancient world. One is that animals could be divided into varieties, according to appearance as well as habits and behaviour. They reliably pass these characteristics down through their offspring, rather than having them be recreated by spontaneous generation or metamorphosis between species. Each animal or bird, in summary, has a predictable nature. The bestiaries regarded birds and animals as archetypal patterns, a bit like Platonic forms, which might also be found in human society. Every bird or animal embodies moral qualities, though some, such as the lion and griffin, can represent either God or the Devil.[10]

From the twelfth century to the fourteenth, bestiaries became increasingly naturalistic.[11] Much of the bestiary format was retained by Holy Roman

Emperor Frederick II of Sicily, whose *De arte venandi cum avibus* (The Art of Hunting with Birds), first set down in the mid-thirteenth century, was arguably not only the first scientific work of ornithology but, even more importantly, the first zoological treatise to supplement text with illustrations. The information about birds is gathered through close observation and experiments, some of which are remarkably modern. To test whether certain vultures find their food through sight or smell, Frederick had the eyes of the vultures sewn shut, while leaving their nostrils open. Since they were then unable to locate food, he concluded that they navigate by sight. He also denied food to vultures so that they would be especially hungry, and then threw live chickens to them, observing that the vultures would not eat living birds. Finally, he killed the chickens and found that the vultures ate them.[12]

The text describes in detail the behaviour, anatomy and uses of birds. As for the illustrations, they are similarly systematic. There are pictures comparing the beaks, necks, shoulders, heads and feet of various species of bird. Other illustrations show how birds protect their young and evade predators. Some of the illustrations reflect close observation, for example with respect to the patterns formed by geese in flight. Nevertheless, the pictures are rather stiff and artistically undistinguished.[13] They even lack the loving attention to detail found in much medieval marginalia, since their purpose is intellectual rather than aesthetic. In any case, the manual of Frederick II, while widely read, did little to inspire further scientific investigation into the natural world over the next few centuries.

Liminal Figures

The worldly concerns, paranoia, laughter, pettiness, anger, raucous humour and so on that had been banished from religious stories come out during the later Middle Ages, at least in Western Europe, in the monstrous creatures high above, on the decorative facades and in the dark corners of churches. Most especially, they appear in the margins of medieval manuscripts. There we find some of the most exuberantly imaginative events that humankind has ever conceived. A knight on horseback charges with his lance at a giant snail, and a monkey sits enthroned with a royal crown and robes. Heads without torsos run about with just a pair of legs. Roots of trees turn into figures of men and women. Mermaids, centaurs and other monsters are everywhere, caught up in events that seem too fantastic and complex for anyone to describe.

Margins of manuscripts became a free space in which artists could indulge in fantasy as well as meticulous observations of the natural world,

which elsewhere might have seemed idolatrous. They contain painstakingly executed miniatures of grasses, caterpillars, moths, butterflies, grasshoppers and other insects, with attention to biological detail that had not been shown previously, even by the ancient Egyptians.

The margins also included birds, especially songbirds and waterfowl. By far the most celebrated example is the Sherborne Missal, produced for the Benedictine abbey of Sherborne in Dorset, England, by the Dominican friar John Siferwas around the end of the fourteenth century. It is a sumptuous book of nearly seven hundred pages, containing texts for the celebration of Mass on every day of the liturgical year. Among the marginal decoration are 48 birds, which are not only carefully painted but, in most cases, labelled by species.[14] All of them are in profile, posed in a dignified and heraldic, though static, sort of way. This is one medieval book with very little whimsy in the marginalia.

Together with *De arte venandi cum avibus*, the Sherborne Missal marks the beginning of modern ornithological illustration. For illustrations to document the physical appearance of birds, it was at first necessary to cleanse them of narrative and symbolic significance. Accordingly, the birds that are most often featured in fables and allegories from Aesop to the bestiaries are absent in the Sherborne Missal. There are no eagles, owls, falcons, hawks or other raptors. Also absent are crows, ravens, jackdaws and other corvids, except for the jay. Even the dove, which has such a central role in Christianity, is not included. None of the birds is depicted engaged in any activity. None is juxtaposed with anything that might arouse curiosity or suggest a fable. Among the birds that are elsewhere most prominent in literature only a few, such as the peacock, swallow and goose, are included.

On the other hand you have many birds that, as folklorists have since amply documented, have been prominent in the folklore of country people. The wren and robin are paired in the same margin, as they were often associated in British and Irish folklore.[15] The wide range of perching birds includes the linnet, titmouse, bullfinch, chaffinch and goldfinch. There are also several water birds such as the herring gull, mallard, moorhen, heron and kingfisher.[16]

The pictures of birds alternate with those of saints and rulers. The text of the missal is organized by time, the largely circular time of the liturgical year. The birds and sages that accompany them belong not to time but to eternity. The vision, of course, is religious, but it has some affinity with science, which also endeavours to reveal an abiding order behind ephemeral events.

Sir Heinrich von Veldeke, from Manessischen Liederhandschrift *(c. 1304). Perhaps because the book containing this picture makes no claim to religious or scientific authority, the birds here seem more animated than those in bestiaries.*

Perhaps the culmination of medieval bird art came not in Europe but in the court of the Mughal emperor Jahangir in India. He was a great lover of the natural world and an enthusiastic patron of the arts who in 1612 began to import a large menagerie of exotic birds and other animals through the

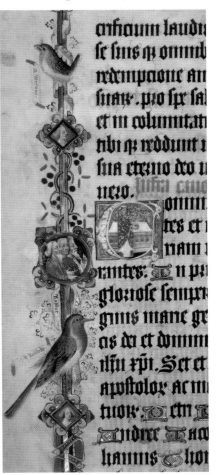

Portuguese colony of Goa. Fascinated by their unfamiliar features, Jahangir commissioned Ustad Mansur and other artists to document them.[17] By that time, Western artists had largely abandoned mineral pigments for organic ones. The artists of India still produced many of their coloured pigments by grinding up gold and various minerals.[18] That enabled them to create pictures that combined the jewel-like surfaces of medieval art with a scientific emphasis on anatomic accuracy. Because Islamic culture has a fairly strict taboo against religious imagery, the pictures of birds are not filled with symbolic and allegorical messages, and so we can enjoy the colours and shapes almost as abstract patterns.

Early Modern Illustration

Symbolism similar to that of the Middle Ages has been used in modern times, and even today, in scientific, particularly ornithological, illustration. When they have backgrounds at all, birds are often detached from them. Often the bird may be shown in colour, while the background is in black and white. While they now often suggest narrative, it is rarely dramatic or complex enough to distract the viewer from the pedagogical content. Creatures of a single species but radically different sizes are often present in the same frame in ways that cannot be attributed to perspective. Birds will be identified by means of symbols: for example, a tropical bird may be placed on top of a palm tree.

Of course, secular painting was a lot flashier, but even the early ornithological illustrations had a subtle appeal, at least for those who

Above: Eurasian wren and English robin from the margin of the Sherborne Missal, c. 1400.
Opposite: Ustad Mansur, painting of an Asian Barbet, Mughal, c. 1615.

contemplated them at length. Not unlike Byzantine icons, they gave us a sort of 'snapshot of eternity'. By removing their subjects a bit from the context of real life, the illustrators may have helped us to appreciate qualities of form and colour, a bit as one does with non-representational art. Ornithological illustration has always been heavily conventionalized, but people gradually developed more ways to be inventive within the elaborate structures, just as they did with those of the Italian sonnet. The backgrounds, while just as symbolic, became more detailed and interesting. The birds themselves, while still intended as types, were shown in an increasing variety of positions and activities.

In the middle of the fourteenth century Konrad von Megenberg wrote his *Buch der Natur* (The Book of Nature) in Augsburg, Germany, the first illustrated encyclopedia of zoology. The copious pictures of birds and other animals were much like those of the bestiaries and may seem naive to us today.

Many birds are simply in profile, but others are in motion, turning, strolling, raising their wings and even flying, sometimes with fluid postures that would seldom be matched over the next few centuries. The book became a medieval bestseller and established the genre of popular natural history.

Most people think of Hieronymus Bosch (1450–1516) as the most phantasmagoric of painters, but the right side of the central panel of his triptych *The Garden of Earthly Delights* shows that he was also adept at the emerging craft of ornithological illustration. In addition to his fantastic creatures, there are several birds that, apart from matters of scale, seem as realistic as any painted by his contemporaries. Many are identifiable, including a mallard, robin, goldfinch, kingfisher, spoonbill, ibis and hoopoe. Bosch also follows the convention of bird illustration by showing all but the short-eared owl, which faces forwards, in profile.[19] These birds are also far more static than his fantastic monsters, which suggests that even Bosch had not entirely figured out how to animate illustrative models.

The conventions of illustration became more established in examples that accompany the works of Early Modern scientists such as the Swiss Konrad

Details of the central panel of The Garden of Earthly Delights *by Hieronymus Bosch, 1503–15, oil on panel, showing oversized but otherwise naturalistic birds.*

Gessner and the Italian Ulisse Aldrovandi, making the pictures more zoologically accurate though a bit less lively. The pictures often have backgrounds, but they are as conventionalized as those in Byzantine icons. Birds, except for owls, are almost always shown in profile and very rarely in motion, much less in flight. A bird will often be perching on a branch of a dying tree with a hollow stump. Very often a single branch will bear a few leaves, while the rest is barren. Around might be a few blades of grass and small shrubs. For water birds, one might have, instead of a tree, a few reeds and the edge of a pond. For birds that frequent beaches, one might have sand and a little grass. The backgrounds, in other words, were mostly symbolic, helping to convey information and make the bird seem a bit more vivid without attracting much attention.

The traditions of symbolism were continually challenged during the Age of Exploration by the discovery of new species that were brought back from exotic parts of the world. These did not only offer new subjects for study and comparison. They also, since they were not surrounded by traditional

Above: Illustration to the diary of Joris Spilbergen showing the Straits of Magellan, c. 1617. The fanciful penguin in the foreground is as large as any of the people. The one seen in the distance resembles a traditional image of a phoenix. Explorers brought back fantastic accounts of birds and animals in distant lands that mixed observation, myth, hopes and fears.
Opposite: 'Birds of Africa', from Charles Middleton, Middleton's Complete System of Geography, *1778, engraving with watercolours. The picture resembles traditional depictions of Adam and Eve in Eden. The illustrators could not avoid using Western paradigms, though perhaps the picture also anticipates later discoveries that humankind had begun on the African continent.*

Engraved for Middleton's Complete System of Geography.

BIRDS of AFRICA

1. Nests of the Bird Kurbalot or Fisher, which are suspended over the Water.

2. The Egret......3 Bustard.

4. Numidian Damsel.

5. Royal Bird.

6. Monoceros of the River Gambia.

7. Guina Hen.

8. African Swan.

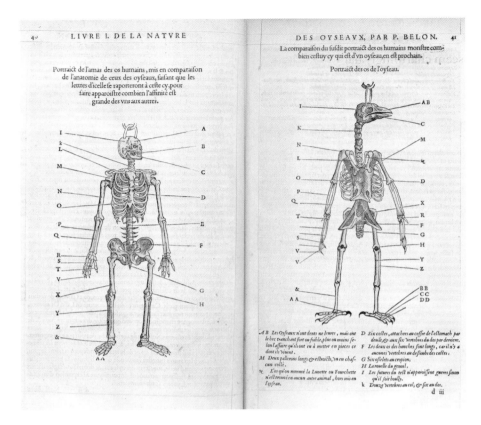

associations, demanded special inventiveness with respect to their presentation. Some were utterly strange, such as the kiwi of New Zealand, a nocturnal bird that navigates mostly by scent, poking for grubs into the moist soil with its long beak. Several newly discovered Asian, New Guinean and African birds so dazzled explorers with their brilliant plumage that it seemed they could only have come from a primeval paradise.

In 1555 Pierre Belon published *L'Histoire de la nature des oyseaux* (The Natural History of Birds), the first comprehensive work of ornithology in Europe since Frederick II of Sicily. A widely travelled scholar and diplomat, Belon adopted a relatively informal style, blending scientific knowledge of birds with folkways, anecdotes, traditions and customs that he had learned about in his journeys. He is best known for his work on comparative anatomy: the most famous illustration from his book is a comparison of an avian and

Above: Comparative skeletons of bird and man, illustration to Pierre Belon, L'Histoire de la nature des oyseaux *(1555).*
Opposite: Ceremonial hornbill mask from the Nuna people of Burkina Faso, painted wood, date unknown.

human skeleton placed side by side and standing upright. His illustrations were utilitarian and strictly subordinate to the text, though today they may seem charmingly naive.

Other Traditions

Due to the vastness of the subject of birds in art, I cannot possibly do justice to more than a very small number of cultures and their artists. The preceding discussion has been somewhat centred on, though not confined to, the highly amorphous tradition that we often call 'the West'. It has less about traditions that, for whatever reason, have been comparatively isolated for long periods, produced art that is not accessible to outsiders, or have constructed art of ephemeral materials. Most representations of birds in almost every culture have been in media that we think of as more utilitarian than artistic, such as textiles, utensils, toys and games. Highly stylized birds have been used to decorate pottery, not only in Egypt but in Mesoamerica, India and elsewhere.

Such items were most likely to be bought, sold and traded, so they often had a surreptitious influence in other lands, perhaps among people who had little idea of their origin. Motifs, styles, media and stories were constantly exchanged along the Silk Road and other trading routes. In most cases, these were not consciously copied so much as absorbed into other cultures, which makes their influence particularly difficult to trace. A good example is the bird art of sub-Saharan Africa. Perhaps even more than that of Egypt, Central and Southern African bird art generally has ceremonial significance, and much consists of costumes, headdresses and masks. The details of the associated rituals are often closely guarded by secret societies and passed on only to carefully chosen heirs. Much of it is also difficult to understand fully without having observed the animals in question, but on less esoteric levels it is not hard to appreciate at all. The art appeals to very basic responses such as humour, affection or fear.

This art was made mostly from organic materials and little has survived from before the last few centuries. Since African communities generally have a strong sense of tradition, we can guess that previous art of the region may not have been terribly different. Though chronologically comparatively recent, the art that has survived seems to record bonds with

253

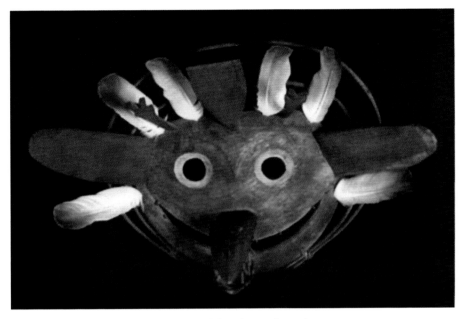

Yupik mask, Pacific Northwest, date unknown.

birds and animals that most people today, even in Africa, have lost though not quite forgotten. The art of Central Africa was in many ways the antithesis of ornithological illustration. It showed little interest in the sort of fine detail needed to distinguish among related species. Instead it would render the spirit of a bird or animal using bold, simple, dramatic designs, with an economy and an elemental power that has been seldom seen in Western art.

Perhaps the most frequently depicted bird in Central and Southern Africa is the hornbill, which many peoples of Central Africa believe to possess great wisdom and to be a bringer of rain. This refers to a family of birds with large beaks that curve downwards, large eyes and long tails, which eat mostly fruit and small animals. Its deep call and gait seem oddly human, and people imitate them on occasions such as initiations and funerals.[20] It is possible that there may be a folkloric relationship between the hornbill and many of the bird deities of Egypt, such as the ibis.

The bird paintings of Native Americans, particularly of the Northwest Coast, are surely among the most sophisticated pieces of art in the world. The raven, especially, in the mythologies of the Tlingit, Haida, Kwakiutl, Yupik and related tribes, is at once a sage, a trickster and a creator deity. To incorporate these and other identities into a single representation is no small task, but tradition has found ways to accomplish it. Images might tease the viewer by showing eyes of the bird on the patterns of wings or tail. The feathers might form complex designs from which shapes of other animals would emerge. But the playfulness did not become frivolity, for the works were full of celestial imagery, and they illustrated stories with cosmic themes such as the creation of the world. The Age of Exploration began a process of globalizing artistic styles, which would extend over many centuries.

Exotic Birds

Europeans in the Age of Exploration felt overwhelmed by the novelty and variety of the newly discovered regions, but this generally only led to greater determination to impose their own cultural order. In the late sixteenth century Bernardino de Sahagún, a Franciscan missionary, produced three volumes that became known as the *Florentine Codex*, an encyclopedic description of the cultures, customs and wildlife in New Spain, a vast area that included territories in North, Central and South America. A chapter was devoted to avifauna and contained systematic descriptions of 130 kinds of birds including their plumage, migratory patterns and relations with human beings.[21] The text was written in the Aztec language of Nahuatl using the Latin alphabet, accompanied by a rough Spanish translation, and the illustrations were by Indians who had been educated in Western traditions. They were almost as scientifically accurate as those of their leading European counterparts of the time, and they followed much the same conventions, though they reflected the styles of Aztec paintings in much the same way as Western zoological illustrations recalled Christian religious art.

There were several subsequent codices, including that of Francisco Hernández, published posthumously in the early seventeenth century, which describes nearly 230 varieties of birds.[22] Translating between the Aztec classification of birds and the European one was as much a matter of culture as language. This was made easier because the traditional symbolism of some birds was similar in both. Eagles in both Europe and Mesoamerica had strong martial associations. The turkey, which the Mesoamericans had domesticated and used as a sacrificial bird, was more or less the equivalent of the cockerel and hen in Europe. In both cultures, the owl was associated with death and its cries were interpreted as omens. Even the resplendent quetzal, with its bright colours and flowing tail, might be an equivalent of the peacock or the mythical phoenix.

To a degree, the two symbolic systems blended in a way that was not scientific but nevertheless, since it conveyed an impression of order, at times made the birds easier to study. Mesoamericans, however, saw the vulture as a

ic moteaiotia Atvneuepo
hie tlatoa, iuhquin aca
naçoa——

¶ Ateponaztli: yoan iba
iotl, yoan atotolin: vel
tliuac, tenvittic, temp
tic, coziaiactic. Inic mie
ateponaztli: inic tlatoa,
conaqueja mieten: iuhqui
teponaçoa iccaquizti. I
va. Atotolin: anoço Acolh
tlaquiani——

¶ Xomotl: omito in impa
¶ Acacalotl omito in impa
¶ Aztatl: omito in impa totm
¶ Acacuiialotl: anoço acue
lotl omito. Iniquem
icaxioa, inic ano: matla
bonvilo, xomecavilo, tlaço
lo.

¶ Injc vme parrapho
teth pa tlatoa inixq
tlein minichtin

¶ Michi: incaço tlein mie

¶ Parrapho segundo delos
peces

¶ Los peces desta tierra son se

sort of eagle, while the Europeans endowed it with macabre associations, so its classification in the codices is not always clear.[23] But perhaps the biggest difference between the illustrations to the *Florentine Codex* and pre-conquest Aztec art lies in the very concept of taxonomy. Identity was relatively fluid in Mesoamerican art, and it is not always easy to distinguish birds from men in costume or avian deities. In the codex, these distinctions are always sharp and unequivocal.

Although the illustrators of the *Florentine Codex* were adept at using Renaissance conventions such as shading and perspective, their world view was not that of either Christianity or Western science. Unlike Europeans, Mesoamericans did not regard separate beings as units of subjectivity. For

Opposite: Birds and fishes from the Florentine Codex, latter 16th century.
Above: Aztec warriors dressed as eagles and panthers from the Florentine Codex, *latter 16th century.*

them, subjectivity was universal, and individuality lay primarily in the physical form. The paintings were not representations of gods, human beings or animals so much as evocations of them.[24] In consequence, paintings of the Aztec deities were in subdued colours, since the artists did not wish to create powerful images to which they would not be able to accord proper honour and respect.[25] Birds such as the quetzal were a form often taken by the gods. This restriction was a sort of Aztec version of the taboo against 'graven images'. While Europeans of the time gloried in showing the brilliant colours of exotic birds, the colours in pictures of birds in the *Florentine Codex* are generally softened.

In the meantime, Europe was in turmoil caused by religious wars, absolutist rulers and peasant revolts. Europeans, like Native Americans, struggled with questions of faith, doubt, reason and imagination. Confronted with the utterly strange creatures in remote lands, the first impulse of explorers had often been to identify them with the figures of old mythologies, such as mermaids, satyrs and phoenixes. For both colonists and indigenous peoples, classification was a way of affirming order and quieting fears.

11 ART OR ILLUSTRATION?

The very idea of a bird is a symbol and a suggestion to the poet.
A bird seems to be at the top of the scale, so vehement and intense
is his life – large brained, large lunged, hot, ecstatic, his frame
charged with buoyancy and his heart with song.

John Burroughs[1]

The goldfinch has traditionally symbolized the Passion of Christ, in part because the red on its face suggests blood. A painting by Raphael of about 1505, known as *Madonna of the Goldfinch*, shows Mary looking on as the child John the Baptist holds out a goldfinch, while the infant Jesus reaches out to pet it. The expressions of all three figures are slightly melancholy, as though troubled by a premonition of their destiny.

Dutch art of the seventeenth century was largely secular though subtly pervaded by Christian imagery. There is an echo of that bird symbolism in *The Goldfinch*, painted by Carel Fabritius, a pupil of Rembrandt, in 1654. His teacher would strip away glamour not only from Dutch burghers but from mythological deities and even Old Testament prophets in order to reach the underlying character of his subjects. Fabritius did much the same with a bird in one of his last paintings.

The goldfinch perches on top of a feeding box to which it is attached by a delicate chain. It has probably been captured for its song. The body of the bird is in profile, as in most ornithological illustrations, but the head is turned halfway towards the viewer. The left eye, which reflects a gleam of light, seems to be looking directly outward at us, as the subjects of portraits often do, while the right eye is just barely visible. One must look very closely to see it, but there is also a faint point of reflected light in the right eye, so perhaps the goldfinch is also looking through a window at the field where it was captured.

The brilliant mask of red, which is the bird's most recognizable feature, is mixed with a dull grey, and the yellow bar on its wing is also softened. The bird may be starting to moult, but the condition could be aggravated by lack of sun or bathing water. The wall in the background is a mottled white, on which the goldfinch and the feeding box cast a shadow. The feeder is directly in the centre of the panel, but the composition is not balanced. In the upper half, the bird itself is far to the right. The faded paint on the wall on the left side is almost like an abstract composition, a sort of space for dreams.

Modern illustration was starting to diverge from art during the sixteenth and seventeenth centuries. Art was primarily about human beings. It focused

Eurasian goldfinch. The bird painted by Fabritius is drab compared with a goldfinch in the natural world.

especially on religious, mythological and historic subjects, but had also begun to embrace portraits. Illustration was devoted to everything else, from planets and minerals to mammals and birds. The goal of art was expression, while that of illustration was documentation.

About halfway between illustration and art were still-life paintings, which had become increasingly popular in the Netherlands and beyond. These canvases provided a place to display virtuosity in accurately rendering shades, textures and modulation of tone. When such paintings contained birds, these were usually dead. Life was represented in such paintings mostly by insects, snails or lizards. The flowers, butterflies and other organisms are all destined for death, but at different times, and the major theme of still-life paintings was transience. Human life expectancy was less than half of what it is today, and awareness of this permeated portraits as well.

The understated style of Fabritius suggests that, despite an unconventional subject, he aspired to produce serious art. By contrast, ornithological illustrations consistently depict the brilliance of avian plumage. But, in making a portrait of

Carel Fabritius, The Goldfinch, *1564, oil on canvas.*

the goldfinch, Fabritius was, from the viewpoint of his contemporaries, raising a bird to the level of humanity and still-life to that of portraiture.

Though far from ecstatic, the bird is imbued with a tragic nobility. All pictures of birds are ultimately also about human beings, simply because they are so intimately bound up with human aspirations and fears. Perhaps, in the picture by Fabritius, the goldfinch may represent the poet or artist who must rely on patrons to live.

Illustration

In 1676 Francis Willoughby and John Ray published *Ornithology*, by far the most encyclopedic work on birds to date. It endeavoured to include all known varieties throughout the world. Previous authors such as Gesner and Aldrovandi had each listed only about two hundred types of bird, yet Willoughby and Ray included five hundred. They classified birds not by habitat or diet but by anatomical features such as the form of their beaks or their feet. They also attempted to standardize terminology by not giving the names of birds in many languages. Perhaps most significantly, as Ray and Willoughby stated in their introduction, they focused purely on science and did not include 'hieroglyphics, emblems, morals, fables, presages, or aught pertaining to divinity, ethics, grammar, or any sort of humane learning'.[2] But the greater scientific aspiration made the subjects seem diminished, reducing scope for artistry in the illustrations. By eliminating story, the authors also largely did away with motion, and the birds in their illustrations were placed in stiff, symmetrical poses.

For artists such as Dürer or Leonardo, there had been little or no distinction between art and scientific illustration, just as there was no distinction between rendering the physical body and the spirit of a subject. By the time of Ray and Willoughby, the sciences and humanities, which had been previously grouped together under the broad heading of 'philosophy', were starting to fragment. As their book on ornithology shows, the separation opened new possibilities for each kind of discipline, but it also left both in ways diminished. For the next several centuries, both artists and illustrators would often try to bridge the divide by creating a work that might show both the physical body and the spirit of its subject.

Well into the Early Modern era illustrations were widely distrusted by scientists, who thought of them as idiosyncratic and subjective. Linnaeus did

Raphael Sanzio, Madonna of the Goldfinch, *1505, oil on wood.*

Phœnicopterus.   *Keratophiton &c.*

not use them in *Systema naturae* (System of Nature), which laid the foundations for modern taxonomy in the eighteenth century. Linnaeus saw natural history as a purely intellectual, even spiritual, pursuit. He wrote of images, 'I absolutely reject them, although I confess that they are more pleasing to children and ... they offer something to the illiterate ... But whoever derived a firm argument from a picture?'[3] Linnaeus was not very consistent on this point, however, since he did include many references to illustrations in other books, and without them many of the species he described would not have been identifiable.[4]

His *Systema naturae*, the first edition of which was published in 1735, arranged living things hierarchically in seven levels, from 'kingdom' to 'species', which corresponded to the seven days of creation in the Bible. It was the most elaborate expression of the Early Modern idea that uncovering the order of a purposefully created universe was a way to better comprehend the will of God. He probably saw himself as the biblical Adam, entrusted with the holy task of naming other creatures. Although he made careful observations, the sort of knowledge that he aspired to was ultimately not empirical. Linnaeus thought of species as ideal, unchanging types, ordained by the Deity. As a very religious man, Linnaeus probably felt some residual inhibition about violating the biblical prohibition against images. Over the following centuries many illustrators were inhibited by this suspicion of frivolity and tried to keep their pictures from overshadowing the accompanying texts. As a result, many zoological pictures were formal and very conventionalized.

At the opposite pole from Linnaeus with respect to illustration was his contemporary Mark Catesby, an Englishman who journeyed to the New World in order to record the fauna and flora and published his major work *The Natural History of Carolina, Florida, and the Bahama Islands* in instalments between 1729 and 1747. He decided the best way to document wildlife was not through writing but through pictures. Accordingly, though he had no background in art, he taught himself drawing and engraving, and used graphics to provide most of the information about natural history, while keeping his texts to a minimum. He ignored perspective, even disregarding the relative sizes of objects in his pictures. With their sharp lines and absence of depth, his hand-coloured etchings can be a bit like diagrams.[5] A flamingo would be striding in front of a coral, which looked rather like a barren tree.[6]

George Edwards learned engraving from Catesby. He also corresponded extensively with Linnaeus, and he combined the approaches of both in his *Natural History of Uncommon Birds*, published between 1741 and 1751. Edwards

Mark Catesby, Flamingo, *c. 1722, engraving with watercolours.*

used his descriptions to name and catalogue about 350 new birds.[7] His pictures were precisely accurate, although, while he was successful in rendering harmonies of line and colour, the life of the bird would at times seem to be lost in the mass of anatomical detail.

Zoological illustration became fully established by Georges-Louis Leclerc, Comte de Buffon, Linnaeus's great rival. His *Histoire naturelle* (Natural History), published in 36 volumes over the second half of the eighteenth century, together with its many revisions, translations, abridgements and adaptions for young people, became a perennial bestseller. All species were illustrated, the mammals and reptiles primarily by Jacques de Sève and the birds mostly by François-Nicolas Martinet. The illustrations to these books were mostly copper engravings, sometimes hand coloured, and they reveal a constant tension between traditional symbolism and scientific innovation.

At times the backgrounds in illustrations to Buffon's books are contrived to the point of being comic. Bats are generally shown amid the walls of ruined castles, like something out of a Gothic novel. Owls were often placed in the bell towers of ruined churches. Monkeys are often shown in Rococo boudoirs, sometimes dressed in human clothes and engaged in childish mischief. Many animals and birds are depicted amid the ruins of ancient temples, perhaps to dramatize their historic association with humankind. Sometimes they are standing on tombs, rather like mounted pieces in a museum.

With only occasional exceptions, the birds and beasts are in rather stiff poses, but a great deal of attention is paid to their textures and anatomic detail. Unlike their East Asian counterparts, Western painters and illustrators of birds would seldom draw birds outdoors. A few artists used captive birds in the zoo as their models. Most used models created through taxidermy, which was very popular in the late eighteenth and nineteenth centuries.

By the middle of the eighteenth century an elaborate set of conventions had been developed for ornithological illustration. Birds were usually placed upright on a single branch protruding from the stump of a dead tree, rather as they were in taxidermy cases. Great care might be taken to draw the avian anatomy correctly, but everything else might be absurdly out of proportion. In many cases a small bird would be larger than the tree that supported it. When there was a lack of space, illustrators would also at times place associated birds from different parts of the world on branches of a single tree, anticipating the 'tree of life' that would later become so important in evolutionary theory.

In 1804 Thomas Bewick published *The History of British Birds*, the first field guide to avian life. The book was easily affordable to people of the

George Edwards, Grackle, c. *1746, engraving with watercolours.*

middle class and compact enough to be easily taken along on a walk through
the countryside. Bewick revived the woodcut, a form of illustration that had
seldom been used since about the end of the Middle Ages. By using boxwood
and cutting against the grain, he adapted the form to modern printing, and his
woodcuts were at times able to produce over a million good impressions. He
did not have his illustrations coloured but emphasized textures instead. Like
his contemporaries, he generally depicted birds standing still, but he knew
how to suggest just enough motion to keep them from appearing rigid. While
other illustrators abstracted the birds from their environment, including only

267

Head of Turkey Buzzard.

Head of Black Vulture.

Drawn from Nature by A.Wilson.

Engraved by W.H.Lizars

1. Turkey Buzzard. 2. Black Vulture. 3. Raven.
75.

symbolic backgrounds or none at all, Bewick placed birds in detailed, rural settings. He paid careful attention to the surrounding vegetation, the water and the soil, often showing homes or church steeples in the background. The birds appealed to a nostalgia for country ways, which, as Britain industrialized, were beginning to vanish.

Other bird illustrators were admired and respected, but none has been loved as much as Bewick. In the opening scene of Charlotte Brontë's novel *Jane Eyre* (1847) the heroine is a neglected child of ten who seeks to relieve the monotony of her life by turning to the bookshelf and opening *The History of British Birds*. She finds adventure in the illustrations and accounts of waterfowl on the cliffs and islands of the North Sea. 'With Bewick on my knee,' she writes, 'I was then happy.'[8]

Near the end of the eighteenth century, Alexander Wilson, a weaver by trade, conceived the ambitious project of documenting all the birds of North America. He travelled around the United States for years in near-poverty, shooting, observing, painting and writing about birds, and then published his nine-volume *American Ornithology* in 1808–14. To economize on space, he would cram several different bird species, oddly oblivious to one another, into a single scene. Wilson, like Catesby before him, sacrificed artistic realism for the cause of science. Their pictures can appear naive, but they express wonder at the profusion of wildlife, still largely undocumented, in the New World.

The expansion of the British Empire had created a taste for grandeur and splendour to which John Gould appealed with huge, expensively produced folios of exotic birds, published in the middle decades of the nineteenth century. Starting with *A Century of Birds from the Himalaya Mountains* (1830–32), he went on to publish books of birds in Europe, parrots, birds of Australia, hummingbirds and others, all illustrated with hand-coloured lithographs. He picked many of the best illustrators of his time as collaborators, including Edward Lear, Joseph Wolf, and his own wife Elizabeth Gould. Like his predecessors, Gould portrayed not individual birds but generic types, but he realized that did not mean the figures needed to be static, as long as the activity they engaged in was representative. Furthermore, showing types did not mean simply showing a single bird at a time. Species might be better represented by two or more birds of the same kind in a single picture, though Gould's birds

Opposite: Alexander Wilson, illustration showing from left to right, a raven, turkey vulture and black vulture in America, early 19th century, engraving with watercolours.
Overleaf: Henry Richter and John Gould, Lyrebird, *1850–83, hand-coloured lithograph.*
Yellow-billed water hen, from William Jardine, The Naturalist's Library *(1830s), hand-coloured engraving.*

MENURA SUPERBA, *Shaw.*

are seldom engaged in any shared activity and often seem barely aware of one another.

Similar to Buffon in format and, to an extent, in popularity as well was *The Naturalist's Library*, a forty-volume series by Sir William Jardine published between 1833 and 1843. The illustrations by James Hope Stewart and others placed greater emphasis on colour than his predecessors. The backgrounds in Stewart's illustrations were less stereotyped than in Martinet's. Stewart would, however, make his subjects stand out by showing the bird in full colour and leaving the background in black and white, a technique adopted by many subsequent illustrators of the nineteenth century. Stewart and Jardine also showed their subjects in comparably active, dynamic poses.

The most popular illustrated book of birds in Britain during the second half of the nineteenth century was probably Francis Orpen Morris's *History of British Birds*, first published in six volumes from 1851 to 1857, illustrated in colour with woodblock prints by Alexander Lydon that were elegant and attractive yet almost entirely utilitarian. The birds were generic examples of the species, almost always in profile against very spare backgrounds.

The Science of Nonsense

In 1830, the same year as Gould's book on birds of the Himalayas, Edward Lear published the first volume of his *Illustrations of the Family of Psittacidae, or Parrots*, at the early age of nineteen. He drew directly from life, sketching parrots at the London Zoo, at a time when almost all other ornithological illustrators used stuffed animals as models. He taught himself lithography and was among the first zoological illustrators to exploit its possibilities. Though without formal training in either art or ornithology, he was able to catch the basic form of the birds, despite their being in constant motion, with a few fluid lines. Instead of always showing the birds in profile, like other illustrators of the time, he portrayed them from a wide range of different angles, on some occasions even from the back.[9] He was able to show the patterns on feathers and their subtle gradations of colour in the most meticulous detail. But what was most remarkable was his feeling for the emotional life of the birds, which he could portray without excessive humanization. He did this in part through their eyes, especially with parrots, but mostly through their postures. The initial books on parrots were enthusiastically received by experts but, since Lear

Edward Lear, 'Sulphur Crested Cockatoo', from a book of natural history (1889). This beautifully drawn bird has a slightly mischievous smile, which may anticipate the illustrated nonsense verse of Lear's later years.

lacked business sense, they were a commercial failure. Lear never completed his ambitious project of covering all the parrots of the world. Within a few years he switched to landscape painting and then to nonsense verse, including the limericks for which he is perhaps best known today.

What is especially remarkable is that he accomplished so much not only without formal training or extensive funds but despite being often sick, epileptic, socially awkward, subject to frequent depressions and morbidly shy. He may also have been on the autism spectrum. Temple Grandin, who is herself autistic and has done seminal work with farm animals, has presented a theory that autistic people have a special affinity with animals because both perceive the world in an analogous way. Animals and autistic people, according to her, do not filter out perceptions and see the world as 'a swirling mass of tiny details'.[10] She also believes that autistic people, like animals, lack ambivalent feelings, adding that 'one thing that I appreciate about being autistic is that I don't have to deal with the emotional craziness my students do.'[11]

I am unable to evaluate to what extent Grandin's theory is correct. It seems to me that at least a few animals focus their attention very intensely, for example a heron scanning a pond for fish. Nevertheless, Grandin's description of autism seems to apply well in the case of Lear. It would help to explain his extraordinary eye for detail, as well as his empathetic connection with birds.

Illustrated limerick by Edward Lear, 1887.

There was a Young Lady whose bonnet came untied when the birds sate upon it;
But she said, " I don't care ! all the birds in the air
Are welcome to sit on my bonnet ! "

It would also explain his alienation from, and difficulty negotiating, human society,[12] which haunted him for his entire life.

The illustrations that Lear made to accompany his nonsense verse often show birds and human-avian composites. His favourite was the owl, and Lear often drew himself as one. He had little interest in small, elegant avians such as warblers and hummingbirds; he preferred large, flamboyant ones such as storks. As his eyesight failed and his waistline expanded, Lear feared he was becoming bizarre and he wanted his birds to be monstrous as well. The graphics that accompany his nonsense verse show an absurd, Alice-in-Wonderland sort of world, in which there is no clear distinction between human beings and animals. There are only individuals, which are all totally idiosyncratic. His birds are grotesque humans, his humans, grotesque birds.

Illustrators, unlike artists, are expected to subordinate their personalities to the subject at hand. Lear seemed to do this in his early illustrations of parrots and other birds, but his eccentricity became increasingly apparent over the decades. If, after looking at the pictures that accompanied his nonsense verse, we return to the parrots, we realize that they are more complex, more innovative and more personal than perhaps they initially seemed.

The American Woodsman

John James Audubon, known in Europe as 'The American Woodsman', managed to bridge, at least temporarily, the gap between illustration and fine art. His *Birds of America*, first published from 1827 through to 1838, was an undertaking that exceeded even the ornithology books of John Gould in ambition and scope. It contained 435 hand-coloured aquatints of American birds, all of them life-size, printed by London publisher John Havell. Though a huge scientific and artistic success, the high printing costs kept it from being a financial one. In the next decade, Audubon followed with a smaller edition consisting of hand-coloured lithographs, and then went on to a similarly elaborate book on North American mammals, which was incomplete at his death in 1851 and finished by his son, John Woodhouse Audubon.

Audubon is the only zoological illustrator in the West whose work is regularly featured in histories of art. He was born on the Caribbean colony of Sainte-Domingue (now Haiti), the illegitimate son of a wealthy French sea captain. At the age of six he joined his father back in France, and at eighteen he emigrated to the United States, at least in part to avoid conscription into Napoleon's army. He settled for a while at his father's farm in Pennsylvania. Much of his subsequent life was spent on the frontier, far from the cultural and economic centres of Europe or the United States, where he developed his knowledge and skills not through formal study but by obsessive shooting and drawing of birds. The fascination in which he was held by his contemporaries, and by us as well, is increased by the many apparent contradictions of his personality. He cultivated his image as a backwoodsman, yet also claimed membership in the French aristocracy, even encouraging rumours that he was the lost dauphin, son of Louis xvi and Marie Antoinette.

Audubon not only painted but wrote romantically of birds, often according them human emotions. Nevertheless, he shot birds on a prodigious scale, killing over one hundred in a day. This was not very different from the practice of other ornithologists and bird artists of his time. John Gould was called by his wife, Elizabeth, 'a great enemy of the feathered tribe, having shot a great many beautiful birds and robbed others of the nests and eggs'.[13] But, unlike Gould and almost all of his contemporaries, Audubon was very open about this contradiction, both with himself and his public. He would sometimes attempt to justify this on the basis or devotion to art or to science, and he would also ask his reader's forgiveness. Christopher Irmscher writes, 'a strange mixture of release and remorse . . . makes Audubon, as a character in his own text, almost as memorable as the birds he describes.'[14]

But perhaps the greatest paradox of all about Audubon is that he managed to depict birds that seemed so dynamic and spontaneous by developing new techniques that were, in many respects, very mechanical. He would first shoot a bird, and then, while the body was still fresh, fasten it to a grid of parallel lines using wires. He would have an identical grid on his canvas. This enabled him to depict the proportions of a bird very exactly, as well as to note how it moved. The new technique enabled Audubon to clearly show birds from unusual angles that revealed normally concealed patterns in their plumage and other features. This sometimes led him to place birds in improbable or contorted positions, but it empowered him to show a wider range of avian activity than any previous artist. The combination of romantic vision and mechanistic technique make Audubon, in many ways, a quintessential figure of the Modern era.

He also found new ways in which species could be represented. Instead of a few rather disconnected individuals in a landscape, he would show dramatic scenes, in some of which his subjects might be either in conflict with one another or working cooperatively. They might be blue jays eating another bird's eggs, barn owls exchanging glances as they prepare to take flight, mockingbirds protecting their nest from a snake, parakeets flirting with one another and so on.

John James Audubon, Northern Mockingbird, *1827–38, aquatint.*

Mocking Bird TURDUS POLYGLOTTUS, Linn. *Male & Female. & Florida Jasmine Gelseminum nitidum.*

Most animal pictures derive much of their fascination from the tension between the human and bestial aspects of their subjects, in other words between our identification with them and their alterity. *The Goldfinch* by Fabritius, discussed above, is a good example. This is certainly also true of Audubon's birds, which seem at once almost human in their activities and their passions yet, at the same time, utterly unknowable.

A good example is Audubon's illustration of a rattlesnake attacking a mockingbird's nest. The reptile has climbed a tree. Its mouth is wide open in a very threatening way, but it is not focused on the egg but on one of four birds that are mobbing it. That bird is rearing backwards to avoid the strike, but it does not seem greatly frightened and its beak is almost ready to retaliate. Another mockingbird has its opened beak directly behind the rattlesnake's head. That mockingbird's eye, which is close to the exact centre of the print, looks directly out at us and appears remarkably human. So, for that matter, does the eye of the rattlesnake. Above to the left, a third mockingbird has its beak wide open and seems to be scolding the rattlesnake, while a fourth in the upper left also appears poised to attack.[15]

Naturalists have questioned whether the drama played out here could actually happen, and it would be unusual at best. But, although Audubon painted indoors, he spent more time in the field than just about any of his contemporaries among artists, so it is possible that he might have witnessed behaviours that others were not aware of. It was especially easy to empathize with the mockingbirds because the crisis they faced was a familiar one to people of the time. It was not terribly unusual, particularly in the American Southwest, for people to find their homes, or at least their gardens, invaded by rattlesnakes, something that still happens occasionally today. The four mockingbirds, caught between fear and fight, represent different human responses to such a crisis. Beyond that, the drama might represent just about any catastrophe of near apocalyptic proportions, from an epidemic to environmental collapse.

Audubon did much to loosen the conventions of bird illustration, but his legacy was otherwise almost impossible to build on. When Audubon began his *Birds of America*, it was still easy to imagine that the bounty of nature in the New World was limitless, and so it was permissible to shoot birds on a prodigious scale. Audubon had inherited this myth of the New Eden, which is why few of his pictures have signs of human habitation even in the backgrounds. As the end of the nineteenth century approached, the frontier was closing and the limits of exploitation were more apparent as many birds became rare. It was no longer permitted, or perhaps even possible, to kill birds in the numbers that Audubon had needed in order to paint them using his grid. No subsequent artist adopted his technique, and Audubon himself became concerned about wildlife preservation.

Modernism

By the late nineteenth and early twentieth centuries, the depiction of birds in the fine arts was moving further away than ever before from that in illustration. Artists questioned the very nature of representation intensely, and this ushered in a period of bold experimentation that went beyond any before or since. In some ways, birds were becoming more important, but major painters showed little or no interest in describing them scientifically or classifying them. Artists such as Odilon Redon, Henri Matisse, Georges Braque, Pablo Picasso and Max Ernst painted birds that were at most identifiable by genus and almost never by species. Others such as Constantin Brancusi depicted birds that were stylized beyond any prospect of identification. They were interested in birds

Johnny Kit Elswa (Haida culture), Raven and Whale, *1881, pencil drawing. Haida ceremonial tattoo. Finding all of the faces in the image can be a sort of divine game.*

primarily as symbols of transcendence and saw Linnaean classification as an obstacle to creativity.

In their effort to move away from academic styles, European artists of the late nineteenth and early twentieth centuries drew inspiration from previously neglected sources. Paul Gauguin was influenced by Tahitian art. Brancusi adapted techniques of peasant artists that he had observed during his childhood in Romania. Picasso took inspiration from African art, while Surrealists such as Ernst, André Breton and Joan Miró looked to that of Native Americans.[16] The Modernists were particularly interested in masks, which make up an important part of both Native American and African art. Worn to communicate with the spirit world, these masks

blended human features with those of birds, terrestrial animals, creatures of the sea and deities. They were originally used in a variety of ceremonial purposes connected with initiation, divination, healing and hunting. In general, Modernists had, and aspired to, no more than a very superficial understanding of the rituals, but they were fascinated by their rejection of fixed identities.

There was certainly a good deal of irony about the Modernist borrowing of indigenous techniques and motifs, since the traditional peoples were struggling to maintain their heritage in the face of massive pressure from colonial powers. The European artists of the time sought precisely the opposite: liberation from tradition. The Modernists shared the Victorian idea of indigenous cultures as 'savage', but they saw that as a badge of honour. Both Europeans and native artists nevertheless struggled with feelings of continuous disorientation. In an era of great anxiety, birds gained additional importance in art as highly ambiguous symbols of freedom from pressures, terrors and demands.

Few artists expressed this distress as obsessively as Max Ernst, whose birds are perversely human. By his own account, his fascination with birds

*Photograph by Edward Curtis of a Kwakiutl dancer
wearing a ceremonial raven mask, 1914.
Opposite: Max Ernst, collage from* Une Semaine de bonté, *1934.*

began in childhood, when his pet cockatoo died and, at the same time, a sister of his was born. In the 1920 Ernst created a monstrous alter ego called 'Loplop, superior of birds', which serves as his symbol and at times his spokesman.[17] His birds are rarely depicted in flight. Consigned to the ground, they retain some of their proverbial freedom, but it takes the form of a life outside of social norms. Often, they are people with the heads of birds, a sort of 'mask' that frees them to act out human fantasies of violence and bizarre sexuality. The avian identity signals the alienation of the artist, which is not terribly different from that of a criminal or other outsider. In summary, for Ernst the definition of 'human being' might be 'a bird deprived of flight'.

By contrast, Ernst's fellow surrealist René Magritte almost always painted birds in flight. While Ernst filled his canvases with extreme melodrama,

René Magritte, The Large Family, *1963, oil on canvas.*

Tony Angell, Pinion Jays, *1975, scratchboard. Bird art has emerged in the latter 20th century as a fairly distinct genre which combines traditions of ornithological illustration and fine art. While there is a lot of precise detail, the birds are more individualized than those you would be likely to find in a popular guide or a scientific work.*

Magritte dispensed with every trace of it. His contemporaries had little but contempt for the blandness they found in popular culture. Perhaps anticipating postmodernism, Magritte embraced blandness, yet looked beyond it to a reality that was utterly strange. For most artists, a huge pigeon filling the sky would be a fairly standard depiction of the Holy Spirit. Magritte would draw such a bird in outline. Within the avian silhouette was an azure surface with tranquil clouds, while darkness loomed outside. By rearranging commonplace motifs in an unfamiliar way, Magritte would make them appear bizarre, at times even threatening. For both Ernst and Magritte, birds in flight were symbols of transcendence. For Ernst this was something missing from contemporary life, while Magritte found it just below the surface in everyday routines.

For the most part, though, avian depiction is, as it has always been, on the boundaries of what we call the 'art world'. It has relatively few celebrity artists and does not command huge sums of money. Bird artists draw on techniques developed by movements such as Impressionism, Fauvism, Abstract Expressionism and postmodernism, but they do not belong to artistic movements. They have little use for the highly abstract, socio-philosophical explanations known as 'artspeak'. Bird artists have their own networks, and perhaps the most important centre for these may be the Woodson Art Museum in Wausau, Wisconsin, which has sponsored an annual exhibition and convention on 'birds in art' since 1976.

Because art focused on human beings has been more extensive, it must constantly contend with the prospect of exhausting the possibilities, which creates a demand for newness. Most art now seems to require a perpetual infusion of new techniques, media and theories. Bird art is never haunted by the prospect of obsolescence, so it can appear relatively conservative. Simply by looking at a piece of bird art, it is often difficult or impossible to tell what period or even what century it was made in.

Birds in Film

Even with the refinements of photography in the twentieth century, illustrations have usually been preferred for field guides to wildlife, since they could provide more generic and easily recognizable images. Such ideal types have always been confined to a Linnaean sort of world, where they effectively exist outside of time. Still photography profoundly impacted our view of birds by individualizing them, while film shifts the emphasis from individuals to their environment.

The development of photographic media coincides historically with an acceleration of extinctions and the disappearance of many animals from our daily lives. This has led to a profusion of animals in culture to fill the void, from monsters of science fiction to nature documentaries.[18] But birds remain, as they have usually been, thought of as belonging to a realm largely separate from the human. Several movies have been made about dogs such as Lassie, but there have been very few films that focused primarily on birds.

The few that have featured birds have found ways to exploit this sense of birds belonging to a domain apart. An example is Alfred Hitchcock's *The Birds*, released in 1963, in which the birds in a seaside community in California suddenly begin attacking human beings. A common practice of horror movies is to shock the audience by making icons of innocence such as adorable children into monsters. In this instance, it is done with birds, which often symbolize the purity of nature. A movie poster for the film quotes Hitchcock as calling it 'the most terrifying picture I ever made'.

A more recent example, which shows the increasing technical sophistication of the medium, is *Legend of the Guardians: The Owls of Ga'Hoole* (dir. Zack Snyder), released by Warner Brothers in 2010, which is made entirely with computer-generated imagery. It is a mostly conventional 'sword and sorcery' tale in which all of the characters are owls of various species rather than human beings. The movie contains no references whatsoever to people or to human civilization, yet it depicts birds with considerable anatomic accuracy, according to a purely human fantasy.

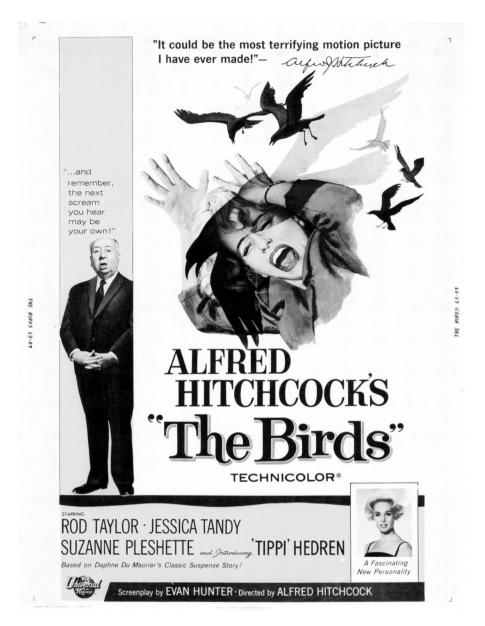

Poster for Hitchcock's The Birds, *1963.*

One film that blends together art and illustration almost perfectly is *Le peuple migrateur* (dir. Jacques Perrin), released in 2001 by the French production company BAC Films and known in the English-speaking world as *Winged Migration*. The film shows, with the barest minimum of commentary, birds of many species undertaking migrations to the southern hemisphere and back again, as they contend with hazards such as storms, hunters, raptors and exhaustion. In one particularly horrifying scene a bird with an injured wing is attacked by crabs on a beach. The film ends in a muted triumph as the birds return home and begin to build or reclaim their nests. The story is told with almost no anthropomorphism or sentimentality, with the camera as a sort of omniscient narrator.

But this seemingly most naturalistic of tales conceals the constant presence of human beings with all their artifice and cunning. About five hundred people worked on the film, divided into six teams, and over a period of more than four years. They made about three hundred trips, repeatedly returning to every continent. The movie consists of footage shot from gliders, air balloons, drones, boats and motorcycles, all meticulously edited and stitched together. At some points the sound of human panting is subtly superimposed on the sound of beating wings. Birds themselves do not pant, but that technique contributes to the illusion that we are watching from the perspective of a bird. Many scenes were filmed with wild birds, but others were shot with birds that had been carefully trained for the purpose from birth.[19]

By comparison with the graphic arts, film gives a creator vastly more control over time and space. The artist can decide the pace of time by showing a scene in either slow or accelerated motion. S/he can flash back or jump ahead to the future. It is possible, and even routine, to zoom in or out from a scene. Movies and related media need not represent time as linear or space as continuous. In this respect, they take us back to a pre-modern, perhaps even the pre-Christian, world. These media give us an organic view of time and space, which may ultimately help us to understand how birds see the world.

12 BIRDS, FLOWERS AND TIME

> Loveliest of trees, the cherry now
> Is hung with bloom along the bough,
> And stands about the woodland ride
> Wearing white for Eastertide.
> **A. E. Housman, 'A Shropshire Lad'**

Huizong (1082–1135) had the misfortune to be the emperor of China, but he was also a painter, poet, scholar and musician. In his painting *Plum Blossom and Mountain Birds*, a plum tree stands on the right, its trunk rising in an 's' curve towards the sky. Some of its buds are just starting to blossom, so we know that the season is early spring. A thick branch extends leftwards, and on it are perched a mated pair of light-vented bulbuls. They are intently gazing to the left, and the viewer wonders what they see. Perhaps they are watching for hawks. A bit further to the left, the branch divides in two. The twig pointing upwards is bursting into blossom, while the one curving towards the ground is not. Animals in the wild face constant threats from predators or lack of food, and their lives are always precarious. Perhaps the two branches in front of them represent the prospects of life and death.

But the curve of the downward-pointing branch points to a poem by Huizong, and the tail of the larger bulbul is pointing to it as well. It tells how the two bulbuls rest comfortably amid the scent of plum blossoms, and then concludes:

> This painting is the promise
> Of hoary age spent together.[1]

The poems that accompany Asian paintings do not always illustrate them in a straightforward way, and this one may contain a hint of irony. Will the promise be kept? Are the birds entirely at ease? In any case, the painting and poem are a complicated meditation on life and death.

As an emperor, Huizong would have thought more than most people in terms of historical time. A Daoist, he would have taken a sceptical view of the trappings of wealth and power. Not being a scholar of Chinese culture, much less an emperor, I am just guessing, but he may have been exasperated with a life at court surrounded by counsellors, eunuchs, flatterers and concubines. It may add a bit of extra pathos to know that Huizong himself came to a tragic end: he was captured in an invasion by the Jin people and spent the last years of

山禽矜逞態

梅粉弄輕柔

已有丹青約

千秋指白頭

宣和殿御製并書

his life in captivity. But the Jin founded what became known as the Northern Song dynasty, which continued Huizong's artistic legacy. Looking at *Plum Blossom and Mountain Birds*, one wonders if the artist had some premonition of what was to come.

Bird and Flower Pictures in Asia

Asian bird and flower paintings are meditations on time, not in terms of units measured by a clock but as experienced in days, seasons and years. Typically, each picture will feature one species of bird and flower, each represented by one or more individuals. Both flowers and many birds are symbols of transience but in contrasting ways. Both have short lifespans compared to human beings, but flowers last only for a season while birds live for years. Understood in a broader and more usual sense, the genre of 'bird and flower paintings' consists of closely observed vignettes of the natural world.

The lives of birds are governed by seasonal cycles. For many birds there is annual migration and return, as well as flocking, nest building, fledging and moulting. But none of these cycles is entirely regular, or completely synchronized with those of vegetation, and subtle variations are shown in pictures. If a blossom is opening early, or birds are gathering late in the season, their juxtaposition also tells us something about avian, and even human, experience. If flowers are just opening or starting to fade, that may be a reference to the stages of human life.

Vegetation was imbued not only with symbolism but with personality. The orchid, plum blossom, chrysanthemum and bamboo were called the 'four gentlemen' of Asian painting. Bamboo was strong but unassuming and divided into segments. Chrysanthemums were optimistic, since they bloomed late in the year as other flowers wilted. The resilient plum blossom not only flowers early but survives most of the year and is even found in snow. The orchid is delicate and aloof, and it prefers secluded spots.[2] Cherry blossoms, which bloom for only a short time in spring, are beloved symbols of transient beauty, especially in Japan. So are morning glories, which open at dawn and close as night comes on, like a door to an illicit love. The peony also blossoms early, and its varied, curvilinear patterns also make it a symbol of feminine refinement.

The symbolism of birds was similarly varied and subtle. As in the West, the return of swallows from their migrations makes them a harbinger of spring.

Huizong, Plum Blossom and Mountain Birds, *early 12th century, ink and colour on silk.*

Mandarin ducks are symbols of faithful, married love. So are cranes, which additionally symbolize longevity. Falcons, especially in Japan, are, because of their dramatic ascent to the sky, associated with both the rising sun and the new year. Quails are known for fighting but also for forming stable, peaceful couples. Magpies are bringers of joy, which form a bridge every year that unites the Herdsman and Weaving Maiden, lovers that, according to Asian legend, were separated in opposite parts of the sky. The kingfisher is beloved for its bright iridescent plumage and associated with the more flamboyant forms of feminine beauty. The peacock represents the splendour of autumn, when the leaves change colour. Sparrows stand out for their constant chirping, rapid motion and gaiety. Pheasants represent royal magnificence and sophistication. But this sort of symbolism is always contextual. One cannot learn what a given bird or blossom represents in a picture simply by looking it up in an inventory, only by reflecting on the specific environment in which an artist has depicted it. Birds are, like human beings, fully individual. Certain birds and plants are regularly paired together, such as the kingfisher and iris, peacock and peony or crane and pine. By varying the conventions even slightly, an artist would subtly change the meaning of a picture.

The distinction between high art and mere technical facility is in many ways the same in East Asia and the West. To be considered 'art' requires a special seriousness of purpose that goes beyond decoration or utility.[3] East Asian culture grounds this exalted concept of art in Buddhism and Daoism, while the West bases it mostly on Neoplatonism. All three philosophies hold that everyday appearances are ultimately an illusion, and they share this with contemporary science.

In Western tradition, the status of serious art was traditionally granted primarily to depictions of historical, mythological and religious subjects. Since about the sixteenth century it has partially been extended to portraits, genre scenes, landscapes and still-lifes. In East Asian art, landscapes and animals have always been among the preferred subjects, and major historical events such as battles have not. But in both traditions high art is expected to penetrate beyond the subject, narrowly conceived, to convey insight into an eternal order. In the West that has, since the Renaissance, generally meant an individual vision. Accordingly, tradition has emphasized personal idiosyncrasy and technical innovation. In Asia, by contrast, people have tended to see individual identity as an obstacle to transcendence. In East Asian graphic arts birds have long been among the most elevated themes. In early Western painting, birds, particularly when without any obvious religious or societal symbolism, have generally not counted as a thoroughly worthy artistic subject.

A Chinese treatise from the late seventeenth century entitled *The Dao of Painting* gave directions for painting birds in many poses, some quirky or unconventional, such as hanging upside down, fighting on the wing and bathing.[4] The Chinese depiction of avian motion in paintings can seem so fluid and effortless as to appear almost magical, but it was a result of centuries of study and experimentation. Already in the first centuries of the common era, treatises were being written about how to paint birds and other creatures. A master painter had to internalize rules so well that they became largely unconscious.

The purpose of Chinese painting was always to convey vitality and so, unlike in the West, dead or captive birds were not used as models. Nevertheless, a good deal of attention was paid to details of the plumage and anatomy of individual species. Huang Quan (*c.* 903–965 CE) was a court artist in Szechuan, a cosmopolitan centre where he was able to obtain access to unusual birds and plants. His painting *Rare Birds from Life* depicts ten birds, two turtles and twelve insects in ink with colours on silk. Almost none of the creatures is interacting with one another, and there is no background. The purpose here seems to be primarily documentation of their appearance. In fact, the birds and other animals, taken in isolation, could almost have been illustrations in a Western book of popular ornithology or zoology from the eighteenth or nineteenth century. As in early European ornithological illustrations, almost all the birds are shown in profile. Only one bird, in the upper left, is flying. Its wings are stretched out symmetrically and a bit stiffly.

Huang Quan, Rare Birds from Life, *c. 960, ink and colours on silk.*

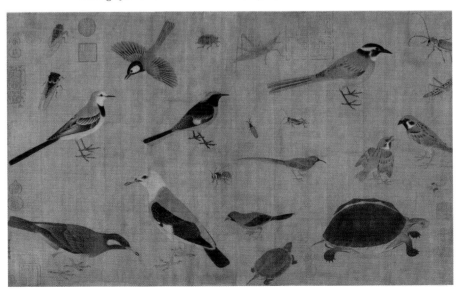

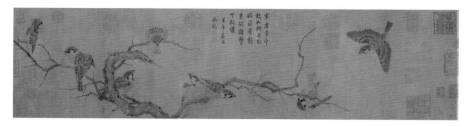

Cui Bai, Sparrows in Winter, c. *1070, ink on silk.*

The brushwork is delicate and the colours subtle, but the birds convey very little sense of motion. There is only one exception. The smaller sparrow in the centre left is not in a symmetrical pose. Its wings are partly raised, one a bit higher than the other, as if about to embark on flight. It has its beak open and seems to be chirping at the larger sparrow beside it. This is the only hint of a story in the painting. My impression is that the little sparrow could be a fledgling, about to take flight for the first time and looking to a parent for guidance.

Asian painters have always specialized, concentrating on specific subjects such as particular species of birds, which they observed with a patience that very few people could summon today. In *Sparrows in Winter* by Cui Bai (*c.* 1040–1080) from 1070 CE, nine sparrows are shown playing on a branch and in the air, each one showing a different side to the viewer. One is upside down, while another has its back turned. Yet another has its head facing directly outward, but the face is not turned towards the viewer but downwards, as though to remind us of the ultimate unimportance of humankind. The birds are calling to one another and not to us. They encounter the onset of winter with a gaiety that, to me at least, brings to mind paintings of Daoist immortals.

The artist Bian Shoumin (1683–1752) specialized in geese and lived beside a lake simply to observe them on their migration routes. His ink painting on paper entitled *One Hundred Geese*, from the early eighteenth century, shows scores of birds, each one highly individualized, interacting with one another and with their environments. Some are on land, engaged in a vast range of activities such as preening, foraging, resting and minding goslings. Several birds are also starting their ascent into the air, landing or in flight. Others still are diving into a lake. No two birds have quite the same posture, and their motions are fluid.[5] The depiction of the birds is not especially anthropomorphic, but the panorama of the activities suggests that, taken together, they might represent humankind.

Bian Shoumin, One Hundred Geese, *late 17th to early 18th century, ink on paper.*

It also shows an impulse towards documentation. Confucian scholars are renowned for their love of order, which entailed making innumerable lists of everything from virtues to energies. Birds and other animals were classified in detail, but the basis of classification was less their biological characteristics than their relationship to human beings. This might be based on practicality, for example classifying horses according to their usefulness in war. It might also be according to their roles in legend or their significance as omens.[6] Classifying was a means of placing things within an intricate matrix of analogies, parallels, signatures and correspondences that constituted the cosmic order.

Many Asian artists from the seventeenth century on were influenced by Western zoological illustration, but their central purpose was still not to document the physical appearance of birds scientifically. They endeavoured to suggest a spiritual reality beyond the corporeal one, while also showing the evanescent beauty of changing colours and forms. The way that figures, a bit like those in cave paintings, are often detached from their backgrounds and surrounded by much empty space gives them an otherworldly aspect.[7] The shapes and colours interact in ways that are, to some extent, comparable to those of Western abstract art. The East Asian depiction of birds is, unlike

House sparrows fighting in the park. Smaller birds often move so quickly and unpredictably that the changes are hard for human beings to register.

Kitagawa Utamaro, Abiding and Fickle Love, *1790, woodblock print.*

the Egyptian, not analytic, in that various parts of the avian anatomy do not appear to be considered separately. A bird does not, in other words, appear as an anagram of parts such as the head, wings, torso and beak, each of which has been studied in isolation. Rather, a bird is drawn holistically as a single organism.

The postures of the birds in some East Asian paintings and prints are, however, so varied, and the foreshortening is so skilful that it seems hard to believe the pictures were made before the development of snapshot photography. One reason artists could capture movement so well is that their tradition of brushwork, which emphasized practised but rapid strokes, was suited to capturing rapid and varied motion, such as that of birds changing direction in flight. East Asian artists were taught to trust their intuition, which enabled them to capture impressions that were fleeting. The outlines of birds in rapid motion may not register consciously, but the painters let their unconscious minds take over.[8]

Many conventions of Chinese bird and flower painting were taken over by the makers of Japanese prints, particularly by masters of ukiyo-e or 'floating world' style in the late eighteenth and nineteenth centuries. About 1791 Kitagawa Utamaro (1754–1806) published a series of bird prints in the Chinese style to illustrate short poems. If the Chinese bird pictures were often subtly anthropomorphic, those of Utamaro were more overtly so, to a point where the birds sometimes seem like stand-ins for human beings. After completing the bird prints he switched to pictures of courtesans, for which he is most famous today, and it is interesting to consider parallels between the two. Both the birds and women are generally depicted alone or in small groups, and they are at times thoughtful yet relatively carefree. Their respective feathers and kimonos are graceful and colourful. Most significantly, both exist on the fringes of male human society, close enough to reflect it yet distant enough to preserve some mystery.

In the early to middle nineteenth century, Utagawa Hiroshige (1797–1858) produced hundreds of bird and flower prints. Hiroshige may not have created his work primarily for naturalists, but he took care to accurately record the appearance of his subjects, and almost all of them are identifiable by species. They cover scores of different birds, some rare and a few not even indigenous to Japan. For the most part they are depicted from life, according to the Asian tradition, but he must have used accounts by naturalists at least to check details of anatomy and coloration. Since he was working with woodblocks rather than painting his images, Hiroshige could not achieve spontaneity in the same way as his Chinese predecessors. A sense of heightened immediacy is achieved, however, by showing his subjects from unusual angles and in dynamic poses. Particularly with smaller birds such as sparrows, he emphasizes playfulness, a quality that has been conspicuously absent in ornithological art of the West. Quite a few of his prints contrast the heedless gaiety of birds with the hazards represented by autumn winds or winter snow. His prints are cheerful but with an undertone of melancholy.

In *Double-petalled Cherry Blossoms and Small Bird*, from the 1830s, a sparrow looks at a cluster of cherry blossoms in full bloom. Behind its head are some blossoms that are unopened and others that have just barely appeared. Finally, above the bird's head is a branch from which all the petals have already fallen, a reminder of transience.[9] *Yellow Bird and Cotton Rose*, printed in 1852,[10] shows a Japanese white eye perched on a rose with buds in four different stages of blossoming, from one that is still closed to another in full bloom. It is looking towards the tips of a large leaf in the foreground, which have begun to turn from green to brown, telling us that winter is coming soon. The bird is like a child that is first becoming aware of mortality.

Opposite: Katsushika Hokusai, Weeping Cherry and Bullfinch, *1834, woodblock print.*
Overleaf: Audubon discovers his work was eaten by a rat in this woodblock print
by an unknown Japanese artist, c. 1875. Audubon has long been a favourite in Japan.
Here he is depicted with Asian features.
Utagawa Hiroshige, Double-petalled Cherry Blossoms and Small Bird,
1830s, woodblock print.

合衆國有名の禽學者嘗て妹珠ある時

旅行せしが又多年思慮を凝して摸寫せる

繪本を箱に親戚に托して置き歡月にして

家に歸り箱を開き見るに鼠其内に巢

ひ畫圖の悉く齧りて碎片となして

鞘皮抔は是と見て大に心を傷ましゝ然り

歡日の間恍惚として失念せる者の如く

既みじく人舊の如く小銃と手ふて記簿繪筆を

携へ林に入て禽鳥を捕へ其形狀を摸寫せんと

至りけれども畫又箱に滿ち摸寫は前時よう更も好さと覺えしとぞ

Utagawa Hiroshige, Yellow Bird and Cotton Rose, *1852, woodblock print.*

The bird illustrators in the modern West absorbed, often unconsciously, the tradition of Asian bird and flower paintings.[11] Starting during the late seventeenth century and the eighteenth, there was a huge vogue in Europe for the style known as 'chinoiserie'. Designers copied motifs from East Asian art, including many from bird and flower painting, on to items such as wallpaper, porcelain, fabrics and pieces of furniture. East Asian motifs and styles were so ubiquitous that one might easily absorb their influence without being consciously aware of it. Europeans discovered Japanese prints in the middle of the nineteenth century, and by 1860 they had become highly fashionable.[12] They would become a major influence on French Impressionists such as Monet and Post-impressionists such as Van Gogh.

Utagawa Hiroshige and his contemporary John James Audubon may arguably have been the pre-eminent bird artists of their times, respectively in East Asia and the West, and the parallels between them are remarkable. They were working at a time when early cameras started to become available yet only with extremely slow shutter speeds. Both specialized in prints rather than in paintings, and, in spite of professional recognition, had to struggle financially for much of their lives. They both favoured bold, asymmetrical compositions and bright colours. They preferred to show birds in unusual, dynamic poses. Finally, both endeavoured to combine systematic documentation with popular appeal and artistic aspiration.

But the similarities highlight the profound difference between Audubon and Hiroshige as well as other artists of Japan and China, particularly with respect to their perspectives on time. Hiroshige, unlike Audubon, constantly reminds us of transience. Like other Japanese and Chinese artists, he emphasizes motifs that show the variation of seasons, such as leaves changing colour as they decay or petals dropping from flowers. These are relatively unusual, though not entirely absent, in the art of Audubon. In the work of Hiroshige it is usually possible to tell not only the season but the more specific time of year, for example whether it is early or late in summer. In the pictures made by Audubon, it is usually summer or winter and occasionally spring, though the season does not seem very important. For East Asian artists, autumn was the most poignant of seasons, with dying trees and chilly winds, but it is rarely the season in which Audubon's bird pictures are set.

Perhaps Audubon could not contemplate the future lives of his subjects simply because they did not have any. They were birds he had killed. Audubon was painting the myth of America as the New World, where nature was endless in its bounty. He was painting in a culture infatuated by newness, in which the past was annulled and the future only vaguely imagined. The unequalled dynamism of his illustrations reflects the adventure and romance that surrounded the American wilderness. But though he was not the least squeamish about showing predation, Audubon seldom or never depicted his birds as threatened by the elements.

Hummingbirds

The motif of birds juxtaposed with flowers first became important in the ornithological art of the West with the illustrations of hummingbirds. They are the bird most closely associated with flowers in the wild, since their major food is nectar, which they suck into their mouths by pushing their beaks deep into a blossom. They are also the smallest of birds and the most continuously active. It is intriguing to consider how traditional Asian artists would have depicted them had hummingbirds been indigenous to their part of the world. In many ways, hummingbirds epitomize what we think of as 'avian'. At least in the popular imagination, flight is the defining characteristic of a bird, and hummingbirds are the great virtuosos of flight. They fly not only forwards and backwards but

COLIBRI COL PETTO ROSSO MASCHIO E FEMMINA

Giuseppe Pazzi, Ruby-throated Hummingbirds, Male and Female, *1763, engraving.*
In this very early depiction of hummingbirds, the artist saw the closest analogue as a butterfly,
pictured on the right. Butterflies were, in fact, sometimes referred to as 'hummingbirds'.

in any other direction as well and can also hover for long periods in the air. But Asian artists of pre-modern times knew of hummingbirds only vaguely if at all, for hummingbirds are native only to the Americas.

In the religion of the Aztecs, the hummingbird represented Huitzilo-pochtli, the god of the sun and war. Aztec warriors wore hummingbird feathers on their headdresses, cloaks and shields. They were associated with battle for their fierceness and for the way they would quickly manoeuvre in the air. They are generally solitary and often fight with one another over flowers, which are their source of food. The Aztecs believed that those who died in battle might return as hummingbirds in the next life. Mayan and Aztec depictions often blend human features with those of hummingbirds, and it can be hard to know if a graphic primarily represents a deity, a bird or a warrior in costume.[13]

The motif of birds together with flowers becomes important in Western graphic art in the early nineteenth century with the documentation of hummingbirds. In 1832 the French doctor René Primevère Lesson published *Les trochilidées ou, Les colibris et les oiseaux-mouches* (Trochilidae: or, Hummingbirds), a book on the hummingbirds that he had seen during a journey around the world.[14] It contained delicate, graceful illustrations by many artists of the birds, but they were perched motionless, and a bit stiffly, on a branch rather than in flight. By far the grandest book on hummingbirds was *Monograph of the Trochidae, or Family of Hummingbirds*, put together by John Gould and published in six volumes between 1849 and 1887. Its illustrators included such distinguished artists as Joseph Wolf, Edward Lear, Elizabeth Gould and Henry Richter. Many of the graphics attempted to show the iridescence of hummingbirds, a very elusive and nearly intangible quality, by use of varnish and transparent oil. They were innovative in other respects as well. In a way close to

'Half-tailed Hummingbird', from William Jardine, The Naturalist's Library *(1834), engraving with watercolours. The bird is drawn in exquisite detail but, like almost all hummingbirds painted at the time, appears static.*

TROCHILUS ENICURUS.
(Half-tailed Humming-Bird.)
Lizars sc.

that of Audubon, they showed not just one but a few birds in every plate in order to document their appearance from many angles. The birds were not simply placed flat on the page or in symbolic landscapes. Instead, they were flying, hovering and perching around blossoms indigenous to their habitat.

Gould's lithographs of hummingbirds are still valued for their beauty and anatomical accuracy, but in some respects they showed a fantasy. They were based not on observation of living birds but on Gould's vast collection of

Henry C. Richter and John Gould, Blue-breasted Sapphire Hummingbird, *1860s, hand-coloured lithograph.*

hummingbird skins. Gould himself had never even seen a live hummingbird until, when the project was already very well underway, he visited Philadelphia and observed one in a botanical garden.[15] The birds in his prints show none of the aggressiveness that had so intrigued the Aztecs. The scenes seem to belong to a paradise, a beautiful, timeless world. At least unconsciously, Gould and his associates may well have been influenced by Asian bird and flower painting, but their work has little of its philosophical dimension.

Around the mid-nineteenth century hummingbirds became a craze in Victorian England. Taxidermized hummingbirds were placed in gilded cabinets, incorporated into hats and even worn as earrings. Their diminutive size and iridescence suggested fairies, as these were imagined during the nineteenth century. The fact that, like fairies, they were almost never seen alive doubtless added to their romance.

Flight

Even Audubon and Gould had trouble depicting birds in flight. In the late nineteenth century researchers began using the new technology of photography to investigate the rapid movement of animals. The disputes centred largely on a posture known as the 'flying gallop', with all the horse's legs stretched out and the hooves pointing either forwards or back, which had been often depicted over the centuries. The Anglo-American photographer Eadweard Muybridge finally settled the matter in the late 1880s using a state-of-the-art camera to take sequences of still photographs of animals in motion. The photographs showed that the flying gallop did not actually occur.[16] Almost all artists throughout history from sculptors of the Tang dynasty in China to Pisanello and Leonardo in Renaissance Italy had misunderstood the motion of horses.

Prehistoric cave painters, however, had by far the best record for accuracy,[17] which indicates that patient, repeated observations might indeed reveal motions that had seemed too fleeting for the human eye. Birds did not present any question that was as simple and tangible as the controversy about the flying gallop, but there was a lot of uncertainty about their motion as well. It turned out that their postures in the photographic sequences were not very different from those painted by Chinese artists over a millennium ago.

Even photographs, however, do not always capture the fluid motion of a bird's flight. A contemporary book for artists on drawing birds advises starting with long observation, adding that, 'The human eye sees differently from a high-speed camera, and the brain always interprets the received image. You will get convincing results from recording this mind's-eye view rather

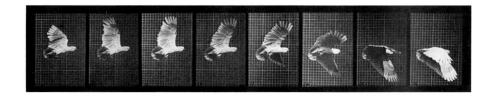

than using photographs as the basis for bird studies.'¹⁸ Chinese, Korean and Japanese bird-and-flower paintings are probably unequalled in their depiction of avian motion. The artists realized that birds do not fly simply by flapping their wings. They coordinate every part of their bodies, especially when taking off, landing or changing direction. The wings change shape as they are spread out or relaxed, and their lithe bodies can seem to be in a constant state of transformation. Smaller birds, especially, are in almost perpetual motion and they are often shy around human beings.

Human perception is not directly registered but edited, simplified and rendered coherent by the intellect. Just as the mind combines the impressions from our two eyes into a single image or the many frames of a strip of film into a single motion, it may synthesize perspectives of a bird in flight. The wings of a hummingbird usually beat over fifty times per second, and they are capable of more than twice that speed, so their wings appear to the eye as a blur. Depicting this is a challenge to the ingenuity of any artist, but can simply painting a hummingbird in flight with clearly delineated wings stretched out to the sides ever be 'realistic'? At any rate, it suggests that the picture was modelled after a dead bird rather than a living one.

Had Gould and his artists depicted hummingbirds after living models and painted what they actually saw, they would have been artistically far more innovative. Quite possibly, they might have developed the techniques of Impressionism, Futurism and Cubism. As it was, they generally showed the hummingbirds with their wings outstretched to form a single plane, a bit like those of a gliding gull. The result was to make illustrations that seemed, in spite of the frenetic activity, nearly static.

Not even Muybridge was able to reveal the secrets of hummingbird flight, since cameras of his time were still not nearly fast enough. It was not until the twenty-first century that scientists, using the latest imaging technology, were able to explain how hummingbirds fly. They do not flap their wings but

Above: Edweard Muybridge, snapshots of cockatoo in flight, USA, late 19th century.
Opposite: Photo by Margaret L. Bodine showing a ruby-throated hummingbird in flight, 1930s.
This was probably taken with what was then a state-of-the-art camera, but the wings of the hummingbird come out as a blur.

rotate them in a figure-of-eight motion, enabling them to get lift from both downward and upward strokes, as well as to hover in place or change direction instantly.[19]

Fog and Mirrors

I close this chapter with an example of how bird and flower painting may be able to incorporate challenges from new media, becoming perhaps even more relevant in the process. *A Hawk Glaring at Its Reflection in a Waterfall*, painted in ink and watercolour on two paper scrolls by Shibata Zeshin only a few years before Muybridge published his seminal photographs of animals in motion, is austere yet provides material for virtually endless meditations. On the left panel is the mother hawk with her fledgling on the edge of a cliff. On the right panel is a similar cliff at the top, with a few suggestions of falling water, much

Above: Martin Johnson Heade, Passion Flowers and Hummingbirds, *1865, oil on canvas, The artist has romanticized the hummingbirds as something like a married pair of settlers building their home on the American frontier. The scene is actually the Brazilian rainforest, but it is 'wild' like the 'Old West'.*
Opposite: Shibata Zeshin, A Hawk Gazing at Its Reflection in a Waterfall, *1870, ink and colours on silk.*

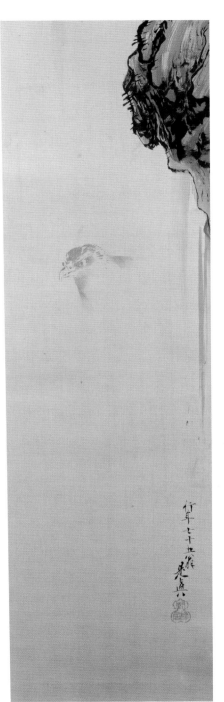

empty space and a spectral image of the head and shoulders of the adult hawk. The mother hawk and her chick are gazing at the reflection of the adult in the falling water.[20]

Would human beings be able to see their faces in water moving so quickly? Perhaps not, but the vision of hawks is far better than ours. Do the mother and chick recognize the face in the waterfall as a mirror image and not an intruder? Perhaps not, since the baby appears scared and the mother appears fiercely protective. The young hawk is spreading its wings and seems as if it may be about to plunge down the cliff, attempting flight for the first time. The falling water symbolizes time and the face represents the self, the constancy of which may, according to Buddhists, be an illusion. The surface of falling water is a bit like a hanging scroll and so the painting is also a reflection, in more than one sense, on the nature of art. The reflection in falling water could also represent photography. Zeshin must have been aware of that emerging technology, which had already been constantly refined over many decades. Like early photographs, which had very slow shutter speeds, the image in the waterfall fails to register whatever is in motion. If the mother shifts her head even momentarily, the image may vanish.

13 THE NIGHTINGALE AND THE ROSE

Wilt thou be gone? it is not yet near day:
It was the nightingale, and not the lark,
That pierc'd the fearful hollow of thine ear;
Nightly she sings on yon pomegranate tree:
Believe me, love, it was the nightingale.
William Shakespeare, *Romeo and Juliet,* Act III, sc. 5

The English cellist Beatrice Harrison was starting to practise her instrument in her garden near Oxted, Surrey, when a bird began to sing. She immediately recognized it as a nightingale and the two improvised a duet. In May 1924, after the same had happened on several occasions, the BBC made a recording of Beatrice playing the 'Londonderry Air', accompanied by a nightingale, and this went out on the radio throughout Britain. The event created an immediate sensation and the concert was repeated many times. New recordings were made of Beatrice and a nightingale every spring for the next twelve years. For many people, including John Reith, managing director of the BBC, the singing was not simply music, even splendid music, but a sort of primeval silence. When Beatrice finally moved, the BBC continued to broadcast the song of a nightingale without her.[1]

The Nightingale as Artist

Nobody will doubt that Beatrice was an artist. Were the nightingales that accompanied her artists as well? According to tradition, a defining quality of art is its lack of obvious utility. Bird calls are close to language, since they tend to have a specific purpose such as warning about the approach of a predator. Birdsong, by contrast, does not necessarily have a clearly defined purpose. In general, it marks off territory and signals a willingness to defend it. Song is also used by a male bird to attract a female.

But these explanations raise as many questions as they answer. Why use a single signal for such disparate purposes? One would expect specialized songs to be more effective. Besides, birds often sing when none of these purposes seem to be in play. At times, in order to sing, songbirds even undertake an unnecessary risk of signalling their location to predators. And even if the three purposes could explain the reason why birds sing, they still would not explain the extreme range and variety of avian melodies. They would also not explain

why these songs appeal to human beings. Is this the expression of an artistic instinct that crosses lines of species?

To some extent, birdsong and human music have co-evolved. Until glass windows became widespread in the Early Modern era, many, probably most, people fell asleep every night listening to nightingales, thrushes or other birds. The trills of opera singers are difficult to learn, and they sound closer to birdsong than to human speech. Composers including Vivaldi, Mozart, Beethoven and, most extensively, Olivier Messiaen have incorporated imitations of birdsong into their works.[2] Many birds incorporate imitations of sounds in their environment, including those of people, into their songs. They could easily have picked up themes from human music and then passed them on to one another. Nevertheless, human tunes progress in a linear way, while the songs of nightingales or mockingbirds have no beginning, middle or end.

The nightingale's song has a reputation not only for beauty but also emotional and even intellectual complexity. It has passages that sound melodious, but it relies far less than human music on graceful transitions. David Rothenberg calls the nightingale's song 'strange and crackly, musical only in a foreign way'.[3] In Graeco-Roman tradition, people have thought of the singer as female and believed it told the traumatic tale of the woman Procne (or, in later versions, her sister Philomela), with gaps, interruptions and changes of tone, rather like a scene of a Greek tragedy in which the frightening narrative of the protagonist alternates with the empathetic pronouncements of the chorus. It has scratchy passages as well as melodious ones, and the former may have suggested something almost too frightening to say.

Caged nightingales have been kept for their songs since the ancient world, and Pliny reported that they fetched the same prices as slaves in Rome.[4] In the Early Modern era, when the wealthy were constructing increasingly elaborate mansions, keeping a caged nightingale became a way of incorporating

Nightingale from Konrad Gesner's Historia animalium *(German edition of 1667).*
Opposite: Beatrice Harrison with mementos of her concerts with the nightingales, c. 1920.

a bit of the natural world into the home. Percy Bysshe Shelley wrote in *A Defence of Poetry*, 'A poet is a nightingale who sits in darkness and sings to cheer its own solitude with sweet sounds.'[5] References to the nightingale as a sublime singer became a standard part of poetic diction.

When people recognized that many birds learn songs from one another, especially beloved singers were assigned the role of teaching others. Here is Jules Michelet's description of a Russian singing school for nightingales:

> The master nightingale, in his cage suspended in the centre of a saloon, has his scholars ranged around him in their respective cages. A certain sum per hour is paid for each bird brought here to learn his lesson. Before the master sings they chatter and gossip among themselves, salute and recognize one another. But as soon as the mighty teacher, with one imperious note, like that of a sonorous steel bell, has imposed silence, you see them listen with a sensible deference, then timidly repeat the strain. The master complacently returns to the principal passages, corrects, and gently sets them right.[6]

The scene is a sort of idealized university classroom with much emphasis on craft and little on spontaneity.

Michelet was very conscious of the freedom that birds have to sacrifice in a domestic setting. He wrote of 'winged voices, voices of fire, angel voices, emanations of an intense life superior to ours, of a fugitive and mobile existence, which inspires the traveller doomed to a well-beaten track with the serenest thoughts and brightest dreams of liberty'.[7] Nevertheless, as a close observer of nature, Michelet was also very aware that birds and other animals can benefit from captivity. They are protected from predators and from the elements. They are given a steady supply of food, and they are liberated from constantly needing to struggle for survival.

Do the negatives outweigh the advantages? Michelet does not say, and perhaps it is impossible to accurately generalize. It depends on the individual bird and the conditions that prevail, both in the wild and in the domestic setting, but Michelet believed the inner conflict added a dimension to the nightingale's song. It changed the nightingale from being a bearer of beauty, like a rose or a peacock, to a creator.

Michelet saw the nightingale as the epitome of the romantic artist – moody, temperamental, naive, timid, solitary, prone to vanity and ultimately good-hearted. He may even have been thinking of Keats and Shelley. Much of

European culture at this time centred on the ideal of freedom and the contrast between nature and society. Michelet found precisely these themes in the song of the nightingale: 'a nightingale, born in freedom, which alone is the true nightingale, bears a very different value from one born in a cage: he sings quite differently, having known liberty and nature, and regretting both. The better part of the great artist's genius is suffering.'[8] For Michelet, the nightingale, and perhaps no other bird, understood human alienation from the natural world, with its privileges and sorrows.

Life and Death

In Islamic, especially Sufi, tradition, the singing nightingale is male. His song is a lament for a distant, unattainable object of desire represented by the rose. The rose is a highly cultivated plant of aristocratic gardens, while the nightingale lives in woodlands. The appearance of the rose is dazzling, while the nightingale is drab apart from its melody. This makes the rose into a sort of princess, courted by a man of humble origins. In a Persian legend, the nightingale presses its breast against a thorn and dies in order to ease the pain of unrequited love.[9]

The motif of the nightingale longing for the rose comes up frequently in the work of Attar, Rumi, Hafiz and many other Sufi poets. It generally symbolizes the vanity of earthly attachments, but it can suggest the virtue of faithfulness or even the longing of the soul for God. In a verse attributed to the eleventh-century Persian mathematician Omar Khayyam and translated in the mid-nineteenth century by Edward FitzGerald, it is a symbol of transience:

> Alas, that Spring should vanish with the Rose!
> That Youth's sweet-scented Manuscript should close!
> The Nightingale that in the Branches sang,
> Ah, whence, and whither flown again, who knows![10]

In the late eighteenth century, Hafiz and other Persian poets were translated into English and became part of a fad for 'Orientalism'. They were valued largely for their exoticism and mystery, but the allegory of the nightingale and the rose became familiar to the English-speaking public.[11] It blended into a long tradition of literary references to the nightingale in Chaucer, Spenser, Shakespeare and many others. In Western tradition as well, the nightingale had at times become a sort of martyr, though more for art than for love. According to St Bonaventure, writing in thirteenth-century Italy, when it was about to die the nightingale would perch in a tree and start

Painted nightingales and roses from the wall of Hasht Behesht Palace, Isfahan, Iran, 1669.

singing before dawn. Its song would become louder and more joyous as the sun rose, but it would die of exertion at noon.[12]

The reputation of the nightingale as the most sublime of singers reached a pinnacle in the romantic cult of the artist in the nineteenth century. For Keats, in 'Ode to a Nightingale', the song of the bird is of unearthly joy. The poet hears, but does not see, a nightingale and tries to follow it in his imagination through meadows and woods, which become landscapes of fantasy. Finally, when he can no longer hear the sound, it is like death and the poem ends with the question, 'Do I wake or sleep?' The song of the nightingale represents life, and yet its song is impersonal, a sort of 'music of the spheres':

> Thou wast not born for death, immortal Bird!
> No hungry generations tread thee down;
> The voice I hear this passing night was heard
> In ancient days by emperor and clown:
> Perhaps the self-same song that found a path
> Through the sad heart of Ruth, when, sick for home,
> She stood in tears amid the alien corn;
> The same that oft-times hath
> Charm'd magic casements, opening on the foam
> Of perilous seas, in faery lands forlorn.[13]

The poet did not realize that nightingales do not sing in flight. He may have falsely attributed some of the variation in its song to change in distance, direction and acoustics as it passed over changing terrain. Even more significantly, Keats did not realize that nightingale songs are largely learned, constantly altered and very individual. Writing about four decades before Darwin's *On the Origin of Species*, he did not know that nightingales evolve, as do their songs, and might be subject to great regional variations. There is virtually no chance that the biblical Ruth or a Roman emperor would have heard the same song as Keats.

For all these anachronisms and errors in ornithology, the poem can be very moving, not only for its evocative imagery but as a personal testament. Keats was suffering from tuberculosis, which was then incurable and would kill him two years later. The perfection he finds in the nightingale's song leads him to melancholy thoughts of human transience and vulnerability, yet finally brings consolation. The bird offers no empathy but the assurance that life, like the song, will continue when he is gone. Whether deliberately or not, Keats suggests the old allegory from Sufi poetry, though used in reverse. The poet becomes the rose, confined to the earth, while the nightingale is the distant object of longing and adoration.

Hans Christian Andersen's story 'The Nightingale' is set in the palace of the emperor of China, where all things, even the flowers, are made of porcelain. The emperor reads in a book that the greatest marvel of his kingdom is the song of the nightingale, but he does not know anything about it. He enquires of his courtiers, but they as well have never heard of it. Finally, the Chamberlain asks a little girl working in the kitchen. She knows the nightingale well and

J. J. Grandville, engraving showing the nightingale and the rose, 1840s.

leads the courtiers to it. They ask the bird, which can speak like a human being, to come to the emperor's palace and it agrees. When the bird sings for the emperor, the monarch is deeply moved. The nightingale refuses any material reward but agrees to stay at the palace. The bird is confined in a cage at court, though allowed to leave twice a day and once at night. Everyone talks about, and even imitates, the nightingale.

Then one day a mechanical nightingale is given to the emperor. Covered with precious gems, the mechanical nightingale is much prettier than the real one, though it can only sing one tune. The people at court transfer all of their attention to the newcomer, and the real nightingale flies away through the window. Eventually the mechanical nightingale breaks down, and the emperor becomes very ill and close to death. The original nightingale returns to sing at his window, restoring him to health. It agrees to sing for the emperor every night, on condition that he never reveal its presence.[14]

In summary, the story is really about two songbirds: the organic nightingale, representing life, and the mechanical nightingale, representing death. They vie for the soul of the emperor, who, apart from his office, seems to be a very ordinary human being. Andersen had no fondness for ambivalence or psychological complexity. His characters, like those in fables attributed to Aesop, are one-dimensional and only become interesting through their interaction. But both birds are aspects of the archetypal nightingale of legend, intimately associated with the source of life and its conclusion.

The China in which the story is set is a fantasy, and the caricatures of people there would be considered racist today, but the story is clearly a satire on the European courts. These were places of manufactured splendour, elaborate manners and obsequious courtiers, which were constantly pervaded by a longing for nature and spontaneity. The atmosphere that prevailed was enough to make Marie Antoinette and her companions pretend to be shepherdesses and milkmaids.

Scientific knowledge and technology are forms of power. The monarchs and aristocrats tried to claim title to this power by creating marvels, which would blend science, craftsmanship and nature. These included instruments such as astrolabes made of gold and decorated with precious stones. Foremost among these wonders were automatons with intricately constructed gears, designed to perform tasks from greeting visitors to drawing and playing music. These were meant not only to dazzle and amaze but to explore the boundaries between humanity, other forms of life and inanimate matter. Descartes, in his *Meditations*, had worried that all the people he saw on the street might be robots.[15] E. T. A. Hoffmann wrote a story entitled 'The Sandman', in which a young man falls madly in love with a girl who turns out to be an automaton.[16] All of the hubris, the exhilaration and the fear that has accompanied the rise of artificial intelligence were already present. The artificial nightingale in Andersen's story may have been inspired by reports of mechanical birds at the court of the Byzantine emperor.[17]

For neo-Romantics such as Oscar Wilde in the late nineteenth century, it was not easy to write of love with the same directness as Andersen or Keats. For the early Romantics, suffering from unrequited love had been a point of pride, but it was becoming more of an embarrassment to be hidden under layers of irony. This problem was compounded by Wilde's homosexuality, something that was largely accepted in artistic circles but nevertheless illegal. Wilde was committed to romantic ideals but dubious about the ability of his society to live up to, or even understand, them.

The living nightingale in Andersen's tale could not only speak like a human being but seemed almost a full member of human society. The one in Wilde's tale 'The Nightingale and the Rose' cannot speak, but it can understand (or, rather, misunderstand) what people say. It is, in other words, on the farthest fringes of the human world, sharing the alienation that Romantics saw as part of the artistic vocation.

Wilde, who clearly identifies with the nightingale, makes the bird female. As the story begins, a young student tells how a girl said that she would dance with him if he brought her a red rose but laments that he has none in his garden. A nightingale overhears him and resolves to bring him the rose. She flies about but can find none. She finally returns to her nest in a rose tree in the student's garden. The tree has been damaged by a storm and had its buds destroyed by frost, and it tells the nightingale that to obtain a rose, 'You must build it by moonlight and stain it with your own heart's blood.'

As instructed by the tree, the nightingale pierces its breast with a thorn and then sings for the entire night. The student listens and responds a little, but he is completely unable to comprehend the song. She 'sang of Love that is perfected by death, of love that dies not in the tomb'. Finally, she perishes with a final burst of song, and a magnificent crimson rose appears on the tree. The student finds the rose and offers it to the girl, but she replies that it will not go with her dress and, besides, the Chamberlain has sent her jewels that are more valuable. She throws the rose into a gutter, where it is crushed by a wagon. The student, with no more than mild regret, goes back to his books.[18]

A theme of the story is how people have allowed their passions to atrophy by failing to appreciate the natural world. Passion seems to exist only in nature, in the bird and even the tree, while the people are almost mechanical. The

Swans in the Wallkill River, New York State. Their pristine white and undulating curves often make swans appear otherwise.

relationship between the student and the girl is not very significant here, since there is no attraction on her side and very little on his. Perhaps 'The Nightingale and the Rose' is really a story of requited love between the nightingale and the tree. A Freudian might contend that the thorn is phallic and the final union between nightingale and rose actually seems like copulation. It could be called 'unnatural', but that is also what people said about Wilde's homosexuality, and the idea may seem less counterintuitive if we remember that birds help to pollinate vegetation. The union of bird and tree does produce at least one child, which is the rose. It could be that the nightingale's sacrifice has revived the tree so that rose was only the first of many.

That seems to be the interpretation of W. B. Yeats, who alludes to Wilde's tale in his poem 'The Rose Tree' about Patrick Pearse and James Connolly, who became leaders of the 1916 Easter Rebellion in Dublin against British rule in Ireland. They observe that a rose tree in a garden is withered and needs to be watered:

> 'But where can we draw water',
> Said Pearse to Connolly,
> 'When all the wells are parched away?
> O plain as plain can be
> There's nothing but our own red blood
> Can make a right Rose Tree.'[19]

Here, the rose tree is Ireland, and the nightingale is the rebels who must sacrifice their lives to revive it.

Swans, according to tradition, also sing a melody of transcendent beauty as they die. The swan's song is alluded to by Plato and Aristotle, but the idea that swans sing at death was already being debunked in antiquity.[20] Michelet believed that swans had ceased to sing due to persecution of swans by humankind. Like many refugees, they had lost part of their heritage in leaving their ancestral home in Italy.[21]

Today, most authorities regard the idea of a swan song as a myth. Nevertheless, there have been occasional reports of this song over the centuries, perhaps just enough to keep it from being entirely dismissed as a legend or hallucination. In 1898 the American zoologist Daniel Giraud Elliot shot a swan and was amazed to hear the song as the bird swam almost a mile away. He described it as 'plaintive' and 'musical' and said that he and his companions stood listening 'in mute astonishment'.[22] One explanation of the song, given by German zoologist Peter Pallas around the start of the nineteenth century, is that the whooper swan has an unusually convoluted trachea that emits a wailing sound as its lungs collapse.[23]

The 'swan song', whether real or just a legend, is like the final song of the nightingale in the story we have looked at by Wilde. In the tales of both swans and nightingales, we find an eroticizing of death. Keats also wrote in 'Ode to a Nightingale':

Victor Mikhaylovich Vosnetsov, Sirin and Alkonost, *1896, oil on canvas. Here the Sirin, on the right, is the bird of joy, while the Alkonost, on the left, is the bird of sorrow, but they are very similar. One might compare them to the organic and mechanical birds in Andersen's 'The Nightingale'.*

Darkling I listen; and, for many a time
I have been half in love with easeful Death,
Call'd him soft names in many a mused rhyme,
To take into the air my quiet breath;
    Now more than ever seems it rich to die,
To cease upon the midnight with no pain,
    While thou art pouring forth thy soul abroad
In such an ecstasy![24]

The same erotic view of death is found in the legends of the Greek sirens. There are also Russian legends of the sirin, a beautiful bird with the head of a woman and the tail of a peacock, whose song is of such unearthly beauty that any man who hears it must die.[25] The ultimate model for these creatures of myth is probably the Egyptian soul bird.

Sorrow and Joy

The song of a bird seems to have a sort of purity that we can seldom if at all find in human art. We know it is not sung for money or prestige (at least among human beings), nor for any political agenda. But the question here is not why birds sing. It is why human beings perceive their sounds as song. Why, in other words, do we find birdsong beautiful? After all, it is not sung for us. We hear the sound very differently from the birds themselves, so our enjoyment probably cannot be called a result of 'communication'.

It may be that birdsong has forms and structures whose aesthetic appeal transcends species or even modes of sensual perception, but the wide range of interpretations indicates that our appreciation is cultural. For Milton, the song of a nightingale was the promise of consummated love.[26] For William Drummond, a contemporary of Milton, the song suggested almost the opposite of what it represented for the Greeks:

What soul can be so sick, which by thy Songs
(Attir'd in sweetness) sweetly is not driven
Quite to forget Earth's Turmoils, Spites and Wrongs.[27]

For Keats, the song evoked melancholy, and for Coleridge it inspired joy.[28] Perhaps the poets were all simply listening to different nightingales, but they very rarely thought of the birds as individuals.

Christina Rossetti expressed this most clearly in her poem 'Pain or Joy':

We call it love and pain
The passion of her strain;
And yet we little understand or know;
Why should it not be rather joy that so
Throbs in each throbbing vein?[29]

Birdsong, especially the nightingale's, taps into some reservoir of emotion on the fringes of the usual human range. It has the ambiguity that was greatly valued in the tumultuous era of European Romanticism when poets were passionately struggling with questions of faith and doubt.

This brings us back to my argument in the initial chapter of this book. The feelings evoked by the song of the nightingale do not fit into the dichotomy of sorrow and joy, arguably the most basic dualism of all. This is an example of how animals, in this instance birds, challenge the categories with which we see the world. If we are honest, I believe we will have a lot of trouble categorizing them as either 'moral' or 'immoral', 'conscious' or 'insentient', 'wild' or 'civilized', 'stupid' or 'intelligent' and so on. Nothing can be taken as a given when we speak of birds, not even time, space, sex, pain, power, status, freedom, dominance, life or death.

Every species is an alternate universe, and each individual creature is another world. Human language begins to break down in reference to birds, because our concepts, developed for interpersonal communication, no longer apply. But since precisely these meanings mark off the boundaries of the human domain, interaction with animals creates our identity as human beings.[30] It also perpetually challenges us to rethink the basic terms with which we describe the world.

On a July day a single beam of sun flashes brightly from the wing of a bird, flying low over a rocky coast. A few people notice it and they are cheered for a moment, after which they get in cars and drive away. This is an avian illumination, if a small one. In a few days, or perhaps even hours, they may no longer remember what they saw. But it will remain in their unconscious, becoming part of them, and merging with many such illuminations. Perhaps one lady may keep visiting the coast without ever knowing why. This is the beginning of a story that may never be told, for the ways in which birds influence our lives are mostly below the threshold of consciousness.

CONCLUSION

BIRDS AND
THE FUTURE

14 EXTINCTION

> O what can ail thee, knight-at-arms,
>   Alone and palely loitering?
> The sedge has withered from the lake,
>   And no birds sing.
> **John Keats, 'La Belle Dame sans Merci'**

We are approaching a climax of the period often called the Anthropocene or 'era of humankind'. In textbooks of the mid-twentieth century the story of this period was told as a sort of epic drama in which the hero is man. He masters fire, learns farming, builds cities and goes on to ever new adventures. Today, however, we often tell the story as a narrative of accelerating extinctions, which scientists now variously put at 100 to 1,000 times the usual or 'background' rate. In *The Sixth Extinction* Elizabeth Kolbert estimates that a quarter of all mammalian species and a fifth of reptilian ones are doomed to vanish soon. The rate of extinction for amphibians is even higher, though she declines to put a number on it. Birds do a little better. Only a sixth of them, in her opinion, are facing imminent oblivion.[1] Compared to many estimates, these figures are conservative. Is man, then, the hero or the villain? Either answer is anthropocentric in that it makes man the focus of the story. For our purposes here, it may be more useful to think of humankind as a mighty yet impersonal force rather like the weather at sea.

Awareness of the possibility of extinction has been gradually building over centuries in spite of intellectual and emotional resistance. When Linnaeus articulated the concept of 'species' in the eighteenth century, he created, for the first time, a unit with which people might measure extinctions. He and his followers believed, however, that species represented eternal forms created by God that could never perish. Around the start of the nineteenth century, Georges Cuvier presented his Theory of Catastrophism (or Theory of Extinction), according to which the Earth underwent periodic upheavals in which many creatures died out. Once the possibility had been established, people could easily observe that, even without an event like the Great Flood in the Bible, many species were being driven to the point of disappearance. In Darwin's *On the Origin of Species* (1859), extinction was recognized as part of the normal process of evolution.

Frans Snyders, Cook at Kitchen Table with Dead Game, *1635, oil on canvas. We have a reminder of the violence of the hunt as the cat tries to eat the goose and the cook raises his arm to strike.*

In *The Bird* by Jules Michelet, first published in 1856 in French, the author comes across a lone heron in a pond of his native France. The bird seems majestic yet melancholy, and he asks it, in his imagination, what is wrong. Instead of a metaphysical complaint, as is so often found in the Romantics, the heron responds by telling how the environment of his tribe has diminished and declined:

> Earth was our empire, the realm of the aquatic birds in this transitional age when, young and fresh, she emerged from the waters. An era of strife, of battle, but of abundant sustenance. Not a heron then but earned his life. There was neither need to attack nor pursue; The prey hunted the hunter; it whistled, or croaked, on every side.

Finally, the heron predicts the extinction of its kind, at least in Europe, within about another hundred years.[2]

In the inaugural issue of *The Audubon Magazine*, published in February 1887, an anonymous editorial expressed similar fears:

> There will soon not be a bird of paradise on earth, and the ostrich has only been saved by private breeders. Man will not wait for the cooling of the world to consume everything in it, from teak trees to hummingbirds, and a century or so hence will find himself perplexed by a planet in which there is nothing except what he makes.[3]

Such statements were not very unusual, and they were mostly lamentations for losses that had not yet even occurred.

Nearly all of the devastation done to birds, particularly in the last five centuries or so, can be traced back to men and women. The extermination of birds has at times been accomplished in a state of emotional intoxication inspired by a sense of divine election. This has also been done in a sombre spirit of submission to duty. Most frequently, people have extirpated birds almost unknowingly, and it was virtually never done with full understanding of the consequences. Humankind began steadily reducing the population of birds around the world during the Neolithic era by over-exploitation, habitat destruction and introduction of invasive species.[4] Up until the Early Modern era, the pressure on birds and other animals was usually not very dramatic, yet it was also steady and almost inexorable. Human beings had spread across the globe, claiming land for homes and crops. They at times actively persecuted birds and occasionally protected them, yet for the most part accepted their presence as part of normal life. But swamps were drained and forests cut down to make room for expanding human settlements.

Prior to the Industrial Revolution most people were still rural, and birds and their products pervaded everyday life, from roosters that woke people at dawn to quills used for writing. Parts of birds were ingredients of many medicines. When birds were served at the table, the cooks would preserve rather than destroy their original form. The roast swan would really look like a swan. When people wanted a ready metaphor, birds were among the first things that came to mind. This visibility and integration into the fabric of everyday life gave the birds at least a degree of security, since it meant that any local populations being killed off might immediately be missed.

Around the sixteenth or seventeenth century, the killing of birds became far more deliberate, systematic and extensive, and it was often done with unprecedented exuberance. Much of the reason was a growing sense of human entitlement. Human beings were no longer resigned to be at the mercy of the elements. Farmers were more determined to maximize profits and less willing to tolerate birds eating even a small amount of grain. With the invention of ever more accurate firearms, they were given the means to realize their aspirations. From 1500 to 2017, 182 known bird species have become extinct,[5] and many others doubtless vanished without ever having been identified.

Revelling in Death

European game paintings of the seventeenth century by artists such as Frans Snyders and Melchior d'Hondecoeter often show great piles of freshly killed birds, including swans, ducks, pheasants, bitterns and many others.[6] Ornithologists have identified fifty different avian species in these paintings by Snyders,[7] which is a testimony to his careful observation, the abundance of avian life and the indiscriminate way birds were killed. These paintings are essentially trophies, but the generally realistic style, with its sober attention to detail, suggests that the amount of game was not greatly exaggerated.

This revelling in death may appear macabre today, but it will be more understandable if we remember that for most people up until that time (and for many afterwards as well) the prospect of going hungry had been a perpetual danger. They had been constantly dependent on local harvests, which might be ruined by droughts or tempests, and meat was a luxury. The emerging middle classes were celebrating their liberation from perpetual insecurity.

By the eighteenth century the birds and animals had become less abundant and ownership of firearms was forbidden to the poorer classes. Orgiastic celebrations of the hunt were continued by royalty and the very rich, who maintained game parks and stocked them with imported quarry.

The genre reached a culmination in France during the eighteenth century in the work of François Desportes, who served Louis xiv, and Jean-Baptiste Oudry, court painter to Louis xv, both of whom were renowned for their skill in depicting feathers.[8] The subject then gradually disappeared from painting, perhaps because even kings could no longer bring down game on such a scale, and there was at least an incipient awareness that the natural world might not be able to recover from the predations. Around the end of the nineteenth century William Henry Hudson wrote that, while some species of British birds had perished due to causes such as draining of marshes, most of those that were lost had been hunted to extinction, adding that, 'Fowlers, gamekeepers, collectors, cockney sportsmen, and louts with guns, pursued them to the death, even as they are now pursuing all our rarer species.'[9]

Jean-Baptiste Oudry, Still-life with Dead Game and Peaches in a Landscape, *1725, oil on canvas. The bird and rabbit are held in place by ropes and sprawled on the ground in contorted poses that highlight the violence of their deaths.*

Frans Snyders, Concert of Birds, c. *1635, oil on canvas.*

At the same time as the game paintings, and frequently in works by the same artists, other canvases celebrated a vast profusion of avian life. In sixteenth- and seventeenth-century Europe people did not yet fully appreciate that different species, even of birds, were adjusted to different environments. Accordingly, these paintings would include dozens of birds from all over the world from great auks to parrots to turkeys in a single canvas. Sometimes these were presented as an allegory of the air, presided over by a goddess of nature.[10] In other cases, the reason for depicting a vast range of birds together is a biblical scene such as the creation of the world, the Garden of Eden or Noah's Ark. In some it is a concert of the birds, usually led by an owl.[11] But often the celebration of birds is presented with no pretext. Such paintings were in part an opportunity for artists to exhibit their virtuosity, but they were also an attempt to reconstruct a world of ornithological abundance that the artists and their patrons at least sensed was vanishing. Its archaic nature was often indicated by including ancient ruins in the background.

Early Extinctions

The arrival of human beings to a new part of the world has always been followed within a span of a few centuries by mass extinctions of flora and fauna, and this has not been confined to people of Western culture. Humans played a major role in mass extinctions in the Americas, Australia, New Zealand and elsewhere. The reason is not simply innate human rapacity. It is that human beings confronting a new environment and unfamiliar forms of life are restrained by neither cultural traditions nor practical experience.[12] Birds, most of which can escape by flight, probably usually did not suffer quite as much devastation as mammals and reptiles, but that begins to change as we start to approach the modern era. The moas, an order of huge, flightless birds similar in appearance to the ostrich and cassowary, were quickly hunted to extinction when the Maori became the first humans to colonize New Zealand in the early fourteenth century CE. The family of elephant birds, arguably the largest birds ever, met a similar fate in Madagascar during the Middle Ages.

The dodo, a large, flightless pigeon with a heavy bill, was discovered by Dutch settlers on the island of Mauritius at the end of the sixteenth century, and it was driven to extinction in less than two hundred years. Much of this was due to excessive hunting, but importation to Mauritius of invasive species such as pigs and dogs, which would eat the bird's eggs, was an important factor as well. In the late 1860s, just after extinction of the dodo, one popular book on natural history, reflecting a kind of anthropocentrism that was common at the time, declared, 'The Dodo did not even possess the merit of being useful after its death, for its flesh was disagreeable and had a bad flavor. On the whole, there is not much reason to regret its extinction.'[13] For a long time the bird had the reputation of being a proverbial 'loser', an anachronism that did not

Moa, illustration to H. N. Hutchinson, Extinct Monsters *(London, 1910).*

Dodo, from a 19th-century book of natural history. The bird was slimmer and more agile than this and most other depictions of the time indicate, as they were almost all based on skins or captive birds.

deserve to survive. Its name became an epithet of contempt. Only gradually did researchers come to realize that it had not been as stupid and awkward as they had initially thought, and its major failing was trust in human beings. It is now remembered largely as a martyr to human rapacity. Today, Mauritius proudly features the dodo on its coat of arms.

Of all the birds that have become extinct over the centuries, the tale of the great auk has perhaps a special pathos, since it had a long and varied history of interaction with human beings. The great auk was a relatively large, flightless bird that looked rather like a penguin, though the two are not closely related. In historic times, the great auk inhabited islands and coasts of the north

Thomas Bewick, Great Auk, *1804, woodblock print.*

Atlantic Ocean, though its range once extended as far south as Spain and the Mediterranean. It was eaten by people of Palaeolithic times, and it is one of very few birds that are depicted in cave paintings. By the sixteenth century it had withdrawn to what were once remote, inaccessible locations, but it was rediscovered in the Age of Exploration. During the sixteenth century auks became a favourite subject in European paintings that endeavoured to show the panorama of avian life. Initially auks were hunted primarily for their feathers and eggs, but, as they became rare, auks also grew more valuable. They were increasingly killed for taxidermy, to be displayed in museums and private collections. The last confirmed great auks were killed on a rock near Iceland in

1844.[14] Before they were finally killed off, moas, elephant birds, dodos and great auk all gradually had their populations and their genetic variation reduced to a level that was unsustainable.

Harvesting Feathers

Feathers have been often used for practical purposes such as filling pillows and mattresses or fletching arrows, but they are more often taken from birds for decorative and ceremonial purposes.[15] Colourful feathers have often been used as decorations, gifts and a medium of exchange in pre-Columbian America, New Zealand, Polynesia and elsewhere.[16] In many ways, feathers in these countries were the equivalent of gemstones and precious metals in medieval Europe. Bright colours and elegant curves make feathers aesthetically appealing, but they are also a way to appropriate symbolic meanings associated with the birds. Feathers, particularly when worn, are used to encode information about the class, role and gender of the human possessor.

In Polynesian myth the creator of the world was the avian god Ta'aora. At the beginning, he was encased in a shell and, like a baby bird, pecked it open. He made its dome into the sky, and then made the feathers that had covered him into trees. The Tahitians, together with other Polynesians, regard birds as embodiments of primeval ancestors and emissaries from the spirit world. They use feathers to make ceremonial headdresses, masks and robes. When Polynesians converted to Christianity, they placed feathers on Christian images.[17]

The Polynesians made garments of feathers. The cape of Kamehameha the Great, who unified Hawaii at the end of the eighteenth century, contained feathers from 80,000 mamo birds.[18] Native peoples of the Solomon Islands, off the coast of New Guinea, used rolls made from the feathers of the scarlet honeyeater as a currency. In the nineteenth and early twentieth centuries about 20,000 male scarlet honeyeaters were sacrificed for this purpose every year.[19] The traditional use of feathers in the South Seas was so extensive that one can wonder why far more birds were not driven to extinction. The reason seems to be that the region was relatively thinly populated by human beings and birds had areas to which they could safely retreat.

The Aztecs of Mexico made elaborate feathered tapestries. The Navajo and Hopi of the American Southwest have traditionally used feathers from the golden eagle and other birds in ceremonies and on garments. The Navajo hunter would hide in a pit beneath a dead rabbit, and then grab an eagle by the legs when it swooped down to take the bait. The Hopi would kidnap young eagles

Inca feathered tabard, Peru, 15th or 16th century.

from a nest. Some of the birds were later returned to the wild,[20] and their capture proved sustainable until the eagles were also threatened by greater hazards: farmers who shot raptors indiscriminately and the pesticide DDT.

Feathers have an especially strong association with war. Peoples from the Plains people of the United States to the Zulu of Southern Africa and tribesmen of New Guinea have used feathers, especially in headdresses, to signify the rank of warriors going into battle. Feathers have also often been used to decorate shields and weapons.[21]

During the late Middle Ages and Renaissance, imported ostrich feathers worn in a hat became an important accessory for aristocratic European ladies and gentlemen. Knights in tournaments often wore huge plumes made up of many such feathers, even though they could cost more than their entire armour. Since the fifteenth century the heraldic symbol of the Prince of Wales has been three ostrich feathers surrounded by a crown. In Victorian and Edwardian times, a lady appearing before a high court was required to wear ostrich plumes in her hat, three feathers for a married woman and two for a single one.[22]

Colourful birds were sacrificed for fashion in the West, especially hats for European and American women in the nineteenth and early twentieth centuries, which became increasingly extravagant. It is likely that these hats were deliberately designed to deliver a piquant sort of shock, to make their wearer seem 'barbaric' in an exciting way. A well-respected book on birds stated that, in 1868,

Illustration to a German translation of Livy's Ab urbe condita *(1514), woodblock print. The illustrations show people in contemporary dress, and the man on the left, with his plumes of ostrich feathers, represents the height of fashion for the start of the 16th century. Lucas van Leyden,* Man with Ostrich Plumes, *1517, engraving. The fashionable feathers here represent earthly vanity. The young man is coming to realize this, for he holds a memento mori in his left hand and points to it with his right.*

R NEWTON del et feat.

the headdress of every votary of fashion was decorated with the
wing of a bird – not confining the demand to birds of paradise,
ostriches, pheasant, and other birds of brilliant plumage . . .
extending to the harmless sea-fowl, which were destroyed by the
thousands only for the sake of their feathers.[23]

Fashionable hats contained not only a profusion of feathers, but entire
stuffed birds. The inaugural issue of *The Audubon Magazine* in 1887 contained

Opposite: Richard Newton, Tippies of 1796, *1796, engraving. A satire on high fashion for women and men in London at the end of the 18th century.*
Above: Adolph Murr, photograph of Bird Head, Sioux, 1899. The profusion of feathers in the subject's hat might elsewhere be simply an indication of status, but they contrast with the tragic nobility of his face and bearing.

Above: Advertisement for J. A. Stein Ostrich Feathers, United States, 1896. Ostrich feathers were used for countless stylish women's accessories.
Opposite: John N. Hyde, 'The Cruelties of Fashion', Frank Leslie's Illustrated Newspaper, *10 November 1883. How a women's hat with taxidermized birds is produced.*

THE CRUELTIES OF FASHION. — "FINE FEATHERS MAKE FINE BIRDS."

SEE PAGE 182.

Ross Gordon, 'The Woman behind the Gun', Puck, 24 May 1911. The woman is probably Coco Chanel, who had recently opened a fashionable millinery shop in Paris. One of the men hiding is labelled 'French Milliner'. As has often happened before and since, the protection of animals becomes a pretext for nationalism.

an article by Celia Thaxter entitled 'Woman's Heartlessness', in which she writes bitterly: 'Today I saw a mat woven of warbler's heads, spiked all over its surface with sharp beaks, set up upon a bonnet and borne aloft by its possessor in pride! Twenty murders in one!'[24] A few years later Hudson wrote, 'there are warehouses in this city [London] where it is possible for a person to walk ankle-deep – literally to wade – in bright plumaged bird skins, and see them piled shoulder-high on either side of him.'[25] Egret plumage was particularly trendy for its brilliant white, gentle curls and wisps of down.

Eradicating Predators

Smaller birds such as warblers have at least been granted some protection because of sentiments aroused by their songs and their lovely colours, but that did not apply to raptors. In the late nineteenth and early twentieth centuries predators in general were often demonized, and several such as the wolf and the peregrine falcon were driven close to extinction in the United States. On a practical level, this was done to protect livestock such as sheep and chickens. Beyond that, the persecutions reflected the resentment by a relatively democratic age against symbols of the old, monarchical and aristocratic order.

Kings and the nobility had generally chosen predators such as the falcon and eagle as their major emblems, and so those birds were later resented.

Alphonse Toussenel believed that different varieties of birds corresponded to sectors of human society. Rather than use the scientific taxonomies of Linnaeus and others, he classified birds according to what they ate. Toussenel considered flesh-eating birds such as the eagle to be oppressors. Birds that ate plants such as the dove were victims, and omnivorous birds such as the magpie could be a bit of both.[26] While he did not explicitly advocate hunting eagles and owls to extinction, his polemics could easily have moved people to shoot them indiscriminately. Jules Michelet, who had been influenced by Toussenel, viewed the killing of raptors as a sign of progress. According to him, the eagle 'lives by murder only' and should be called the 'minister of death'.[27] Drawing on the now discredited discipline of physiognomy, which endeavoured to determine the character of both human beings and animals by the shape of their skulls, Michelet claimed that the flattened skulls of raptors showed their stupidity and brutality.[28]

Hunting birds such as partridges, grouse and pheasants has long been a highly ritualized sport of the British upper classes, analogous to fox hunting. In the early nineteenth century it was an all-male event, though women were in attendance, and each participant had a role commensurate with his class. Beaters would startle birds into flight; men of status would shoot the birds,

Hobby, from William Jardine, The Naturalist's Library *(1830s), engraving with watercolours. Predation was generally ignored in most ornithological illustrations of the Victorian era, but, when depicted, it was usually dramatized as cruel.*

VOL. LVIII. No. 1488.   PUCK BUILDING, New York, September 6, 1905.   PRICE TEN CENTS.

"What Fools these Mortals be!"

𝒫uck

CORPORATE VULTURE

DOUGH

"OUR" SENATORS   "OUR" LEGISLATURES   "OUR" JUDGES

THE NATIONAL BIRD OF PREY.

Cover of Puck, *6 September 1905. Just as raptors were stigmatized for cruelty, vultures were associated with financial exploitation. The cap on the mother vulture adds to the suggestions of antisemitism. Opposite: 'Comparative Anatomy of the Skulls of Men, Apes and Birds', from Charles Linnaeus and Ebenezer Silby,* A Universal System of Natural History Including the History of Man *(1803 edn). Physiognomy, a racialist discipline, held that the mental capacities of human beings, animals and birds could be ascertained from their 'facial angles'. Here, descending from the top left, they are ranked accordingly.*

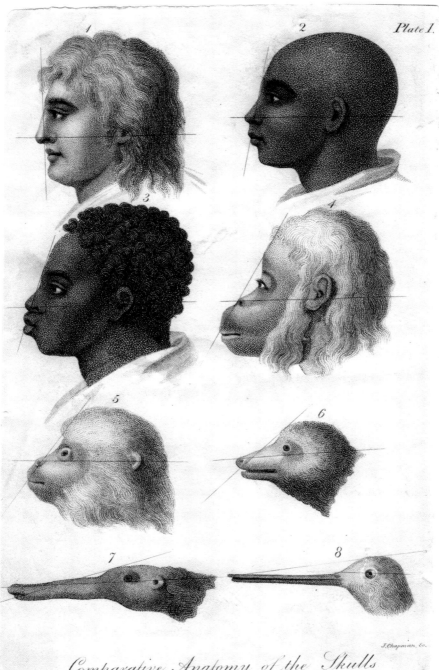

1   2   Plate I.

3

4

5   6

7   8

J. Chapman, Sc.

Comparative Anatomy of the Skulls
of Men, Apes, and Birds.

Publish'd as the Act directs June 11th 1803.

and dogs would retrieve the fallen bodies. The opening of the shooting season was a major social event. In Jane Austen's *Pride and Prejudice*, the foolish Lydia, infatuated with her new husband, 'was sure he would kill more birds on the first of September than anybody else in the country'.[29]

When aristocratic hunters faced a lack of game birds, gamekeepers in Britain began stocking the countryside with millions of pheasants. Because these were not indigenous, such birds were not protected by law, but they were potential meals for birds of prey. Having provided the game, hunters felt an especially strong sense of ownership, and having their 'birthright' usurped by raptors aroused a sort of primal fury. Gamekeepers joined farmers in shooting any raptors. As a result, about half of the large birds of prey, including the goshawk and osprey, were extinct in Britain by the end of the nineteenth century, and another six species were reduced to fewer than a hundred pairs.[30]

Collecting for Science

Added to the hazards faced by birds in modern times were the scientists themselves. Much like the subjugation of indigenous peoples by colonial powers, the conquest of nature by scientists was accomplished largely by violence. Before the advent of efficient binoculars and high-speed cameras, the only way they could closely observe birds over an extended period was to shoot them with guns, which scientists did in great numbers. A guide to collecting and preserving specimens of birds from the early 1870s advises, 'While visiting a remote region . . . one should not neglect to shoot numbers of every bird met with.' It tells us that when a male and female bird are seen together, a collector should shoot the female first, since those are more difficult to find. It also says that 'A good collector . . . must always keep his gun in readiness, for at any moment a bird that he desires may start up at his feet or peer from the bushes.' The book also gives detailed directions for preserving birds one has shot, and they are not for the squeamish. If the bird has not yet died, one should press

Hector Giacomelli, illustration to The Bird *by Jules Michelet (1869). Eagles and other raptors were associated with the old aristocracy and often vilified for their violence.*

its body to make the lungs collapse. All traces of blood should be wiped away to avoid staining the feathers. After plugging the mouth, nostrils and other orifices and taking careful notes, the bird should be left to dry before being skinned and treated with arsenic.[31]

Older natural history museums still usually contain a profusion of taxidermized birds from the period, often gazing rather macabrely at the visitor. Amateurs imitated the scientists, and wealthy collectors competed to see who could obtain the most birds, the rarest birds or the most perfect specimens. In the early twentieth century Hudson wrote that, 'Many a time on visiting a great house, the first thing the owner has drawn my attention to has been his stuffed birds in a glass case.'[32]

Nests and eggs were also taken by scientists, as well as for exhibits in science classes and museums. And, as scientists bestowed their prestige on these activities, they were copied by countless amateurs. Eggs were valued for their delicate tones, textured surfaces and patterns of dots or lines. Killing birds

Above: Hector Giacomelli, illustration to The Bird *by Jules Michelet (1869). Michelet kept an English robin in his house, and the illustrator probably intends the bird to represent Michelet himself, staring longingly out of the window. Though a passionate advocate of bird protection, Michelet apparently saw no problem with taking bird nests and eggs into his home to study.*
Overleaf: 'Albatrosses Driven from Their Nests', from Mary and Elizabeth Kirby, The Sea and Its Wonders *(1890). Collectors of eggs and nests often would not use guns for fear of damaging their finds. Instead, they drove the birds away with clubs.*
'Hawfinch Nest', from A Natural History of the Nests and Eggs of British Birds, *by F. O. Morris (1871), engraving with watercolours. In Victorian books of natural history, nests and eggs were illustrated with the same care as the birds themselves.*

ALBATROSSES DRIVEN FROM THEIR NESTS.

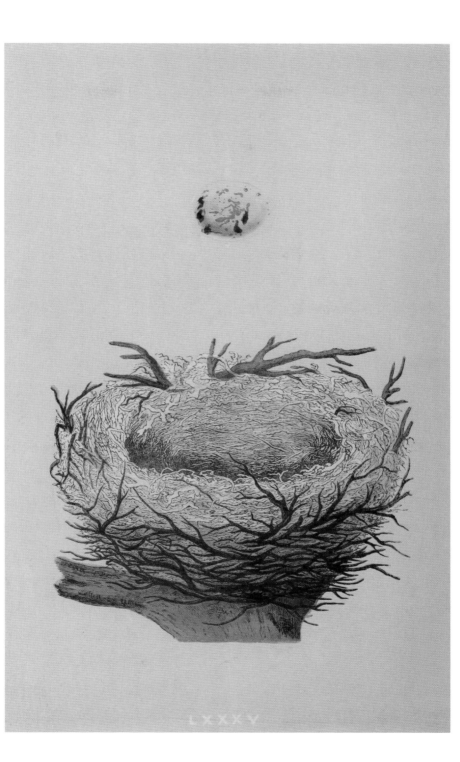

LXXXV

Men with stuffed birds, photo by Harris & Ewing, 1922. The subjects show a gravity befitting the vocation of science.

and pilfering their eggs was practised on such a massive scale throughout most of the modern period that it was impossible to tell just where science left off and sport began. For all their frequently professed love of birds, those who engaged in these activities showed remarkably little awareness of the ecological or humane consequences of their collecting.[33]

The vast number of bird skins, eggs and nests available to scientists enabled ornithology to grow very rapidly, and it became one of the first subfields to spin off from zoology in the later eighteenth century. Nevertheless, it is doubtful whether the knowledge was worth the price in devastation. In general, the study of birds was a very violent occupation and it became more violent as one approached the top of the scientific hierarchy. But this was an era in which the more bucolic European view of nature, which had prevailed around the start of the nineteenth century, seemed to be discredited by reports from exotic lands of contemporary cannibalism, violent typhoons, starvation and, most significantly, predatory behaviour of animals. Nature seemed to be pervaded with violence and, in accord with a post-Romantic aesthetic, participation in that violence seemed to be a sort of communion with the natural world.[34] Audubon, who shot birds by the hundreds in order to paint them, constantly depicted birds and mammals engaged in killing or eating prey.[35]

Protecting Crops

The sort of mental compartmentalization the killing of birds sometimes required is shown by the case of the Carolina parakeet, the only member of the parrot family indigenous to the northern regions of the United States. It was small, with a blue-green body and bright yellow-and-red head. If pictorial representations are any indication, this may have been the most beloved bird ever in America. At the start of the nineteenth century it was constantly featured, especially by the Pennsylvania Germans, on jars, furniture, textiles, baptismal certificates, marriage certificates and so on.

Unfortunately, the Carolina parakeet had a liking for crops, especially fruit, and its beauty did not make farmers hesitate to shoot. According to Audubon, it was easy to kill in great numbers. When hit by a bullet, a bird would cry out, which made the rest of a flock fly in its direction, bringing them as well in easy range of a gun.[36] They were already rare by the mid-nineteenth century and became extinct in the early twentieth. Curiously, its image remained popular long after the bird ceased to be common.

PASSENGER PIGEON.

The passenger pigeons in the United States may once have been the most numerous bird ever. It was about the size of other pigeons, but noted for its long tail, blue-grey plumage, and bronze, iridescent breast. Alexander Wilson estimated that a flock seen in Frankfort, Kentucky, in 1808 contained at least 2.25 billion birds.[37] Audubon once tried to count the passenger pigeons passing over in an hour but soon gave up, for they were far too numerous. He reported, 'The air was literally filled with them. The daylight, in full mid-day, was obscured as by an eclipse; the dung fell like flakes in a fall of snow.'[38] Huge parties of men were convened to hunt the birds, in part for meat but also to

'Passenger Pigeon', from F. O. Morris, Birds of Britain *(1863–40), engraving with watercolours.*

PLATE. XX

prevent them from eating grain in cultivated fields. The hunters would fire into the passing flocks for hours, creating large piles of dead and dying birds, before the flocks began to diminish and retreat.[39] Audubon saw large boats loaded with heaps of dead passenger pigeons in New York, where they were sold for one cent apiece.[40] By the end of the nineteenth century the passenger pigeon had almost completely disappeared from the wild; the last-known passenger pigeon died at the Cincinnati Zoo in 1914.

A highly respected book on birds published in 1869 gave a graphic account of the way passenger pigeons were being slaughtered but immediately added that, nevertheless, Audubon claimed some decades earlier that the number of passenger pigeons in the United States was actually increasing.[41] That comforting reassurance is quite a testimony to the way Americans at the time had come to take the bounty of nature for granted as a manifestation of divine favour, in rather the same way that many Americans deny the reality of climate change today.

Not many people at the time realized that the birds were needed to keep insects in check. Just as the passenger pigeons approached their demise, from the mid-1870s until almost the end of the nineteenth century, huge clouds of locusts passed the American Midwest, darkening the sky.[42] They destroyed grain far more completely than birds ever could, since they would eat not only seeds but entire plants. The locusts were responsible for $200 million in crop damage between 1874 and 1877, which comes to well over $100 billion in today's currency.[43] They also consumed fabrics and even flesh.[44]

A similar campaign, though against sparrows rather than pigeons, was begun in China during 1958 and the results were at least as catastrophic. Mao Zedong, who had recently come to power, was fascinated by mass mobilization in the service of building industry. He believed that sparrows were eating too much grain, so he called for their eradication. Almost the entire population, including children, was mobilized in some rural areas. They beat drums to startle the sparrows into flight, shot them, chased them until the birds collapsed from exhaustion, crushed their eggs and destroyed their nests. At least millions, possibly billions, of sparrows were killed, and for a time they were virtually extinct in much of China. Their extirpation was followed by swarms of locusts and other insects, which destroyed crops and seriously contributed to what may have been the greatest famine in human history.[45]

John James Audubon, Carolina Parakeets, *1827–38, aquatint.*

Imported Exotics

The modern period brought an increasing globalization of wildlife, and many indigenous species were compelled to compete with imported ones for their survival. The acclimatization movement of the mid- to late nineteenth century sought to spread birds and other wildlife to British settlements throughout the world. This was a way of making people of British descent feel at home in exotic places. Environmental imperialism was a way of claiming distant places as their own. Accordingly, rooks were deliberately introduced in New Zealand in the 1870s, and European starlings were brought to Australia around the same time.

Hudson, who led the movement to conserve British birds in the late nineteenth century, advocated importing and acclimatizing exotic birds in Britain, especially those renowned for their songs or their plumage. He hoped these would not only replace the birds that had become extinct or rare but promote the cause of bird protection. In his words, 'If we can spare the rare,

Thomas Bewick, Starling, *1804, woodblock print.*

lovely birds brought hither at great expense from China or Patagonia, can we not also spare our own kingfisher and the Golden Oriole?'[46] Attempts to establish colourful and melodious birds from distant lands in Britain were, except for the common pheasant first imported from Asia at the end of the Middle Ages, unsuccessful. Had they been so, the exotics would probably, contrary to Hudson's expectation, have not only competed with indigenous birds but attracted more hunters.

In the mid-nineteenth century the Natural History Society of America released European songbirds in New York City and Cincinnati, including nightingales, English robins, skylarks and blackbirds, none of which appear to have survived. The society also brought in a flock of house sparrows (which are, strictly speaking, not classified as 'sparrows' at all) to stop the proliferation of worms in a Brooklyn cemetery. Those birds spread in a spectacular way to become one of the most numerous birds in North America. The pharmacist Eugene Schiefflin conceived the plan of releasing all the birds mentioned in Shakespeare in New York, but, once again, they mostly failed to survive. In 1890, however, he released forty pairs of European starlings, which accommodated themselves splendidly to the new continent.[47]

House sparrows are aggressive birds that can attack other birds of comparable size, kill them and take over their nests. Starlings are powerful, assertive birds that nest in cavities. Many blame the spread of house sparrows for the decline of several indigenous sparrows and finches. The starlings may have been able to thrive only at the expense of native species such as bluebirds and woodpeckers that prefer the same nesting sites. Both imported species are widely resented in the United States, where some people even find arrogance in the way starlings cock their heads. The birds have defenders who say that, after a century and a half in America, the starlings and house sparrows should be considered indigenous and, in any case, their damage to native species has not been as extensive as their critics claim.

But the animal most threatening to bird life is the domestic cat. One recent study, sponsored by the Smithsonian Institution and endorsed by most conservation organizations, estimates that feral and free-ranging domestic cats kill about 2.4 billion birds each year in the United States alone.[48] Perhaps more than any other issue, this has pitted the animal rights movement, which centres mostly on domestic animals, against the environmental movement, which emphasizes wild ones.

Chemicals, Plastics and Glass

In the opening passage of *Silent Spring* (1962), Rachel Carson describes an idyllic, rural community beset by a mysterious malady. The chickens and then other livestock begin to sicken and die. Farmers and their families begin to feel the blight as well: 'There was a strange stillness. The birds, for example – where had they gone? … The feeding stations in the backyards were deserted.' What is the cause of this mysterious blight? The book starts as a sort of murder mystery, and the tension gradually builds. There are plenty of potential culprits, in fact the perpetrator could have been not one suspect but a gang.

Like many crime novelists, Carson has chosen an offender that her readers would not suspect – the use of pesticides that had been spreading poisons, particularly DDT, throughout the environment.[49] DDT had initially been used to control lice and diseases like malaria among troops fighting overseas during the Second World War under relatively unsanitary conditions. Later, it was publicized as an agricultural wonder drug and sprayed on crops to destroy insect pests.

People were easily seduced by its promise because the increasing industrialization of agriculture had brought with it a change in standards. Prior to the Second World War, imperfections in fruits and vegetables were tolerated. People expected, for example, occasional wormholes in a bag of apples, but they could easily be cut out, and rural people carried a pocketknife partly for that purpose. The aesthetic that prevailed after the Second World War emphasized uniformity, and people increasingly viewed such flaws as signals of poor quality and even as repulsive. Spraying crops with pesticides seemed more hygienic than more organic ways of controlling insects such as encouraging their predators.

As might have been expected, the pesticide industry vehemently attacked Carson and her thesis that DDT was killing birds, other wildlife and livestock, but researchers confirmed her findings. Today, chemicals that could potentially be poisonous are released into the environment by many industries far more quickly than they can be tested or regulated.

Chemicals like DDT are generally invisible, which can imbue them with a special horror. Plastics, by contrast, are usually extremely visible, to a point where people can take them for granted as part of normal life. There is some dispute over whether they eventually degrade or simply break down into ever smaller particles, remaining as microplastics in the ecosystem indefinitely.

Birds can inadvertently swallow plastic objects, especially those that find their way into bodies of water. While skimming the surface of bodies of water for fish with their beaks, some such as the albatross can easily swallow floating objects. Others ingest plastic while diving rapidly. Discarded fishing lines and synthetic fibres can become tangled around their organs. Sharp edges can wound them internally, and then the accumulation of plastic objects can clog their digestive systems. By 1980 plastic was found in the digestive systems of 80 per cent of seabirds, and soon it will be in nearly all of them.[50] Death from ingesting plastic is likely to be especially painful.

Most hazards to bird life go back, as already noted, to Neolithic times and perhaps earlier, but technology has brought others that are new. Hundreds of millions of birds die in the United States every year by crashing into glass windows. Other hazards created, or at least greatly aggravated, by technology, particularly for migratory birds, include smog, light pollution and noise pollution.

The Crisis

Farmers and other citizens may have realized intellectually that they were not acting in their own self-interest when they indiscriminately shot huge numbers of passenger pigeons and other birds. The continuing carnage was driven by quiet fury, a sense of outrage that the birds were taking grain that farmers believed should rightly belong to them. Particularly in the United States they were emotionally shielded from the consequences by a sense of manifest destiny. The birds were attacked in much the same way as other animals such as the buffalo and the wolf, but that required a state of emotional intoxication that was hard to sustain. After the American frontier was officially closed in 1890, many people felt increasingly troubled by the devastation of the natural world. Finally, starting around the end of the twentieth century, people realized that extinction was not simply a problem but a crisis.

'Terror Bird', illustration to H. N. Hutchinson, Extinct Monsters *(London, 1910).*

By the start of the twentieth century the ideal of human dominion was no longer pursued with such passion and excitement. It was by then universally recognized that birds were necessary for farmers to control the predations of insects against crops. This was constantly stressed in scientific publications, farmers' almanacs, government reports and so on. People were also entirely aware of other services provided by birds, such as spreading vegetation or consuming carrion. The foundations of environmental science were already firmly in place. Killing was no longer celebrated with orgiastic abandon, and protection of birds, animals and the environment became more common, but the pace of habitat destruction, importing of invasive species, chemical pollution and use of plastics steadily increased. This sets in motion a chain of extinctions that may eventually threaten the demise of humankind.

The extinction of the passenger pigeon, which had numbered in the billions, in less than a century should warn human beings that, with respect to extinction, we will find no safety in numbers. Intelligence as well gives us no guarantees. If there has ever been an animal in evolutionary history that corresponded to humankind today, a sort of 'man before man', it was the 'terror birds' or Phorusrhacidae. These huge, flightless birds were the apex predators in South America from about 60 to 2 million years ago. We can, perhaps, think of them as a combination of dinosaur and human being. They had, like other flightless birds such as the ostrich, the basic morphology of a therapod dinosaur with abilities to match. They had enormous beaks, long legs and sharp claws, and some could run at speeds of almost 113 km/h (70 mph). They also had huge skulls and were probably among the most intelligent animals ever.[51] Neither their physical nor their intellectual abilities could save them when a land bridge opened between North and South America, allowing large, mammalian predators such as sabre-tooth cats to cross.[52]

15 PROTECTION AND REVIVAL

But now they drift on the still water,
Mysterious, beautiful;
Among what rushes will they build,
By what lake's edge or pool
Delight men's eyes when I awake some day
To find they have flown away?
W. B. Yeats, 'The Wild Swans at Coole'

Helen Macdonald has written in reference to ornithologists of early seventeenth-century Italy, 'The sheer abundance of bird life that Cassano, Olina, Leonardi and their peers would have encountered is almost impossible to imagine.'[1] The profusion of birds that those Renaissance artists and thinkers experienced was, in turn, less than that in medieval and ancient times. In *The Birds*, Aristophanes mentions 79 avian species and includes a lot of information about their habits and behaviour.[2] Ornithologists can identify about eighty varieties of birds in the Roman mosaics at Pompeii.[3] Shakespeare refers to sixty varieties of birds in his works,[4] far more than most people would be able to identify now. To search for avian life like a birdwatcher of today was hardly necessary before the modern era, since birds were everywhere.

Not everyone in the late eighteenth and early nineteenth centuries was pleased about urbanization and industrialization, but early objections generally took the form of mourning rather than protest. The momentum of what was called 'progress' seemed overwhelming and beyond challenge. Most European and American Romantics sublimated any uneasiness about the direction of society in a melancholy veneration of the natural world. They may well have intuitively sensed the environmental damage created by industry, but, without the conceptual tools of contemporary environmentalism, they had no means to challenge it.

Romantic poets have often described the experience of seeing or hearing a bird as an ecstatic annihilation of the self, not unlike falling in love or religious ecstasy. Their medieval and Renaissance forebears such as Walther von der Vogelweide or Geoffrey Chaucer would write of meadows with many birds singing in a joyful harmony. Keats and Shelley, by contrast, would focus on a solitary bird singing in a field. The bird would seem alienated from nature, in much the same way as the poets felt alienated from society. This isolation shows the increasing rarity of songbirds by that time.

The increasingly elaborate description and classification of birds, starting around the seventeenth century, was in tension with the view of them as otherworldly creatures. This is illustrated by two of the most grandly awkward lines of English Romantic poetry. Shelley's 'To a Skylark' begins:

> Hail to thee, blithe spirit!
> Bird thou never wert . . .[5]

Of course, the skylark really is a bird, but the author found it hard to reconcile physical reality with an ethereal song. This is not simply an isolated, rhetorical excess, since much the same tension between lyrical effusion and objective description runs through the work of illustrators of the time such as John James Audubon. But, in retrospect, it can almost seem as if Shelley, by removing birds to the realm of spirits, was making an excuse for not worrying about the possibility of their extinction.

Watching and Feeding Birds

Birdwatching grew out of the popular craze for natural history in Victorian times, when scientific amateurs explored woods, meadows and shorelines in the effort to find and document new species. That pursuit had a foundation in natural theology, essentially a monotheistic variant of what Cicero called 'natural divination'. Victorian naturalists believed that, in learning the plan of creation, they would better understand the will of God. Today birdwatching seems entirely secular, though it is still based on the veneration of nature.

It is not an accident that birding became most popular in the most heavily industrialized countries, particularly the UK and the United States. On one level it is a way to enjoy the environment, while doing no damage and even helping to monitor the ecosystem. At the same time, it shares many features of industrial society such as pervasive competition, quantification and the incessant quest for novelty. Some birders compete with one another to see who can see the most birds in a season, a year or a lifetime. A few spend hefty sums travelling around in the hope of seeing a rare bird that has been reported in a distant location.

One critic of birdwatching is Paul Shepard, who has called it 'a perversion of natural history'. He writes, 'Birds have always been wonderful metaphoric symbols, but the new, technological, unionized pursuit is "by the numbers". They (birders) identify them against a "life list" and keep score.'[6] Shepard belonged to a generation of Americans for whom the frontier was still a fairly vivid memory.

Americans celebrated pristine landscapes and large, fierce animals such as the bear and buffalo. For many during this period and immediately afterwards, it seemed as if intimacy with nature could only be achieved though conflict, in something like the way some couples believe fighting brings them closer together. The popular models for this were rugged frontiersmen such as Daniel Boone and Davy Crockett together with idealized Native Americans. By comparison, birdwatching seemed decadent, lazy and effeminate.

Shepard's criticism of birdwatching contains some truth. As currently practised, birding places too much emphasis on species identification and too little on storytelling, but 'keeping score' is of major importance only to relatively few practitioners. Birdwatching puts people in touch with the rhythms of the seasons. They learn when birds migrate and return, change the colour of their plumage, mate and bear new chicks. They see how these cycles are affected by storms, intense winds, unseasonable heat or cold, and, more generally, by climate change. Watching birds is a prelude to, and in ways even a prerequisite for, environmental activism on their behalf.

An immediate consequence of watching birds can be wanting to feed them, a practice that doubtless goes back in an informal way to very early times. People of all social levels probably always left out scraps and leftovers that could not be disposed of in any other way for birds. For the Greeks, Romans and many other peoples, animal sacrifice was essentially a form of bird feeding, for they would leave skin, bones, gristle and small portions of meat from an animal on an altar, where the immediate recipients were likely to be not gods but birds.

Bird feeding became recognized as a recreation in Britain, Continental Europe and the United States around the end of the nineteenth century. It steadily grew in popularity, becoming a major industry around the end of the Second World War, with heavily marketed, competing brands of birdseed. In 2006 the u.s. Fish and Wildlife Service estimated that 56 million American fed birds as a hobby.[7] The consensus among ornithologists is that feeding birds generally does them little harm or good, but it is a way to relieve the loneliness that comes with our estrangement from the natural world.[8] The next step, which is far more difficult, is protecting birds.

Protecting Birds

A few birds were protected by law or custom from very early times. Among the Lenca and Maya of Central America, killing the quetzal bird, which was central to their mythologies, was punishable with death.[9] Both Aristotle and Pliny the Elder reported that to kill a stork was a capital crime in Thessaly, at least in part because the birds performed a service by eating snakes.[10] In 1457 King James II of Scotland made it illegal to kill partridges, plovers, wild ducks and similar birds during the breeding season.[11] Flora Thompson, in her memoir of growing up in a poor community in rural England during the nineteenth century, wrote that even boys who made a sport of killing birds and destroying their nests would never harm a robin, wren, martin or swallow, for they believed those birds were under the protection of God.[12]

Some birds gained security through association with the high and mighty. In 1482 the English monarchy decreed that only select people of wealth could own swans, which had to be marked by an authorized symbol carved or branded on their beaks, a privilege retained even today on the River Thames by the guilds of vintners and dyers. All unmarked swans automatically belonged to the Crown, and there were heavy fines for killing swans, stealing their eggs or cutting grass near a swan's nest.[13] The swan, with its graceful curves, luminous white feathers and literary importance, would have made a very attractive target for trophy hunters. Because of its protection by royalty, it is the only large bird in Britain that has never become endangered.

People have also protected birds for their contribution to hygiene. Until around the end of the sixteenth century ravens in Britain were guarded both by custom and law for their service by devouring carrion.[14] Kites were also protected, especially in London, and remained a familiar part of city life, often mentioned by Shakespeare and other writers, until about the end of the eighteenth century.[15] Vultures have provided a similar service in India up through much of the twentieth century. Hindus keep cows for milk, ploughing and bearing loads but generally do not eat beef, so they leave the carcasses of cattle at roadsides for vultures to consume. Since they prevented the stench of decaying bodies, the killing of vultures was strictly forbidden.[16] But new methods of sanitation eventually made these prohibitions appear anachronistic, while industrial poisons in the ecosystem killed birds in ways that often go almost unnoticed.

Other birds were protected for their utility in protecting crops from insects. In 1848 the Mormons in Utah had their harvest saved from katydids that were destroying their crops by a flock of gulls, and they maintain the birds were sent by God especially for that purpose. Insectivorous birds such as quails, prairie chickens and turkeys proved to be an effective means of destroying locusts when they ravaged the American Midwest in the late nineteenth century, and many states revised their game laws to protect them.[17]

Attempts to protect birds in the early twentieth century, when a very substantial part of the American population still lived from farming, emphasized their importance for the rural economy. A 1919 flyer produced by the Bird Sanctuary Campaign in America contained very specific agricultural information, such as that the cuckoo is the only bird that eats the hairy caterpillar, so, 'A cuckoo is worth $100 to any orchardist for the production of fruit trees.' When the First World War created food shortages in Europe, and to a lesser extent America as well, Herbert Clark Hoover, the American Food Administrator and future President, said, 'I hope the people of the United States will be able to realize how closely to this whole question of food saving is the protection and encouragement of migratory birds.'[18] But new chemical sprays would soon make the use of birds for that purpose appear outmoded.

In the late nineteenth and early twentieth centuries upper-class American women led a boycott of feathered hats. In 1918 the protest culminated in the passing of the Migratory Bird Treaty Act by the United States Congress, which outlawed the trade in feathers. The act was legally challenged and brought before the Supreme Court, where Justice Oliver Wendell Holmes, writing the majority opinion, declared that without such legislation all birds might eventually become extinct.[19] In 1954 the British Parliament passed the Protection of Birds Act, which made it illegal to kill wild birds, capture them, take their eggs or damage their nests. It made several exceptions, however, by allowing for people to be licensed to perform those acts for certain purposes such as falconry, scientific investigation or the protection of other birds.[20]

Ten years after the publication of *Silent Spring*, in 1972, use of DDT as an agricultural spray was banned in the United States. Britain followed suit in 1984, though DDT is still used in a few countries such as India. In 1973 the U.S. Congress passed the Endangered Species Act, which provided a large range of protections for indigenous species that were at risk. The law prohibited interfering with their habitat, killing them, taking them as pets or selling them.

The application of the Endangered Species Act and other legislation for the protection of birds to indigenous people, who use eagle feathers in religious ceremonies, has been a sensitive issue. The bald eagle, the national bird of America, had been driven to the point of extinction in the United States by reproductive problems associated with DDT. In 1892 there had been an estimated 50,000 mated bald eagle pairs in the United States, and by 1963 the number was down to 417.[21] Today it is illegal in the United States to kill or capture eagles, with a partial exception made for the Hopi people,[22] but people are asked to send any eagle feathers they find to the Bureau of Indian Affairs for distribution to various tribes. Native Americans generally feel that refraining from capturing the birds is a small price for their preservation.

Reviving Birds

Henry Wadsworth Longfellow criticized the agriculturalists' short-sighted focus on profits in his narrative poem 'The Birds of Killingworth', first published in 1863. It begins with an idyllic celebration of birdsong. Then it tells how the thrifty farmers were alarmed at the call of the crow. After a village assembly, the townspeople shoot all the birds, to find their crops are destroyed by insects instead. A teacher ('preceptor') addresses them, using imagery much like that Rachel Carson would later employ in *Silent Spring*:

> 'Think of your woods and orchards without birds!
> Of empty nests that cling to boughs and beams
> As in an idiot's brain remembered words
> Hang empty 'mid the cobwebs of his dreams'!
> Will bleat of flocks or bellowing of herds
> Make up for the lost music, when your teams
> Drag home the stingy harvest, and no more
> The feathered gleaners follow to your door?
> (lines 129–37)

Faced with devastation, they realize their mistake. They bring new birds in wicker cages and release them to their fields, where they sing for the teacher's wedding.[23] The happy ending does not seem convincing today in view of our current difficulty in reintroducing vanished species.

By about the end of the nineteenth century concentrated efforts began to not only protect but bring back birds such as the American turkey and the Eurasian bittern, which had been driven close to extinction. These were initially nothing like the effortless repatriation that Longfellow had described in 'The Birds of Killingworth' and resulted in qualified failures at best. People at the time had little understanding of the difficulty and complexity of the task. They did not appreciate, for example, how the absence of birds could change the environment, rendering it less welcoming on their return.

The Endangered Species Act gave new impetus to the movement to not only protect but revive or even reintroduce many species that had been driven almost to the point of extinction. Particularly in the United States, conditions for the revival of many forest birds had become more favourable over the past half century or so. Urbanization and the abandonment of farms had vacated much land that could serve as wildlife habitat. By the twenty-first century trees had gradually grown back to a point where they covered about two-thirds of the area that had been woodland in 1630.[24]

Wildlife managers had also learned from earlier, mostly unsuccessful attempts to bring back species from the brink of disappearance. They appreciated that it took far more than releasing them from a wicker cage, as in Longfellow's 'The Birds of Killingworth', and they approached the task with new sophistication and resources. The challenge often seemed quixotic, but they showed enormous dedication and resourcefulness. Earlier attempts to bring back the American turkey had failed, largely because those raised on farms were unable to survive when released into the wild.

Starting in the 1950s, environmentalists began to restock the woods by capturing wild birds from the few remaining areas where they might still be found and then relocating them in areas where they had been extirpated. It worked spectacularly. By 2009 the number of turkeys in the United States had grown to 8 million.[25] Similar programmes involving transplanting captive birds

Thomas Bewick, Bittern, 1804, woodblock print.

and habitat protection have brought back the bald eagle in America from near extinction to a point where it is no longer endangered and may easily be seen on both the Atlantic and Pacific coasts of the United States as well as around many lakes and rivers.[26]

From Colonial times educated Americans had felt jealous of the literary and folkloric richness of Britain and Continental Europe, where just about any stream or mountain was connected to a tale. They saw the primeval splendour of American landscapes as compensation. Accordingly, their efforts at conservation emphasized charismatic megafauna such as condors, wolves and cranes, which they preferred to think of as outside of human history. The British, who had to address the needs of a smaller and more densely populated territory than the United States, approached the challenge from a very different point of view. They tended to think of fauna as part of an organic community that also included vegetation, and human beings, which had been inscribed in hedgerows and pastures. Protecting wildlife was a matter of preserving history, not escaping from it.

A good example is the revival of the Eurasian bittern, a marshland bird with a long beak and a booming call. The bittern had been in steady decline since the 1500s, and it had ceased to breed in Britain by the early twentieth century. Hudson called it 'one of the most fascinating of the British birds on account of its solitary, mysterious habits, its strange, richly coloured and beautifully pencilled plumage, and that booming cry, once familiar in our land, that "shakes the sounding marsh".'[27] The Royal Society for the Protection of Birds (RSPB), founded in 1889, lobbied to protect the bittern by emphasizing its importance as an integral part of the English countryside as reflected in custom and folklore. Once bitterns had begun to breed at a marsh in Minsmere, Suffolk, conservationists worked in the last decades of the twentieth century to entice the birds to nearby areas. To encourage cooperation from local people, they deliberately created a 'bittern brand'. A local beer and a railway line were named after the bird. The strategy of reintegrating the bird into the fabric of a community, ruled largely by custom, has been largely successful and the number of nesting sites has steadily increased.[28]

The success with a few species is cheering, but it is far from enough to reverse the general trend towards increasing extinction. According to a recent, highly regarded study, 29 per cent of birds in the United States and Canada vanished between 1970 and the end of 2019, as have 31 species. The two countries have lost 53 per cent of grassland birds, such as meadowlarks, 37 per cent of shorebirds, such as plovers, 33 per cent of boreal forest birds, such as warblers, and 23 per cent of Arctic tundra birds, such as puffins. The one encouraging trend, apart from the revival of turkeys and many raptors, has been that of wetland birds such as ducks, whose numbers have actually increased.[29]

Resurrecting Birds

Far more complicated and ambitious than the case of the American turkey or Eurasian bittern was that of the California condor, a vulture with a wingspan of more than 3 metres (9 ft). By the early 1980s it was extinct in the wild. Only 22 individual condors were left, all of them in captivity. Re-establishing them involved the seemingly impossible task of not only teaching the chicks the skills necessary to survive in the wild but, in addition, how to cope with humans and their technology. So that the condors would not become overly dependent on human beings, they were taught by people who concealed their identity by using puppets with the heads of adult vultures. Using electric shocks for negative reinforcement, they taught the chicks to avoid simulated power lines and garbage cans. After vaccinating and releasing them, the wildlife experts, assisted by Native American volunteers, carefully monitored their progress and occasionally recaptured a few to examine them for lead poisoning.[30] Amazingly, the birds did become increasingly independent and, in the third decade of the twenty-first century, a little over four hundred individuals live in the wild, a very impressive number though still not nearly enough to ensure the survival of the species.

The attempt to revive the whooping crane has involved even greater artifice. Around the end of the twentieth century there were fewer than twenty left in the world. Several attempts were made to release captive cranes into the wild, but they met with little success, because the captive birds did not know how to migrate. Rehabilitators at the start of the twenty-first century tried a radical new method. They approached captive baby cranes wearing elaborate costumes, in effect impersonating their parents. They then taught them to migrate from Wisconsin to Florida by getting the chicks to follow an ultralight aircraft.[31] Today there are 669 whooping cranes in the wild and another 163 still in captivity. They are still classified as 'endangered' in part because their population, while carefully monitored, could be devastated by a natural disaster such as a hurricane.[32]

For all the heroic effort and ingenuity that has gone into their revival, California condors and whooping cranes remain functionally extinct. They provide a magnificent spectacle, a sort of monument to their former glory, but they are not numerous or established enough to have a significant impact on the environment. They would probably not survive long without elaborate monitoring by human beings, something that could easily be withdrawn in the event of a serious recession or a political change in fashion. But nature is full of surprises, so perhaps one or both species may provide us with one. They may come up with ingenious ways to survive that their trainers did not anticipate and increase their numbers dramatically.

PL. CXI

Besides, even as just a memorial, the surviving populations of cranes and condors may be important. In terms of the expenditure of time, money, emotion and ingenuity, preserving these populations may at first not seem to be a very pragmatic approach to conservation, but then we can factor in their inspirational power. It is not rare to spend great effort and artistry on monuments, and their purpose is to remind people of what they have lost and, by implication, what they should now work to preserve. A handful of birds might do that far better than any statues made of bronze.

Even bringing back whooping cranes and California condors is modest compared to some of the projects that are now being initiated. A group of scientists called 'Revive and Restore' is working to insert reconstructed DNA of passenger pigeons into the eggs of a related species. In this way, they hope to hatch a new flock of passenger pigeons and then release them, so that birds can multiply and rejuvenate American forests with their dung.[33] The challenges here are not purely scientific, since the project, if initially successful, would risk reviving the old animosities that moved people to kill the passenger pigeons in the first place. And would the newly resurrected species compete with other birds, perhaps either driving its rivals to extinction or facing oblivion a second time? Would the birds, whatever their DNA, really be passenger pigeons at all, having been raised in a very different environment from their genetic forebears? In all of these projects to resurrect extremely rare or extinct species, is conservation being used as a pretext for ever more aggressive intervention into natural processes?

Theodore Jasper, 'American Vultures', chromolithograph from Studer's Popular Ornithology *(1881). The large bird on the tree stump is a California condor. Below it are a black vulture and a turkey vulture.*
John James Audubon, Whooping Crane, *1827–38, aquatint.*

PLATE CCXXVI

Hooping Crane. GRUS AMERICANA. *Adult Male.*

Which Species to Save?

Killing predators and competitors has long been a standard practice of those seeking to protect or restore endangered species. American government contractors have shot foxes to protect seabirds on the coast of Alaska. At the end of the twentieth century, conservationists had 140,000 goats shot on the Galapagos Islands to protect indigenous plants and the native animals that feed on them. Between 2010 and 2015, 300 tonnes of poisoned food were left on the island of South Georgia in the South Atlantic to save endangered birds by killing the rats that eat their eggs.[34] In the forests of the American Northwest, the u.s. Fish and Wildlife Service is attempting to protect the spotted owl by systematically killing thousands of barred owls, which have been moving westwards and forcing out their relatives.[35] More radical still is the decision of the Australian government, undertaken in 2015, to extirpate hundreds of thousands of feral cats in order to preserve native wildlife, especially birds.[36]

I have mentioned only a few of the recent attempts to protect and revive endangered birds, but they will illustrate some of the risks, dangers, demands, problems and opportunities of such programmes. Because ecosystems have become increasingly fragile, extreme measures may be required. Many programmes to preserve or return wildlife involve manipulation, deception or killing. As Thom van Dooren has noted, 'it seems that care and hope are frequently saturated with, perhaps even grounded in, unavoidable and ongoing practices of violence.'[37] As the problem of mass extinctions grows more desperate, conservationists will probably cast off many inhibitions, and the violence of their methods will increase.

Elizabeth Kolbert concludes *The Sixth Extinction* by stating that, 'We are deciding, without quite meaning to, which evolutionary pathways will remain open and which will be forever closed.'[38] As she observes, this is a massive responsibility. Decisions about which species to concentrate on saving involve complex balancing of personal loyalties, environmental considerations, sentiment, economic feasibility and aesthetic appreciation. There are profound differences, even within the environmentalist community, as to how the limited resources available should be used to at least limit mass extinctions. Should we concentrate on preserving individual species or ecosystems? Should we try to protect the greatest possible number of birds or just concentrate on a few keystone species?

Kolbert exaggerates the power of humankind. If all 7 billion human beings on this planet could entirely coordinate our efforts, we would come closer to being able to choose which creatures survive, but that is not likely to happen. Humankind is divided by culture, geography and, even more, by individual experience. Birds like pigeons, starlings, house sparrows and crows have proliferated in the Anthropocene, the supposed 'Age of Man', not because people chose them, but because they could adjust to urban environments. People may have created the conditions for them to thrive, but that was not conscious or intentional.

Meanwhile, birds such as parrots that have been especially beloved by human beings have not been flourishing. Often the favour of human beings has even hurt their chances of survival. Those in the ecotourism industry often destroy avian habitats in order to build luxury hotels. Beloved birds may also be captured as part of the clandestine, and mostly illegal, trade in exotic pets. Large numbers of birds are taken from their natural habitats for falcon races, which are popular in Arab countries, and birdsong competitions, which are popular in Indonesia.[39]

Kolbert, after presenting an apocalyptic vision of the future, probably wished to avoid sounding preachy. She hoped that concluding with a passage on human power might simultaneously offer some readers reassurance, while also inspiring them to a commensurate sense of responsibility. We have yet to see how effective this approach will prove. With respect to mass extinctions and the closely associated problem of climate change, neither detached analysis, dire warnings nor appeals to guilt have proved sufficiently effective to overcome public inertia and denial.

Epilogue

On an emotional level, extinction is an intensification of death, and in ways it is just as mysterious. Just as people constantly dream of reviving the dead, they aspire to bring back extinct species. We mourn species, just as we do individuals. But it is not only birds that are now becoming extinct. It is also other animals, plants, cultures, ways of life, religions, languages, crafts, technologies and almost everything. The cumulative impact can be terrifying.

The losses are interconnected in complex ways. Rachel Carson had objected to ways of killing insects in *Silent Spring*,[40] but not even she had realized that their demise, when it had attained a sufficient scale, could by itself constitute a threat to the environment. Early in the twenty-first century farmers and ornithologists in Europe noticed a precipitous decline in birds, similar to the one Rachel Carson had written about. There were huge drops in the number of partridges, nightingales and turtle doves among others. This time it turned out that the birds were starving, since the insects they relied on for food were

Robert Rauschenberg, Tracer, *1964, oil and silkscreen on canvas. The bald eagle finds itself surrounded by the discarded paraphernalia of human civilization on the sea, on land and in the air.*

not available. There had been a precipitous decline in insect numbers and diversity.[41] In a way, this is not a separate cause of bird decline so much as an elaboration of the familiar ones. The insects were being killed for much the same causes as the birds had been such as habitat destruction and poisons. Birds were partially protected from the most direct effects of climate change, since they generally possessed the ability to relocate over substantial distances, but the insects that they relied on for food could not.

What is strange, perhaps unprecedented, is that the environmental crisis is at once so desperately urgent and yet, in many ways, so amorphous. We habitually compare major causes to war, but, in this case, there is no clearly defined enemy and we have only a vague idea of what 'victory' would be. Furthermore, though people measure the decline of biodiversity in terms of numbers of species, there is no consensus among scientists about what species are or even whether they exist. And what is this 'human civilization', which we are so concerned with protecting? People may variously think of it in terms of business and politics as usual, a few hundred cultural monuments, folk traditions or abstract principles, but few would even attempt a succinct definition. Survival is not simply a matter of passing on a physical form. Far more fundamentally, it is a matter of preserving identity, something that has always been tenuous.

I believe the crisis is ultimately not precisely about biodiversity. It is about restructuring our relationship as human beings with the natural world, and birds are an excellent place to start. Their flourishing or demise can serve as an environmental conscience for us, an indicator of whether we are doing the right thing. What I have called an 'avian illumination', the intense identification of a person with a bird, is not, and has never been, a particularly unusual, much less exotic, experience. Such epiphanies pervade human civilization, and they are central to building both individual and collective notions of identity, even though we are not always conscious of them. What can be baffling, however, is how different people identify with songbirds or raptors as well as other birds in a vast range of ways.

As this book has, I believe, shown, this identification may be expressed in divination, falconry, activism, storytelling, music and art, to name just a few of the most easily recognizable ways. Our relationships with birds and other animals are every bit as elusive, layered, ambivalent and nurturing as those with other human beings. Even our sense of dominion is not as simple as it may seem, as it is tied, in both philosophy and myth, to suspicions of human inferiority.[42]

Because of this complexity, I do not try to tell people whether or not they should farm, eat meat, hunt, patronize zoos or keep pets. Such decisions

Thomas Bewick, Rook, *1804, woodblock print.*

often go directly to the core of personal identity in ways that can be extremely difficult to discuss, whether in sedate academic journals or noisy public forums. I ask only that people carefully consider the implications of their choices and remain open to other possibilities.

In many respects, our drive to collective survival does not seem particularly strong, for we constantly engage in pointless and suicidal wars. Yet birds embody many of our values, at times adding a grace that can seem otherworldly. If we will not address environmental problems for our own survival, we might still do it for them. Birds also have a remarkable ability to confer hope in times of adversity.

Reminiscing about her experience living in Cambridge during the Second World War, the novelist Celia Dale wrote in a letter to the magazine *Country Life*:

> I find there is nothing more soothing than the cawing of Rooks. During the war when disaster after disaster seemed to be England's lot, I would look out of the window and see the nests of the rooks and hear the birds' voices, and I used to think: 'The Rooks are still there, at any rate.'[43]

REFERENCES

Introduction

1 Boria Sax, 'Swan Maiden: The Animal that Adam Could not Name', in *Goddesses in World Culture*, ed. Patricia Monaghan (New York, 2012), vol. II, pp. 183–92.

2 Daniel Ward, ed. and trans., *The German Legends of the Brothers Grimm* (Philadelphia, PA, 1981), vol. II, legends 541–5, pp. 179–84.

3 Mircea Eliade, *Shamanism: Archaic Techniques of Ecstasy* (Princeton, NJ, 1964), p. 403.

4 Herman Melville, *Moby-Dick* (New York, 1902), p. 166.

5 Graeme Gibson, 'Some Blessed Hope: Birds and the Nostalgic Human Soul', in *The Bedside Book of Birds: An Avian Miscellany*, ed. Graeme Gibson (New York, 2005), pp. 304–5.

6 Gerard Manley Hopkins, 'The Windhover', in *On Wings of Song: Poems about Birds*, ed. J. D. McClatchy (New York, 2000), p. 224.

7 Boria Sax, *Dinomania: Why We Love, Fear and are Utterly Enchanted by Dinosaurs* (London, 2018), pp. 227–46.

1 Parallel Worlds

1 John Ayto, *Dictionary of Word Origins: The Histories of More than 8,000 English-Language Words* (New York, 1990), pp. 64, 239, 289.

2 Claude Lévi-Strauss, *The Savage Mind* (Chicago, IL, 1966), pp. 204–5.

3 Ibid., p. 204.

4 Ibid., p. 184.

5 Sian Lewis and Lloyd Llewellyn-Jones, *The Culture of Animals in Antiquity* (Oxford, 2017), pp. 45–6.

6 Roel Sterckx, *The Animal and Daemon in Early China* (Albany, NY, 2002), pp. 43–9.

7 P'u Sung-ling, *Strange Stories from a Chinese Studio*, trans. Herbert A. Giles (New York, 1926), pp. 171–6.

8 John Cummins, *The Hound and the Hawk: The Art of Medieval Hunting* (London, 2001), pp. 187–8.

9 Alphonse Toussenel, *Le monde des Oiseaux, Ornithologie Passionnelle* (Sydney, 2019), pp. 1–7. The translations are my own.

10 Levi-Strauss, *Savage Mind*, pp. 137–8.

11 Philippe Descola, *Beyond Nature and Culture*, trans. Janet Lloyd (Chicago, IL, 2013), pp. 144–71.

12 Edward O. Wilson, 'Biophilia and the Conservation Ethic', in *The Biophilia Hypothesis*, ed. Stephen R. Kellert and Edward O. Wilson (Washington, DC, 1993), p. 31.

13 Roberto Marchesini, *Over the Human: Post-humanism and the Concept of Animal Epiphany* (Cham, Switzerland, 2017), pp. 93–114.

14 Donna Haraway, *The Companion Species Manifesto: Dogs, People and Significant Otherness* (Chicago, IL, 2003), pp. 16–17.

15 Lisa Nocks, *The Robot: The Life Story of a Technology* (Baltimore, MD, 2008), p. 17.

16 Apollodorus, *The Library of Greek Mythology*, trans. Robin Hard (Oxford, 1997), pp. 140–41.

17 M. C. Howatson, ed., 'Daedalus', *The Oxford Companion to Classical Literature* (Oxford, 1989), p. 167.

18 Plato, 'Euphyphro', trans. Hugh Tredennick and Harold Tarrant, in *The Last Days of Socrates* (London, 1993), section 11C, p. 20.

19 Plato, *The Republic*, trans. Robin Waterford (Oxford, 1998), section 620a-b (p. 378).

20 Mircea Eliade, *Myth and Reality* (New York, 1963), pp. 124–5.

21 Mircea Eliade, *Shamanism: Archaic Techniques of Ecstasy* (Princeton, NJ, 1964), p. 403.

22 Giorgio Vasari, *The Lives of the Artists*, trans. Julia Conaway and Peter Bondanella (Oxford, 2008), p. 286.

23 Smithsonian National Air and Space Museum, 'Leonardo da Vinci's Codex on the Flight of Birds', http://airandspace.si.edu, 22 October 2013.

24 Ibid.

2 Phoenix and Thunderbird

1 Graziella Arazzi, 'I segni dell'universo animale. Zooantropologia e zoosemiotica in Gaston Bachelard', *Zooantropologia: Storia, etica e pedagogia dell'interazione uomo/animale*, ed. Claudio Tugnoli (Milan, 2003), pp. 185–93.

2 Gaston Bachelard, *Air and Dreams: An Essay on the Imagination of Movement*, trans. Edith R. Farrell and C. Frederick Farrell (Dallas, TX, 2002), pp. 19–110.

3 Gaston Bachelard, *The Poetics of Space*, trans. Maria Jolas (New York, 2014), pp. 124–37.

4 Bachelard, *Air and Dreams*, pp. 247–8.

5 Geoffrey Chaucer, 'Prologue to *The Canterbury Tales*', in *Chaucer: Complete Works*, ed. Walter W. Skeat (London, 1973), lines 9–10, p. 419.

6 Tim Birkhead, *Bird Sense: What It's Like to Be a Bird* (New York, 2012), pp. 30–31.

7 Joseph Nigg, *The Phoenix: An Unnatural Biography of a Mythical Beast* (Chicago, IL, 2016), p. 19.

8 Roel Sterckx, *The Animal and the Daemon in Early China* (Albany, NY, 2000), pp. 178, 288.

9 Adam McLean, 'The Birds in Alchemy', *Hermetic Journal*, 5 (Autumn 1979), pp. 15–18, available at http://levity.com, accessed 14 November 2019.

10 Sabine Baring-Gould and Edward Hardy, *Curious Myths of the Middle Ages* (New York, 1987), pp. 27–34.

11 Antonio Pigafetta, *Magellan's Voyage around the World*, ed. James Alexander Robertson, 3 vols (Cleveland, OH, 1906), II, p. 105.

12 Willy Ley, *Dawn of Zoology* (Englewood Cliffs, NJ, 1968), p. 140.

13 Ibid., p. 140.

14 Sterckx, *Animal and Daemon*, p. 181.

15 Ibid.

16 Edward A. Armstrong, *The Folklore of Birds* (London, 1958), pp. 109–10.

17 Hieronymus Megiser, *Warhafftige, gründliche und außführliche so wol Historische alß Chorographische Beschreibung der uberauß reichen, mechtigen und weitberhümbten Insul Madagascar* (Altenburg, 1609), p. 22.

18 Husain Haddawy, trans., *Sindbad and Other Tales from the Arabian Nights* (New York, 1995), p. 12.

19 Evan T. Pritchard, *Bird Medicine: The Sacred Power of Bird Shamanism* (Rochester, VT, 2013), p. 207.

20 Bachelard, *Air and Dreams*, p. 16.

* The nebulous identity of fantastic birds often makes it uncertain whether their names should be treated as proper nouns. I have not capitalized them on that ground except in cases where, as with Garuda, it is clear in the legends that there is only one.

3 Bird Divination

1 Homer, *Odyssey*, trans. Stanley Lombardo (Indianapolis, IN, 2000), X.514–17, p. 115.

2 Apollodorus, *The Library of Greek Mythology*, trans. Robin Hard (Oxford, 1997), 1.9, pp. 46–7.

3 Anonymous, 'The Lay of Fafnir', in *The Poetic Edda*, trans. Carolyne Larrington (Oxford, 1996), pp. 157–65.

4 Jacob Grimm and Wilhelm Grimm, *The Complete Fairy Tales of the Brothers Grimm*, trans. Jack Zipes (New York, 1987), tale 33, pp. 127–9.

5 Mircea Eliade, *Shamanism: Archaic Techniques of Ecstasy* (Princeton, NJ, 1964), p. 98.

6 Rebecca Ann Bach, *Birds and Other Creatures in Renaissance Literature* (New York, 2018), p. 42.

7 Jared Diamond, 'The Worst Mistake in the History of the Human Race', www.discovermagazine.com, 1 May 1999.

8 Marie V. Lilly, Emma C. Lucore and Keith A. Travin, 'Eavesdropping Grey Squirrels Infer Safety from Bird Chatter', *PLoS One*, https://journals.plos.org, 4 September 2019.

9 Hesiod, *Works and Days*, in *Theogony, Works and Days*, trans. M. L. West (Oxford, 1988), lines 448–50, p. 50.

10 J. Pollard, *Birds in Greek Life and Myth* (New York, 1977), p. 111.

11 Hesiod, *Works and Days*, lines 484–5, p. 51.

12 Ibid., line 828, p. 61.

13 Pollard, *Birds in Greek Life and Myth*, p. 113.

14 Apollodorus, *The Library of Greek Mythology*, 1.9, pp. 52–3.

15 Boria Sax, *City of Ravens* (London, 2011), p. 28.

16 Debra Hermann, *Avian Cognition: Exploring the Intelligence, Behavior and Individuality of Birds* (Boca Raton, FL, 2016), p. 17.

17 Paul Shepard, *Thinking Animals: Animals and the Development of Human Intelligence* (Athens, GA, 1998), p. 34.

18 Jeremy Mynott, *Birds in the Ancient World* (Oxford, 2018), p. 10.

19 Herodotus, *The History of Herodotus*, trans. G. C. Macaulay, vol. 1 (London, 1890), II.55.

20 Homer, *The Iliad*, trans. Stanley Lombardo (Indianapolis, IN, 1997), X.282–301, pp. 188–9.

21 Ibid., XII.201–57, pp. 230–31.

22 Ibid., XXIV.336–42, p. 477.

23 Homer, *Odyssey*, II.161–72, p. 19.

24 Homer, *Illiad*, VII.58–60, p. 130.

25 Homer, *Odyssey*, V.333, p. 39.

26 Hans Blumenberg, *Work on Myth*, trans. Robert M. Wallace (Cambridge, MA, 1985), pp. 131–2.

27 Ibid., pp. 136–7.

28 Plutarch, *Plutarch's Lives*, trans. John Dryden, ed. Arthur Hugh Clough [1864] (New York, *c.* 1930), p. 141.

29 Ibid., pp. 820, 852.

30 Sian Lewis and Lloyd Llewellyn-Jones, *The Culture of Animals in Antiquity: A Sourcebook with Commentaries* (London, 2018), p. 518.

31 Suetonius, *The Twelve Caesars*, trans. Robert Graves (New York, 2007), p. 38.

32 Aelian, *On Animals*, trans. A. F. Scholfield (Cambridge, MA, 1958), III.9, pp. 165–6.

33 Ibid., III.23, p. 185.

34 Ovid, *Metamorphoses*, trans. Rolfe Humphries (Bloomington, IN, 1955), XIV.310–96, pp. 348–50.

35 Ibid., XI.408–761, pp. 272–84.

36 Rozenn Bailleul-LeSuer, ed., *Between Heaven and Earth: Birds in Ancient Egypt* (Chicago, IL, 2012), p. 134.

37 Caroline Bugler, *The Bird in Art* (London, 2012), p. 50.

38 Armstrong, *Folklore of Birds*, p. 80.

39 Apuleius, *The Golden Ass: The Transformations of Lucius*, trans. Robert Graves (New York, 2009), pp. 122–3.

40 Cicero, *On Divination*, Book One, in *On Old Age. On Friendship. On Divination*, trans. W. A. Falconer (Cambridge, MA, 1923), VI.10–11, p. 235.

41 Elijah Judah Schochet, *Animals in Jewish Tradition: Attitudes and Relationships* (New York, 1984), p. 128.

42 Anthony S. Mercatante, *Zoo of the Gods: Animals in Myth, Legend and Fable* (New York, 1974), pp. 169–70.

43 *The Koran*, with parallel Arabic text, trans. N. J. Dawood (New York, 2000), 5:31, p. 111.

44 Anon., *The Nibelungenlied*, trans. A. T. Hatto (New York, 2004), p. 18.

45 Kakuichi, *The Tale of the Heike*, trans. Helen Craig McCullough (New York, 1988), chap. 11, #7, p. 372.

46 J. V. Andrea, *The Chemical Wedding of Christian Rosenkreutz*, trans. Joscelyn Godwin (Boston, MA, 1991), p. 25.

47 J. Simpson and S. Roud, 'Magpies', in *Oxford Dictionary of English Folklore* (Oxford, 2000), pp. 222–3.

48 Grimm and Grimm, *The Complete Fairy Tales of the Brothers Grimm*, pp. 22–8.

49 Iona Opie and Moira Taten, eds, *A Dictionary of Superstitions* (New York, 1989), pp. 90–91.

50 Ibid., pp. 25–6.

51 Ibid.

52 Evan T. Pritchard, *Bird Medicine: The Sacred Power of Bird Shamanism* (Rochester, VT, 2013), p. 22.

53 Ibid., pp. 69–70.

54 Ibid., p. 105.

55 Jacob Grimm and Wilhelm Grimm, *The German Legends of the Brothers Grimm*, trans. Donald Ward, 2 vols (Philadelphia, PA, 1981), legend 23, 1, p. 33.

56 Sax, *City of Ravens*, p. 34.

57 W. M. Patterson & Company, eds, *The Growing World* (Philadelphia, PA, 1882), p. 196.

58 Anonymous, 'Official France is Worried to Death', *Boston Post*, 28 November 1922, p. 15.

59 Anonymous, 'Raven of Ill Omen Reappears in Paris', *New York Times*, 21 November 1921.

60 Sax, *City of Ravens*, pp. 15–35, 49–55.

61 Ibid., pp. 36–40, 62–73, 56–88.

62 Sarah Marsh, '"Bored" Ravens Straying from Tower of London as Tourist Numbers Fall', *The Guardian*, 20 August 2020.

63 Peter Doherty, *Their Fate Is Our Fate: How Birds Foretell Threats to Our Health and Our World* (New York, 2013), p. 181.

4 Bird Souls

1 Sherif Bana El Din, 'The Avifauna of the Egyptian Nile Valley: Changing Times', in *Between Heaven and Earth: Birds in Ancient Egypt*, ed. Rozenn Bailleul-LeSuer (Chicago, IL, 2015), p. 125.

2 Francis Klingender, *Animals in Art and Thought to the End of the Middle Ages* (Cambridge, MA, 1971), p. 49.

3 Juliet Clutton-Brock, *Animals as Domesticates: A World View through History* (East Lansing, MI, 2012), p. 66.

4 Patrick F. Houlihan, *The Animal World of the Pharaohs* (New York, 1996), p. 136.

5 Ibid.

6 Klingender, *Animals in Art and Thought*, p. 32.

7 Rozenn Bailleul-LeSuer, 'Pharaoh the Living Horus and His Subjects', in *Between Heaven and Earth,* ed. Rozenn Bailleul-LeSuer, p. 136.

8 Aaron H. Katcher, 'Man and the Environment: An Excursion into Cyclical Time', in *New Perspectives on Our Lives with Companion Animals*, ed. Aaron H. Katcher and Alan M. Beck (Philadelphia, PA, 1983), p. 526.

9 Bailleul-LeSuer, 'Nina de Garis Davie's Facsimilies from the Painted Tomb-chapel of Nebamun', in *Between Heaven and Earth*, ed. Bailleul-LeSuer, pp. 152–3.

10 S. Peter Dance, *The Art of Natural History: Animal Illustrators and their Work* (New York, 1978), p. 10.

11 Dorothea Arnold, *An Egyptian Bestiary* (New York, 1995), p. 24.

12 Edward Bleiberg, Yekaterina Barbash and Lisa Bruno, *Soulful Creatures: Animal Mummies in Ancient Egypt* (New York, 2015), pp. 66–7.

13 Rozenn Bailleul-LeSuer, 'From Kitchen to Temple: The Practical Role of Birds in Ancient Egypt', in *Between Heaven and Earth*, ed. Rozenn Bailleul-LeSuer, p. 30.

14 Bleiberg, Barbash and Bruno, *Soulful Creatures*, p. 64.

15 Patrick F. Houlihan, *The Birds of Ancient Egypt* (Cairo, 1988), p. 140.

16 Ibid., pp. 84–5.

17 Bleiberg, Barbash and Bruno, *Soulful Creatures*, pp. 91–4.

18 Bailleul-LeSuer, 'Introduction', in *Between Heaven and Earth*, ed. Bailleul-LeSeur, p. 16.

19 Bleiberg, Barbash and Bruno, *Soulful Creatures*, p. 83.

20 Dorothea Arnold, *An Egyptian Bestiary* (New York, 1995), p. 45. I have slightly altered the lines on poetic grounds, without changing the meaning.

21 Ibid.

22 Joseph Nigg, *The Phoenix: An Unnatural Biography of a Mythical Beast* (Chicago, IL, 2016), pp. 3–17, 38–41.

23 Homer, *Odyssey*, trans. Stanley Lombardo (Indianapolis, IN, 2000), XII.1109–14, pp. 179–82.

24 Apollodorus, *The Library of Greek Mythology*, trans. Robin Hard (Oxford, 1997), I.9, pp. 52–3.

25 Louis Charbonneau-Lassay, *The Bestiary of Christ*, trans. D. M. Dooling (New York, 1991), p. 230.

26 Pliny the Elder, *Natural History: A Selection*, trans. John F. Healey (London, 1991), p. 100.

27 Mircea Eliade, *Shamanism: Archaic Techniques of Ecstasy* (Princeton, NJ, 1974), pp. 477–82.

28 Bede, *A History of the English Church and People*, trans. Leo Sherley-Price (London, 1976), p. 127.

29 Mary Webb, *Precious Bane* (New York, *c.* 1930), p. 29.
30 Suzana Marjanić, 'Croatian Notions of the Post-mortal and Cataleptic Soul', trans. Nina Antojak, in *Body, Soul and Supernatural Communication*, ed. Eva Pócs (Newcastle, 2019), p. 110.
31 Jakob Grimm and Wilhelm Grimm, 'The Juniper Tree', in *The Annotated Brothers Grimm*, ed. and trans. Maria Tatar (New York, 2004), pp. 208–23.
32 Jan Knappert, *African Mythology* (London, 1995), p. 38.
33 Pedro Pitarch, *The Jaguar and the Priest: An Ethnography of Tzeltal Souls* (Austin, TX, 2010), pp. 21–2.
34 John Marzluff and Tony Angell, *In the Company of Crows and Ravens* (New Haven, CT, 2005), pp. 137–8.
35 Elisabeth de Fontenay, *Le silence des bêtes* (Paris,1998), p. 244.
36 Anon., *Physiologus*, trans. Michael J. Curley (Austin, TX, 1979), pp. 13–14.
37 Ibid., pp. 7–8.
38 Randy Shonkwiler, 'Sheltering Wings: Birds as Symbols of Protection in Ancient Egypt', in *Between Heaven and Earth*, ed. Bailleul-LeSuer, pp. 49–54.
39 Horapollo Niliarcus, *The Hieroglyphics of Horapollo*, trans. George Boas (Princeton, NJ, 1993), p. 50.
40 Anon., *Physiologus*, pp. 47–9.
41 Anon., *Bestiary: Ms. Bodley 764*, trans. Richard Barber (Woodbridge, 1993), p. 126.

5 Migration and Pilgrimage

1 Joseph Campbell, *The Hero with a Thousand Faces* (Princeton, NJ, 1973), pp. 36–7.
2 Gaston Bachelard, *The Poetics of Space*, trans. Maria Jolas (New York, 2014), p. 137.
3 Dale Serjeantson, *Birds* (Cambridge, 2009), p. 14.
4 Edward A. Armstrong, *The Folklore of Birds* (London, 1958), p. 99.
5 Anon., *The Tain*, trans. Thomas Kinsella (London, 1972), pp. 21–3.
6 Boria Sax, *City of Ravens: London, The Tower and Its Famous Birds* (New York, 2011), p. 41.
7 George N. Allen, *Ocean Burial: Song and Quartette* (Boston, MA, 1850), p. 5.
8 Richard J. King, *Ahab's Rolling Sea: A Natural History of Moby Dick* (Chicago, IL, 2019), p. 100.
9 Armstrong, *The Folklore of Birds*, pp. 209–13.
10 Roel Sterckx, *The Animal and the Daemon in Early China* (Albany, NY, 2002), pp. 71–2.
11 J. Pollard, *Birds in Greek Life and Myth* (London, 1977), pp. 43–4.
12 Aristotle, *The History of Animals*, trans. D'Arcy Wentworth Thompson (Oxford, 1910), VIII.16.
13 J. F. Lyle, 'John Hunter, Gilbert White and the Migration of Swallows', *Annals of the Royal College of Surgeons of England*, LX (1978), pp. 485–91.
14 Lynn Barber, *The Heyday of Natural History* (New York, 1980), p. 42.

15 Gilbert White, *The Natural History of Selbourne* [1789] (New York, 1895), p. 30.

16 Lyle, 'John Hunter, Gilbert White', p. 490.

17 Gordon C. Aymar, *Bird Flight* (New York, 1938), p. 97.

18 Per Christiansen, *Encyclopedia of Birds: 400 Species from around the World* (London, 2009), p. 177.

19 Clive D. L. Wynne and Monique A. R. Udell, *Animal Cognition: Evolution, Behavior and Cognition*, 2nd edn (New York, 2013), pp. 18–23, 32–4.

20 R. A. Holland, 'True Navigation in Birds: From Quantum Physics to Global Migration', *Journal of Zoology*, 293 (2014), pp. 1–15.

21 Tim Birkhead, *Bird Sense: What It's Like to Be a Bird* (London, 2012), pp. 61–2.

22 Debra Hermann, *Avian Cognition: Exploring the Intelligence, Behavior, and Individuality of Birds* (North Bethesda, MD, 2014), pp. 15–16.

23 Jennifer Ackerman, *The Genius of Birds* (New York, 2016), pp. 192–232.

24 Antonio Demasio, *Descartes' Error: Emotion, Reason, and the Human Brain* (New York, 1994), p. 145.

25 Ibid., pp. 150–51.

26 Sterckx, *The Animal and the Daemon*, pp. 178–9.

27 William Cullen Bryant, 'To a Waterfowl', in *On Wings of Song: Poems about Birds*, ed. J. D. McClatchy (New York, 2000), pp. 225–6.

28 Jules Michelet, *The Bird*, trans. W. H. Davenport Adams (London, 1869), p. 183.

29 William T. Hornaday, *Popular Official Guide to the New York Zoological Park*, 17th edn (New York, 1921), p. 138.

30 W. G. Sebald, *Austerlitz*, trans. Anthea Bell (New York, 2001), pp. 50, 68.

31 Rosi Braidotti, *The Posthuman* (Cambridge, 2003), p. 86.

6 Nature-cultures

1 Jeremy Black and Anthony Green, 'Tower of Babel', in *Gods, Demons and Symbols of Ancient Mesopotamia: An Illustrated Dictionary* (Austin, TX, 1992), p. 179.

2 Nigel Barley, *Grave Matters: A Lively History of Death around the World* (New York, 1995), pp. 9–29.

3 Bruno Latour, *We Have Never Been Modern*, trans. Catherine Porter (Cambridge, MA, 1993), p. 17.

4 Boria Sax, 'What is this Quintessence of Dust? The Concept of the Human and its Origins', in *Anthropocentrism: Humans, Animals, Environments*, ed. Rob Boddice (Boston, MA, 2011), pp. 21–36.

5 David Quamen, *Natural Acts: A Sidelong View of Science and Nature* (New York, 2009), p. 27.

6 Katy Sewall, 'The Girl Who Gets Gifts from Birds', BBC News, www.bbc.com, 25 February 2015.

7 Jacob Grimm and Wilhelm Grimm, *The Complete Fairy Tales of the Brothers Grimm*, trans. Jack Zipes (New York, 1987), pp. 67–70.

8 John Marzluff and Tony Angell, *Gifts of the Crow: How Perception, Emotion, and Thought Allow Smart Birds to Behave Like Humans* (New York, 2012), pp. 169–92.

9 Anon., 'The Twa Corbies', in *On Wings of Song: Poems About Birds*, ed. J. D. McClutchy (New York, 2000), p. 89.

10 Boria Sax, *City of Ravens: London, the Tower, and Its Famous Birds* (London, 2011), p. 26.

11 Dale Serjeantson, *Birds* (Cambridge, 2009), p. 362.

12 Marzluff and Angell, *Gifts of the Crow*, pp. 137–46.

13 Sax, *City of Ravens*, p. 101.

14 Black and Green, *Gods, Demons and Symbols*, frontispiece.

15 J. C. Cooper, 'Owl', *Symbolic and Mythological Animals* (London, 1992), p. 173.

16 Ashley E. Sharpe, 'A Reexamination of Birds in the Central Mexican Codices', *Ancient Mesoamerica*, xxv/2 (2014), pp. 317–36.

17 Cooper, 'Owl,' *Mythological Animals*, pp. 173–4.

18 Sonia Tidemann and Tim Whiteside, 'Aboriginal Stories: The Riches and Colour of Australian Birds', in *Ethno-ornithology: Birds, Indigenous Peoples, Culture and Society*, ed. Sonia Tidemann and Andrew Gosler (Abingdon, 2010), pp. 168, 176–8.

19 Steve Pavlik, *The Navaho and the Animal People: Native American Traditional Ecological Knowledge and Ethnozoology* (Golden, co, 2014), pp. 189–91.

20 Allen F. Roberts, *Animals in African Art: From the Familiar to the Marvelous* (New York, 1995), p. 72.

21 Viviane Backe, 'Les hommes et leurs "doublures animals"', in *Animal*, ed. Christiane Falgayettes-Leveau (Paris, 2007), p. 260.

22 Roberts, *Animals in African Art*, p. 72.

23 Aristotle, *The History of Animals*, trans. D'Arcy Wentworth Thompson (Oxford, 1910), ix.1.

24 Aelian, *On Animals*, trans. A. F. Scholfield (Cambridge, ma, 1958), 1.29, available at www.attalus.org.

25 T. H. White, trans., 'Owl', *The Book of Beasts* (Mineola, ny, 1984), pp. 133–4.

26 J. L. Schrader, *A Medieval Bestiary* (New York, 1986), p. 38.

27 Boria Sax, *Imaginary Animals: The Monstrous, the Wondrous and the Human* (London, 2013), p. 127.

28 J. J. Grandville, text by Albéric Second et al., *Les Métamorphoses du jour* (Paris, 1854), p. 144.

29 'Owlery', *Harry Potter Wiki*, https://harrypotter.fandom.com, accessed 6 September 2020.

30 Desmond Morris, *Owl* (London, 2009).

31 Ibid.

32 George Eliot, *Middlemarch* (Edinburgh and London, 1872), pp. 297–8.

33 Luca Impelluso, *La natura e i suoi simboli* (Milan, 2003), p. 193.

34 Boria Sax, 'When Adam and Eve Were Monkeys: Anthropomorphism, Zoomorphism, and Other Ways of Looking at Animals', in *The Routledge*

Companion to Animal-Human History, ed. Hilda Kean and Philip Howell (Abingdon, 2019), pp. 273–97.

35 Arthur W. Ryder, trans., *The Panchatantra* (Chicago, IL, 1964), pp. 179–82.

36 Aelian, *On Animals*, XIII.18.

37 Richard H. Randall Jr, 'A Gothic Bird Cage', *Metropolitan Museum of Art Bulletin*, XI/10 (June 1953), p. 292.

38 Sian Lewis and Lloyd Llewellyn-Jones, eds, *The Culture of Animals in Antiquity: A Sourcebook with Commentaries* (Abingdon, 2018), pp. 268, 271.

39 Serjeantson, *Birds*, p. 313.

40 Martin Schongauer, *Madonna and Child with the Parrot*, http://metmuseum.org, accessed 18 April 2020.

41 Colin Eisler, *Dürer's Animals* (Washington, DC, 1991), pp. 47–52.

42 Impelluso, *La natura e i suoi simboli*, pp. 302–3.

43 Caroline Bugler, *The Bird in Art* (London, 2012), pp. 215, 219, 221.

44 Paul Carter, *Parrot* (London, 2008).

45 Clive D. L. Wynne and Monique A. R. Udell, *Animal Cognition: Evolution, Behavior and Cognition*, 2nd edn (New York, 2013), pp. 79–80, 292–3.

46 Irene M. Pepperberg, *Alex and Me: How a Scientist and a Parrot Uncovered a Hidden World of Animal Intelligence – and Formed a Deep Bond in the Process* (New York, 2008), pp. 4–32, 242.

47 Purbita Saha and Claire Spottiswoode, 'Meet the Greater Honeyguide, the Bird that Understands Humans', *Audubon*, 22 August 2016, www.audubon.org.

48 Mercy Njeri Muiruri and Patrick Maundu, 'Birds, People and Conservation in Kenya', in *Ethno-ornithology: Birds, Indigenous Peoples, Culture and Society*, ed. Sonia Tidemann and Andrew Cosler (Abingdon, 2010), pp. 279–90.

49 Jake Page and Eugene S. Morton, *Lords of the Air: The Smithsonian Book of Birds* (New York, 1989), p. 32.

50 Ibid., p. 31.

51 Mark Bonta, 'Ethno-ornithology and Biological Conservation', in *Ethno-ornithology: Birds, Indigenous Peoples, Culture and Society*, ed. Sonia Tidemann and Andrew Cosler (Abingdon, 2010), pp. 13–30.

52 Tidemann and Whiteside, 'Aboriginal Stories', pp. 168–9.

7 Avian Politics

1 Evan T. Pritchard, *Bird Medicine: The Sacred Power of Bird Shamanism* (Rochester, VT, 2013), pp. 73–9.

2 Edward T. C. Werner, *Ancient Tales and Folklore from China* (London, 1986), pp. 189–91.

3 Hollym International, *Long, Long Ago: Korean Folk Tales* (Seoul, 1997), pp. 23–9.

4 Hesiod, *Works and Days, in Theogony, Works and Days*, trans. M. L. West (Oxford, 1988), lines 203–20, pp. 42–3.

5 Aesop, *The Complete Fables*, trans. Olivia and Robert Temple (London, 1998), p. 8.

6 Hesiod, *Works and Days*, line 568, p. 54.

7 John Pollard, *Birds in Greek Life and Myth* (London, 1977), p. 165.

8 Aristophanes, *The Birds*, trans. Peter D. Arnott (Wheeling, IL, 1986), pp. 1–58.

9 Stephanie Dalley, ed. and trans., *Myths from Mesopotamia: Creation, The Flood, Gilgamesh and Others* (Oxford, 1992), pp. 203–27.

10 Edward A. Armstrong, *The Folklore of Birds* (London, 1958), pp. 161–2.

11 René Girard, *Violence and the Sacred*, trans. Patrick Gregory (Baltimore, MD, 1993), pp. 124–30.

12 Dalley, ed., *Myths from Mesopotamia*, pp. 230–31.

13 Aesop, *Three Hundred Aesop's Fables*, trans. Geo. Fyler Townsend (London, 1867), pp. 45–6.

14 Anon., *Jātaka Tales*, trans. H. T. Francis and E. J. Thomas (Cambridge, 1916), pp. 30–32.

15 Arthur W. Ryder, trans., *The Panchatantra* (Chicago, IL, 1953), pp. 304–8.

16 Anon., 'The Owl and the Nightingale', in *The Owl and the Nightingale/ Cleanness/ St Erkenwald*, trans. Brian Stone (London, 1988), pp. 181–244.

17 Walther von der Vogelweide, 'Weltklage', in *Werke*, vol. 1: *Spruchlyrik. Mittelhochdeutsch/Neuhochdeutsch*, ed. Günther Schweikle and Ricarda Bauscke-Hartung (Stuttgart, 1994), pp. 74–5.

18 Geoffrey Chaucer, 'The Parliament of Fowles', in *The Complete Works*, ed. Walter Skeat (London, 1973).

19 Joyce E. Salisbury, *The Beast Within: Animals in the Middle Ages* (London, 1994), pp. 117–33.

20 Dalley, *Myths from Mesopotamia*, pp. 189–202.

21 Sian Lewis and Lloyd Llewellyn-Jones, *The Culture of Animals in Antiquity: A Sourcebook with Commentaries* (Abingdon, 2018), pp. 505–6.

22 Ibid., pp. 510–11.

23 Dante Alighieri, *La Divina Commedia di Dante Alighieri*, (Milan, 1962), canto XVIII, lines 106–11, p. 484.

24 Janet Backhouse, *Medieval Birds in the Sherborne Missal* (Toronto, 2001), p. 43.

25 Lewis and Llewellyn-Jones, *The Culture of Animals in Antiquity*, p. 417.

26 Elizabeth Lawrence, *Hunting the Wren: Transformation of Bird into Symbol* (Knoxville, TN, 1997), pp. 23–7.

27 Beryl Rowland, *Birds with Human Souls: A Guide to Bird Symbolism* (Knoxville, TN, 1978), p. 185.

28 Jacob Grimm and Wilhelm Grimm, *The Complete Fairy Tales of the Brothers Grimm*, trans. Jack Zipes (New York, 1987), pp. 548–9.

29 Ibid., pp. 36–7.

30 Ibid., pp. 107–8.

31 Armstrong, *The Folklore of Birds*, pp. 160–65.

32 Grimm and Grimm, *Complete Fairy Tales*, p. 549.

33 Armstrong, *The Folklore of Birds*, pp. 159–60.

34 Francis Klingender, *Animals in Art and Thought to the End of the Middle Ages*, ed. and trans. Evelyn Antal and John Harthan (Cambridge, MA, 1971), pp. 471–2.

35 Réné Girard, *The Scapegoat*, trans. Yvonne Freccero (Baltimore, MD, 1989), pp. 198–212.

36 Elizabeth de Fontenay, *Le silence des bêtes* (Paris, 1998), p. 249.

37 Benjamin Franklin, 'From Benjamin Franklin to Sarah Bache', 26 January 1784, https://founders.archives.gov, accessed 4 October 2020.

38 Jack Santino, *All Around the Year: Holidays and Celebrations in American Life* (Chicago, IL, 1995), p. 173.

39 Jim Sterba, *Nature Wars: The Incredible Story of How Wildlife Comebacks Turned Backyards into Battlegrounds* (New York, 2012), p. 165.

40 Jim Sterba, *Nature Wars: The Incredible Story of How Wildlife Comebacks Turned Backyards into Battlegrounds* (New York, 2012), pp. 165–9.

41 Girard, *Violence and the Sacred*, pp. 274–308.

42 Sterba, *Nature Wars*, pp. 206–10.

43 Thorleif Schjelderup-Ebbe, 'Beiträge zur Sozialpsychologie des Haushuhns', *Zeitschrift für Psychologie*, 88 (1922), pp. 225–52.

44 Thorleif Schjelderup-Ebbe, 'Social Behavior of Birds', in *A Handbook of Social Psychology*, ed. Carl Murchison (Worcester, MA, 1935), pp. 947–72.

45 Donna Haraway, *Primate Visions: Gender, Race, and Nature in the World of Modern Science* (London, 1989), pp. 54–8.

46 Ibid., p. 164.

47 Lorenz Konrad, *Man Meets Dog*, trans. Marjorie Kerr Wilson (Boston, MA, 1955), pp. 147–9.

48 Boria Sax, 'Konrad Lorenz and the Mythology of Science', in *What Are the Animals to Us?: Approaches from Science, Religion, Folklore, Literature, and Art*, ed. Dave Aftandilian, Marion W. Copeland and David Scofield Wilson (Knoxville, TN, 2007), pp. 269–76.

8 Falconry

1 Helen Macdonald, *Falcon* (New York, 2016), p. 103.

2 Dale Serjeantson, *Birds* (New York, 2009), p. 320.

3 Sian Lewis and Lloyd Llewellyn-Jones, *The Culture of Animals in Antiquity: A Sourcebook with Commentaries* (Abingdon, 2018), pp. 501–2.

4 Leslie V. Wallace, 'Representations of Falconry in Eastern Han China (25–220 ACE)', *Journal of Sport History*, XXXIX/1 (Spring 2012), p. 101.

5 Alexandra Marvar, 'As Things Fall Apart, Falconers Hear Opportunity Call', *New York Times*, 26 April 2020, Style Section, p. 9.

6 Helen Macdonald, *H is for Hawk* (New York, 2014), p. 90.

7 Johan Huizinga, *The Waning of the Middle Ages: A Study of the Forms of Life, Thought and Art in France and the Netherlands in the XIV and XV Centuries* (1924) (London, 2016), p. 77.

8 Anon., 'The Gay Goshawk', in *Old English Ballads and Folk Songs*, ed. William Dallam Armes (London, 1924), pp. 16–21.

9 Linda Woolley, *Medieval Life and Leisure in the Devonshire Hunting Tapestries* (London, 2002), pp. 8–9, 39–70.

10 Francis Klingender, *Animals in Art and Thought to the End of the Middle Ages* (Cambridge, MA, 1971), pp. 461–76.

11 Frederick II of Hohenstaufen, *The Art of Falconry*, trans. Casey Albert Wood and F. Marjorie Fyfe (New York, 2010), vol. II, pp. 273–311.

12 Giovanni Pietro Olina, *Pasta for Nightingales: A 17th Century Handbook of Bird Care and Folklore*, trans. Kate Clayton (New Haven, CT, 2018), p. 108.

13 Farid ud-Din Attar, *The Conference of Birds*, trans. Afkham Darbandi and Dick Davis (New York, 1984), pp. 29–32, 45–6.

14 Anon., *Bestiary: Ms. Bodley 764*, trans. Richard Barber (Woodbridge, 1993), pp. 154–7.

15 Louis Charbonneau-Lassay, *Bestiary of Christ* (New York, 1991), p. 204.

16 John Cummins, *The Hound and the Hawk: The Art of Medieval Hunting* (London, 2001), pp. 230–32.

17 Vicki Hearne, *Adam's Task: Calling Animals by Name* (New York, 2016), p. 262.

18 Macdonald, *H is for Hawk*, p. 110.

19 Patrick F. Houlihan, *The Animal World of the Pharaohs* (London, 1996), pp. 160–65.

20 Shihab Al-Din Al-Nuwayri, *The Ultimate Ambition in the Arts of Erudition: A Compendium of Knowledge from the Classical Islamic World*, trans. Elias Muhanna (New York, 2016), p. 174.

21 Frederick II, *Falconry*, vol. I, pp. 5–6.

22 Serjeantson, *Birds*, p. 321.

23 Macdonald, *Falcon*, p. 100.

24 John Julius Norwich, *Four Princes: Henry VIII, Francis I, Charles V, Suleiman the Magnificent and the Obsessions that Forged Modern Europe* (New York, 2016), p. 68.

25 Macdonald, *Falcon*, p. 97.

26 Theodor Echtermeyer and Benno von Wiese, eds, *Deutsche Gedichte: Von den Anfängen bis zur Gegenwart* (Düsseldorf, 1956), p. 31.

27 Aldo Leopold, *A Sand County Almanac: And Sketches Here and There* (London, 1968), pp. 129–30.

9 Plato's 'Man'

1 Diogenes Laertius, *Lives and Opinions of Eminent Philosophers*, trans. C. D. Yonge (London, 1901), p. 231.

2 Allen F. Roberts, *Animals in African Art: From the Familiar to the Marvelous* (New York, 1995), p. 102.

3 Donna Haraway, *The Companion Species Manifesto: Dogs, People, and Significant Otherness* (Chicago, IL, 2007), pp. 2–5.

4 Juliet Clutton-Brock, *Animals as Domesticates: A World View through History* (East Lansing, MI, 2012), pp. 110–11.

5 Ibid.

6 Sian Lewis and Lloyd Llewellyn-Jones, *The Culture of Animals in Antiquity: A Sourcebook with Commentaries* (Abingdon, 2018), p. 244.

7 Patrick F. Houlihan, *The Birds of Ancient Egypt* (Cairo, 1988), pp. 79–81.

8 Patrick F. Houlihan, *The Animal World of the Pharaohs* (London, 1996), pp. 205–6.

9 Lewis and Jones, *The Culture of Animals in Antiquity*, pp. 251–2.

10 Pliny the Elder, *Natural History: A Selection*, trans. John F. Healy (London, 1991), p. 144.

11 Dale Serjeantson, *Birds* (Cambridge, 2009), p. 273.

12 Andrew Lawler, *Why Did the Chicken Cross the World: The Epic Saga of the Bird that Powers Civilization* (New York, 2014), p. 1.

13 Edward Topsell, *The Fowles of Heaven or History of Birds* (Austin, TX, 1972), p. 26. I have modernized the spelling in the quotation.

14 Fred Hawley, 'The Moral and Conceptual Universe of Cockfighters: Symbolism and Rationalization', *Society and Animals*, I/2 (1993), pp. 162–3.

15 Lewis and Llewellyn-Jones, *The Culture of Animals in Antiquity*, p. 742.

16 Hawley, 'The Moral and Conceptual Universe of Cockfighters', pp. 163–4.

17 Clifford Geertz, 'Deep Play: Notes on the Balinese Cockfight', *Daedalus*, 134/4 (Fall 2005), p. 62.

18 Lawler, *Why Did the Chicken Cross the World*, pp. 102–3.

19 Geertz, 'Deep Play', pp. 71–82.

20 Hawley, 'The Moral and Conceptual Universe of Cockfighters', p. 163.

21 Lawler, *Why Did the Chicken Cross the World*, p. 106.

22 Hal Herzog, *Some We Love, Some We Hate, Some We Eat: Why It's So Hard to Think Straight about Animals* (New York, 2010), pp. 149–74.

23 Plato, 'Phaedo', in *The Last Days of Socrates*, trans. Hugh Tredennick and Harold Tarrant (London, 1993), p. 185.

24 Lewis and Jones, *The Culture of Animals in Antiquity*, p. 253.

25 Ruth Q. Sun, *The Asian Animal Zodiac* (Edison, NJ, 1974), p. 162.

26 Ibid., pp. 173–5.

27 T. H. White, trans., *The Book of Beasts: Being a Translation from a Latin Bestiary of the Twelfth Century* (Mineola, NY, 1984), p. 151.

28 Geoffrey Chaucer, 'The Nonne Preestes Tale', in *The Complete Works of Geoffrey Chaucer*, ed. Walter W. Skeat (1894–1900) (Oxford, 1973), pp. 542–51.

29 Ibid., p. 543.

30 Giovanni Pico della Mirandola, *Oration on the Dignity of Man*, trans. A. Robert Caponigri (Washington, DC, 1996), p. 23.

31 Ulisse Aldrovandi, *Aldrovandi on Chickens*, trans. R. Lind (Norman, OK, 1963), pp. 178–9.

32 Adam Nossiter, 'On the Front Lines of Culture War in France: Maurice the Rooster', *New York Times*, 23 June 2019, pp. 1, 17.

33 Lewis and Llewellyn-Jones, *The Culture of Animals in Antiquity*, p. 247.

34 Houlihan, *The Birds of Ancient Egypt*, p. 81.

35 Lewis and Llewellyn-Jones, *The Culture of Animals in Antiquity*, pp. 249–51.

36 Aelian, *On Animals*, trans. A. F. Scholfield (Cambridge, MA, 1958), XVII/46, III, p. 381.

37 Boria Sax, 'The Basilisk and Rattlesnake, or a European Monster Comes to America', *Society and Animals*, II/1 (1994), pp. 6–7.

38 Mark Dash, 'On the Trail of the Warsaw Basilisk', *Smithsonian Magazine*, 23 July 2012, www.smithsonianmag.com.

39 Lawler, *Why Did the Chicken Cross the World*, pp. 120–26.

40 Herman Melville, 'Cock-a-Doodle-Doo!' (1853), in *The Apple Tree Table and Other Sketches* (Princeton, NJ, 1922), pp. 211–56.

41 Robert G. Breunig and Jeffrey Crespi, *Animal, Bird and Myth in African Art* (Phoenix, AZ, 1985), p. 22.

42 Allen F. Roberts, *Animals in African Art*, p. 110.

43 Ibid., pp. 38–9.

44 Ibid., p. 40.

45 Lawler, *Why Did the Chicken Cross the World*, pp. 192–6.

46 Maryn McKenna, *Big Chicken: The Incredible Story of How Antibiotics Created Modern Agriculture and Changed the Way the World Eats* (Washington, DC, 2017), pp. 55–8.

47 Ibid., pp. 164–5.

48 Lawler, *Why Did the Chicken Cross the World*, p. 210.

49 McKenna, *Big Chicken*, p. 32.

50 These and other early menus have been reproduced by Love Menu Art and may be found at https://vintagemenuart.com, accessed 9 September 2020.

51 McKenna, *Big Chicken*, p. 265.

52 Ibid., pp. 265–7.

53 Ibid., pp. 271–6.

54 Donna Haraway, *When Species Meet* (Minneapolis, MN, 2008), p. 268.

55 Ibid., p. 273.

56 Lawler, *Why Did the Chicken Cross the World*, p. 5.

57 Diogenes Laertius, *Lives and Opinions of Eminent Philosophers*, p. 61.

10 From Caves to Cathedrals

1 Maxime Aubert et al., 'Earliest Hunting Scene in Prehistoric Art', *Nature*, 11 December 2019, www.nature.com.
2 Linda Kalof, *Looking at Animals in Human History* (London, 2007), p. 6.
3 Bruno David, *Cave Art* (London, 2017), p. 38.
4 Francesco d'Errico, 'Birds of the Grotte Cosquer: The Great Auk and Palaeolithic Prehistory', *Antiquity*, LXVIII/258 (1994), pp. 39–47.
5 Edward A. Armstrong, *The Folklore of Birds* (London, 1958), pp. 19, 277.
6 David, *Cave Art*, p. 178.
7 Roger F. Pasquier and John Farrand, *Masterpieces of Bird Art: 700 Years of Ornithological Illustration* (New York, 1991), p. 24.
8 Pliny the Elder, *Natural History: A Selection*, trans. John F. Healy (London, 1991), p. 330.
9 Anon., *Bestiary: Ms. Bodley 764*, trans. Richard Barber (Woodbridge, 1993), p. 150.
10 Janetta Rebold Benton, *The Medieval Menagerie: Animals in the Arts of the Middle Ages* (New York, 1992), pp. 124–30.
11 Ibid., p. 171.
12 Frederick II of Hohenstaufen, *The Art of Falconry*, trans. Casey Albert Wood and F. Marjorie Fyfe (New York, 2010), vol. I, p. 22.
13 Ibid., vol. I, pp. 35–8, 65–8, 85–8.
14 Janet Backhouse, *Medieval Birds in the Shelborne Missal* (Toronto, 2001), pp. 13–15.
15 Ibid., pp. 40, 43–4.
16 Ibid., pp. 62–3.
17 Caroline Bugler, *The Bird in Art* (London, 2012), p. 203.
18 Sanjeev P. Srivastara, *Janahgir: A Connoisseur of Mughal Art* (Maharasta, India, 2001), pp. 74, 89.
19 Ibid., pp. 59, 72–3.
20 Allen F. Roberts, *Animals in African Art: From the Familiar to the Marvelous* (New York, 1995), pp. 69–70.
21 Mark Bonta, 'Transmutation of Human Knowledge about Birds in 16th-century Honduras', in *Ethno-ornithology: Birds, Indigenous Peoples, Culture and Society*, ed. Sonia Tidemann and Andrew Gosler (Abingdon, 2010), pp. 90–91.
22 Ibid.
23 Ashley E. Sharpe, 'A Reexamination of Birds in the Central Mexican Codices', *Ancient Mesoamerica*, XXV/2 (2014), pp. 317–36.
24 Diana Magaloni Kerpel, *The Colors of the New World: Artists, Materials, and the Creation of the Florentine Codex* (Los Angeles, CA, 2014), p. 13.
25 Ibid., p. 47.

11 Art or Illustration?

1 John Burroughs, 'Birds and Poets', in *Birds and Poets with Other Papers* (New York, 1877), p. 10.

2 Tim Birkhead, *The Wisdom of Birds: An Illustrated History of Ornithology* (New York, 2008), p. 24.

3 David Freedberg, *The Eye of the Lynx: Galileo, His Friends, and the Beginnings of Modern Natural History* (Chicago, IL, 2002), pp. 6, 349–66, 412–13.

4 S. Peter Dance, *The Art of Natural History: Animal Illustrators and their Work* (Woodstock, NY, 1978), pp. 62–3.

5 Susan Owens, 'Mark Catesby: A Genius for Natural History', in *Amazing Rare Things: The Art of Natural History in the Age of Discovery*, ed. David Attenborough (London, 2009), pp. 190–91.

6 Ibid., pp. 192–3.

7 Jonathan Elphick, *Birds: The Art of Ornithology* (New York, 2017), p. 35.

8 Charlotte Brontë, *Jane Eyre* (New York, 1984), p. 3.

9 Susan Hyman, *Edward Lear's Birds* (Secaucus, NJ, 1980), pp. 19–20.

10 Temple Grandin and Catherine Johnson, *Animals in Translation: Using the Mysteries of Autism to Decode Animal Behavior* (Orlando, FL, 2005), p. 67.

11 Ibid., p. 89.

12 Hyman, *Edward Lear's Birds*, pp. 82–3.

13 Esther Woolfson, *Between Light and Storm: How We Live with other Species* (London, 2020), p. 173.

14 Christopher Irmscher, *The Poetics of Natural History* (New Brunswick, NJ, 2019), pp. 2019–20.

15 Lynn Barber, *The Heyday of Natural History, 1820–1870* (New York, 1980), p. 97.

16 Alina Cohen, 'How the Native Americans of Alaska Influenced the Surrealists', www.artsy.net, 30 April 2018.

17 Charlotte Stokes, 'Surrealist Persona: Max Ernst's *Loplop, Superior of Birds*', *Simiolus: Netherlands Quarterly for the History of Art*, XIII/3–4 (1983), pp. 226–8.

18 John Berger, 'Why Look at Animals', in *The Animals Reader: The Essential Classic and Contemporary Writings*, ed. Linda Kalof and Amy Fitzgerald (New York, 2007), pp. 256–61.

19 'Making of Winged Migration', DVD extra in *Winged Migration* (dir. Jacques Perrin, 2001).

12 Birds, Flowers and Time

1 Sophia Suk-mun Law, *Reading Chinese Painting: Beyond Forms and Colors, a Comparative Approach to Art Appreciation*, trans. Tony Blishen (New York, 2016), p. 109.

2 Ibid., pp. 99–101.

3 Ibid., pp. 30–39.

4 Christine E. Jackson, *Dictionary of Bird Artists of the World* (Woodbridge, 1999), pp. 508–9.

5 Caroline Bugler, *The Bird in Art* (London, 2012), p. 189.

6 Roel Sterckx, *The Animal and the Daemon in Early China* (Albany, NY, 2002), pp. 34–43.

7 Law, *Reading Chinese Painting*, pp. 111–17, 130–31.

8 Ibid., pp. 119–40.

9 Katsushika Hokusai et al., *120 Japanese Prints* (Mineola, NY, 2006), print 102 (CD-ROM and book).

10 Israel Goldman, ed., *Hiroshige: Birds and Flowers*, trans. Alfred H. Marks, intro. Cynthea J. Bogel (New York, 1988), plate 44.

11 Annette Blaugrund, *The Essential John James Audubon* (New York, 1999), pp. 66–9.

12 Christine E. Jackson, *Bird Artists*, p. 513.

13 Ashley E. Sharpe, 'A Reexamination of Birds in the Central Mexican Codices', *Ancient Mesoamerica*, XXV/2 (2014), pp. 316–36.

14 Daisy Paul, 'A Bird Book in the Hand Is Worth Two in the Bush', www.metmuseum.org, 14 November 2018.

15 Jonathan Elphick, *Birds: The Art of Ornithology* (New York, 2013), pp. 236–7.

16 Eadweard Muybridge, *Muybridge's Animals in Motion* (Mineola, NY, 2007), pp. 1–21.

17 Gabor Horvath et al., 'Cavemen Were Better at Depicting Quadruped Walking than Modern Artists: Erroneous Walking Illustrations in the Fine Arts from Prehistory to Today', *PLoS One*, https://journals.plos.org, 5 December 2012.

18 Richard Bell, *Ways of Drawing Birds: A Guide to Expanding Your Visual Awareness* (Philadelphia, PA, 1994), p. 34.

19 Oregon State University, 'Hummingbird Flight, an Evolutionary Marvel', https://phys.org, 22 June 2005.

20 Joe Earle and Sebastian Izzard, *Zeshin: The Catherine and Thomas Edson Collection* (San Antonio, TX, 2007), pp. 94–5.

13 The Nightingale and the Rose

1 Michael Guida, 'Surviving Twentieth-century Modernity: Birdsong and Emotions in Britain', in *The Routledge Companion to Animal-Human History*, ed. Hilda Kean and Philip Howell (London, 2019), pp. 370–74.

2 David Rothenberg, *Why Birds Sing: A Journey into the Mystery of Bird Song* (New York, 2005), pp. 188–208.

3 Ibid., p. 27.

4 Pliny the Elder, *Natural History: A Selection*, trans. John F. Healy (London, 1991), X.84, p. 146.

5 Percy Bysshe Shelley, 'A Defence of Poetry' (1821), in *The Norton Anthology of Theory and Criticism*, ed. Vincent B. Leitch et al. (New York, 2018), p. 601.

6 Jules Michelet, *The Bird*, trans. W. H. Davenport Adams (London, 1869), p. 270.

7 Ibid., p. 236.

8 Ibid., p. 281.

9 J. C. Cooper, *Symbolic and Mythological Animals* (London, 1992), p. 167.

10 Omar Khayyam (attrib.), *The Rubaiyat of Omar Khayyam*, trans. Edward FitzGerald [1859] (New York, 1942), poem 72, p. 45.

11 John D. Yohannan, 'The Persian Poetry Fad in English Literature', *Comparative Literature*, IV/8 (Spring 1952), pp. 137–60.

12 Louis Charbonneau-Lassay, *The Bestiary of Christ*, trans. D. M. Dooling (New York, 1991), p. 225.

13 Hans Christian Andersen, 'The Nightingale', *The Annotated Hans Christian Andersen*, ed. Maria Tatar (New York, 2008), pp. 78–97.

14 Ibid.

15 René Descartes, *Meditations on First Philosophy with Selections from the Objections and Replies*, trans. Michael Moriarty (Oxford, 2008), meditation 2, section 32, p. 23.

16 E. T. A. Hoffmann, 'The Sandman', *The Best Tales of Hoffmann*, trans. J. T. Bealby, ed. E. F. Bleiler (Mineola, NY, 1967), pp. 183–214.

17 Wolfram Koeppe, 'Technological Marvels in Motion', in *Making Marvels: Science and Splendor at the Courts of Europe*, ed. Wolfram Koeppe (New York, 2020), pp. 200–201.

18 Oscar Wilde, *The Happy Prince* (Mineola, NY, 2006), pp. 14–19.

19 W. B. Yeats, 'The Rose Tree', *W. B. Yeats: The Poems, a New Edition* (New York, 1983), p. 182.

20 W. Geoffrey Arnott, *Birds in the Ancient World from A to Z* (London, 2007), p. 123.

21 Michelet, *The Bird*, p. 114.

22 Celia Fisher, *The Magic of Birds* (London, 2014), p. 32.

23 Arnott, *Birds in the Ancient World*, p. 123.

24 John Keats, 'Ode', in *On Wings of Song: Poems about Birds*, ed. J. D. McClatchy (New York, 2000), p. 220.

25 Catherine Phillips, *Birds of a Feather* (St Petersburg, 2019), pp. 38–9.

26 John Milton, 'To a Nightingale', in *On Wings of Song*, ed. McClatchy, p. 107.

27 William Drummond, 'To a Nightingale', ibid., p. 108.

28 Rothenberg, *Why Birds Sing*, pp. 23–4.

29 Christina Rosetti, 'Pain or Joy', in *On Wings of Song*, ed. McClatchy, p. 116.

30 Boria Sax, *Imaginary Animals: The Monstrous, the Wondrous, and the Human* (London, 2013), pp. 251–3.

14 Extinction

1 Elizabeth Kolbert, *The Sixth Extinction: An Unnatural History* (New York, 2014), p. 21.

2 Jules Michelet, *The Bird*, trans. W. H. Davenport Adams (London, 1869), pp. 111–14.

3 Anon., 'Man the Destroyer', *Audubon Magazine*, I (1 February 1887), p. 9.

4 Dale Serjeantson, *Birds* (Cambridge, 2009), pp. 380–92.

5 BirdLife International, 'We Have Lost over 150 Bird Species Since 1500', www.birdlife.org, 25 September 2020.

6 Roger J. Lederer, *The Art of the Bird: The History of Ornithological Art through Forty Artists* (Chicago, IL, 2019), pp. 18–19, 25.

7 Caroline Bugler, *The Bird in Art* (London, 2012), p. 216.

8 Christine E. Jackson, *Bird Artists of the World* (Woodbridge, 1999), pp. 221–2, 382–3, colour plate 50.

9 Hudson and Gardiner, *Rare, Vanishing and Lost British Birds* (London, 1923), p. xii.

10 Bugler, *The Bird in Art* (London, 2012) p. 100.

11 Ibid., p. 193.

12 E. O. Wilson, *The Future of Life* (New York, 2002), p. 98.

13 Louis Figuier, *Reptiles and Birds: A Popular Account of the Various Orders* (Springfield, MA, 1869), p. 396.

14 W. H. Hudson and Linda Gardiner, *Rare, Vanishing and Lost British Birds*, pp. 28–34.

15 Serjeantson, *Birds*, p. 184.

16 Ibid., p. 189.

17 Maia Nuku, ATAE: *Nature and Divinity in Polynesia* (New York, 2019), pp. 24–34.

18 David Quammen, 'Feathered Capes', in *The Bedside Book of Birds: An Avian Miscellany*, ed. Graeme Gibson (New York, 2005), pp. 246–7.

19 David C. Houston, 'The Impact of Red Feather Currency on the Population of the Scarlet Honeyeater on Santa Cruz', in *Ethno-ornithology: Birds, Indigenous Peoples, Culture and Society*, ed. Sonia Tidemann and Andrew Cosler (Abingdon, 2010), pp. 5–66.

20 Steve Pavik, *The Navajo and the Animal People: Native American Traditional Ecological Knowledge and Ethnozoology* (Golden, CO, 1914), pp. 183, 189.

21 Ibid., p. 185.

22 Evangeline Holland, 'The Court Presentation', www.edwardianpromenade.com, 7 December 2007.

23 Figuier, *Reptiles and Birds*, pp. 205–6.

24 Celia Thaxter, 'Woman's Heatlessness', *Audubon Magazine*, I (1 February 1887), p. 14.

25 W. H. Hudson, *Birds in a Village* (London, 1893), p. 89.

26 Alphonse Toussenel, *Le monde des Oiseaux, Ornithologie Passionelle* (Sydney, 2019), p. 11.

27 Jules Michelet, *The Bird*, trans. W. H. Davenport Adams (London, 1869), p. 159.

28 Ibid., p. 158.

29 Jane Austen, *The Annotated Pride and Prejudice*, ed. David M. Shapard (New York, 2012), vol. III, chap. 9, p. 606.

30 Simon Barnes, *The Meaning of Birds* (New York, 2018), p. 82.

31 C. J. Maynard, *The Naturalist's Guide in Collecting and Preserving Objects of Natural History* (Boston, MA, 1873), pp. 6–8.

32 W. H. Hudson, *Birds and Man* (London, 1920), p. 267.

33 Tim Lowe, *Where Song Began: Australia's Birds and How They Changed the World* (Melbourne, 2014).

34 Daniel Worster, *Nature's Economy: A History of Ecological Ideas*, 2nd edn (New York, 1997), pp. 126–9.

35 Christopher Irmscher, *The Poetics of Natural History* (New Brunswick, NJ, 2019), pp. 230–39.

36 Donald Culross Peattie, ed., *Audubon's America: The Narratives and Experiences of John James Audubon* (Cambridge, MA, 1940), pp. 219–20.

37 William Dutcher, 'The Passenger or Wild Pigeon', National Association of Audubon Societies Educational Leaflet no. 6 (New York, 1913), n.p.

38 Peattie, ed., *Audubon's America*, p. 454.

39 Ibid., p. 455.

40 Dutcher, 'The Passenger or Wild Pigeon'.

41 Figuier, *Reptiles and Birds*, p. 456.

42 Jeffrey A. Lockwood, *Locust: The Devastating Rise and Mysterious Disappearance of the Insect that Shaped the American Frontier* (New York, 2004), pp. xv–xx, 1–100.

43 Ibid., p. xvii.

44 Ibid., pp. 12–13.

45 Frank Dikotter, *Mao's Great Famine: The History of China's Most Devastating Catastrophe* (London, 2018), pp. 186–8.

46 Hudson, *Birds in a Village*, pp. 111–12.

47 Ibid., p. 30.

48 Peter P. Marra and Chris Santella, *Cat Wars: The Devastating Consequences of a Cuddly Killer* (Princeton, NJ, 2016), p. 68.

49 Rachel Carson, *Silent Spring* [1962] (Boston, MA, 2002), pp. 1–7.

50 Laura Parker, 'Nearly Every Seabird on Earth Is Eating Plastic', www.nationalgeographic.com, 2 September 2015.

51 Peter Ward and Joe Kirschvink, *A New History of Life: The Radical New Discoveries about the Origins and Evolution of Life on Earth* (New York, 2016), pp. 327–8.

52 Lowe, *Where Song Began*.

15 Protection and Revival

1 Helen Macdonald, 'Foreword', in Giovanni Pietro Olina and Cassiano dal Pozzo, *Pasta for Nightingales: A 17th-century Handbook of Bird Care and Folklore*, trans. Kate Clayton (New Haven, CT, 2018), p. ix.

2 J. Pollard, *Birds in Greek Life and Thought* (London, 1977), p. 13.

3 Jeremy Mynott, 'Winged Words: The Importance of Birds in the Ancient World', *OUPblog*, 24 May 2018, https://blog.oup.com.

4 Jane O'Brien, 'The Birds of Shakespeare Cause Us Trouble', www.bbc.com, 24 April 2014.

5 Percy Bysshe Shelley, 'To a Skylark', in *On Wings of Song: Poems about Birds*, ed. J. D. McClatchy (New York, 2000), p. 231.

6 Paul Shepard, *Man in the Landscape: A Historic View of the Esthetics of Nature* (New York, 1967), pp. 137–8.

7 Jim Sterba, *Nature Wars: The Incredible Story of How Wildlife Comebacks Turned Backyards into Battlegrounds* (New York, 2012), p. 242.

8 Ibid., pp. 244–5.

9 Mark Bonta, 'Transmutation of Human Knowledge about Birds in 16th Century Honduras', in *Ethno-ornithology: Birds, Indigenous Peoples, Culture and Society*, ed. Sonia Tidemann and Andrew Cosler (Abingdon, 2010), p. 98.

10 Jeremy Mynott, *Birds in the Ancient World* (Oxford, 2018), p. 200.

11 Dale Serjeantson, *Birds* (Cambridge, 2009), p. 393.

12 Flora Thompson, *Lark Rise to Candleford: A Trilogy* [1945] (London, 1973), p. 153.

13 Emily Cleaver, 'The Fascinating, Regal History behind Britain's Swans', *Smithsonian Magazine,* 31 July 2017, www.smithsonianmag.com.

14 Boria Sax, *City of Ravens: London, the Tower and Its Famous Birds* (London, 2011), pp. 41–5.

15 Roger F. Pasquier and John Farrand Jr, *Masterpieces of Bird Art: 700 Years of Ornithological Illustration* (New York, 1991), p. 165.

16 Thom van Dooren, *Flight Ways: Life and Loss at the Edge of Extinction* (New York, 2014), pp. 52–7.

17 Jeffrey A. Lockwood, *Locust: The Devastating Rise and Mysterious Disappearance of the Insect that Shaped the American Frontier* (New York, 2004), pp. 58–9.

18 *People's Home Journal*, 'Origin, Development and Importance of the Bird Sanctuary Campaign' (1919) [flyer].

19 William Souder, 'How Two Women Ended the Deadly Feather Trade', *Smithsonian Magazine*, March 2013, www.smithsonianmag.com.

20 UK Parliament, 'Protection of Birds Act, 1954', www.legislation.gov.uk, accessed 30 December 2019.

21 Steve Pavlik, *The Navajo and the Animal People: Native American Traditional Ecological Knowledge and Ethnozoology* (Golden, CO, 1914), p. 186.

22 Ibid., pp. 169–94.

23 Henry Wadsworth Longfellow, 'The Birds of Killingworth', in *Henry Wadsworth Longfellow: Poems and Other Writings* (New York, 2000), pp. 440–47.

24 Sterba, *Nature Wars*, p. 74.

25 Ibid., p. 169.

26 u.s. Fish & Wildlife Service, 'History of Bald Eagle Decline, Protection and Recovery', 5 May 2020, www.fws.gov.

27 W. H. Hudson and Linda Gardiner, *Rare, Vanishing and Lost British Birds* (London, 1923), p. 45.

28 Maan Barua and Paul Jepson, 'The Bull of the Bog: Bittern Conservation Practice in a Western Bio-cultural Setting', in *Ethno-ornithology: Birds, Indigenous Peoples, Culture and Society*, ed. Sonia Tidemann and Andrew Gosler (Abingdon, 2010), pp. 301–12.

29 Gustave Axelson, 'Vanishing', *Living Bird: Cornell Lab of Ornithology*, XXXVII/4 (2019), pp. 44–52.

30 Elizabeth Kolbert, *The Sixth Extinction: An Unnatural History* (New York, 2014), pp. 224–5.

31 Van Dooren, *Flight Ways*, pp. 89–92.

32 Matt Mendenhall, 'A Cloudy Future: Whooping Cranes Have Made a Steady Return from the Brink of Extinction, But Sea-level Rise Due to Climate Change Poses a Serious Risk', *Birdwatching*, XXXIII/5 (September/October 2019), pp. 14–19.

33 Ed Young, 'What DNA says about the Extinction of America's Most Common Bird', *The Atlantic*, 16 November 2017, www.theatlantic.com.

34 Emma Marris, 'When Conservationists Kill Lots (and Lots) of Animals', *The Atlantic*, 26 September 2018, www.theatlantic.com.

35 Sarah Deweerdt, 'Killing Barred Owls to Keep Spotted Owls Breathing', *Newsweek* (17 May 2017).

36 Jessica Camille Aguirre, 'The Culling: Australia Has Become Deadly Serious about Killing Millions of Feral Cats', *New York Times Magazine*, 28 April 2019, pp. 34–41.

37 Van Dooren, *Flight Ways*, p. 93.

38 Ibid., p. 231.

39 Joshua Hammer, *The Falcon Thief: A True Tale of Adventure, Treachery and the Hunt for a Perfect Bird* (New York, 2000), pp. 37–40; Richard C. Paddock, 'Where Poachers Feed a Craze for Songbird Contests', *New York Times*, 19 April 2020, p. 19.

40 Rachel Carson, *Silent Spring* [1962] (Boston, MA, 2002), pp. 1–7.

41 Brooke Jarvis, 'The Insect Apocalypse Is Here: What Does It Mean for the Rest of Life on Earth?', *New York Times Magazine*, 27 November 2018, pp. 41–5, 67–9.

42 Boria Sax, 'What Is this Quintessence of Dust? The Concept of the "Human" and Its Origins', in *Anthropocentrism: Humans, Animals, Environments*, ed. Rob Boddice (Leiden, 2011), pp. 21–36.

43 Celia Dale, 'The Cawing of Rooks', *Country Life* (17 March 1955), p. 746.

FURTHER READING

The literature about birds is virtually endless, but the following books are suggested for further reading. I have not included highly specialized books, books in languages other than English, books that discuss birds only tangentially, works of fiction or books that could be especially difficult to obtain. Reaktion Books, the publisher of this volume, also publishes a series entitled Animal, which contains books on individual varieties of birds including the albatross, crow, chicken, peacock, parrot, duck, eagle, falcon, ostrich, pigeon, sparrow, swallow, swan, vulture and woodpecker. They are an excellent source of information on specific kinds of birds, but they are not listed individually here.

General Books on Birds

Fisher, Celia, *The Magic of Birds* (London, 2014). A wide-ranging discussion of the traditional roles played by birds in myth and other aspects of human culture throughout the world.

Gibson, Graeme, ed., *The Bedside Book of Birds: An Avian Miscellany* (New York, 2005). An anthology of thought-provoking quotations and short essays relating to birds.

Nozedar, Adele, ed., *The Secret Language of Birds: A Treasury of Myths, Folklore and Inspirational True Stories* (London, 2006). Anecdotes, vignettes and bits of curious information about birds.

Phillips, Catherine, et al., *Birds of a Feather* (St Petersburg, 2019). An introduction to birds in history, which is especially strong in the area of Russian mythology.

Birds in Anthropology

Serjeantson, Dale, *Birds* (Cambridge, 2009). A history of bird-human relations from a zooarchaeological perspective.

Tidemann, Sonia, and Andrew Gosler, eds, *Ethno-ornithology: Birds, Indigenous Peoples, Culture and Society* (Abingdon, 2010). A collection of essays on human relations with birds in various cultures as well as ways in which ornithologists, anthropologists and indigenous peoples can work together.

Birds in the Arts

Bogel, Cynthea J., Israel Goldman and Alfred H. Marks, *Hiroshige: Birds and Flowers* (New York, 1988). Focuses on the art of Hiroshige but also contains a discussion of traditional Oriental bird and flower painting.

Bugler, Caroline, *The Bird in Art* (London, 2012). Birds in art, including works of both fine artists and scientific illustrators, with insightful commentaries.

Elphick, Jonathan, *Birds: The Art of Ornithology* (New York, 2017). A meticulously detailed history of bird illustration.
Jackson, Christine E., *Bird Artists of the World* (Woodbridge, 1999). An encyclopedia covering hundreds of bird artists in both Western and Asian cultures.
Lederer, Roger J., *The Art of the Bird: The History of Ornithological Art through Forty Artists* (Chicago, IL, 2019). A history of bird illustration focusing particularly on how artists responded to scientific developments.
Roberts, Allen F., *Animals in African Art: From the Familiar to the Marvelous* (New York, 1995). The many relationships that Africans have had with birds and other animals, especially as reflected in their art.
Rothenberg, David, *Why Birds Sing: A Journey into the Mystery of Bird Song* (New York, 2005). A multidisciplinary study of the relationships between birdsong and music.

Birds and the Environment

Doherty, Peter, *Their Fate Is Our Fate: How Birds Foretell Threats to Our Health and Our World* (New York, 2013). Birds as indicator species that can help predict changes in the environment.
Dooren, Thom van, *Flight Ways: Life and Loss at the Edge of Extinction* (New York, 2014). The cultural, social and philosophical implications of the avian extinction crisis.

Birds in History

Arnott, W. Geoffrey, *Birds in the Ancient World from A to Z* (London, 2007). An encyclopedic compilation of references to birds in early writings and art.
Bailleul-LeSuer, Rozenn, ed., *Between Heaven and Earth: Birds in Ancient Egypt* (Chicago, IL, 2012). Scholarly essays on birds in every aspect of ancient Egyptian life.
Houlihan, Patrick F., *The Birds of Ancient Egypt* (Cairo, 1988). A scholarly survey of birds in ancient Egyptian life and art.
Mynott, Jeremy, *Birds in the Ancient World* (Oxford, 2018). A comprehensive reference on birds in the ancient Mediterranean.
Pollard, J., *Birds in Greek Life and Myth* (New York, 1977). A very thorough survey of birds in ancient Greek literature and art.

Birds in Literature

Bach, Rebecca Ann, *Birds and Other Creatures in Renaissance Literature* (New York, 2018). An illuminating discussion of birds in the work of Shakespeare and his contemporaries.
Bachelard, Gaston, *Air and Dreams: An Essay on the Imagination of Movement*, trans. Edith and Frederick Farrell (Dallas, TX, 2011). An essay on the significance of birds in literature and dreams by an influential philosopher.

Collins, Billy, ed. *Bright Wings: An Illustrated Anthology of Poems about Birds* (New York, 2013). An anthology of poems for birdwatchers that emphasizes individual species and includes illustrations by David Allen Sibley.

McClatchy, J. D., ed., *On Wings of Song: Poems about Birds* (New York, 2000). An anthology of poetry about birds containing the traditional favourites as well as others that are not well known.

Rowland, Beryl, *Birds with Human Faces: A Guide to Bird Symbolism* (Knoxville, TN, 1978). A comprehensive guide to birds in literature, especially that of Britain.

Birds in Myth and Folklore

Armstrong, Edward A., *Folklore of Birds* (London, 1958). This book, while somewhat dated, remains perhaps the most comprehensive discussion of avian folklore available.

Lawrence, Elizabeth, *Hunting the Wren: Transformation of Bird into Symbol* (Knoxville, TN, 1997). A scholarly exploration of the cult of the wren and, more broadly, the theme of animal sacrifice.

Nigg, Joseph, *The Phoenix: An Unnatural Biography of a Mythical Beast* (Chicago, IL, 2016). A very thorough history of the phoenix in Egypt, China, Greece and other parts of the world.

Pritchard, Evan T., *Bird Medicine: The Sacred Power of Bird Shamanism* (Rochester, VT, 2013). An Algonquin, Native American perspective on birds.

Birds in Science

Ackerman, Jennifer. *The Genius of Birds* (New York, 2016). A scientific discussion of ways in which birds find their way during migration.

Birkhead, Tim, *Bird Sense: What It's Like to Be a Bird* (London, 2012). A scientific discussion of the senses of birds.

——, *The Wisdom of Birds: An Illustrated History of Ornithology* (New York, 2008). The history of ornithology as told from the perspective of a scientist.

Hermann, Debra, *Avian Cognition: Exploring the Intelligence, Behavior and Individuality of Birds* (Boca Raton, FL, 2016). Not only discusses scientific studies of the cognition of many avian species but contains an interesting discussion of the concept of intelligence.

WEBSITES ABOUT BIRDS

The following are a few of the most important national and international websites about birds. There are numerous local sites that provide information about birdwatching in a limited geographic area or explore avian life from a more specialized point of view, but they are not included here for reasons of space.

Birds of a Feather
http://birdsofafeather.feralscribes.org
A website that contains information on birds from many disciplines but specializes in poetry and stories.

Birdlife International
www.birdlife.org
The website of a large, international organization devoted to all aspects of bird conservation.

Cornell Lab of Ornithology
www.birds.cornell.edu
A website of the ornithology programme at Cornell University, which is the most extensive in American higher education. It specializes in scientific study and contains extensive information on avian behaviour and habitats.

Leigh Yawkey Woodson Art Museum
www.lywam.org
The website of an art museum in Wisconsin that specializes in depictions of birds. It sponsors yearly conferences and special exhibitions devoted to contemporary bird artists.

National Audubon Society (USA)
www.audubon.org
The Audubon Society represents a vast network of nature centres, birdwatching clubs and other organizations devoted to the conservation of birds and other forms of wildlife. It contains a huge database on birds, their identification and current distribution, together with many suggestions for ways to promote their conservation.

Ornithology

www.ornithology.com

A very extensive website covering just about all aspects of birds and their interaction with human beings, including material on a variety of specialized subjects such as bird rehabilitation and birds on stamps and coins.

Royal Society for the Protection of Birds (UK)

www.rspb.org.uk

Founded in 1889, the RSPB may be the oldest organization in the world for the protection of birds. Its website contains extensive information on avian conservation, birdwatching, environmental history and related topics.

ACKNOWLEDGEMENTS

Many thanks to my wife Linda Sax, who proofread the manuscript and offered many very useful suggestions. Thanks also to Reaktion Books for their confidence in me to complete this fascinating yet daunting project.

PHOTO ACKNOWLEDGEMENTS

The author and publishers wish to thank the organizations and individuals listed below for authorizing reproduction of their work:

© ADAGP, Paris and DACS, London 2021: p. 282; Adobe Stock: p. 89; Alamy: p. 247 (Album); Tony Angell: p. 283; The Art Institute of Chicago: pp. 11 (Henry Field Memorial Collection), 297 (Clarence Buckingham Collection); Ashmolean Museum, Oxford: p. 142; John James Audubon, *Birds of America* (1827–38): p. 352; author: pp. 46, 76, 186, 187, 320; author's collection: pp. 2, 10, 19, 21, 30, 34, 39, 41, 42, 45, 106, 107, 115, 125, 132, 138, 144, 145, 146, 154, 155, 168, 173, 174, 177, 189, 197, 202, 203, 207, 215, 220, 221, 222, 224, 228, 229, 230, 246, 251, 267, 268, 270, 271, 273, 302, 303, 313, 332, 337 left, 343, 345, 351, 354, 357, 368; Gordon C. Aymar, *Bird Flight* (Garden City Publishing, New York, 1938): pp. 33, 52 (photo by Underwood & Underwood), 55 (photo by C. L. Welsh), 105, 166, 307; Bibliothèque nationale de France: p. 59; Birmingham Museum of Art: p. 330; Boston Public Library: p. 277; Museum of Fine Arts, Boston: p. 308; British Museum, London: pp. 83, 88 (© The Trustees of the British Museum), 218 (© The Trustees of the British Museum); Brooklyn Museum, New York: p. 293; Catherine Calhoun, *Egyptian Designs* (1983). International Design Library, Stemmer House: p. 82; Caren Caraway, *Northwest Indian Designs* (1982). International Design Library, Stemmer House: p. 49; clipart.com: pp. 9, 13, 80; Dover Pictorial Archives: pp. 6, 12, 20, 26, 37, 38, 51 (A. G. Smith, Viking Designs), 85, 92, 157, 159, 209, 238, 264, 274, 281 (© ADAGP, Paris and DACS, London 2021), 300, 304, 306, 317, 333, 334, 337 right, 365, 374; Dreamstime: pp. 14 (Ivkuzmin), 27 (Zatletic), 31 (Feathercollector), 58 (Alaskaphoto), 61 (Perseomedusa), 99 (Prathabphotography), 110 (Carlijnbrands), 180 (Rannoch), 185 (Vladsokolovsky), 188 (Stevebyland), 223 (Fuchsphotography), 240 (Lindacaldwell2), 257 (Jgaunion), 294 (Nataba16), 316 (Radiokafka); Fenimore Art Museum, Cooperstown, New York: p. 254; Louis Figuier, *Reptiles and Birds* (Springfield, MA, 1869): p. 210; Gallica Digital Library: p. 252; Germanisches Nationalmuseum, Nuremberg, Germany: p. 141; J. Paul Getty Museum, Los Angeles: p. 56; Jacob and Wilhelm Grimm, *Household Stories* (Dover Publications, New York, 1963): p. 73; Hermitage Museum, St. Petersburg: p. 326; Internet Archive: p. 100; From Mary and Elizabeth Kirby, *The Sea and Its Wonders* (T. Nelson and Sons, 1890): p. 348; Library of Congress, Washington, DC: pp. 29, 136, 176, 204, 280, 298, 299, 312, 338, 339, 340, 341, 342, 344, 350; Metropolitan Museum of Art, New York: pp. 68 (Gift of Harry G. Friedman, 1960), 86 (Rogers Fund, 1944), 87 (Rogers Fund, 1907), 104 (Fletcher Fund, 1963), 124 (The Crosby Brown Collection of Musical Instruments, 1889), 129 (Harris Brisbane Dick Fund, 1937), 131 (Purchase, Bashford Dean Bequest, 1969), 137 (Purchase, Oscar L. Tang Family and The Vincent Astor Foundation Gifts, 1998), 139 (Harris Brisbane Dick Fund, 1937), 140 (Fletcher Fund, 1919), 143 (H. O. Havemeyer Collection, Bequest of Mrs. H. O. Havemeyer,

1929), 195 (Purchase, 2017 NoRuz at The Met Benefit, 2017), 226 (Bequest of Mary Stillman Harkness, 1950), 236 (The Cesnola Collection, Purchased by subscription, 1874–76), 295 (H. O. Havemeyer Collection, Bequest of Mrs. H. O. Havemeyer, 1929), 336 (Fletcher Fund, 1959); Jules Michelet, *The Bird*, 1869: pp. 346, 347; Museo del Prado, Madrid: pp. 134, 248, 249, 331; National Palace Museum, Taipei: p. 288 (CC BY 4.0); The Nelson-Atkins Museum of Art, Kansas City: p. 130; The Palace Museum, Beijing: pp. 291, 292; University of Pittsburgh: p. 369; Courtesy of the Robert Rauschenberg Foundation: p. 372; Rijksmuseum, Amsterdam: p. 250; Royal Picture Gallery Mauritshuis, The Hague: p. 261; Jasper Theodore Studer, *Popular Ornithology* (Rockville, MD, 1881): p. 22; Uffizi Gallery, Florence: p. 262; Universitätsbibliothek Heidelberg (Codex Manesse): pp. 161, 182, 190, 244; Van Gogh Museum, Amsterdam: p. 153; Victoria and Albert Museum: p. 192 (Photo by Henry Townsend); The Wellcome Library, London: p. 349; Wikimedia Commons/BabelStone: p. 127 (CC0 1.0 Universal Public Domain Dedication) (British Museum); Wikimedia Commons/Roman Bonnefoy (Romanceor): p. 253 (Creative Commons Attribution-Share Alike 4.0 International, 3.0 Unported, 2.5 Generic, 2.0 Generic and 1.0 Generic license); Wikimedia Commons/Mushki Brichta: p. 53 (CC Attribution-Share Alike 4.0 International license); Wikimedia Commons/British Library: p. 242 (CC0 1.0 Universal Public Domain Dedication); Wikimedia Commons/© Francis C. Franklin: p. 260 (CC-BY-SA-3.0); World Digital Library: p. 256; Yale University Library: p. 279 (Franz R. and Kathryn M. Stenzel Collection of Western American Art. Yale Collection of Western Americana, Beinecke Rare Book and Manuscript Library).

INDEX OF BIRDS

albatross 8, *8*, 237, *348*, 357
alkonost 321
American robin *14*, 15, 54
Anzu 157–8, *157*, *218–19*, 219
archaeopteryx 12
Arctic tern 97, *99*
auk *see* great auk

basilisk 34, 218–19, *218*
benu bird 36, 37, 64, 88, 89, 90, 94
    see also heron
bird of paradise 43–4, *41, 43, 44,*
    136, 328
blackbird 355
black-capped chickadee 54
bulbul 287, *288*
bullfinch 245, *297*

California condor *see* vulture
canary *see* finch
cave art 294, 305, 334–7, *235*
charadrius 95
chicken 201–31, *202, 203, 204,*
    207, 209, 210, 215, 220,
    224, 226, 228–9, 230, 240,
    242, 243, 256, 362
    Andalusian *221*
    Araucana 295
    Captain Heaton's cock *222*
    cochin 220, *223*
    see also red jungle fowl,
    grey jungle fowl
cockerel *see* chicken
cockatrice 219
common poorwill *see* nightjar
crane 7, 54, 193, 290
    whooping crane 367–8,
    369

crow 9, 14, 22, 23, 40, *59*, 60, 64, 69,
    71, 93–4, 98, 117, 119–20, 124,
    125, 150, 151, *153*, 156, 159,
    160, 211, 364
    see also raven
cuckoo 23, 162, 363

dodo *see* pigeon
dove 7, 57, 60, *61*, 65, 66–7, *68*, 69,
    70, 74, 94, 118, 194, 245, 343
    turtle dove 163
duck 106
    mallard 245, 249
    mandarin duck 159

eagle 9, 22, 23, 24, 25, *29*, 32, *38*,
    48, 62–5, 67, 69, 89, 94, 95, 98,
    153, 157, 160, 162–3, 164–7, 169,
    170, 171–2 241, *257*
    bald eagle 363, 366, *372*
    black eagle 48, 74
    eagle of Zeus 48
    golden eagle 62, *185*,
    335–6, 363
egret 342
elephant bird 48, 332, 335
English robin 21, 119, 245, *247*, 362

falcon 10, 14, 21, 22, 69, 79, *80*, 87,
    95, 165, 183–200
    aplomado *186*
    gyrfalcon 22
    hobby *343*
    merlin 22, 162, 185
    peregrine falcon 21, 22, 194, 342
    saker falcon 22
fenghuang 34, *37*, *38*, 40, *45*, 106
    see also phoenix, luan

finch 106
    canary *145*, 147
    hawk finch *349*
firebird 36
flamingo *264*, 265

Garuda 48, *159*, 160, 164, 377
golden oriole 355
goldfinch 245, 249, 259–61, *260*, *261*
goose 79, 81, *110*, 245, *293*, *326*
great auk 234, 237, 333–4, *334*, 335
grackle 93, *267*
grey jungle fowl 205
    see also chicken
grouse 343
gull *55*, 306
    herring gull 245

hawk 21, 46, 54, 87, 100, 106, 114, 122,
    154–6, *154*, 160, 167, 184, 185,
    191, 193, 194, 196, 198, 199, 219,
    237, 245, 287, 308–10, *309*
    eagle hawk 150
    goshawk 185, *188*, 191, 346
    harris hawk 57
    sparrowhawk 21, 185
    red-tailed hawk 72, 103
hen *see* chicken
ho-ho 36
honeyguide 148–9
hoopoe 87, 95, 106, *107*, 155, *155*,
    156, 193, 249
hornbill 252–3, *253*, 254
    rufous-necked hornbill
    frontispiece
house sparrow *294*, 335, 371
hummingbird 302–5, 306–8, *307–8*
    blue-breasted sapphire
    hummingbird *304*
    half-tailed hummingbird *303*
    ruby-throated hummingbird
    307

ibis 80, 84, 88, 211, 254

jackdaw *30*, 158
Japanese white-eye *296*, *300*
jay 14, 245
    blue jay 8, 54, 276
    pinion jay *283*

kestrel 9–10, *10*, 103
kingfisher 64, 245, 249, 290, 355
    kookaburra 146
kite 60, 100–101, 193, 362

lark *11*
luan *106*
    see also fenghuang
lyrebird 146, *270*

magpie 23, 70–71, 152, 290, 343
man-o'-war *52*
meadowlark 22, 366
merlin *see* falcon
mockingbird *see* northern
    mockingbird

nightingale 25, 106, 154–6, *154*,
    155, 160, 310–23, *313*, *316*,
    317
nightjar 102
    common poorwill 102
northern mockingbird 276–8, *277*,
    313
nuthatch 50

osprey 346
owl 12, 14, 18, 23, *34*, 63, 72, 87, 91,
    95, 106, 126–33, *127*, *129*,
    130–31, *131*, *132*, 150, *159*, *169*,
    169
    barn owl 133, 184, 276
    great-horned owl *187*

parakeet 23, 276
 budgerigar 147
 Carolina parakeet 351, *352*
parrot 21, 133–5, *134*, 137–8, *137*,
 138, 139, 140, 141, 142, 150,
 158–9, 269, 272, 274, 275, *275*,
 331, 351, 371
 cockatoo *144–5*, 150, *273*,
 282, *306*
 macaw *144, 146*, 149
 see also parakeet
partridge 21, 25, 106, 343, 362, 371
pelican 40, 95
penguin *250*, 333
petrel 54, 99
pheasant 40, 119, 290, 329, 338, 343,
 346, 355
phoenix 21, *34*, 36–40, *37, 38, 39*, 43, 44,
 45, 46, 48, 49, 88, 89, 93, 94,
 106, 250, 255, 258
 see also fenghuang, luan
phorusrhacidae see terror birds
pigeon 21, 24, 60, 66, 72, 93, 100,
 103, 111, 114, 132, 185, 283, *295*,
 332, 371
 dodo 322–3, *323*
 passenger pigeon 351–3, *351*,
 357–8, 368
 rock dove 24
 wood pigeon 21
plover 362
prairie chicken 362

quetzal bird 255, 258, 361

raven 9, 18, 23, 24, 32, 54, 57, *56–7,
 58*, 62, 63, 64, 69, 70–77, *72–3,
 76*, 90, 93, 97, 98, 114, 119–24,
 121, 122–3, 124, 126, 151, 164,
 165, 245, 254, 268–9, *280*, 362
red jungle fowl 205, 231
 see also chicken

robin *see* American robin, English robin
rooster *see* chicken
roc *see* rukh
rook 354, 374, *374*
rukh 34, 36, *47*, 48

shearwater 63
simorgh 34, 36, 106, 108
 see also luan
siren 90, 241, 322
shrike 21
sirin *321*, 322
skylark *11*, 355, 360
sparrow 54, 63, 74, 114, 119, 237,
 290–92, *292*, 296, 353, 355
spoonbill 249
starling 57, 180–81, *180*, 354, *354*,
 355, 371
swallow 20, 40, 54, 72, 79, 87, *87*, 97,
 100–102, *100, 115*, 148, 155–6,
 155, 245, 289, 362
 tree swallow 151
swan 7, *13*, 24, 26, 40, 63, 160, *320*,
 321, 329, 359, 362
 whooper swan 321
swift 101
swiftlet 31
 glossy swiftlet *31*

tern *see* Artic tern
terror birds, 358
thrush 43, 50, 160, 191, 313
Thunderbird 46, 48–9, *49*, 165
toucan 146

vulture 14, 21, 23, 60, 64, 79, 80,
 90, 95, 117, 237, 243, 255, *344*,
 362, 367
 black vulture *268, 368*
 California condor 367–8,
 368
 turkey vulture *268, 368*

warbler 275, *339–41*, 342, 360
waterfowl 108–9
woodpecker 48, 98, 160
     pileated woodpecker 9
wren 14, 21, 23, 60, 63, 64, 79, 80,
     90, 95, 117, 237, 243, 255, 257,
     345, 362, 367

yellow-billed water hen *271*

GENERAL INDEX

Aelian 64, 128, 217

Aesop 109, 153–4, 155, 157, 158, 167,
  212, 245, 318

Africa 64, 79, 93, 102, 124, 128, 146,
  148–9, 201, 224–5, *226*, 234, *251*,
  252–4, 280, 336
  see also Egypt, Madagascar

Aldrovandi, Ulisse, *89*, 214, 250,
  264

American Indians *see* Native
  Americans

Americas 8, 20, 23, 48, 71, 102, 111, 117,
  118–19, 122, 124, 137, 138, 146–7,
  148, 152, 158, 165, 171–7, 186, 205,
  223, 224–31, 234, 253, 255–8,
  264–9, 275–9, 301, 302, 308,
  332, 335, 337, 351–5, 357, 358, 359,
  360–61, 362–3, 364–9, 370–71
  see also Mexico, Native
  Americans, United States

Andersen, Hans Christian 317–18,
  319

Angell, Tony 93–4, 124, 283

angels *6*, 8, 34, 67, 72, 87, 116

animal paramour 7, 148

Apollo *59*, 63, 64

Apollodorus of Rhodes 25, 50, 90

Arabia 43, 36, 37, 40, 371

Aristophanes 156–7, 359

Aristotle 100–101, 128, 135, 155, 167,
  184, 201, 238, 321, 361

Armstrong, Edward 48, 169

Athena 58, 60, 62, 63, 126, 127

Attar, Farid ud-Din *104*, 195–8,
  193, 315

Audubon, John James 275–9, *277*, *298*,
  300–301, 304, 305, 350–51, *352*, 353,
  360, *369*

Australia 24, 27, 43, 48, 118, 128, 146, 147,
  150, 234, 269, 332, 354, 370

avian illuminations 7, 9, *10–11*, 323, 373

ba 85–90, 85, *86*, *88*, 94

Babel, Tower of 114–15, 116, 117, 149

Bachelard, Gaston 32–5, 46, 49, 97

Bali 208–9

Belon, Pierre 44, 101, 252–3, *252*

Bernini, Gian Lorenzo *61*

Bewick, Thomas 266–9, *334*, *365*, *374*

Bian Shoumin 292–4, *293*

Bill and Coo (film) 23

bird divination *see* divination

Birds, The (film) 284, *285*

bird-woman figurines 236, *236*

Blumenberg, Hans 63

Braidotti, Rosi 111

Breton, Jules *10–11*

Britain 72, 74, 75, 76, 169, 172, 180–81, *215*,
  221, 222, 269, 272, 311, 346, 354–5,
  361, 362, 363
  see also England

Brueghel, Jan the Younger 133–5, *134*

Bryant, William Cullen 108–9

Buddhism 290

Buffon, Georges-Louis Leclerc, Comte
  de *21*, 266, 272

cages 137–8, *137*, *138*, *146*, 148, 225, 314, 364

Campbell, Joseph 97, 111

Carson, Rachel 356, 364, 371

Catesby, Mark 264–5, *265*

cave art 79, 82, 234–6, *235*

Chaucer, Geoffrey 35–6, 161–3, 178,
  212–13, 219, 315, 356

China 38, 46, 106, 165, 184, 205, 220,
  287–95, 301, 305, 317–18, 353, 355

Chinese dragon *see* dragon
Christ Jesus 84, 94, 95, 101, *138–9, 140, 141,*
    142–3, 169, 170–71, 193–4, 214, 259
    see also Christianity
Christianity 66, 70, 74, 88, 89, 91, 93,
    94–6, 101, 118, 165, 192, 231, 245,
    257, 335
    see also Christ Jesus
Cicero 70, 74, 77, 161, 360
Courbet, Gustave *143,* 146
Crane, Walter *72–3*
Cui Bai 292, *292*

Daedalus 25–6, *26, 27,* 28, 30
Dale, Celia 374
Damian, John 30
Daoism 22, 287, 290, 292,
Darwin, Charles 119, 179, 208, 316, 327
DDT 336, 356, 363
Der von Kürenberg 200
Descartes, René 90, 96, 135, 318
Detmold, Edward Julius *47*
Devonshire tapestries 191–2, *192*
dinosaurs 12–13, *12,* 150, 203, 358
Diogenes of Sinope 201–2, *204,* 206,
    231
divination 23, 50–78, 183, 205, 280, 373
dragon 32, 38, 50, 135
    Chinese dragon 38, *44, 5,* 46–8, *46*
dreams 25, 32, 35, 36, 69, 161–3, 212–13,
    223, 231, 236, 259, 314, 364, 371
Dreamtime 24, 27
Dürer, Albrecht *26, 140,* 143, 263

Eden, Garden of *42, 43, 44,* 133–5, *134,*
    140, 143, 149, 162, 171, 194, *251,* 278,
    331
Edwards, John 265–6, *267*
Egypt 37, *41,* 60, 63, 79–96, 137, 165, 184,
    196, 205, 211, 216, 231, 237–8, 239,
    253, 254
Eliade, Mircea 8, 50

Eliot, George 133
England 23, 51, 70–71, 72, 102, 163, 165,
    184, 196, 209, 210, 245, 305, 362, 374
    see also Britain
Ernst, Max 279, 280–82, *281*

Fabritius, Carel 259–63, *261*
falconry 23, 182–200, 182–200, *182, 185,*
    186, 187, 189, 188, 190, 192, 195, 363,
    373
feathers 18, 25, 28, 35, 36, 38, 40, 43, 44, *53,*
    77, 100, 101, 106, 128, 133, 158, 167,
    170, 193, 199, 200, 201, 206, 213,
    214, 220, 254, 272, 296, 302, 330,
    334, 335–42, *336, 337, 338, 339, 340,*
    340, 341
film 23, 35, 132, 284–6, *285*
Florentine Codex 255–8, *256–7, 257*
France 23, 74, 75, 163, 169, 170, 183, 191,
    216, 234, 275, 328, 330
Frederick II (Holy Roman Emperor)
    163, 193, 196, 243, 252

Germany 74, 77, 101, 110, 161, 179, 248
Gesner, Konrad 36, 44, 250, *313*
Gheeraerts, Marcus *203*
Giacomelli, Hector *346, 346, 347*
Gibson, Graeme 9
Gilgamesh, Epic of 55, 80, 97
Gogh, Vincent van *153,* 300
Gordon, Ross *342*
Gould, Elizabeth 269, 276, 303
Gould, John 269–70, 275, 276, 303–5,
    304, 306
Goya, Francesco 130–31, *131*
Grandville, J. J. *19, 30, 34, 115,* 131, *132, 154,*
    155, 207, 317
Greece 60, 63, 100, 137, 156, 184, 205, 207,
    216, 237, 239
Grien, Hans Baldung *141,* 143
Grimm, Jacob and Wilhelm 50, 71, *73,*
    74, 91, *92,* 120, 167–9

Habiballah of Sava *104*
Hafiz 315
Haraway, Donna 24, 179, 201, 203, 229
Harrison, Beatrice 311, *312*
harpy *89*, 90
hawking *see* falconry
Heade, Martin Johnson 308
Heike, Tale of the 69
Herodotus 36, 37, 40, 59, 60, 88, 93, 95
Hesiod 37, 54, 59, 155
Hiroshige, Utagawa *20*, 296, *299*, 300–301, *300*
Hitler, Adolf 179–80
Hokusai, Katsushika *297*
Holy Spirit *61*, 66–7, *68*, 74, 94, 194, 283
Homer 25, 50, 59, 60, 61–3, 65, 67, 74, 90, 187
Hopkins, Gerard Manley 9–10
Horthemels, Frédéric *68*
Horus *80*, 88, 95, 165, 196
Huang Quan 291, *291*
Hudson, William Henry 330, 342, 347, 354–5, 366
Huizong 287–8, *288*

Icarus 25, *26*, 28
India 8, 37, 40, 43, 94, 137, 138, 184, 205, 214, 247, 253, 362, 363
Indonesia 40, 118, 234, 371
Islam 8, 69, 70, 106, 108, 183, 194, 247, 315
Italy 163, 184, 193, 240, 305, 315, 321, 359

Japan 7, 98, 289, 290, 296, 301
Jardine, William *106*, *144*, *168*, *269*, 271, 272, *303*, *343*
Jasper, Theodore *22*, *368*
Jatakas 158–9

Keats, John 314, 316–17, 319, 321, 322, 327, 359
Kolbert, Elizabeth 327, 370–71

Lear, Edward 269, 272–4, *273*, *274*
Leonardo da Vinci 18, 25, 27, 28–30, 263, 305
Lévi-Strauss, Claude 20–21, 24
Leyden, Lucas van *337*
Linnaeus (Carl von Linné) 44, 101, 263, 265, 266, 327, 343, 344
Lorenz, Konrad 179
Lydon, Alexander 272

Macdonald, Helen 187, 194, 199, 359
Madagascar 48, 332
Magritte, René 282–3, *282*
Mann, Gabriella 120
Mansur, Ustad *246*, 247
Marchesini, Roberto 24
Marzluff, John 120, 124
Mary (mother of Jesus) 17, 63, 67, 95, *139*, *141*, 143, 149, 194, 259, *262*
masks 193, 224, *253*, 253, *254*, *280*, 280, 282, 335
Melampus 50
Melville, Herman 8, 222–3
Mexico 93, 97, 98, 102, 138, 164, 205, 209, 335
Michelet, Jules 109–10, 314–15, 321, 328, 343, *346*, 347, *347*
migration 52, 97–111, 285, 289, 292
Migratory Bird Treaty 363
Milton, John 36, 322
Morris, F. O. 272, *347*, *349*, *351*
Muybridge, Eadweard 305, 306, *306*, 308

Native Americans 48, 72, 90, 122, 151, 152, 175, *175*, 176–7, 199, 208, 254, 258, 280, 361, 363, 367
Nebamun, tomb painting of 81–3, *83*
Neolithic Age 48, 51–2, 98, 147, 169, 328, 357
New Guinea 43, 118, 146, 252, 335, 336
New Zealand 252, 332, 335, 354
Nibelungenlied, the 69

Nielsen, Kay *92*
Noah *56*, 57, 331

Odysseus 50, 62–3, 90
Omar Khayyam 315
Oudry, Jean-Baptiste 330, *330*
Ovid 21, 36, 63

Panchatantra 137, 159
Parmigiano *204*
Parker, Agnes Miller *201*
Pazzi, Giuseppe *301*
Pepperberg, Irene 147–8
Physiologus 94–6
Pico della Mirandola 213–14
Pisano, Andrea *27*
Plato 25–8, 31, 50, 201, 211, 231,
 242, 290, 321
Pliny the Elder 40, 90, 205, 238,
 239, 313, 361
Plutarch 167
Polynesia 205, 335

Queen of the Night relief 126, *127*

Rackham, Arthur *123*
Raphael Sanzio 259, *262*
Rauschenberg, Robert *372*
Ray, John 101, 263
Rembrandt van Rijn 259
Richter, Henry C. 303, *304*
Rome 8, 23, 36, 50, 61, 116, 137,
 138, 163, 164, 184, 216,
 239, 313
Rossetti, Christina 322–3
Rumi 315

Schjelderup-Ebbe, Thorleif 178–9
Schongauer, Martin 138, *139*, 143
Sebald, W. G. 110–11
Shakespeare, William 36, 311, 315, 355,
 359, 362

Shelley, Percy Bysshe 314, 359
Sherborne Missal 165, 245–7, *247*
Shepard, Paul 58, 360–61
Sigurd 50, *51*
Snyders, Frans *326*, 329, *331*
Socrates 25–8, 211
 see also Plato
Sufis 105, 108, 193, 325, 317

Thanksgiving (American holiday)
 171–7, *173*, *174*, *176*, *177*
Tiepolo, Giambattista *142*, 146
Tiresias 50
totemism 23–5, 27, 80
Toussenel, Alphonse 23, 243

United States 48, 97, 170, 171–7, 179, 180,
 184, 208, 209, 219, 221, 225, 269,
 275, 276, 336, 340, 342, 351–3, 355,
 357, 360, 361, 363, 364, 365–7
Utamaro, Kitagawa 295–6, *295*

Vilgerðarson, Flokki 57
Vosnetsov, Victor Mikhaylovich *321*

Walther von der Vogelweide 161, *161*,
 178, 359
Wilde, Oscar 319, 321
Willoughby, Frances Kay 263
Wilson, Alexander 268–9, *269*, 351
Wilson, Edward O. 24
Winged Migration (film) 285–6
Wolf, Joseph *2*, 303

Yahweh 65–7, 100, 114–15, 211
Yeats, W. B. 183, 320–21

Zeshin, Shibata 308–10, *308–9*
Zeus 48, 54, 58, 60, 62–4, 65, 67, 74, 81,
 156, 164